Advance ~~Praise for~~

Investing in the Educational Success of Black Women and Girls

"[This book] demonstrates, from our own lived experiences, the multifaceted and continued need to look critically at the historically and present day exclusionary policies, practices and structure of U.S. education that serve to predetermine our success. This anthology pushes us all to dig deeper into the organizational intent of learning as a transformational and liberatory practice, and to cast aside its role as indoctrination."—***Clarice Bailey***, *Faculty, Organizational Development and Leadership, Saint Joseph's University*

"What an amazing collection of essays! What a profound acknowledgment and powerful testament of the lives, histories, brilliance, beauty, and perseverance of Black women and girls. For too long, others have tried silencing, disempowering, and erasing Black women and girls within inequitable educational systems. This collection brings to light these realities while placing needed attention on mattering for Black women and girls who will never stop working for our liberation, freedom, justice, and wellbeing."—***Valerie Kinloch***, *Renée and Richard Goldman Dean and Professor, School of Education at the University of Pittsburgh*

"Centers the significant challenges Black girls and women face in schools and society while simultaneously bringing forth the beauty in them being their 'full selves.' It is a timely book that provides educators, leaders, and policymakers—across the educational pipeline—yet another chance to provide schooling experiences worthy of Black girls, their magic, and their brilliance. Perhaps someday soon they will get it right."—***Yolanda Sealey-Ruiz***, *Associate Professor, Teachers College, Columbia University*

"This book ... pushes our understanding of Black women and girls beyond the stereotypical model minority myths of magic. The authors unpack the complexities of experiences that includes injustice and resilience within education and across intersecting systems. This critical resource positions Black women and girls at the center, which is where they belong, in postsecondary research and beyond."—***Tiffany Jones***, *Deputy Director of Measurement Learning and Evaluation for Postsecondary Success at the Bill and Melinda Gates Foundation*

INVESTING IN THE EDUCATIONAL SUCCESS OF
BLACK WOMEN AND GIRLS

INVESTING IN THE EDUCATIONAL SUCCESS OF BLACK WOMEN AND GIRLS

Edited by Lori D. Patton,

Venus E. Evans-Winters, and

Charlotte E. Jacobs

Foreword by Cynthia B. Dillard

1996–2021 25TH ANNIVERSARY

Sty/us
PUBLISHING, LLC.

STERLING, VIRGINIA

Published by Stylus Publishing, LLC.
22883 Quicksilver Drive
Sterling, Virginia 20166-2019

Library of Congress Cataloging-in-Publication Data
Names: Patton, Lori D., editor. | Evans-Williams, Venus E., editor. | Jacobs,
    Charlotte E., editor.
Title: Investing in the educational success of Black women and girls / Edited
    by Lori D. Patton, Venus E. Evans-Winters, and Charlotte E. Jacobs ;
    Foreword by Cynthia Dillard.
Description: First edition. | Sterling, Virginia : Stylus Publishing, LLC,
    [2022] | Includes bibliographical references and index. | Summary: "The
    purpose of this book is to illuminate scholarship on Black women and girls
    throughout the educational pipeline. The contributors--all Black women
    educators, scholars, and advocates--name the challenges Black women
    and girls face while pursuing their education as well as offer implications
    and recommendations for practitioners, policymakers, teachers, and
    administrators to consider in ensuring the success of Black women and
    girls"-- Provided by publisher.
Identifiers: LCCN 2021045673 (print) | LCCN 2021045674 (ebook) |
    ISBN 9781620367964 (cloth) | ISBN 9781620367971 (paperback) |
    ISBN 9781620367988 (pdf) | ISBN 9781620367995 (epub)
Subjects: LCSH: African American women--Education--Social aspects.
    | African American girls--Education--Social aspects. | Academic
    achievement--United States. | Education and state--United States. |
    Discrimination in education--United States.
Classification: LCC LC2717 .I58 2022 (print) | LCC LC2717 (ebook) |
    DDC 371.829/96073--dc23/eng/20211006
LC record available at https://lccn.loc.gov/2021045673
LC ebook record available at https://lccn.loc.gov/2021045674

13-digit ISBN: 978-1-62036-796-4 (cloth)
13-digit ISBN: 978-1-62036-797-1 (paperback)
13-digit ISBN: 978-1-62036-798-8 (library networkable e-edition)
13-digit ISBN: 978-1-62036-799-5 (consumer e-edition)

Printed in the United States of America

All first editions printed on acid-free paper that meets the American National
Standards Institute Z39-48 Standard.

Bulk Purchases

Quantity discounts are available for use in workshops and for
staff development.

Call 1-800-232-0223

First Edition, 2022

I dedicate this book to the collective of Black women and girls who deserve to be loved, to be seen, to be heard, and to simply . . . be. —Lori D. Patton

I dedicate these words of wisdom and scholarly ideas inscribed on the sheets of this book to all the Black women scholars who have tenaciously endured the ebb and flow of what we know plainly as education. —Venus E. Evans-Winters

I dedicate this book to all of the Black women and girls who came before me and in whose footsteps I follow, and to all of the Black girls who come after me. Thank you for your brilliance, your power, and your joy. —Charlotte E. Jacobs

CONTENTS

I grew up as a Black girl in Seattle, Washington. Given the rather small population of Black people in the Pacific Northwest, understanding who we were both individually and as a collective was mostly the purview of our immediate and extended families and the precious few other places where Black people gathered. And whenever we could, we definitely *gathered*. One of those sites of gathering was in our church, an important space and place of Black spiritual and social life both then and now. As a curious child, I learned and grew tremendously in this space. But when I became an adolescent and started teaching Sunday school, I heard a story that has served as a touchstone throughout my academic career as a scholar who cares deeply about the lives of little Black girls and the Black women they become, an echo of the voices gathered in this book.

My children and I were talking one Sunday morning about jobs and opportunities. About how, as you grew into adulthood, there was a need to make contributions not only to your own family but to others, to the larger society. As we went around the circle, children of all races and hues shared their desires and dreams of what that becoming would look like. I remember one young Chinese child shared that he wanted to be a fireman so he could "save peoples' lives if there was a fire." Another young Black child shared that he wanted to be a minister "like his father." But it was an amazing little Black girl who taught me a profound lesson about the role that freedom plays in our becoming as Black women. In response to my question about what she wanted her contribution to be (and in a voice profoundly wise for her age), she exclaimed this truth: "I want to be *full of myself!*"

I want to be full of myself. Not full of someone else, but full of myself. This little girl understood deeply what Audre Lorde had already taught us: That when all of our energy is focused and integrated in being all parts of ourselves, we will bring forth success *on our terms*, unrestricted by the definitions and limits of others. And the book you hold in your hands holds the wisdom and stories we need to create spaces that encourage us to become full of ourselves as Black women and girls.

Frankly, despite it all, we are *still* here. We are still standing. We are finding ways to remain visible, vigilant, and victorious. In the powerful essays that make up *Investing in the Educational Success of Black Women and Girls,*

Black women and girls are listened to, appreciated, and valued in recognition of the unrelenting challenges to our existence in a world that continues to be committed to stifling our voices. What these authors know intimately is that such stifling is not because what Black women and girls are saying isn't important: It is precisely because it *is*.

Reading this book is the wisdom we need at this moment. It is a collection that is not truncated, a full rendering of the experiences that Black women and girls for millennia have understood and endured. It articulates the ways we have been hushed, silenced, made invisible and the ways we have found joy, persevered, survived, thrived, and stood so beautifully full of ourselves. This book names the challenges Black women and girls continue to experience as we pursue our education and offers implications and recommendations for practitioners, teachers, administrators, and policymakers. If we have the courage to take these recommendations to heart and implement them fully, we can create spaces and conditions that animate the success of Black women and girls. Importantly, the voices gathered in this book make clear that Black families and communities are absolutely essential advocates and change leaders in the lives of Black girls and women who are *able* to become full of themselves, to take their place in a more just and equitable society.

The wisdom of that little Black girl I met in church all those years ago serves as a touchstone for all of us in this moment of global pandemics, racial reckoning, economic challenges, and enduring educational inequities. Her message was crystal clear: *The desire for Black women and girls is to be full of our God-given potential, brilliance, creativity, and beauty.* This book calls us all to hold a mirror up to our teaching, policies, and practices at the same time that it very definitively reminds us that the broader society will only be just and equitable when the sociocultural, emotional, economic, and political condition of Black girls and women are taken up in a just and equitable manner. *Investing in the Educational Success of Black Women and Girls* needs to be read widely and deeply, studied as much for its formations and beautiful representations of Black women and girls as its recommendations. It is the truth-telling we need today and a groundbreaking resource we need today and beyond.

Cynthia B. Dillard

ACKNOWLEDGMENTS

This project has been years in the making, and I'm so glad to have been on this journey alongside two amazing thought partners and sista scholars: Venus and Charlotte. Charlotte thank you so much for your organizational skills and keeping the book on track. Thanks to our contributors for your words, passion, and scholarly insights that illuminate Black women and girls along their educational trajectories. Your thoughtfulness, patience, and dedication to this project has been tremendous. Thank you to the village of Black women and girls who sustain me personally and professionally. Special thanks to my graduate assistant, Jasmine Akubar, for helping me with some finishing touches and a quick first read! —Lori D. Patton

I want to extend a long-overdue "thank you" to my coeditors, Lori D. Patton and Charlotte Jacob. We successfully and collaboratively coedited a book together during a pandemic! You are definitely two of the most thoughtful Black women scholars that I know, and I am not surprised that it was the three of us that could get the work done with so much adroitness and diligence. I would also like to thank all the Black women authors presented in this book who dared to pen a project on the education of Black girls and women during a moment in time when the world was once again reminded of people of African ancestry's sociopolitical vulnerability and collective wisdom. I further acknowledge all the girls and women I have come in contact with throughout my career as a racial and gender justice educator. Together we stand! —Venus E. Evans-Winters

I am truly honored to have been invited to work on such an important book project with the brilliant scholar–activists Lori D. Patton and Venus Evans-Winters. Thank you for bringing me into the fold of your ideas, scholarship, and visions for Black women and girls. I couldn't have asked for a better team of thought partners and hype women to sustain the momentum needed to get this book over the finish line. Also, a warm thank you to all of the contributors of this book. Thank you for saying "yes" when we asked, and for sharing your expertise and love for Black girls and women with us and with the world. —Charlotte E. Jacobs

Cover photos:

Row 1, l to r: "Goals, Dreams and Melanin" by Alex Nemo Hanse on Unsplash; "Braids With Graffiti in the Background" by Etty Fidele on Unsplash; "Afro Puff" by Suad Kamardeen on Unsplash.

Row 2, l to r: "Woman Holding Girl" by Eye for Ebony on Unsplash; "Future Leader" by Kiana Bosman on Unsplash; "Woman Looking Up" by Tachina Lee on Unsplash.

Row 3, l to r: "Green Graduation Robe" by Andre Hunter on Unsplash; "Woman Writing on Whiteboard" by Thought Catalog on Unsplash; "Woman Braiding Girl's Hair" by Shingi Rice on Unsplash.

INTRODUCTION

Establishing a Context for Centering Black Women and Girls in Education

Lori D. Patton

Black women and girls matter. They matter in our communities. They matter in our families. They matter in schools. They matter in colleges and universities. Black women and girls matter regardless of context. Yet, speaking their mattering into existence is critical because Black women and girls are overwhelmingly subjected to processes of erasure. The conditions under which erasure occurs consistently make it difficult to locate Black women and girls in policies, practices, and spaces where their well-being and humanity are deemed worthy of investment. As coeditors of this volume, we wanted to engage in a project that not only named the challenges and issues Black women and girls face but also yielded the space to imagine and consider what it means to invest in Black women and girls, particularly within the realm of education.

Using the educational system as a launching point, this book allowed each contributor to articulate what it means for Black women and girls to be seen in spaces that have often ignored and marginalized them. This book reveals the distinctive conundrum in which many Black women and girls are enmeshed as they pursue education. On one hand, some Black women and girls manage to thrive in educational spaces, leading to the ever-present headlines that Black women are the most educated group in the United States. However, this "good news" for Black women often results in the presumption that they are "okay" or somehow "magical" due to their accomplishments. The focus on these perceptions overshadows the fact that Black women and girls persevere without equitable resources (e.g., investments). Ultimately, Black women and girls are subjected to tropes centered on resilience and success, without deeper examination of their struggles; the mental, physical, and emotional toll of these struggles; and failures of educational institutions to provide adequate support. As Patton and Croom (2016) stated:

1

While the purpose of the Black Girl Magic message across Black women's communities is rooted in self-empowerment and uplift, the message has also been mishandled and used as a trope to diminish the complexity of its meaning for Black women, who are almost always forced to define and redefine themselves beyond stereotypical notions of resilience and success. (p. 7)

When #BlackGirlMagic is positioned as a trope, attention to the pervasive impact of the racism, sexism, classism, and violence they face is diminished. Such tropes make Black women's and girls' challenges forgettable, promoting a failure to see that their lives matter in ways that are seldom acknowledged. When Black women and girls are viewed as "magical" it becomes easy to dismiss the following:

- Black girls were "held back" a grade or "retained" at a rate of 21% in 2013, compared to 10% of girls overall (Smith-Evans et al., 2014).
- During the 2011/12 academic school year, Black girls were suspended from K–12 schools at the highest rate among girls, more than six times as often as their White female peers (Crenshaw, 2015). Wisconsin was the state with the highest out-of-school suspension rate (21%) for Black girls that year (Smith-Evans et al., 2014).
- In 2013, 39% of Black female high school seniors scored "below basic" in reading and 63% scored "below basic" in math (Smith-Evans et al., 2014).
- Black girls graduate from high school at rates lower than their Asian American and Pacific Islander, Latina, and White female classmates (Smith-Evans et al., 2014).
- Only 44% of Black women who began college in 2006 received bachelor's degrees within 6 years, compared to 61% of all female collegians (Smith-Evans et al., 2014).
- Black women earn less than most other groups in the United States ($34,000/year; DuMonthier et al., 2017).
- Black women's earnings are the primary foundation of Black families, with 80.6% of them bringing the primary financial support (DuMonthier et al., 2017).
- Black women experience poverty at rates greater than Black men and women of other races (DuMonthier et al., 2017).
- Black women are imprisoned at twice the rate of White women (DuMonthier et al., 2017).
- Black girls experience greater school discipline, representing 45% of all girls suspended during 2011–2012 (DuMonthier et al., 2017).

- 60% of Black girls are sexually assaulted before turning 18 (Black Women's Blueprint, 2018).
- Normalized negative characterizations of Black women (e.g., angry, aggressive, hypersexual) are routinely projected onto Black girls (Blake & Epstein, 2019).
- Black girls as young as 5 were "more likely to be viewed as behaving and seeming older than their stated age; more knowledgeable about adult topics, including sex; and more likely to take on adult roles and responsibilities than what would have been expected for their age" (Epstein et al., 2017, p. 8).
- In the 2011/12 school year, despite being only 28% of the female population, Black girls accounted for 61% of all girls disciplined in Boston (Crenshaw, 2015).
- Moreover, nationwide, Black girls in K–12 are:
  - seven times more likely to receive one or more out-of-school suspensions (National Black Women's Justice Institute, 2019);
  - four times more likely to be arrested (National Black Women's Justice Institute, 2019); and
  - over three times more likely to receive corporal punishment or be referred to law enforcement (National Black Women's Justice Institute, 2019).

Efforts to serve, support, and better understand Black women and girls require scholarship that raises important questions about their experiences in education. However, understanding their experiences means rethinking and reconsidering how issues are framed. Sociologist L'Heureux McCoy Lewis explained:

> If we think about the narrative of mass incarceration, we think about the ways in which black men and black boys have been locked up at increasing rates since the 1980s. While this is true, the fastest growing incarceration rate is among Black and Latino women. And because we haven't thought seriously about what's happening with Black girls and Latina girls, we tend to make the issue of incarceration solely male, and we miss the different ways in which we need to be intervening not just for our young boys, but also our young girls. (Martin, 2010, 2:14)

Kimberlé Crenshaw (2014) made a similar argument, sharing that policy reports and research data rarely attend to the challenges of Black girls or whether their challenges resemble or look completely different from those of Black boys. As an outspoken advocate on the need to center Black women and girls, Crenshaw addressed the White House's My Brother's Keeper Initiative, stating:

> Perhaps the exclusion of women and girls is the price to be paid for any race-focused initiative in this era. "Fixing" men of color—particularly young black men—hits a political sweet spot among populations that both love and fear them. Judging from the defense of My Brother's Keeper by many progressives and the awkward silence of their allies, the consequent erasure of females of color is regarded as neither politically nor morally significant. (para. 4)

She further declared:

> Gender exclusivity isn't new, but it hasn't been so starkly articulated as public policy in generations. It arises from the common belief that black men are exceptionally endangered by racism, occupying the bottom of every metric: especially school performance, work force participation and involvement with the criminal justice system. Black women are better off, the argument goes, and are thus less in need of targeted efforts to improve their lives. The White House is not the author of this myth, but is now its most influential promoter. (para. 5)

When we think of Black women and girls, it is easy to identify their successes, while never naming the disinvestments in that success. Conversely, when Black women and girls struggle, they are blamed and presumed to be deserving of their predicament. They expressly become their own disinvestment, rather than the unjust and inequitable educational system that has fundamentally failed them.

The purpose of this book is to illuminate scholarship on Black women and girls throughout the educational pipeline. The contributors, all Black women educators, scholars, and advocates, name the challenges Black women and girls face while pursuing their education as well as offer implications and recommendations for practitioners, policymakers, teachers, and administrators to consider in ensuring the success of Black women and girls. This book is divided into four sections, each offering a strategy for how readers should think about the educational success of Black women and girls.

In the first section of this book, "Mattering for Black Women and Girls in Schooling Contexts," the contributors call for stakeholders (e.g., educators, policymakers, communities) to invest in their educational success. Ruth Nicole Brown and Aria S. Halliday invite readers to stop and consider what success means for Black girls beyond dominant notions of achievement. They reflect on their work with Black girls and share lessons that emerge when

Black girls' lives are centered and when their voices (laughing) and movement (twerking) become the starting point for understanding success. Gholnescar E. Muhammad advocates for Black girl literacy spaces that encourage them to thrive personally and academically. She offers the Black girl literacies framework and its six critical components to engage Black girls in literacy pedagogies across the educational spectrum. Black girls and women should also matter in science, technology, engineering, and mathematics (STEM), yet they face significant barriers in these spaces. Nicole Joseph explains efforts underway to make STEM more accessible, their promises and pitfalls, as well as strategies to engage Black girls and women in these areas across the P–20 educational context. Charlotte E. Jacobs's chapter centers Black girls' emotions and emotional literacy as one way to ensure they matter. She explains that the way we tell Black girls about their emotions can either disempower them or promote their sense of agency to navigate educational contexts.

In Part Two, contributors engage in "Naming and Challenging the Violence and Criminalization of Black Women and Girls," issues that must be addressed if investments in their educational success are to be realized in a substantial way. Erin Corbett describes how the "mis"education of Black girls and women is rooted in limiting structural realities. She links the pushout of Black girls from schools to how Black women are situated in the justice system and the manner in which the educational system and justice system collude and fail them. Venus E. Evans-Winters and Dorothy E. Hines write about Black women and girls' erasure through a framework of "nobodyness." Nobodyness, they argue, is a form of erasure that disregards Black women and girls and leaves them absent from the same educational policies that deeply affect their lives and well-being in educational spaces. They further discuss educational policy discourses and school discipline that leads to violence and victimization of Black women and girls. Whereas Erin Corbett sheds light on education while incarcerated and the process of rehabilitation and reentry, Tiffany L. Steele discusses the outcomes of school disciplinary action on women who pursue college. She shares how these early schooling experiences inform Black women's navigation of collegiate environments. LaWanda W.M. Ward, Ayana T. Hardaway, and Nadrea R. Njoku specifically focus on how Title IX policy promotes intersectional failures that erase Black women and girls. They reimagine Title IX in a way that supports Black women and girls as they pursue their educational endeavors.

Part Three of this book focuses on "Navigating Politics and the Politicization of Black Women and Girls in Higher Education" contexts. Lori D. Patton, Keeley Copridge, and Sacha Sharp discuss how Black women navigate their pathways to college and theorize the notion of disinvestments in Black women's education. Such disinvestments often require

Black women to navigate without resources that could make their collegiate pathways smoother. Historically and in the present day as well, Black girls are subjected to hair politics that follow them into adulthood. Jamila L. Lee-Johnson provides a perspective on hair politics that affect Black women undergraduates who successfully obtain leadership roles while in college, particularly at historically Black colleges and universities (HBCUs). Janice A. Byrd and Christa J. Porter illuminate the importance of social/emotional and mental health for Black undergraduate women while examining the consequences to their identity and overall development when institutions fail to provide adequate resources to meet these needs. Mercedes Adell Cannon's discussion of how Black women with disabilities navigate higher education reveals that one essential way to center them is through privileging their narratives as knowledge and allowing their voices to be heard. This section concludes with Mildred Boveda as she reflects on her mother's socialization and its influence on her life. Boveda uses this reflection, along with the work of Audre Lorde, to engage readers in considering Black women's responsibilities for Black girls who attend college.

The final section of this book, "Still We Rise: Black Women and Girls Lifting and Loving Black Women and Girls," invites readers to think deeply about how we can and should position love and care for Black women and girls as the most significant investment in their educational success. Maisha T. Winn offers a transformative justice framework as one opportunity for educators to shift their mindset toward supporting the educational needs of Black girls. Monique Lane introduces the politicized ethic of care as a philosophy to address the invisibility and hypervisibility of Black girls. Rooted in Black women's pedagogical practices, Lane suggests this philosophical approach to support Black girls in dealing with the challenges they face in and beyond schools. Tykeia Robinson and Brittany Williams explore how Black women in higher education support one another and construct communities within digital environments. They argue that Black women use these spaces to retain each other in physical environments that are rarely supportive of their experiences. The final chapter, by Toby S. Jenkins and Vivian Anderson, speaks to the vital need for intergenerational love, commitment, and dialogue between Black women and girls. The authors lift up community-based educators, familial connections, and others within intergenerational villages who operate to ensure Black girls and women thrive.

We view this book as one of many efforts to make Black girls and women more visible in educational discourses. Too often, their voices are silenced or ignored rather than appreciated and valued. Although Black women and girls have accomplished amazing educational feats, they are not a monolithic group. Moreover, how they navigate the educational system is not because the system treats them well, but instead exists in resistance to the barriers and inequities the system reproduces that disproportionately affect them. The chapters presented in this book will explain how Black women and girls experience education and how such experiences can be both liberating and stifling in terms of their life trajectory. Although focused on education, each chapter will present broader societal implications for their success and well-being. Our hope is that readers will consider the challenges and issues Black women and girls encounter, but also juxtapose them with sound strategies that are ultimately implemented to support Black women and girls in achieving success, contributing to their families and surrounding communities, and engaging in leadership and advocacy for change.

References

Black Women's Blueprint. (2018). *Home page.* https://www.blackwomensblueprint. org/

Blake, J. J., & Epstein, R. (2019). *Listening to Black women and girls: Lived experiences of adultification bias.* Georgetown Law Center on Poverty and Inequality. https:// genderjusticeandopportunity.georgetown.edu/wp-content/uploads/2020/06/ Listening-to-Black-Women-and-Girls.pdf

Crenshaw, K. W. (2014, July 29). The girls Obama forgot. *New York Times.* https:// www.nytimes.com/2014/07/30/opinion/Kimberl-Williams-Crenshaw-My-Brothers-Keeper-Ignores-Young-Black-Women.html

Crenshaw, K. W., Ocen, P., & Nanda, J. (2015). *Black girls matter: Pushed out, over-policed and underprotected.* African American Policy Forum & Center for Inter-sectionality and Social Policy Studies. https://www.atlanticphilanthropies.org/ wp-content/uploads/2015/09/BlackGirlsMatter_Report.pdf

DuMonthier, A., Childers, C., & Milli, J. (2017). *The status of Black women in the United States.* Institute for Women's Policy Research. https://iwpr.org/wp-content/ uploads/2020/08/The-Status-of-Black-Women-6.26.17.pdf

Epstein, R., Blake, J. J., & González, T. (2017). *Girlhood interrupted: The erasure of Black girls' childhood.* Georgetown Law Center on Poverty and Inequality. https:// www.law.georgetown.edu/poverty-inequality-center/wp-content/uploads/ sites/14/2017/08/girlhood-interrupted.pdf

Martin, M. (2010, March 4). *Black male privilege?* [Radio Broadcast]. NPR. https:// www.npr.org/templates/story/story.php?storyId=124320675

National Black Women's Justice Institute. (2019). *End school pushout for Black girls and other girls of color: Federal, state and local policy recommendations.* https://950b1543-bc84-4d80-ae48-656238060c23.filesusr.com/ugd/0c71ee_7d 6b6469aa144b0397a4d7cd5d0f8051.pdf

Patton, L. D., & Croom, N. N. (2016). Critical perspectives on undergraduate Black women. In L. D. Patton & N. N. Croom (Eds.), *Critical perspectives on black women and college success* (pp. 1–13). Routledge.

Smith-Evans, L., George, J., Goss Graves, F., Kaufmann, L. S., & Frohlich, L. (2014). *Unlocking opportunity for African American girls: A call to action for educational equity.* NAACP Legal Defense and Educational Fund & National Women's Law Center. https://www.nwlc.org/sites/default/files/pdfs/unlocking_opportunity_for_african_american_girls_final.pdf

PART ONE

MATTERING FOR BLACK WOMEN AND GIRLS IN SCHOOLING CONTEXTS

I

MID-TWERK AND
MID-LAUGH

Ruth Nicole Brown and Aria S. Halliday

Another way

Create for Black girls opportunities to experience happiness.
Allow Black girls capacious good feelings for how they see a situation.
Black girls' ability to defy what you think, is possible, every day.
Do not settle in a moment that isn't yours.

Take pause.

Observe your surroundings, note the conditions, and resist white supremacist logics.

During a walk back to the conference hotel in Baltimore, Maryland, for the National Women's Studies Association Annual Meeting in 2017, we found a point of connection between us. Our research is undeniably informed by the love we have for Black girls. Love informs how we see each other and the research questions we find worthwhile to pursue. On our walk, mutual excitement about each other's work fueled collaborative possibilities between us. We were motivated in the best possible way by dance and laughter, our own and the Black girls we met through our respective research and public engagement processes. Those pleasures, in and outside of the school, academic, and writerly routine, ought not to be met with skepticism. This essay is our opportunity to write into curiosity about Black girl affect, to slow down, pause, and stretch the moments for what they might disclose and reveal about meanings of success for Black girls in educational spaces. Prescriptive notions of success seemingly fail everyone, and make issues and problems out of the ways student behaviors do not measure up to unappealing norms. We wanted to think about success for Black girls in education—grounded in something we felt. Therefore, we deliberately began with what we believe. We questioned dominant notions of success and wondered out loud what that very idea means to and for us as Black women. An unapologetic walking withness gave entrée to what matters to us outside of the regularly scheduled program and well-worn routine. It is with this insight that we write: When with Black girls, there is something about the sound of Black girl pleasures that can't ever really be *capturedcodedarchived* as productive or profitable by the school as industry and industrial complex—we aim to stay there, in the sounds of pleasure. We believe those possibilities hold authority.

As scholars of Black girlhood, we are enlivened by the opportunity to reflect on our respective research that is, for Brown—working for more than a decade with Black girls in collective decision-making spaces to celebrate Black girlhood via Saving Our Lives, Hear Our Truths (SOLHOT)—and for Halliday, working within popular culture and digital humanities to make Black girls visible as creators and as audiences. Together, we decided to write as we walked, with the walk as the writing, and then document the ways our distinct personal and professional experiences gave way to shared beliefs in Black girls. This text expresses our desire to make good on the collaborative promise of Black Girlhood Studies scholarship.

In this chapter, we pause to consider two very socially engaged moments of pleasure we have seen, felt, and been with where Black girls are enjoying themselves—laughing and twerking. The laugh and twerk, sometimes considered ruptures to schooling, offer those who believe in education a chance to take to task underlying beliefs about standard measures of social and emotional well-being, which implicate and inform "behavior discourse" at the very least; we are admittedly, however, reaching for something more radical than that—transformative epistemological shifts in the ways adults engage Black girls' happiness so that education is not also without the freedom and pleasure of Black girls' heads thrown back in laughter, feeling joy in their bodies, in the company of others who are also in on the joke yet never the joke itself.

Education is more than schooling. The educational system must redefine itself as Grace Lee Boggs (2011) wrote:

> Instead of trying to bully young people to remain in classrooms isolated from the community and structured to prepare them to become cogs in the existing economic system, we need to recognize that the reason why so

many young people drop out from inner-city schools is because they are voting with their feet against an educational system that sorts, tracts, tests, and rejects or certifies them like products of a factory because it was created in the age of industrialization. They are crying out for another kind of education that gives them opportunities to exercise their creative energies because it values them as whole human beings. (p. 49)

Boggs's critique of the system gives language to the kind of paradigm shift necessary and that we are after. We want to think more about the creative energies of students as Boggs suggested together with what Brown (2013) called creative potential, the artistry of Black girlhood, already occurring in classrooms—of all kinds—as representations of shifted values and meanings of education. In the examples that follow, we offer a critical thinking through of Black girl affective responses to schooling which both centers and hinges on what is believed of them, and a creative imaginative articulation of something other than what the rules and evaluations demand.

Advocating for a Pause

Consider us, for this moment, together and still. This intentional pause is useful for administrators, teachers, and youth workers who seek to more deeply interrogate dominant conceptualizations of schooling as punishment. If you've been paying attention to daily injustices, then you already know an epistemological time out is needed. According to Evans-Winters and Esposito (2010), "Because of racism, sexism, and class oppression in the U.S., African American girls are in multiple jeopardy of race, class and gender exclusion in mainstream educational institutions" (p. 13). And so we must ask if you've thought about Black girls, specifically, at all. These authors and others continue to make the case that it is necessary to address the ways identity and difference matter for Black girls in schools and society. A slowing down to think first, and then again, about the structural conditions that seemingly justify punishing Black girls in schools and other public spaces requires considering what was before, future speculations, and what was also going on at the same time as a way to grasp the emotional landscape (often ignored) on its widest continuum.

Criminalization and respectability are useful concepts for explaining responses to unequal structural conditions that too often and wrongly characterize and reduce Black girls to stereotypes. In educational spaces, Black girls are routinely criminalized for the typical behavior of children (Winn, 2011). Characterized as too loud and too aggressive, Black girls are systematically harassed and ushered into the prison industrial complex through higher numbers of suspensions and expulsions than any other children in schools (African American Policy Forum, 2015; Morris, 2019). Recent executive reports and popular education have pointed our attention to the disproportionate statistics and punitive discipline policies and other school-related decision-making that affect the well-being and life chances of Black girls. According to *Inequities Affecting Black Girls in Pittsburgh and Allegheny County* by Sara Goodkind (2016), "Black girls in Pittsburgh public schools are more than 3 times as likely as White girls to be suspended from school" (p. 3). Likewise, much of school policy from Black girls' dress to social behavior is constructed as issues to be dealt with, rather than engaging Black girls, imaginative here-and-now capacities to create worlds beyond what is known today. According to *The School Girls Deserve Report* (Girls for Gender Equity, 2017),

> to actualize the school that girls and TGNC [trans gender and nonconforming] youth of color deserve, we must flip the conversation from what do we need to do to keep young people from being pushed out of school to focusing on how we create the schools that girls and TGNC youth of color want and need in order to succeed. (p. 43)

They also note the need for stronger support systems in the form of "a shift in teaching culture and teacher education that would make teachers more respectful and caring" (p. 29). In this way, we point to the usefulness in Black girls' own epistemological frameworks, particularly around pleasure as necessary foundations in creating transformative pedagogical spaces that not only acknowledge Black girls as fully human but also position education as a site for affirmation and humane transformation for all kids.

While Butler (2018), Evans-Winters (2005), Morris (2019), Richardson (2007), and others have articulated important shifts in pedagogical standards to account for the multiplicity and dearth of experiences that Black girls have in educational spaces, we argue that there need to be shifts, also, in the epistemological references used to learn Black girlhood. What remains necessary is a conceptualization of Black girlhood powerful enough for us to forgo the tacit understandings that contribute to carceral conditions. Slippery institutional language does not harvest enough texture for a concept of Black girlhood, as we hold on to Black girls who insist on holding on to each other. In spite of many valuations of diversity (multiculturalism, inclusion, etc.) to create knowledge that may undo oppressive structures, we must articulate our beliefs about what is educationally possible, beyond the distrustful expectations in part that come about because of recognition, that keep the status quo going strong.

The challenge to us all is to create educational spaces that respect another way of challenging current arrangements of power so that the oppression of Black girls is no longer. We can love boldly enough to grow other kinds of power. Not for them, but with them because it's necessary. On our walk, there is no behavioral problem. We are not defined by drama. We paused all of that. We are thinking together of different ways of learning, listening, and teaching. Believe with us. Picture us laughing. Today and tonight, we twerk.

Believe Black Girlhood
Believe Black girlhood songs made possible because the demands of schooling require them remaking the unknowable in crevices of the known.
Believe in Black girlhood holding everything we are and are not, our individual and collective fantasies and failures.
Believe in Black girlhood wonderment. Favor frameworks of pleasure just as much as you wish to tackle problems. I wonder & what if secret passwords to better days.
Believe in Black girlhood
Radical   Decolonized   Deprivatized   Embodied
Not easily, because it is not easy.
Not quickly, because it does not happen in an instant.
Believe in Black girls' laughter, an imaginative context for rehearsal and improvisation of which is most sincerely calling us and we obsessively yearn to answer back with our truths, fomented by idiosyncratic stylings that live beneath the skin.
Believe in Black girls' dance as promise to consistently resound and cherish. Before all, there is no justice in Black girlhood without them who name themselves Black girls and femmes. After all, Black girls realize what words and meanings are at the bottom of the locker, needing to be thrown away.
Believe in Black girlhood preferences. Believe in the nonimperialistic knowledge of I am and I am not a girl.

The poetic reflection, written by Brown, foregrounds and mirrors the deeply held conviction we have about Black girls: Black girls' creativity is too often devalued and punished by adult interpretations that also sometimes miss the educational possibilities of how Black girls see and understand themselves. Yet, even in institutional spaces like schools, there are ruptures and moments of freedom that reveal a greater arts and humanities of everyday life than can be governable and ordered. As educators who care deeply about Black girls' experiences in our presence and as they navigate public spaces, we found it especially generative to think together about our beliefs specifically, and the relationship between belief and action.

We want to know what you, dear reader, believe about Black girls because such information is at the heart of this matter. The matter being the ideas you have about Black girls as a group and the singular Black girl whose life you desire to positively influence. Black girls, and our beliefs about who they are, are absolutely worth naming, thinking more about, and expressing out loud. Following Gwendolyn Brooks (1993) in her novel *Maud Martha*, "what was unreal to you, you could deal with violently" (p. 153). By making Black girls real, through the centering of their pleasure, we invite you to recognize Black girls for who they are. We are absolutely for who Black girls say they are, as they say they are.

Mid-Laugh

You already know

we had just finished up in the bathroom

She held me up right angle and smiled hugged up close to a friend I could tell they were having fun really enjoying each other fits of laughter and giggles

She pushed down   I did what I always do   Record

Next thing I know it was eight or nine beautiful Black girl smiles in view

The lighting did them right   they sent one of my files to Facebook

I love being held by her   she's more fun than the other one   As we were walking back to the group   I knew someone was following us   Right as her game was about to start back up she put me in the pocket   everything got quiet Dr. Brown was stuttering looking into another one of my kind   I heard the girls say   "Ohhh weeee" as soon as we came up in here   my system automated to theirs

it's automatic   I can't help it   It was set up like that

I told you   my old owner was into some dirt I was passed down now I'm in the hands of she   who keeps me busy   There is so much sweet and sour gossip in seventh grade   I hear them inquiring about my whereabouts   who I am   who I belong to they sound so mean   Full-breasted authorities   my innocent new owner loyal to me

she already know

     this gift gonna cost

Our bathroom session was used against us   Privacy   illusion   I knew that   but why should she assume   Those smiles   I recorded were sent   Facebook   we know now,   showed up on screen   to some people   could not see   who definitely   saw us.   I could not even help   it.

     I did not know the system knew when I entered the building

They took me away from her   I'm glad they just took me with
them and not her
     I'll miss her smile

     Seems like the sound of Black girls' laughter can't ever last longer than
my charge without them showing up and separating us from each other.

     The sound of Black girls' laughter can't ever last longer than my charge
without them showing up and separating us from each other.

     Black girls' laughter can't ever last longer than my charge without them
showing up
     and separating us from
     each
     other

One time we decided to go bowling and the police appeared, questioned
us, and took her phone. A phone is for many seventh-graders a social world
they can plug into and the police unplugged it, attempting to unplug her
power which is exactly how respectability coconstitutes corporate surveillance which coconstitutes increased criminalization, and coconstitutes segregation with the Black girls I live, love, and work with in Saving Our Lives
Hear Our Truths. I wrote a persona poem for this girl's iPhone because that
technology, I believe, if it could speak would talk first about her smile and
give receipts—all those selfies and usies as documentation of a kind of peace
and happiness that grows from the inside. If phones could talk, it could tell
the police of her innocence and it's only because of the world we currently
live in that a persona iPhone poem is necessary because you too know that
technology is sometimes trusted more than human interaction. This again,
is the horror.

     Black girls' laughter can't ever last longer than my charge without them
     showing up
     and separating us from
     each
     other.

Racialized gendered surveillance means technological devices and online
platforms can be taken, the algorithms are not neutral, and somebody can
decide to hack and derisively use our words, our lives, our school routine.
But Black girlhood can repurpose technologies like cell phones so that we can

still call who we need to call. What I learned that day is they took her phone, but we were still able to call each other and answer. Listen to us expressing each other and you hear Grace Lee Boggs's (2011) wisdom at work and play as we have already "transitioned to a new postindustrial world based on partnership among ourselves and with our environment rather than patriarchal and bureaucratic domination" (p. 43). Ultimately, we want to suggest a new vision: Where there is Black girls' laughter uninterrupted, there is education happening, powerful knowledge being shared and enjoyed.

Mid-Twerk

Like laughing, Black girls' bodily expression is criminalized by authoritarian teachers, administrators, and community workers. However, we contend that the recapitulation of twerking in education as education provides the knowledge teachers hope students learn about community and connection. In classrooms and in social areas of schools, Black girls face particularly difficult odds because of the authoritarian attitudes attached to their bodily behaviors. Matching contemporary representations of Black girls as *ghetto* or *ratchet*, adults in schools recreate binaries of behavior that always situate Black girls negatively. Teachers and administrators construct Black girls as dangerous to the learning environment and therefore racially code them as deviants despite their educational success, marked as inherently *loud* because of their skin (Shange, 2019).

Despite Black girls' understanding and reception of racialized ideas of their bodies in educational settings, they find solace and even joy in the social activity of twerking. Much like the process of learning to write one's own name, Black girls learn, elevate, collapse, retool, extend, push, and pull on ideas of dance in what we today consider *twerking*. YouTube provides hundreds of "black girl dance ciphers" that illustrate joy, laughter, and creativity formed through twerking (Brown, 2008).

When we believe Black girls and the creativity informed by their experiences, we shift our pedagogical frameworks to include dance and breaks as forwarding educational success. As a type of pep rally—or social space where people gather to inspire, insight allegiance, and excite for future occurrences—Black girl twerk sessions in schools in the past, presently, and in the future provide the bodily opportunity and physical space for cultural expression. I call us to pause mid-twerk—mid-booty isolation, hip movement, back elongation. When we stop the struggle for the control of Black girls' bodies and allow them to see the joy and pleasure in the creative bodily movement of twerking, we as bystanders and they as participants witness how every dancer imbues each movement with their own signature, their own originality, their own distinctiveness. Dancing together in a cipher engenders a proximity to others, an intentional closeness, through experiencing together (Halliday, 2020). When we allow Black girls to pause and take control of their own bodies, pleasure, and self-expression, we witness the transformative power of education.

Black girls find their own expressive possibilities through dance and recognize the ingenuity of others as they mimic, celebrate, and challenge one another. For example, in the Vine video "Carver Twerk Girls," three Black girls twerk in an empty hallway with book bags and matching outfits. Jubilant and laughing, Black girls are at the center of this video portraying similar but differing booty popping moves. They energize each other's moves with the prevailing call "Aye!" The gleeful smile and laughter at the end portray the 6 seconds of joy they were able to bring to each other. "High School Musical in the Hood," another Vine set in a lunch room with kids of all ages and potentially parents, shows how Black girls can platonically energize and excite others with their moves. The camera focuses on one girl in the foreground; however, behind her are multiple girls dancing happily on tables and on the floor. The video cuts to the same girl dancing on a table, elevated for others to see how dedicated she is to her moves. More people—boys and girls—join her on the table and soon the room is alive with dancing and celebrating. As the song "All in This Together" plays happily on top of the dancers, we indeed witness a community fostered by twerking.

In both videos, we see how twerking has developed and changed to encompass all the variety that Black girls express in other ways such as hair and fashion. Twerking, as they do in groups and to different audiences, then is an assembly of individuality and originality, a coming together of different bodies and connections to dance. Twerking bridges knowledge of self, connection to others, and the creation (and/or negotiation) of community.

Conclusion

Twerking and laughing are human expressive behaviors, yet through the ways that Black girls are criminalized in contemporary educational spaces, there is little room for the full belly laughter and body contouring that they exhibit in other spaces. There should be an intentional educational shift that allows for a fuller range of human expression that isn't regulated and criminalized in schools. We challenge the idea that twerking and laughing are inherently oppositional to education. To pause mid-twerk and mid-laugh—before the consequence of crime and punishment come into place—regards that we as an educational community must look at other possibilities of feeling the movement.

There are a number of strategies of incorporating epistemological positionalities of Black girls within the classroom or school environment. For example, the videos of teachers incorporating dance in the classroom presents the possibilities of regarding twerking as pep rally, which enfolds experiences of laughter, joy, and community building within the cipher. When the school environment comes together to encourage, recognize, and celebrate, as illustrated from the rise of these popular videos mostly by teachers of color, we see an excitement for education as well as a maintenance of human dignity for all involved. We challenge educators and administrators to review the questions and bibliographic information we have included to further their beliefs of Black girlhood to the moment of pause.

Discussion Questions

1. What do you believe about Black girls? Who and what has shaped those beliefs?
2. How does your school promote creative expression and unregulated movement?
3. What emotions do you regularly experience in the company of Black girls? How might those feelings be structured by school policies?
4. How can we sustain uninterruptable spaces of Black girls laughing in public so as to create the conditions from which then to educate each other about coming undone as a way to learning something more about happiness?

Further Reading

The following recommended readings take up the radical possibilities of education in ways that we believe value Black and Latina girls as whole human beings.

African American Policy Forum & Center for Intersectionality and Social Policy Studies. (2015). *Black girls matter: Pushed out, overpoliced and underprotected.* http://static1.squarespace.com/static/53f20d90e4b0b80451158d8c/t/54dcc1ece 4b001c03e323448/1423753708557/AAPF_BlackGirlsMatterReport.pdf
Brown, R. N. (2008). *Black girlhood celebration: Toward a hip-hop feminist pedagogy.* Peter Lang.

Carney, C., Hernandez, J., & Wallace, A. (2016). Sexual knowledge and practiced feminisms: On moral panic, Black girlhoods, and hip hop. *Journal of Popular Music Studies, 28*(4), 412–426. https://doi.org/10.1111/jpms.12191

Carrillo, R. (2006). Humor casero mujerista (womanist humor of the home): Laughing all the way to greater cultural understandings and social relations. In D. D. Bernal, C. A. Elenes, F. E. Godinez, & S. Villenas (Eds.), *Chicana/ Latina education in everyday life: Feminista perspectives on pedagogy and epistemology* (pp. 181–196). SUNY Press.

Ford, T. (2019). *Dressed in dreams: A Black girl's love letter to the power of fashion.* St. Martin's Press.

Halliday, A. (2019). *The Black girlhood studies collection.* Women's Press.

Hernandez, J. (2021). *Aesthetics of excess: The art and politics of Black and Latina embodiment.* Duke University Press.

Jarmon, R. (2013). *Black girls are from the future: Essays on race, digital creativity and pop culture.* Jarmon Publishing.

Kwakye, C. J., Hill, D. C., & Callier, D. M. (Eds.). (2017). 10 years of Black girlhood celebration: A pedagogy of doing. *Departures in Critical Qualitative Research, 6*(3), 1–10. https://doi.org/10.1525/dcqr.2017.6.3.1

Lindsey, T. B. (2014). Let me blow your mind: Hip hop feminist futures in theory and praxis. *Urban Education, 50*(1), 52–77. https://doi.org/ 10.1177/0042085914563184

McMillan-Cottom, T. (2019). *Thick: And other essays.* The New Press.

Pérez, E. (2015). The ontology of Twerk: From "sexy" Black movement style to Afro-diasporic sacred dance. *African and Black Diaspora: An International Journal, 9*(1), 16–31. https://doi.org/10.1080/17528631.2015.1055650

References

Boggs, G. L. (with Kurashige, S.). (2011). *The next American revolution: Sustainable activism for the twenty-first century.* University of California Press.

Brooks, G. (1993). *Maud Martha.* Third World Press. Originally published 1953 by Harper & Row.

Brown, R. N. (2008). *Black girlhood celebration: Toward a hip-hop feminist pedagogy.* Peter Lang.

Brown, R. N. (2013). *Hear our truths: The creative potential of Black girlhood.* University of Illinois Press.

Butler, T. (2018). Black girl cartography. *Review of Research in Education, 42*(1), 28–45. https://doi.org/10.3102/0091732X18762114

Evans-Winters, V. (2005). *Teaching Black girls: Resiliency in urban classrooms.* Peter Lang.

Evans-Winters, V., & Esposito, J. (2010). Other people's daughters: Critical race feminism and Black girls' education. *Educational Foundations, 24*(1), 11–24. https://files.eric.ed.gov/fulltext/EJ885912.pdf

Girls for Gender Equity. (2017). *The schools girls deserve report.* http://www.ggenyc
.org/the-schools-girls-deserve/

Goodkind, S. (2016). *Inequities affecting Black girls in Pittsburgh and Allegheny County.* FISA Foundation & the Heinz Endowments. http://www.heinz.org/ UserFiles/Library/Inequities_Affecting_Black_Girls_in_Pittsburgh_and_Allegheny_County

Halliday, A. S. (2020). Twerk sumn: Theorizing Black girl epistemology in the body. *Cultural Studies, 34*(6), 874–891. https://doi.org/10.1080/09502386.2020 .1714688

Morris, M. (2019). *Sing a rhythm, dance a blues: Education for the liberation of Black and Brown girls.* The New Press.

Richardson, E. (2007). "She was workin like foreal": Critical literacy and discourse practices of African American females in the age of hiphop. *Discourse and Society, 18*(6), 789–809. https://doi.org/10.1177/0957926507082197

Shange, S. (2019). *Progressive dystopia: Abolition, anthropology, and race in the new San Francisco.* Duke University Press.

Winn, M. (2011). *Girl time: Literacy, justice, and the school-to-prison pipeline.* Teachers College Press.

2

BLACK GIRLS LITERACIES FRAMEWORK

Gholnecsar E. Muhammad

We, the Sister Authors, will promise to push the boundaries of our existence to learn from the past, act on our present and improve our future. We can teach others as our history has taught us. By putting our pens to paper and our voices to action, we can defy all stereotypes put on Black girls by society. As Black girls, we will replace guns with pens and revive the broken spirits within ourselves and our race to break through societal barriers. We, as Black queens, will build kingdoms with our language using the strong identities of our Sisters as pillars of guidance. We are more than enough. Remember, nothing is placed upon us that we cannot handle. We will not allow the chains of injustice to tie us down. We must strive to be the living embodiment of Black excellence. We will juxtapose ignorance with our intellect and fight through our struggles and challenges through the power of words. We are smart and strong and we express our feelings by writing.

Over the past 8 years, I have been developing a program called Black Girls W.R.I.T.E ("Writing to Represent our Identities, our Times, and our Excellence"). Each summer, a group of 8–25 girls (we call each other "Sister Authors") aged 9–17 come together to read and write. We typically meet for 3 days a week, 3 hours per session, on a college campus. During this time, the girls and I read from and discuss Black women's literature typically found on college-level syllabi. For example, we have read from authors such as Toni Morrison, Audre Lorde, Maria Stewart, Frances Harper, and Alice Walker. Our readings lead to the study and composition of various genres of writing such as protest poetry, personal narratives, short stories, public addresses, editorials, and letters. Black Girls W.R.I.T.E was created for girls in elementary, middle, and high school to gather to read, write, and think, with three distinct purposes: (a) to define their identities, (b) to resist oppression and misrepresentations, and (c) to write toward social change. One of the first literacy practices we engage in is writing a preamble to what is essentially a powerful manifesto. On the 1st day, I ask the girls to write statements that speak to the purpose and power of their pens. Then, after sharing, they collectively decide where they want each statement to be placed. In the summer of 2018, 25 girls penned the preamble beginning the chapter.

Honoring the past, validating the present, and looking toward the future, their preamble exemplifies the importance of using their pens toward resistance to ways in which society negatively depicts Black girls. In contrast, they write to define their lives so that others do not tell their stories. Referring to themselves as *queens*, they explain that they will use language in ways to acknowledge their imposed challenges but to also express their standpoints. The line "We are more than enough" perhaps serves as a reminder that Black girls are often told that they are not enough or good enough to thrive personally and academically. They conclude their writing by stating their desire and aim to be an embodiment of Black excellence.

A Reflection of History

Black Girls W.R.I.T.E. reflects Black women's literary societies of the 19th century. Throughout the 1800s, a central objective among Black people was to improve and elevate themselves through literary means. The ways in which they set out to counter the conditions they endured during a time of racism and oppression was through reading, writing, and engaging in literary texts. As part of a broader struggle against countering multiple attacks of oppression with violence, they used their minds and their pens as weapons to battle injustice. Books and other forms of texts became ammunition to fuel their progress. They worked toward cultivating the minds and hearts within themselves and among others, which led them to being equipped to face and alter the nation's harshest realities and countless attacks of terror placed upon Black people. Literacy became beyond a set of skills to possess but also the instruments used to define their lives and the tools used to advocate for their rights. To this end, Black people developed literary societies in the urban northeast of the United States, essentially collaborative spaces used to construct knowledge and engage one another toward nurturing a literary culture. The earliest of these societies were led by Black males, and then Black women created spaces of their own (McHenry, 2002; Porter, 1936).

The Need for Black Girl Literacy Spaces Today

The need to create such spaces for Black girl literacies stems from mismatches in education and within the broader society, as we know that schools are a reflection of the wider sociopolitical landscape across communities. One of these mismatches includes the dichotomy between how Black women and girls define themselves and how the public and media view them. While

Black women have traditionally seen themselves as beautiful and complex, the public has depicted them in polar opposite ways. For example, through their writings, Black women have written out the complexity of Black womanhood/girlhood. Valerie Lee (2006) reviewed over 150 examples of Black women's writings, ranging from colonial and antebellum periods to the 21st century. She reviewed several genres of text such as poetry, short stories, autobiographies, memories, and essays and found that Black women expressed themselves across several identities and themes, including beauty; gender; race; education and intellect (including writing about literacy and language); arts and creativity; global, national, regional, and local identities; religion; family, friendships, relationships, and intergenerational representations; and health, life, and death. As they were writing across these diverse topics, they were writing in resistance to the ways others have oppressed them. They did so to create awareness, self-advocacy, and move toward social justice. Black women sought to represent themselves in literary traditions to make their voices public. Their writings exhibited a quest and display of the multiplicity of their lives. Writing also served as a social platform to write to wide audiences about critical issues that were important to them. Their representations about diverse topics affecting their lives signified the plurality of their voices. Their writings were expressions of "self, of society, and of self in society" while also the means to "write themselves into being" (Royster, 2000, p. 5). Black women's writing practices were not merely skills to obtain or acts of participation but instead embodied a purposeful significance to their lives (Peterson, 1995). This is in contrast to the racist and sexist media ads aimed at Black women and girls. From the historic tropes of the hypersexualized Jezebel, the hyperangry Sapphire, and the servant woman who did not receive love she deserved, these visual and written assaults have held a dominant force in the ways others see Black women and girls (Harris & Hill, 1998; Ladson-Billings, 2009; Stephens & Phillips, 2003; West, 2008).

In addition to the mismatch to the ways Black women and girls have defined themselves compared to how others have, there is also a divergence to how Black women were educated historically compared to how they are taught in classrooms today. While in the past Black women came together in environments that offered care, healing, and education that attended to their lives, current educational practices are static, linear, and deficient for who Black girls are (Crenshaw et al., 2015). Literacy groups such as Black Girls W.R.I.T.E are key due to the growing number of Black girls in classrooms across the United States and the rate in which they are being underserved in literacy education, particularly when it comes to reading and writing achievement (Muhammad, 2012a). Classroom spaces are not currently providing Black girls with the most effective literacy education. This is evident by low achievement rates and the growing and disproportionate number of school suspensions and expulsions of Black girls compared to other racial and gendered populations of youth (M. Morris, 2016). Further, Black girls are more likely to experience school punishments, receive lower grades, experience grade-level retention, and have their behavior as the focal point rather than their academic aptitude (E. Morris, 2007). In contrast, when a historical perspective is taken on the literacy development of Black girls, there exists a narrative of excellence and high achievement—one that is responsive to the cultural identities of Black girls and the social times. Creating literacy spaces for Black girls returns to this historical excellence that is less visible in schools and classrooms. This may reduce and eliminate the disparaging statistics that do not paint a complete picture of Black girls' literacies and education.

Purpose of the Chapter

From my direct community work with Black Girls W.R.I.T.E (Muhammad, 2014), historical and archival research on Black literary societies (Muhammad 2012b, 2015), and from conducting a literature review over the past 25 years of Black girls' literacies (Muhammad & Haddix, 2016), I found that Black girls' literacies are reflective of the ways in which Black women have historically practiced literacy. Black girl literacies are consumed in defining self, practices of resistance, and changing communities for the better. More pointedly, they were embedded within six components of literacy, which I define as the *Black girls literacies framework* (BGLF). These six components are useful and necessary for engaging Black girls in literacy pedagogies across grade levels and contexts. They include an understanding that Black girls' literacies are:

1. multiple
2. tied to identities
3. historical
4. collaborative
5. intellectual
6. political/critical

The purpose of this chapter is to discuss the BGLF and its components and affordances for framing literacy in learning. In doing so, I draw upon several writings of Black girls throughout 8 years of Black Girls W.R.I.T.E institutes that illustrate each of the six components of the BGLF. The framework takes up a multiple literacies perspective and moves beyond the emphasis of defining literacy as *just* reading and writing skills. Instead, it compasses a view of literacy as plural and as a set of diverse practices. If literacy practices in classrooms are multiple and diverse, then students have a greater potential to achieve both personally and academically. Specifically, Black girl epistemologies are multidimensional, multilayered, nuanced, and complex (Muhammad & Haddix, 2016). In the following section, I will define each of the components of the framework and connect the component to an example from research and to a sample piece of writing from Black Girls W.R.I.T.E. It is important however to note that these components are intended to work together and not in isolation. Collectively, when Black girls have engaged within these six literacies, they have advanced in cognitive, sociocultural, and critical literacies.

Black Girl Literacies Are Multiple

Black girls do not practice literacies in isolation. Their literacies are multiple both in practice and theoretical orientations. Historically, Black women would come together to read, discuss literature, write about literature, and then speak (and often debate) about the concept found in the literature read. Thus, they were engaged in literacy practices that were intertwined and interwoven. As an extension to traditional literacies that focus on reading, writing, thinking, and language development in seclusion, Black girls thrive when they are collectively practiced together. In addition, Black girls also engage in digital literacies to influence their meaning-making of the world (Price-Dennis, 2016). For example, in Greene's (2016) study, she examined social media and how adolescent Black girls made sense of their identities through an online book club. Through digital spaces, the girls were afforded opportunities to have discussions about the text and talk about their own positionalities and subjectivities in the world.

During Black Girls W.R.I.T.E, the girls naturally engaged in multiple acts of literacy as they often shifted between reading, talking, researching, and writing about critical topics that were urgent from their pens. In one example during the 2016 institute, 14-year-old Dorothy (all names are pseudonyms) was interested in the topic of the appropriation of Black women and girls' beauty. She spent a great deal of time researching the concept of appropriation and its history. After reading, she talked about what she read, took notes, and wrote several pieces (from poetry to a public address) to create awareness of the topic. In her journal, she wrote:

> *What if the hairstyle that you wore as a child suddenly became chic?* Well this is happening to the black community. White people have been taking things from us from the beginning of time. And know they have taken something they once ridiculed. As Jesse Williams said, "Whiteness uses and abuses us, burying black people out of sight and out of mind while extracting our culture, our dollars, our entertainment like oil—black gold, ghettoizing

and demeaning our creations then stealing them, gentrifying our genius and then trying us on like costumes before discarding our bodies like rinds of strange fruit." He is completely right. But, why? Why has it become suddenly desirable? I believe it is because recently we have all been more accepting of our looks, and even loving ourselves. But some might say that even we appropriate white culture—the culture that was forced upon us for hundreds of years. So I ask, who is wrong?

Dorothy follows this by penning the following poem:

Everywhere I look
And the places I go
I see black people
No mo'
I see black skin
But . . .
No black sin
Whites want to be our identical twin
But . . .
Have you been?
Has your kin
Been taken away because of your skin
But . . .
They could never be black
Never copy our melanin
Go ahead and play your tiny violin
Dwelling in your tiny violin
But . . .
In this social weigh-in
They will always have leeway
But . . .
Will never win

Both pieces of writing embody the multiplicity of literacy practices from her reading, research, and thinking about appropriation, and she captures the inner disturbance of taking Black culture.

Black Girl Literacies Are Historical

Black girl literacies are embedded in history. Specifically, they are wrapped up in the histories of African people and Black women. Throughout centuries, Black women's writings have been connected to each other in the concepts written about and the ways in which they are written for both collective and self-advocacy. Royster (2000) referred to this historical connection in discussing the *zamani* (meaning "past") *dimension* of Black women literacies. She found that Black women have drawn upon the writings of other Black women to shape their own writings and their literate self-expressions are similar to the writings of other Black women. Black women were introduced to one another through their writings, and their language provided comfort and mentorship for readers. This connection is intricately woven into the culture and is then conveyed across generations of women and girls. Royster (2000) posited that it is through the zamani dimension that Black women learn who they are, and this transmission (to other women and girls) may occur intuitively, instinctively, spiritually, or through social and cultural practices of storytelling and writing. This connection speaks to the historic and linguistic continuity of writings among Black women and it carries over into the literacies of young Black girls. I found this to be true in a study where I examined the instructional variables when I designed a summer institute that in ways mirrored the historical literacy practices of Black women's literary societies (Muhammad, 2015). Similar to history, girls of different age groups and backgrounds came together to read, write, and think for the advancement of themselves and society. I noted three central contextual variables that the girls found most beneficial to their writings when connecting their ideas to history: (a) reading mentor texts, (b) possessing the freedom to write openly without censorship, and (c) having uninterrupted writing time. In addition, designing a writing space grounded in history created opportunities for girls to cultivate their writing development.

When leading the Black Girls W.R.I.T.E institute, I found it beautifully interesting how the writings of Black women historically connected to Black girls' writings today. They connected in style, structure, and theme. For example, I found the topics of hair, colorism, and flowers to describe the multiplicity of oneself to be a common theme in writings. In one example from the 2010 institute, 15-year-old Violet writes about both her hair and history in the poem "My Roots":

My seed was planted into this American soil in 1994
Nourished with assimilation
My roots began to grow
Until I blossomed into America's favorite flower,
The rose
My rich red petals pleased society
Until my roots expanded and grew into the Motherland
Drinking from the Nile River

Taking in the proper nutrition
I became the flower I was meant to be
The African Violet
Uniqueness standing out among beautiful roses

In her poem, Violet complicates the word *roots* by describing both her heritage (history and lineage) and her *hair-itage* (hair). In this writing, she alluded to the history of her ancestors coming to America who became, quote, "nourished with assimilation," or forced and encouraged to become like the White Americans. Although the assimilation she described was forced, she wrote that people sharing her racial background began to flourish into beautiful flowers. This agentic "flower," as she sees herself, was enriched with traits from the "Motherland" as well as from her current land, America. She writes among the history of her ancestors and uses literary devices and metaphors to define self.

Black Girl Literacies Are Tied to Their Identities

There has hardly been a time when Black women and girls have practiced literacy without making sense of who they are. As Black girls read, write, and think, they are defining their identities, which includes the ways in which others perceive them. Identity development is intricately woven into practices of literacy that enable engagement in a deeper sense of self. Identities are ever-changing and dynamic; therefore, girls practicing literacies are in a constant state of shaping and reshaping the ways in which they see their lives. Examples of identities include racial, ethnic, cultural, gender, kinship, academic/intellectual, personal/individual, sexual, and community selves. Young people especially need opportunities in literacy pedagogy to not only explore multiple facets of self-identity but also learn about the identities of others who are different from them. Typically, each researcher who centers Black girls in their studies has somehow focused on identity. Richardson (2007) examined how Black girls explore various identities of Black women presented in the media, specifically music videos, because mass media has played a significant role in the construction of ideals and cultural conceptions about Black people. Richardson gave examples of the

> bad black girl, video vixen imagery linked to historic controlling images of the wench and the jezebel; the wench, commonly exchanged with bitch which was used to refer to an enslaved (and sometimes free) female, whose sexual behavior was deemed to be loose and immoral. (p. 790)

She explored how some of these same historical depictions are rendered and exploited in media and how Black women and girls construct meaning from them. She found that providing space for them to use their language to "critique and identify the social situatedness of black youth" demonstrated their ability to critically examine how they view the messages (Richardson, 2007, p. 806).

In the 2010 Black Girls W.R.I.T.E institute, 16-year-old Iris penned a poem on the importance of being "my sister's keeper":

I am my sister's keeper because I am my sister. We are bound together through our shared ancestry as well as the ambiguity of the same. Together we walk the spoken steps of those that came before us tracing a line from yesterday's past to today's present that paints our future. When I look in the mirror it is not only my own reflection that stares back at me but hers as well. Our sun kissed skin may come in different shades and the curls that spiral from the crowns of our heads may differ in texture but the blood that courses through our veins is no different. I am my sister's keeper because even if I tried not to be and acted with only what I thought were intentions concerning my benefit I would only be deceiving myself. If I trampled over my sisters dreams in order to obtain what I thought were mine alone in actuality my dreams would suffer the same fate. We are one. My struggle is her struggle. My triumph is her triumph. My pain is her pain. There is no action I can ever take or any decision that I could ever make that would not affect her. If a picture could be drawn to someway represent our interconnectedness the roots of the most ancient tree in the entire world would be shown and just as its roots are so intertwined the beginning cannot be separated from its end so are we. I must do for her as I would do for myself. If I see the hand of my sister stretched out to me in need I must grasp it and help her carry on. If I see the eyes of my sister filled to the brim with tears I must wipe them away and provide the words to heal her soul. If I see the empty mouth of my sister match her aching belly I must reach into my cupboards and give unto her because that is what it means to be your sister's keeper. An unconditional positive regard and a willingness to ameliorate whatever situation I may find her is a true keeper because if she is nothing I am also nothing. In order to be something I must elevate her along with me. No matter what amount of success I achieve or honors I receive, if my sister is not of the equivalent they mean nothing. I am my sister's keeper because I am my sister. To be a true keeper of one's sister one must consider their self and her to be one in the same and therefore take actions regarding both.

In this piece of writing, Iris captures the essence of Black girlhood and how our existence is bound within each other. Having an opportunity to write to make sense of Black girls' identities, she captures the history, brilliance, and potential of Black girl identities. In doing so, she acknowledges the various shades of Black girls and our interconnectedness.

Black Girl Literacies Are Collaborative

Black girl literacies are collaborative in nature and they advance in their education when they work together. Collaboration is more than just working in groups or pairs but is also a shared understanding of collective responsibility. In the Black Girls W.R.I.T.E institute, we took up the Islamic hadith of "wanting for your sister what you want for yourself." This was something that the girls naturally engaged in when the space of collaboration was created. As they were making sense of their lives through literature and text, they were coconstructing ideas together. In an example from research, McArthur (2016) engaged girls in a critical media program called Beyond Your Perception. With eight high school girls, this 14-week program was designed to push beyond the limited boundaries or perceptions that others sometimes have about Black girls. Through multiple meetings, the girls critiqued media images and messages related to Black womanhood/girlhood to engage in personal identity construction. Together they examined popular culture and tied it to historical representations of Black women and girls. She found that when girls worked collaboratively, a space was created for meaning-making, healing, and self work.

There are several examples of collaborative writing within Black Girls W.R.I.T.E. The girls have coauthored pieces of writing and written together. In one particular example, I have asked girls to write kinship poetry. Kinship writing is when one piece of writing has a relationship with another (Muhammad et al., 2017). In kinship writing, the texts that writers read serve as mentors to help *them* write their own pieces. Black women have been kinship writers to each other throughout time. In one example of kinship writing between Black women writers, Rita Dove used the Black ideology–centered writings of her mentor, Gwendolyn Brooks, to write the poem "Teach Us to Number Our Days." Both poets wrote to depict the violence in the lives of Black youth.

In 2016, 14-year-old Nikki wrote the poem "Strangled":

Peeking through a small hole, where nobody seems to hear my cry
Hating myself for something I didn't do
Beating myself, worrying why I can't get out
I'm Strangled

I'm Stuck
My brain is tightening, worrying if I would die if I tried to make one buck
I'm Strangled
I'm Stuck
No one seems to understand
The pain I cry in every hand
Set me free, let me be
I'm Strangled
Stuck

12-year-old Jackie read Nikki's poem and responded with "Lack of Love":

In my heart I see nothing
As I watch it I see nothing
No movement
Not strong
Not healthy
My heart is like a piece of steel that can't be moved
As I watch and watch I still get nothing
As I say to myself, I wish I get some type of love
I want to see something I never seen before
As I hear a little voice going in circles around me
As it says what haven't you heard before
I have never seen a heart beat because of the lack of love

Both poems are affirmations of what happens when Black girls write together. Taking up issues of feeling constrained and having a lack of freedom, they both talk about an internal struggle and pains that many Black women and girls experience. Jackie's poem feels like a continuation of the language used in Nikki's poem about feeling strangled and helpless in a world full of oppression. Because of this continuation, they write in the same spirit of one another to express their thoughts around their personal liberties.

Black Girl Literacies Are Intellectual

Black girl literacies are highly intellectual and connected to learning new concepts and knowledge. Intellect or knowledge is what we learn or understand about various topics, concepts, and ideals. Black women have used writing as an intellectual exercise and as they were reading, writing, speaking, and thinking, they were seeking knowledge. In one example, Brooks et al. (2010) conducted a close reading of several young adult novels featuring Black female protagonists. Among these texts were included *November Blues* (Draper, 2007), *The Skin I'm In* (Flake, 1998), *Bronx Masquerade* (Grimes, 2002), *Like Sisters on the Homefront* (Williams-Garcia, 1995), and *Maizon at Blue Hill* (Woodson, 1992). They found intellectual representations of the protagonists as they engaged in dialogue about intellectual ability, feelings of academic work, academic goals, and academic aspirations. Near the conclusion of each text, protagonists experienced a commitment to continued education and greater possibilities of academic success. The authors of these young adult texts are all Black women, so in keeping with the literary tradition, they wrote along the same topics related to historical representations of Black women (including intellectualism).

During the 2016 institute, after reading from Toni Morrison's 1993 Nobel Prize in Literature speech, 14-year-old Rosa considered the deeper meaning and power of language. In Morrison's speech, she wrote,

> The systematic looting of language can be recognized by the tendency of its users to forgo its nuanced, complex, mid-wifery properties for menace and subjugation. Oppressive language does more than represent violence; it is violence; does more than represent the limits of knowledge; it limits knowledge.

Taking up the ideal of language and power, Rosa elaborated on the same concept. She entitled her poem "Language Is the Tool of an Empire":

LANGUAGE IS POWER
POWER IS CONTROL
CONTROL IS GOVERNMENT
GOVERNMENT IS CONTROL
CONTROL IS POWER
POWER IS LANGUAGE
LANGUAGE IS POWER

Before writing this, Rosa learned that one of the first things stripped from enslaved Africans was their language and, during the institute, I told the group that "if you want to control a group of people, you control their language," as I was speaking to the violent assaults White oppressors put upon Black people during enslavement. Her poem is an expression of intellect as she so simply yet brilliantly breaks down language, control, and power.

Black Girl Literacies Are Political and Critical

Criticality is the ability to read print and nonprint text to understand how power, oppression, and privilege are present. As Black girls engage in reading, writing, thinking, and speaking, they are doing so to make sense of how authority is held in texts, communities, and the wider society. This calls readers to think outside of themselves, including the cultural identities and values that they have come to know, and consider multiple standpoints—including those of marginalized groups. Sociopolitical and critical literacy also calls for seeing, reading, and naming the world to make sense of inequality and social justice. This goes beyond deep thinking (which I refer to lower case "c" *critical*); with *Criticality* (upper case "C"), students are pushed to read between the lines and seek to understand what is not in print (Muhammad, 2020).

Carter (2007) studied racial and textual representations of two Black adolescent girls in a British literature classroom. She examined the influence of Eurocentric curriculum on girls as they read William's Shakespeare's sonnet "My Mistress' Eyes" and examined representations of beauty. The Black girls did not see themselves in the text. As the class read the poem, images of beauty were discussed that did not affirm physical characteristics of Black girls. One Black girl participant stated, "She [the teacher] don't do nothing but base the class on White people. . . . Reading all that White crazy stuff" (Carter, 2007, p. 50). The teacher certainly did not teach her to have a political or critical lens when reading, but it was something already practiced within the literacies of Black girls in class.

In Black Girls W.R.I.T.E, I would often ask the girls, "What issues warrant the urgency of your pens?" and they would follow by creating and researching a list of sociopolitical issues that were important to their lives. In 2014, 15-year-old Raja wrote a poem called "Human Rights":

I'm told that I'm free
But what's free when my environment isn't free?
I mean it is but it isn't because it's never at peace
Gunshot
Child Shot
I'm shot
Out
I'm told I'm protected
But what's protection when I'm terrorized by authorities because of my religious decisions
Half the time can't ful-feel my own soul
It hurts to know

That what they said will help us was
Brought to us to take the peace out of our souls
Gun shot
Child shot
I'm shot
Out

Her writing was offered to create awareness and shed light on fighting and killing in the larger Black community. She told the story of those experiencing warlike violence in their homes and neighborhoods. Her writing is a practice of political and critical literacies because she wrote to bring attention to social injustice. In her language she questions freedom and implicitly asks, *If Black people were truly free in the sense of the word, why are their neighborhoods filled with children and adults being killed?*

Conclusion

The Black girls literacies framework draws upon the intellectual thought of Anna Julia Cooper, who contended that it is through Black women and girls that larger social, economic, and civic progress can be measured and advanced. Thus, if we focus on excellent pedagogies for Black women and girls, given their distinct histories, then Black women and girls lay the foundation for advancing education for all (Muhammad & Haddix, 2016). This historically resonant framework is useful for responding to the achievement of all youth and encourages the teaching of skills, identity development, intellectualism, and criticality. In each of the examples, Black girls used literacy practices—namely, writing—to express a component of the BGLF. Along with each prominent component in the examples, other parts of the framework could be observed, which is a reminder that Black girls often engage in these practices of literacy together.

Black girl literacies are not singular or monolithic. Instead they are multiple and complex. Even when returning to the Sister Authors' 2018 preamble, there is a clear presence of (a) multiple literacy practices (as the girls wrote, read, and recited the words in the preamble), (b) historical literacy practices (as the girls referred to the past in the language in the preamble), (c) collaboration (by the way in which the preamble was composed), (d) intellectual methods, and (e) political/critical literacy practices (as the girls discussed issues of stereotypes, social justice, and societal barriers). Importantly the BGLF is beneficial for framing pedagogy for Black girls and engaging them in literacy practices. When these six components are involved and serve as the foundation to their literacy learning, they hold great benefit for advancement in all of the key areas. Further, the BGLF encompasses multiple theories of learning, including cognitive, sociocultural, critical, and sociohistorical theories. When engaging in the classroom, teachers can use the BGLF as criteria for text selection as well as the conduit for developing learning goals. In addition, future research could take up the framework and use it as an instructional model as well as a framework to understand how Black girls practice each of the six dimensions. I am currently seeing the framework being taken up in dissertation work. Finally, the girls' writings in this chapter are examples of the creativity and brilliance that happens when spaces are created for them. When engaging Black girls and centering the BGLF, it gives girls the opportunity to return to their history and lineage, which is truly, as the Sister Authors put it, "a living embodiment of Black excellence."

Discussion Questions

1. Why do Black girl literacies matter?
2. Why were Black literary societies important historically?
3. How can the literacy of Black women writers serve as a road map for engaging young Black girls today?
4. What are the benefits for creating literacy spaces for Black girls?
5. How can the BGLF advance literacy development in and out of schools?

Further Reading

Foster, F. S. (1993). *Written by herself: Literary production by African American women, 1746–1892*. Indiana University Press.

Lee, V. (Ed.). (2006). *The Prentice Hall anthology of African American women's literature*. Pearson.

McHenry, E. (2002). *Forgotten readers: Recovering the lost history of African American literary societies*. Duke University Press.

Richardson, E. (2002). "To protect and serve": African American female literacies. *College Composition and Communication, 53*(4), 675–704. https://doi.org/10.2307/1512121

Royster, J. J. (2000). *Traces of a stream: Literacy and social change among African American women*. University of Pittsburgh Press.

References

Brooks, W., Sekayi, D., Savage, L., Waller, E., & Picot, I. (2010). Narrative significations of contemporary Black girlhood. *Research in the Teaching of English, 45*(1), 7–35. https://www.jstor.org/stable/25704894

Carter, S. P. (2007). "Reading all that White crazy stuff": Black young women upacking Whiteness in a high school British literature classroom. *Journal of Classroom Interaction, 41*(2), 42–54. https://www.jstor.org/stable/23869447

Crenshaw, K., Ocen, P., & Nanda, J. (2015). *Black girls matter: Pushed out, overpoliced, and underprotected.* African American Policy Forum & Center for Intersectionality and Social Policy Studies. http://static1.squarespace.com/static/53f20d90e4b0b80451158d8c/t/54dcc1ece4b001c03e323448/1423753708557/AAPF_BlackGirlsMatterReport.pdf

Draper, S. (2007). *November blues.* Atheneum.

Flake, S. (1998). *The skin I'm in.* Jump at the Sun.

Greene, D. D. (2016). "We need more 'US' in schools!!": Centering Black adolescent girls' literacy and language practices in online school spaces. *The Journal of Negro Education, 85*(3), 274–289. https://doi.org/10.7709/jnegroeducation.85.3.0274

Grimes, N. (2002). *Bronx masquerade.* Penguin.

Harris, T. M., & Hill, P. S. (1998). "Waiting to exhale" or "Breath(ing) again": A search for identity, empowerment, and love in the 1990s. *Women and Language, 11*(2), 9–20. https://www.researchgate.net/profile/Tina-Harris-3/publication/267834247_Waiting_to_Exhale_or_Breathing_Again_A_Search_for_Identity_Empowerment_and_Love_in_the_1990%27s/links/554351710cf23ff716838d2f/Waiting-to-Exhale-or-Breathing-Again-A-Search-for-Identity-Empowerment-and-Love-in-the-1990s.pdf

Ladson-Billings, G. (2009). "Who you calling nappy-headed?" A critical race theory look at the construction of Black women. *Race Ethnicity and Education, 12*(1), 87–99. https://doi.org/10.1080/13613320802651012

Lee, V. (Ed.). (2006). *The Prentice Hall anthology of African American women's literature.* Pearson.

McArthur, S. A. (2016). Black girls and critical media literacy for social activism. *English Education, 48*(4), 362–379. https://www.jstor.org/stable/26492574

McHenry, E. (2002). *Forgotten readers: Recovering the lost history of African American literary societies.* Duke University Press.

Morris, E. W. (2007). "Ladies" or "loudies"? Perceptions and experiences of Black girl classrooms. *Youth & Society, 38*(4), 490–515. https://doi.org/10.1177/0044118X06296778

Morris, M. W. (2016). *Pushout: The criminalization of Black girls in schools.* The New Press.

Muhammad, G. E. (2012a). Creating spaces for Black adolescent girls to "write it out!" *Journal of Adolescent & Adult Literacy, 56*(3), 203–211. https://doi.org/10.1002/JAAL.00129

Muhammad, G. E. (2012b). The literacy development and practices within 1800s African American literary societies. *Black History Bulletin, 75*(1), 6–13. https://www.jstor.org/stable/24759714

Muhammad, G. E. (2014). Black girls write! Literary benefits of a summer writing collaborative grounded in history. *Childhood Education, 90*(4), 323–326. https://doi.org/10.1080/00094056.2014.937321

Muhammad, G. E. (2015). Inducing colored sisters of other places to imitate their example: Connecting historic literary societies to a contemporary writing group. *English Education, 47*(3), 276–299. https://www.jstor.org/stable/24570936

Muhammad, G. E. (2020). *Cultivating genius: An equity model for culturally and historically responsive literacy.* Scholastic.

Muhammad, G. E., Chisholm, G., & Starks, F. (2017). Exploring #BlackLivesMatter and sociopolitical relationships through kinship writing. *English Teaching: Practice & Critique, 16*(3), 347–362. https://www.emerald.com/insight/content/doi/10.1108/ETPC-05-2017-0088/full/html

Muhammad, G. E., & Haddix, M. (2016). Centering Black girls' ways of knowing: A historical review of literature on the multiple literacies of Black girls. *English Education, 48*(4), 299–336. https://www.jstor.org/stable/26492572

Peterson, C. L. (1995). *"Doers of the word": African-American women speakers and writers in the North (1830–1880).* Rutgers University Press.

Porter, D. (1936). The organized educational activities of Negro literary societies, 1828–1856. *Journal of Negro Education, 5,* 555–576. https://doi.org/10.2307/2292029

Price-Dennis, D. (2016). Developing curriculum to support Black girls' literacies in digital spaces. *English Education, 48*(4), 337–367. https://www.jstor.org/stable/26492573

Richardson, E. (2007). "She was workin like foreal": Critical literacy and discourse practices of African American females in the age of hip hop. *Discourse & Society, 18*(6), 789–809. https://doi.org/10.1177/0957926507082197

Royster, J. J. (2000). *Traces of a stream: Literacy and social change among African American women.* University of Pittsburgh Press.

Stephens, D. P., & Phillips, L. D. (2003). Freaks, gold diggers, divas, and dykes: The sociohistorical development of adolescent African American women's sexual scripts. *Sexuality & Culture, 7*(1), 3–49. https://link.springer.com/article/10.1007%2FBF03159848

West, C. (2008). Jezebel, Sapphire, and their homegirls: Developing an "oppositional" gaze toward the images of Black women. In J. Chrisler, C. Golden, & P. Rozee (Eds.), *Lectures on the Psychology of Women* (4th ed., pp. 287–299). McGraw Hill.

Williams-Garcia, R. (1995). *Like sisters on the homefront.* Puffin.

Woodson, J. (1992). *Maizon at Blue Hill.* Putnam.

3

INSTITUTIONALIZED EFFORTS TO INCREASE THE PARTICIPATION OF BLACK WOMEN AND GIRLS IN STEM

Nicole M. Joseph

I think the reason why it's [Black women and girls in STEM] not emphasized is because I don't think they [Whites] want it to be available.

I definitely feel like there's a lot of not knowing about institutions and programs, and even things within your own institution that you can do.

So I feel like the school [counselors] trips up and fails [Black girls] in that way that they're not giving 100 percent of the information. And you have someone assessing you based on what they believe what is right for you instead of giving you the information and letting you make the decision on your own.

The Subtleness (and Not so Subtleness) of Hegemony in STEM

A growing number of researchers are committed to studying and respecting the intersectional experiences of Black women and girls in science, technology, engineering, and mathematics (STEM; see Gholson, 2016; Joseph, 2016; Joseph, 2021; Joseph & Alston, 2018; Joseph et al., 2017; McGee & Bentley, 2017); nevertheless, a large majority of current research on the educational experiences of women and girls in STEM is based on the experiences of their White peers (Gholson, 2016; Joseph et al., 2017). By focusing on White women and girls, researchers establish a monolithic portrait of women's and girls' experiences, overlooking the nuances presented by Black and other racial and ethnic women and girls. Moreover, the experiences of White women and girls are normalized as representative of all girls, which erases Black women and girls in plain sight, and places them in deficit positions when they do not look and behave like White women and girls. Such normalization prevents math and science teachers, principals, policymakers, curriculum developers, and others from fully understanding Black women's and girls' humanity in their development of enriching STEM educational experiences (Joseph, 2021; Joseph & Alston, 2018). It is from this tension that this chapter situates key problems embedded in the U.S. STEM education system that affect Black women and girls. Black women and girls face several challenges in STEM education, yet they navigate these spaces sometimes with community and individual agency and resilience, and other times by succumbing to pressures and experiencing trauma, signaling the need for institutions, communities, policymakers, and other stakeholders to pay attention and act (McGee & Bentley, 2017).

The three opening quotes are from a focus group conducted as part of a larger study that explored undergraduate Black women's mathematics identities. Mathematics identities are the values, attitudes, and beliefs students take up that reflect both self-assessment and assessment by others (such as teachers, peers, and parents) about their mathematics abilities and achievement. Some scholars suggest that interest, recognition, and competence/performance are constructs that influence students' long-term mathematics identities (Cribbs et al., 2015), whereas others point out that mathematics identities are racialized (Varelas et al., 2012), gendered (Leyva, 2017a), and intersectional (Gholson & Martin, 2014; Joseph et al., 2017; Leyva, 2016). What we know from the literature is that mathematics identity development cannot be understood without examining larger social and historical contexts (Gholson, 2016; Joseph, 2021; Joseph et al., 2017; Nasir & Cobb, 2002; Walker, 2012), that they are dynamic across situations, can transform from one moment to the next, and that productive or positive mathematics identities are associated with longer persistence in the mathematics pipeline (Boaler & Greeno, 2000). I have investigated how Black women and girls, in particular, engage in mathematics identity development as a way to contribute to the national conversation about their underrepresentation in STEM (Joseph et al., 2017). Finding connections between mathematics identity development; what we know about the intersectional lives of Black women in society, in K–12, and in higher education settings (Crenshaw, 1989; Patton & Ward, 2016; Patton et al., 2016); and what we know about the culture of mathematics (Gholson, 2016; Joseph et al., 2016) was a key aim of that larger study. Data sources included one-to-one semistructured interviews, annotated artifacts that represented a time of affirmation and connectedness to mathematics, and focus group discussions.

Prior to the focus group, the seven young women watched *Hidden Figures* and discussed the film—issues, implications, and possibilities—related to Black women and girls, their racial identities, and math. These women were undergraduates from both historically Black colleges and universities (HBCUs) and traditionally White institutions (TWIs) in Tennessee. Although many of the questions focused on the participants' ideas about what influences a math identity and what that process might look like for Black women and girls, the quotes at the beginning of this chapter are in response to the questions "What does our math education system do right for Black girls?" and "What do you think our math education system does wrong when it comes to Black girls?" Their comments illuminate a theme of exclusion. Unfortunately, all the young women in the focus group agreed that they could not find anything that the system does right for Black girls; after all, they speak from a place of lived experiences as undergraduate mathematics and science majors who had come through the P–12 system with many negative experiences, such as low teacher expectations and less rigorous math courses, which put them in precarious positions once they got to college.

What Are the Key Challenges in Our STEM Education System?

One important challenge that is linked to our education system is that STEM is perceived as objective and neutral, yet research has shown that it is exclusionary, a racialized project—structured by whiteness and White supremacy (Battey & Leyva, 2016; Joseph et al., 2017; Martin, 2008, 2009, 2010). STEM is also perceived as masculine (Leyva, 2017b) and serves as a space where who one is and what one identifies with is often devalued and dehumanized (Joseph et al., 2019). Black women and girls are significantly affected by this notion in large part because of the subtle and not so subtle signs in classrooms, media, or interactions with peers that all lead to clues about who belongs in STEM. These messages to Black girls begin early and have been going on for generations. For example, in *Girlhood Interrupted*, Epstein et al. (2017) found that everyday well-educated Americans (n = 325) view Black girls as more adult than their White peers, a phenomenon called *adultification*. This study showed that Black girlhood is erased by a segment of broader society because at all stages of childhood, beginning at age 5 through 19, mainly White American adults (75% of the sample) think that Black girls need to be comforted and supported less, are more independent, and know more about adult topics, such as sex. These adults place views and expectations on Black girls that make them distinct as developmentally older than their White peers. These viewpoints are rooted in American history, particularly slavery, when Black women were stereotyped as mammies (nurturing and self-sacrificing), Sapphires (emasculating, loud, aggressive, angry, stubborn, and unfeminine), and Jezebels (hypersexualized). Consequently, when educators such as teachers or counselors take up, accept, and believe these perspectives as fact, their interactions with and expectations of Black girls can negatively influence Black girls' life outcomes. Examples of social life outcomes most people value include graduation from high school and college, job and career opportunities, and physically and mentally healthy lives.

When teachers regard Black girls as "older" than they are, they may expect Black girls to "know better" when it comes to certain behaviors such as talking back, and are therefore more likely to engage in zero tolerance policies, putting Black girls at risk for entering the criminal justice system (Morris, 2015). Schools perpetuate intersectional violence against Black girls through discipline (Annamma et al., 2016; Crenshaw et al., 2015; Joseph et al., 2016; Morris, 2016) and there have been cases where this has occurred in STEM classrooms. The Spring Valley High School case of a 16-year-old student named Shakara is an important example. Shakara was the student observed in the video that went viral being assaulted by a school resource officer for passively refusing to leave her algebra class after being caught with her cell phone out. When the teacher and assistant principal were both unsuccessful in getting Shakara to hand over her cell phone, school officials called in Officer Ben Fields to assist with the incident. Upon his arrival, Shakara passively sat in her desk and avoided eye contact with the officer before he grabbed her around her neck, flipped her over on her desk, and dragged her across the floor as if she were a rag doll. The recording of this unbelievably violent incident was played countless times on both traditional and social media outlets, providing a residual effect, traumatizing not only Shakara, but any other student who might see themselves in her as the only individual who received a consequence in this incident. Officer Fields was never charged and was determined to be justified for adding to the ongoing subjection of Black women and girls to violence (Associated Press, 2016). This type of trauma results in lost instructional time in mathematics, perpetuates the stereotypes about Black girls, but most of all sends messages to Black girls that they do not belong in mathematics. Consequently, rather than seeing, developing, and nurturing future chemists, computer scientists, or mathematicians, for the inherent brilliance that is within Black girls, educators and the general society see them as little adults, undeserving of a childhood, or care.

Another key issue embedded in the STEM education system that negatively affects Black girls is the structure of tracking. Tracking in mathematics is a long-standing practice in most U.S. public schools that designates students for separate educational paths based on student performance. In some schools, tracking begins with kindergarten screening and continues each year with IQ testing and other early assessments designed to measure students' purported "ability" in order to determine track placement in the early years (Burris & Garrity, 2008). Because it is subject-specific, a kindergartener could be in a "high" reading group and a "low" group in math, and this process is ongoing throughout students' schooling experiences. Although there are cases of students moving up or down a level in math, most often the word *track* is a metaphor for fixed trajectory—students generally remain on that assigned track for 12 years of schooling. In other schools and particularly at the middle school level, math tracking is a meritocracy that relies on teacher recommendations, prior math courses, grades, and student motivation to determine placement, but other factors can come into play. These recommendations are often influenced by teachers' perceptions of the student. Either way, tracking perpetuates a modern system of segregation that favors White students and keeps students of color, particularly Black girls, from long-term equal achievement (Campbell, 2012). What we know is that White and Asian students have access to and enroll in advanced math and science courses at significantly higher rates than Black students (Oakes et al., 2004). Consequently, tracking is a structural contribution to unequal schooling and future opportunities for careers in STEM.

As such, Black girls are most likely to attend tracked public primary and secondary schools (National Center for Education Statistics, 2015); thus, understanding math tracking and its long-term effects on future educational and career opportunities is salient for the STEM field, particularly those who engage in curricula design, program development, and policymaking. Because tracking can be less overt, and parents are often not brought into the decision-making process, many parents do not understand the long-term implications for these decisions until it's too late. Consequently, Black girls and their families are important constituents for understanding the consequences of tracking to better advocate for themselves in schools that are unequal, subtractive, and wrought with institutionalized racism (Valenzuela, 1999).

It is important to highlight the significance of advanced mathematics courses and their connections to college access assessments. What is significant about Algebra II, for example, and other advanced mathematics courses is their high predictability of greater success on the mathematics section of standardized exams such as the American College Testing offering (ACT, 2005). Advanced mathematics courses being predictive of future successful ACT scores holds true because the scoring design of the exam necessitates student mastery of higher-level mathematics content standards to score in the upper ranges of the exam (see Joseph & Cobb, 2019). In short, what can be concluded is that White students compared to Black girls, on average, are enrolling in advanced courses at higher rates, suggesting greater access to these courses and better preparation for the college admissions process.

This phenomenon is realized in the data shown in Table 3.1, based on the National Center for Education Statistics' (n.d.) High School Longitudinal Study (HSLS) of 2009, a nationally representative sample of 23,000 ninth-grade students who were then followed up with during their senior year of high school (2012) and then again in their senior year of college (2016). Students and their parents were surveyed as well as math and science teachers, school administrators, and school counselors. The table includes the percentages of Black girls taking their highest mathematics courses in the pipeline compared to their White peers. The percentages

TABLE 3.1
**Percentages of Black Females Enrolled in Pipeline Mathematics Courses
Compared to White Students**

	Black Girls	*White Girls*	*White Boys*	*Whites Total*
No Math	23.7	38.7	34.5	36.2
Basic Math	16.2[a]	46.4	52.9	50.3
Other Math	32.1[b]	41.1	49.0	45.9
Prealgebra	11.2[a]	59.8	47.2	51.5
Algebra I	10.4	39.6	40.1	39.9
Geometry	11.4	45.4	42.9	43.9
Algebra II	**16.7**	**48.4**	**52.5**	**50.4**
Trigonometry	**27.3**	**46.3**	**51.4**	**48.7**
Probability & Statistics	**18.1**	**57.6**	**58.2**	**57.9**
Precalculus	**12.2**	**59.2**	**61.5**	**60.3**
Calculus	**4.3[b]**	**69.2**	**74.8**	**71.8**
AP/IB Calculus	**7.5[b]**	**54.8**	**63.0**	**59.0**

[a] Interpret data with caution. Estimate is unstable because the standard error represents more than 50% of the estimate.

[b] Interpret data with caution. Estimate is unstable because the standard error represents more than 30% of the estimate.

Note. From NCES (n.d.).

in Table 3.1 demonstrate underrepresentation in advanced math courses (Algebra II and above) among Black girls in comparison to White students. Looking at an example, the data suggest that 16.7% of Black girls took Algebra II as their highest math course in high school. In contrast, 50.4% of White males and females stopped at Algebra II. Moreover, when the White student group is further disaggregated by gender, we see that for example only 12.2% of Black girls took Precalculus and then stopped compared to 59.2% of White girls enrolled in Precalculus. Therefore, in looking at each of these examples, one can observe that Black girls are disproportionately underenrolled in higher level math courses because their selection rate is far lower than that of White students.

These low enrollment numbers that start in the early grades only magnify through the undergraduate and graduate experience, resulting in even lower numbers at the doctoral level. Between 2004 and 2014, on average, eight Black women earned doctorates in mathematics, which is about 1% of the average of all mathematics doctorates given across the same time (NSF, 2016). Reasons for why Black women and girls are not enrolled in advanced mathematics courses and earning STEM college degrees at similar rates to White students is a contentious question that includes reasons such as tracking, disinterest, fear, negative previous math experiences, low teacher expectations, and several others. Expectations teachers hold about Black girls is a significant contributor in recommendation decisions for advanced math courses, even after controlling for achievement (Campbell, 2012).

Researchers have also conducted studies on the *type of instruction* that happens in low- and high-level tracked mathematics courses. For example, scholars such as Anyon (2006), Darling-Hammond (2000), and Oakes et al. (2004) have conducted foundational studies about the track-level differences in content and teacher quality both between and within schools. For example, high-poverty elementary school curricula often focus on basic facts and skills, whereas affluent school curricula provide access to challenging, problem-based learning and enrichment (Oakes et al., 2004). Anyon (2006) and Oakes (1990) found that overall, teachers in low socioeconomic status (SES) elementary schools emphasize problem-solving and inquiry skills less than in higher SES schools. At low SES schools, in science, students were never called upon participate in experiments or to give explanations for facts or concepts (Anyon, 2006). In contrast, at the elite schools, teachers expected students to develop their analytical thinking skills. Similarly, in math, teachers encouraged their students to evaluate each other's decision-making strategies. When the Common Core State Standards for Mathematics were created, they were designed to establish one set of challenging academic expectations for all students that would improve achievement, college readiness, and eliminate the variation described previously in tracking; however, it has been almost 10 years since its official launching in 2009 and the disheartening news is that its goals have not been realized in most mathematics classrooms (Editorial Projects in Research, 2015).

A final issue connected to our STEM education system shaping Black girls' experiences is the limited support in higher education institutions. For the Black girls who actually make it through the secondary mathematics pipeline and continue taking math courses in their undergraduate programs, many still face challenges. For example, in the same study I conducted and discussed previously, some of the young women talked about differences between their mathematics courses and the courses their White peers took. One participant noted that the White students in her math courses at her current TWI had been learning math through the Socratic method since they were in grade school, whereas her math instruction included traditional teacher lectures and memorization, resulting in her struggling in the college mathematics courses. This participant noted that Louisiana overall did not have a good education system and a move to Georgia required adjustments. She stated:

> So I'm from New Orleans. And I've always liked school since I was a little girl. And then after Hurricane Katrina my mom and I moved to Fayette-ville, Georgia. And the school—the public school system in Fayetteville was way better. Of course, New Orleans does not have a good public education system. So it was a little adjustment when I moved to Fayetteville academi-cally, but I made the adjustment very shortly.

Later, she described the type of math instruction:

> They [White students] don't have desks and sit at a board. They have a big round table, and they all sit at the table and just talk. It's Socratic style. And I did that in eighth grade for my English course. I talked to this girl who came from one of the most expensive private boarding schools in America. And she was like, we don't have desks, we sit at a big table, and it's just like my learning style is totally different from kids at [University]. And she's one of the top students here.

The ongoing consequences for Black girls and women majoring in STEM fields who have these experiences in their secondary schooling are exacerbated because university mathematics departments employ exclusionary practices, such as weed-out courses. Additionally, most of the mathematics profes-sors in higher education are White males and often have not thought about socially affirming pedagogy (Leyva, 2017b, Tuitt et al., 2016) nor the ways in which the low racial consciousness of White faculty members in particular is inextricably linked to the preservation of whiteness and White supremacy (Haynes, 2017; Joseph et al., 2016). Thus, Black girls and women rarely get to engage in STEM environments that are humanizing and value their perspectives and ways of knowing (Joseph et al., 2017; Joseph & Alston, 2018); rather, they are constantly having to prove their worth, strip themselves of their identities, and resist stereotypes (McGee & Bentley, 2017).

Overall, what we know from the literature is that from the moment Black girls enter kindergarten, they are intellectually and behaviorally surveilled by a system rooted in institutionalized racism, hegemony, and whiteness. Because of this system that is racist, gendered, and full of other oppressive practices, rich and meaningful STEM experiences, in large part, elude many Black girls. In the next section, I discuss the efforts and initiatives organizations such as the National Science Foundation have offered to increase Black women's and girls' participation in STEM. Although I highlight these efforts, I also critique many of these efforts because they focus on "fixing" Black girls rather than dismantling the oppressive structural systems that created the conditions of their underrepresentation in the first place.

Efforts to Increase Black Women and Girls in STEM: We Keep Getting It Wrong

Guided by its strategic plan, the National Science Foundation (NSF) established a performance area focused on broadening participation to expand efforts to increase participation from underrepresented groups throughout the United States. NSF (n.d.) took up this mission to broaden participation in STEM because they realized that STEM was a White male–dominated space that needed to be disrupted. NSF has bold initiatives, such as the one on developing and implementing an effective preK–20+ system of STEM pathways (CEOSE, 2017). The Committee on Equal Opportunities in Science and Engineering's 2015–2016 biennial report to Congress stated that NSF requested $592.53 million for both focused and emphasis programs in broadening participation. A keyword search in NSF's funded awards and review of abstracts suggested that although they have invested billions of dollars in broadening participation for underrepresented minorities, *the projects that have specifically focused on Black women and girls have been few and far between.* Of the projects that have been funded that centered on Black girls in STEM, the predominant emphasis is Black girls' motivation (e.g., Swinton et al., 2011). That is, most of the studies located sought to answer some form of the question "How can we motivate more Black girls to participate in STEM?" Other large foci were stereotype threats, equipping Black girls with foundational skills, and increasing Black girls' self-concepts and improving their STEM identities. Although some of these efforts looked at features of the systems that impede Black girls' advancement in STEM (e.g., looking at ways to reduce stereotype threat in the institution, access to resources), many remained focused on how to change the *girls themselves* to be more motivated, or have a higher self-perception, or be more interested in STEM. Moreover, even those who turned their lens to institutional structures tended to "add on" programs like summer academies or school clubs, rather than implicating the taken-for-granted features of U.S. high schools and universities.

Few if any STEM programs and organizations center Black women and girls in ways that address intersectionality. Intersectionality is a framing mechanism that examines how multiple systems of oppression collude to the detriment of multiply minoritized populations (King, 1988). Most notably, when Crenshaw (1989, 1991) introduced the concept of intersectionality, she addressed the complex, latent power relations shaping the lives of women of color, and Black women in particular. Power relations are the relationships in which one person or group has some type of power over another person or group, and is able to get the other person(s) to do what they wish (whether by compelling obedience or in other subtler ways). Thus, power relations in STEM can be disciplinary, social, and economic (Collins & Bilge, 2016). For example, the interrogation of the practice of mathematics tracking in U.S. schools illuminates social power relations, because we see that Whites are the majority decision-makers about school tracking. These decision-makers continue to ignore over 30 years of research conducted by Jeannie Oakes (1990, 1992, 2005) and colleagues that clearly state mathematics tracking is an inequitable practice and system that relegates many Black girls and other students of color to lower-level math courses, which sets up extremely limited opportunities for future STEM success (i.e., majoring in STEM or establishing a career in STEM). Black girls experiencing these low-level courses may feel like they are not only bad at math, but also that having a STEM major in college or a STEM career is not possible. So, continuing with this example, how do STEM efforts and initiatives (a) connect with, provide opportunities for, and support Black girls who have a blind spot about their mathematics or STEM abilities because of their experiences with tracking; (b) give Black girls tools to empower and see themselves as legitimate knowledge producers; (c) disrupt the normativity of what it means to be a leader in STEM; and (d) normalize Black girls' full spectrum of femininities and humanity in STEM spaces? This is an example of what I mean by addressing intersectionality.

Black Girls Code (BGC) is a nonprofit organization that has aimed to change the trajectory of Black girls by focusing on providing technology education for Black girls. BGC was founded in 2011 by Kimberly Bryant, an electrical engineering graduate from Vanderbilt University who before establishing her organization had worked in the biotech industry for 20 years (BGC, 2020). BGC offers programs in computer programming, coding, as well as website, robot, and mobile application building, with the goal of providing African American youth with the skills to occupy some of the 1.4 million computing job openings expected to be available in the United States in 2020 (BGC, 2020). BGC has expanded significantly into seven major cities, including Johannesburg, South Africa, and has reached over 3,000 Black girls. This organization centers Black girls and helps them create their own ways of knowing in a technological world—thus BGC's tag line: "Imagine, build, create." Although BGC is a phenomenal organization that is reaching many Black girls, there is a need for additional research on how BGC uses its programming to address intersectionality.

Supporting computational algorithmic thinking (SCAT) is a longitudinal between-groups research project that explores how Black middle school girls develop computational algorithmic thinking (CAT) capabilities over time (i.e., 3 years) in the context of game design for social change (Thomas, 2018; Thomas et al., 2015, 2017). SCAT is also a free enrichment program designed to expose middle school girls to game design. Spanning 3 years, participants develop CAT capabilities as they design more and more complex games that address issues or problems identified by the scholars themselves. Thus, Black girls are decision-makers in this process. Each year, scholars engage in three types of activities: (a) a 2-week intensive game design summer experience; (b) 12 technical workshops where scholars implement the games they designed using visual and programming languages in preparation for submission to national game design competitions; and (c) field trips where scholars learn about applications of CAT in different industries and careers. These robust activities suggest that Black girls are positioned as leaders and creators of knowledge. Scholars also had several scaffolds in the learning environment to support them in the ways apprenticeship suggests, including a facilitator, four undergraduate assistants, and a *Design Notebook*, as well as support from other scholars. Black girls therefore have physical and mental model possibilities for what they can become in computer science.

SCAT meets the intersectional needs of scholars in several ways. First, the environment is designed to reflect the intersectional identities of the scholars. Particularly, the facilitator, undergraduate and graduate assistants, and special guests who work with the scholars are Black women in computing, representing a pipeline of Black women engaging in the field at all levels: middle school (scholars), high school (e.g., students from regional YWCAs talk about their experiences in computing and intentions to major in computing), undergraduate (undergraduate assistants), graduate (graduate assistants), and professional (facilitator, who has a PhD in computer science). Second, SCAT elevates the experiences, culture, and community of the scholars as experts by encouraging and supporting them as they look at their community to identify issues or topics that they want to bring awareness to or address through their games. For example, scholars design and implement games on a variety of topics ranging from bullying to environmental sustainability to Black history (e.g., the role of the Tuskegee airmen in World War II). Third, SCAT highlights the paths that are available to the scholars creatively and professionally because of their CAT capabilities through field trips to places like the Georgia Tech Aware Home that show the application of CAT capabilities to solve real-world problems as well as the kinds of career opportunities they can pursue. Finally, SCAT supports the development of scholars' positive perceptions of themselves as game designers, critical thinkers, and problem-solvers, something that is often not supported among Black women and girls who pursue computer science as a major or persist to pursue computing careers (Thomas et al., 2016, 2018). Overall, SCAT is an example of how programming is being designed and used to disrupt oppression and the normative discourse about Black girls' intelligence and enfranchise Black girls' experiences and product development through leadership. In the next section, I discuss strategies for readers to consider for future practice and research.

Implications

Creating inclusive STEM learning environments that value Black women and girls' perspectives from early childhood through higher education requires due diligence to learn about and deeply appreciate their full humanity. Appreciating their full humanity means that educators see Black girls' and women's lives as intrinsically valuable. Valuing Black girls' and women's lives dismantles disposability and opens up the possibility models. Inclusive STEM environments need intersectional strategies and interventions such as the ones shown in the following, and the implications of such strategies are that they require truth telling, vulnerability, and power relinquishment. So, whether one is designing pipeline programs, transforming a curriculum, creating partnerships, or even writing a policy or law, the following strategies embody the spirit of what needs to be seriously taken into consideration when trying to increase the participation of Black women and girls in STEM. This is not an exhaustive list, but serves as a consideration for future practice, praxis, discourse, and research.

1. Implement emancipatory pedagogies as a core idea of teaching or instruction (Joseph, 2021; Joseph & Alston, 2018). This means that one must rely less on traditional methods of math or science teaching and seek to

forge a cultural democracy where Black girls are treated with respect and dignity (Macadeo & Bartolome, 1999).

2. Self-interrogate biases and take action to dismantle them. This means STEM educators and other stakeholders who make their commitment to equity for Black women and girls in STEM must have courage and take risks to name whiteness and White supremacy and examine how it operates within one's interactions with Black women and girls. Note that this strategy does not deal directly with STEM content knowledge, but rather thinks about how one teaches those who have been silenced and ignored in STEM.

3. Know that a humanizing pedagogy is a coconstructed experience and that it is critical for Black girls' academic and social resiliency for school success (Fránquiz & Salazar, 2004). This means that STEM educators, teachers, curriculum designers, and others need to be prepared to silence hegemony and elevate Black women's and girls' development of themselves as STEM knowledge producers, even when it looks different.

4. Engage in consciousness raising through dialogue using knowledge grounded in personal experience, relationship building, and a view of students as emotional and social beings, not solely cognitive learners (Jennings & Da Matta, 2009). This means helping Black girls name oppressions they experience in STEM spaces both in and outside of classrooms. Black girls need to know that how they know what they know is real and sanctioned and that they have agency to challenge things in their lives that are negative.

5. Give Black girls more STEM content, not less. Require that they think and engage with real-life problems for a purpose. This means that stakeholders must move beyond a textbook and learn to innovate at the intersection of relevance and high expectations.

I end this chapter by posing a few questions to promote dialogue and provide further readings.

Discussion Questions

1. Why do you think stereotypes about Black women and girls are so difficult to dismantle?
2. How do you think these stereotypes show up in STEM spaces?
3. What do you already know about Black woman and girlhood? How have you conceptualized these ideas to critique and/or affirm the gendered and racialized culture of STEM?

4. What ideas do you have for disrupting structural oppression in STEM spaces?
5. In what ways should professional development for STEM instructors or other stakeholders be structured to advance equitable, inclusive, and ultimately more intersectional pedagogical reform?

Acknowledgments

I would like to acknowledge Floyd Cobb, adjunct faculty in teaching and learning sciences at the University of Denver, and Mariah Harmon, Micaela Y. Harris, and Samantha Marshall, doctoral students in teaching and learning at Vanderbilt University, for their invaluable input into this chapter, including providing ideas and reading drafts for editorial purposes.

Further Reading

American Mathematical Society. (n.d.). *Inclusion/exclusion* [Blog]. https://blogs.ams.org/inclusionexclusion/2017/06/14/feminist-theory-and-methodologies-for-more-socially-affirming-undergraduate-mathematics-education/

Booker, K. C., & Lim, J. H. (2016, May 30). Belongingness and pedagogy: Engaging African American girls in middle school mathematics. *Youth & Society.* Advance online publication. https://doi.org/10.1177/0044118X16652757

Collins, P. H. (2017). The difference that power makes: Intersectionality and participatory democracy. *Investigaciones feministas: Papeles de estudios de mujeres, feministas y de género, 8*(1), 19–39. link.gale.com/apps/doc/A501079078/IFME?u=anon~f0d7e48e&sid=googleScholar&xid=7b80a893

Gholson, M., & Martin, D. B. (2014). Smart girls, Black girls, mean girls, and bullies: At the intersection of identities and the mediating role of young girls' social network in mathematical communities of practice. *Journal of Education, 194*(1), 19–33. https://doi.org/10.1177/002205741419400105

Hanson, S. (2008). *Swimming against the tide: African American girls and science education.* Temple University Press.

Lane, M. (2017). Reclaiming our queendom: Black feminist pedagogy and the identity formation of African American girls. *Equity & Excellence in Education, 50*(1), 13–24. https://doi.org/10.1080/10665684.2016.1259025

References

ACT. (2005). *Courses count: Preparing students for postsecondary success.* ACT Policy Report. Act, Inc. https://files.eric.ed.gov/fulltext/ED500454.pdf

Annamma, S. A., Anyon, Y., Joseph, N. M., Farrar, J., Greer, E., Downing, B., & Simmons, J. (2016, May 19). Black girls and school discipline: The complexities of being overrepresented and understudied. *Urban Education*. Advance online publication. https://doi.org/10.1177/0042085916646610

Anyon, J. (2006). Social class and the hidden curriculum of work. In G. Handel (Ed.), *Childhood socialization* (2nd ed., pp. 369–394). Aldine Transaction.

Associated Press. (2016). Deputy who tossed a S.C. high school student won't be charged. *New York Times*. https://www.nytimes.com/2016/09/03/afternoonup-date/deputy-who-tossed-a-sc-high-school-student-wont-be-charged.html

Battey, D., & Leyva, L. A. (2016). A framework for understanding whiteness in mathematics education. *Journal of Urban Mathematics Education*, *9*(2), 49–80. https://files.eric.ed.gov/fulltext/EJ1124962.pdf

Black Girls Code. (2020). *About our founder*. https://www.blackgirlscode.com/about-bgc.html

Boaler, J., & Greeno, J. G. (2000). Identity, agency, and knowing in mathematics worlds. In. J. Boaler (Ed), *Multiple perspectives on mathematics teaching and learning* (pp.171–200). Apex Publishing.

Burris, C. C., & Garrity, D. T. (Eds.) (2008). *Detracking for excellence and equity.* Association for Supervision and Curriculum Development.

Campbell, S. L. (2012). For colored girls? Factors that influence teacher recommendations into advanced courses for Black girls. *The Review of Black Political Economy*, *39*, 389–402. https://doi.org/10.1007/s12114-012-9139-1

Collins, P. H., & Bilge, S. (2016). *Intersectionality: Key concepts*. John Wiley & Sons.

Committee on Equal Opportunities in Science and Engineering. Biennial report to congress 2017–2018: Investing in diverse community voices. https://www.nsf.gov/od/oia/activities/ceose/reports/2017-2018-ceose-biennial-report-508.pdf

Crenshaw, K. (1989). Demarginalizing the intersection of race and sex: A Black feminist critique of antidiscrimination doctrine, feminist theory and antiracist politics. *University of Chicago Legal Forum*, *140*(1), 139–167. https://is.muni.cz/el/fss/podzim2016/GEN505/um/Crenshaw_Black_Feminist_Critique_of_Anti-discrimination_Law.pdf

Crenshaw, K. (1991). Mapping the margins: Intersectionality, identity politics, and violence against women of color. *Stanford Law Review*, *43*(6), 1241–1299. https://doi.org/10.2307/1229039

Crenshaw, K., Ocen, P., & Nanda, J. (2015). *Black girls matter: Pushed out, overpoliced and underprotected*. African American Policy Forum. https://44bbdc6e-01a4-4a9a-88bc-731c6524888e.filesusr.com/ugd/b77e03_e92d6e80f7034f30b-f843ea7068f52d6.pdf

Cribbs, J. D., Hazari, Z., Sonnert, G., & Sadler, P. M. (2015). Establishing an explanatory model for mathematics identity. *Child Development*, *86*(4), 1048–1062. https://doi.org/10.1111/cdev.12363

Darling-Hammond, L. (2000). Teacher quality and student achievement. A review of state policy evidence. *Education Policy Analysis Archives*, *8*(1), 1–44. https://doi.org/10.14507/epaa.v8n1.2000

Editorial Projects in Education Research Center. (2015, September 28). Issues A-Z: The Common Core explained. *Education Week*. http://www.edweek.org/ew/issues/common-core-state-standards/

Epstein, R., Blake, J., & González, T. (2017). *Girlhood interrupted: The erasure of Black girls' childhood.* Georgetown Law Center on Poverty and Inequality. http://dx.doi.org/10.2139/ssrn.3000695

Franquiz, M. E., & del Carmen Salazar, M. (2004). The transformative potential of humanizing pedagogy: Addressing the diverse needs of Chicano/Mexicano students. *The High School Journal, 87*(4), 36–53. https://www.jstor.org/stable/40364283

Gholson, M. L. (2016). Clean corners and algebra: A critical examination of the constructed invisibility of Black girls and women in mathematics. *The Journal of Negro Education, 85*(3), 290–301. https://doi.org/10.7709/jnegroeducation.85.3.0290

Gholson, M., & Martin, D. B. (2014). Smart girls, Black girls, mean girls, and bullies: At the intersection of identities and the mediating role of young girls' social network in mathematical communities of practice. *Journal of Education, 194*(1), 19–33. https://doi.org/10.1177/002205741419400105

Haynes, C. (2017). Dismantling the White supremacy embedded in our classrooms: White faculty in pursuit of more equitable educational outcomes for racially minoritized students. *International Journal of Teaching and Learning in Higher Education, 29*(1), 87–107. https://files.eric.ed.gov/fulltext/EJ1135971.pdf

Jennings, L. B., & Da Matta, G. B. (2009). Rooted in resistance: Women teachers constructing counter-pedagogies in post-authoritarian Brazil. *Teaching Education, 20*(3), 215–228. https://doi.org/10.1080/10476210903096047

Joseph, N. M. (2016). What Plato took for granted: Examining the biographies of the first five African American female mathematicians and what that says about resistance to the western epistemological canon. In B. Polnick, B. Irby, & J. Ballenger (Eds.), *Women of color in STEM: Navigating the workforce* (pp. 3–38). Information Age.

Joseph, N. M. (2021). Black Feminist Mathematics Pedagogies (BlackFMP): A curricular confrontation to gendered antiblackness in the US mathematics education system. *Curriculum Inquiry, 51*(1), 75–97. https://doi.org/10.1080/03626784.2020.1813002

Joseph, N. M., & Alston, N. V. (2018). I fear no number: Black girls' experiences in eModelearning math academy. In I. Goffney, R. Gutierrez, & M. Boston (Eds.), *Rehumanizing mathematics for Black, indigenous, and Latinx students* (pp. 51–62). National Council of Teachers of Mathematics.

Joseph, N. M., & Cobb, F. (2019). Antiblackness is in the air: Problematizing Black students' mathematics education pathways from curriculum to standardized assessments. In J. Davis & C. Jett (Eds.), *Critical race theory in mathematics education research* (pp. 140–163). Routledge.

Joseph, N. M., Hailu, M., & Boston, D. L. (2017). Black girls' and women's persistence in the P–20 mathematics pipeline: Two decades of children and youth education research. *Review of Research in Education, 41*(1), 203–227. https://doi.org/10.3102/0091732X16689045

Joseph, N. M., Hailu, M., & Matthews, J. (2019). Normalizing Black girls' humanity in mathematics classrooms. *Harvard Education Review, 89*(1), 132–155. https://doi.org/10.17763/1943-5045-89.1.132

Joseph, N. M., Haynes, C., & Cobb, F. (Eds.). (2015). *Interrogating whiteness and relinquishing power: White faculty's commitment to racial consciousness in STEM classrooms.* Peter Lang.

Joseph, N. M., Viesca, K. M., & Bianco, M. (2016). Black female adolescents and racism in schools: Experiences in a colorblind society. *The High School, 100*(1), 4–25. https://doi.org/10.1353/hsj.2016.0018

King, D. K. (1988). Multiple jeopardy, multiple consciousness: The context of a Black feminist ideology. *Signs: Journal of Women in Culture and Society, 14*(1), 42–72. https://www.jstor.org/stable/3174661

Leyva, L. A. (2016). An intersectional analysis of Latin@ college women's counterstories in mathematics. *Journal of Urban Mathematics Education, 9*(2), 81–121. https://files.eric.ed.gov/fulltext/EJ1124964.pdf

Leyva, L. (2017a, June 14). *Feminist theory and research methodologies for more socially affirming undergraduate mathematics education.* https://blogs.ams.org/inclusionexclusion/2017/06/14/feminist-theory-and-methodologies-for-more-socially-affirming-undergraduate-mathematics-education/

Leyva, L. A. (2017b). Unpacking the male superiority myth and masculinization of mathematics at the intersections: A review of research on gender in mathematics education. *Journal for Research in Mathematics Education, 48*(4), 397–452. https://doi.org/10.5951/jresematheduc.48.4.0397

Macedo, D., & Bartolomé, L. I. (1999). Dancing with bigotry. In D. Macedo & L. Bartolome (Eds.), *Dancing with Bigotry* (pp. 1–33). Palgrave Macmillan.

Martin, D. B. (2008). E (race)ing race from a national conversation on mathematics teaching and learning: The national mathematics advisory panel as white institutional space. *Montana Mathematics Enthusiast, 5*(2–3), 387–391. https://scholarworks.umt.edu/tme/vol5/iss2/20

Martin, D. B. (2009). In my opinion: Does race matter? *Teaching Children Mathematics, 16*(3), 134–139. https://doi.org/10.5951/TCM.16.3.0134

Martin, D. B. (2010). Not-so-strange bedfellows: Racial projects and the mathematics education enterprise. In U. Gellert, E. Jablonka, & C. Morgan (Eds.), *Proceedings of the Mathematics Education and Society 6th International Conference* (pp. 42–64). Freie Univesitat Berlin.

McGee, E. O., & Bentley, L. (2017). The troubled success of Black women in STEM. *Cognition and Instruction, 35*(4), 265–289. https://doi.org/10.1080/07370008.2017.1355211

Morris, M. W. (2015). The relevance of sacred inquiry in the education of delinquent Black girls. *International Journal of Human Resources Development and Management, 15*(2–4), 185–193. https://doi.org/10.1504/IJHRDM.2015.071156

Morris, M. (2016). *Pushout: The criminalization of Black girls in schools.* The New Press.

Nasir, N. I. S., & Cobb, P. (2002). Diversity, equity, and mathematical learning. *Mathematical Thinking and Learning, 4*(2–3), 91–102. https://doi.org/10.1207/S15327833MTL04023_1

National Center for Education Statistics. (n.d.). *High School Longitudinal Study (HSLS) of 2009.* https://nces.ed.gov/surveys/hsls09/

National Center for Education Statistics. (2015). *Back to school statistics.* https://nces.ed.gov/fastfacts/display.asp?id=372

National Science Foundation. (n.d.). *Broadening participation.* https://www.nsf.gov/od/broadeningparticipation/bp.jsp

National Science Foundation. (2016). *Women, minorities, and persons with disabilities in science and engineering.* https://www.nsf.gov/statistics/2017/nsf17310/data.cfm

Oakes, J. (1990). *Multiplying inequalities: The effects of race, social class, and tracking on opportunities to learn mathematics and science.* Rand.

Oakes, J. (1992). Can tracking research inform practice? Technical, normative, and political considerations. *Educational Researcher, 21*(4), 12–21. https://doi.org/10.3102/0013189X021004012

Oakes, J. (2005). *Keeping track.* Yale University Press.

Oakes, J., Joseph, R., & Muir, K. (2004). Access and achievement in mathematics and science: Inequalities that endure and change. In J. A. Banks & C. A. M. Banks (Eds.), *Handbook of research on multicultural education* (2nd ed., pp. 69–90). Jossey-Bass.

Patton, L. D., Crenshaw, K., Haynes, C., & Watson, T. N. (2016). Why we can't wait: (Re)examining the opportunities and challenges for Black women and girls in education [Guest editorial]. *The Journal of Negro Education, 85*(3), 194. https://doi.org/10.7709/jnegroeducation.85.3.0194

Patton, L. D., & Ward, L. W. (2016). Missing Black undergraduate women and the politics of disposability: A critical race feminist perspective. *The Journal of Negro Education, 85*(3), 330. https://doi.org/10.7709/jnegroeducation.85.3.0330

Swinton, A. D., Kurtz-Costes, B., Rowley, S. J., & Okeke-Adeyanju, N. (2011). A longitudinal examination of African American adolescents' attributions about achievement outcomes. *Child development, 82*(5), 1486–1500. https://doi.org/10.1111/j.1467-8624.2011.01623.x

Thomas, J. O. (2018). The computational algorithmic thinking (CAT) capability flow: An approach to articulating CAT capabilities over time in African-American middle-school girls. In T. Barnes & D. Garcia (Eds.), *Proceedings of the 49th ACM Technical Symposium on Computer Science Education* (pp. 149–154). ACM Digital Library.

Thomas, J. O., Joseph, N., Williams, A., & Burge, J. (2018). Speaking truth to power: Exploring the intersectional experiences of Black women in computing. In *2018 Research on Equity and Sustained Participation in Engineering, Computing, and Technology (RESPECT)* (pp. 1–8). IEEE.

Thomas, J. O., Minor, R., & Odemwingie, O. (2016). Exploring African-American middle school girls' perceptions of computational algorithmic thinking and of themselves as game designers. In C. K. Looi, J. L. Polman, U. Cress, & P. Reimann (Eds.), *Transforming learning, empowering learners: The International Conference of the Learning Sciences (ICLS) 2016 Proceedings* (Vol. 1, pp. 960–962). International Society of the Learning Sciences.

Thomas, J. O., Odemwingie, O. C., Richmond, A., Saunders, Q., & Watler, M. (2015). Understanding the difficulties African-American middle school girls face while enacting computational algorithmic thinking in the context of game design. *Journal of Computer Science and Information Technology, 3*(1), 15–33. https://doi .org/10.15640/jcsit.v3n1a2

Thomas, J. O., Rankin, Y. A., Minor, R., & Sun, L. (2017). Exploring the difficulties African-American middle school girls face while enacting computational algorithmic thinking over three years while designing games for social change. *Journal of Computer Supported Cooperative Work, 26*(5), 389–421. https://doi .org/10.1007/s10606-017-9292-y

Tuitt, F., Haynes, C., & Stewart, S. (Eds.). (2016). *Race, equity, and the learning environment: The global relevance of critical and inclusive pedagogies in higher education*. Stylus.

Valenzuela, A. (1999). *Subtractive schooling: U.S.-Mexican youth and the politics of caring*. SUNY Press.

Varelas, M., Martin, D. B., & Kane, J. M. (2012). Content learning and identity construction: A framework to strengthen African American students' mathematics and science learning in urban elementary schools. *Human Development, 55*(5–6), 319–339. https://doi.org/10.1159/000345324

Walker, E. N. (2012). Cultivating mathematics identities in and out of school and in between. *Journal of Urban Mathematics Education, 5*(1), 66–83. https://www. tc.columbia.edu/faculty/walker/Cultivating.pdf

4

RESISTANCE, SILENCE, AND ARMORING

Black Girls' Navigation of the Intersections of Schools, Emotions, and Emotional Literacy

Charlotte E. Jacobs

I n the history of Black girls' and women's lives, education has always been a cornerstone of liberation, community, survival, and identity formation (Hull et al., 1982). Although the tendency of mainstream media is often to hold up the success stories of Black girls and women who were pioneers, such as Ruby Bridges and Melba Patillo Beales, or who have overcome great odds to be accepted into multiple Ivy League institutions (Criss, 2017), there is also another narrative that frequently appears. Videos and stories of Black girls being handcuffed for pushing a teacher, being expelled for wearing their hair in a natural hairstyle, and being physically assaulted by school resource officers also dominate news headlines on a regular basis (see M. Morris, 2016, 2019).

Although the news media creates a picture of extremes—portraits of success juxtaposed with snapshots of victimhood, the true story of the experiences of Black girls in schools is much more nuanced and requires an analysis beyond achievement and behavior. Seminal research studies conducted by Joyce Ladner (1971), Janie Ward and Tracy Robinson-Wood (2006), and Monique Morris (2016), and more recent reports produced by organizations such as the African American Policy Forum (AAPF; Crenshaw et al., 2015) and Girls for Gender Equity (2017) highlight the agency that black girls employ in strategically navigating their educational environments.

This chapter builds on previous research by applying a more nuanced lens to understand the experiences of Black girls in schools. In particular, this chapter explores how the phenomena of emotions and emotional literacy (Roffey, 2008) serve as an additional contextual layer that is part of Black girls' experiences in schools, and how the messages that Black girls receive about their emotions from their families, schools, and larger society influence both their agency and disempowerment when navigating their school lives.

In this chapter I will first present an overview of the research about the role of emotions in schools and research on the current status of Black girls in schools. Next, I will describe the two theories that serve as guideposts for this chapter: Black girl critical literacies (Jacobs, 2017) and armoring (Edmondson Bell & Nkomo, 1998). Following that, I will illustrate how Black girls engage in the emotional literacy component of Black girl critical literacies and armoring as a way to emotionally navigate through their daily school lives. I will close the chapter by discussing the implications of emotional literacy and armoring in the emotional development of Black girls and how families, educators, and practitioners can support their positive development.

Reviewing the Literature: Black Girls, Emotions, and Schooling

This literature review begins broadly by presenting a short history of how the emotions of teachers as well as students have been situated within schools, and how emotions have moved from the margins to more of a central role in school curriculum and practices through the rise of social and emotional learning. The literature review then narrows its focus to examine the status of Black girls in schools and their related emotional experiences as told by Black girls themselves.

The Role of Emotions in Schools

Historically, emotions and emotion work have always been on the periphery of U.S. education (Osher et al., 2016). When U.S. public education was implemented *en masse* in the early 20th century, social and emotional development were not factors that were believed to be important in terms of how schools were organized and what types of instruction took place in the classroom (Osher et al., 2016). Stemming from these beliefs, for the many decades that followed, a stance of hyperrationality in relation to emotions dominated policies and practices within U.S. schools. Gordon (2006) describes hyperrationality in schools as a process that "hides emotions that are a part of daily life there" (p. 4). Instead of acknowledging how teaching, learning, and leading are "emotional practices," many school administrators and policymakers focus on the "increasingly rationalized, cognitively driven and behavioral priorities of knowledge, skill, standards, targets, performance, management, planning, problem-solving, accountability, decision-making, and measurable results" (Hargreaves, 2000, p. 812). Seminal works in the girls' studies field such as Orenstein (2013) and Pipher (1994/2019) highlight how the focus on hyperrationality in schools has a particularly negative effect on girls. Their research illustrates how girls experienced ongoing episodes of anxiety, depression, and self-harm as an emotional outlet due to not getting the supports they needed in school. Where this leaves us, then, is that schools often become a place where core components of humanity, emotions and emotion work, are often ignored, discounted, or devalued.

That being said, since the creation of public schooling, there have been educators and theorists who believed that meaningful education in schools could not take place without acknowledging and taking emotions into account (Osher et al., 2016). The fact that emotions have always been a part of school life is the foundation of the field of social and emotional learning (SEL), a field that itself is only roughly 20 years old. Though SEL has become more prominent in schools in response to the increased occurrence of bullying and school shootings, it is still firmly situated within the debates of educators and policymakers about the role of schools (particularly those in the public arena) in promoting "nonacademic outcomes" such as skills associated with social and emotional well-being (Osher et al., 2016).

The points of debate surrounding the importance and prioritization of emotions and emotion work in schools serve as a significant backdrop to the daily lives of youth and educators in schools. On the one hand, no one's emotional needs may be getting met in an effort to maintain a sense of rationality and accountability from all members of the school community. On the other hand, if emotions are taken into account, then the question arises of whose emotions are noticed, who notices those emotions, and how those emotions are interpreted. The next section examines this context in relation to the experiences of Black girls in school.

The Status of Black Girls in Schools Through the Lens of Emotion: Reports From the Field

As schools often serve as microcosms of society, they have the latent function of social reproduction (Bowles & Gintis, 1976), and the status of Black girls in school often mirrors what we see in society, which is that of the "other" (Collins, 1986). Research shows that because of the bias of teachers and administrators in schools, Black girls are viewed as less feminine, more aggressive, more disruptive, hypersexual, and less academically capable than their White girl peers (E. Morris, 2007; M. Morris, 2016). These biases then translate into discriminatory practices on behalf of teachers, administrators, and schools, in which Black girls are suspended from school at six times the rate of White girls (Crenshaw et al., 2015), experience harsher disciplinary consequences than their peers as a result of being viewed as being older than they really are (Epstein et al., 2017), and underperform academically (Jacobs, 2018; NWLC & NAACP, 2014).

A recent set of research reports and studies focused on the experiences of Black girls in schools not only highlight the themes listed previously, but also are significant because they center the voices of Black girls as a part of their findings (Crenshaw et al., 2015; Girls for Gender Equity, 2017; M. Morris, 2016). This represents a shift in the ways that research studies about Black girls have been conducted. Whereas in the past the experiences of Black girls in schools were documented in detail by researchers, the actual voices of Black girls largely remained absent. In the reports from the African American Policy Forum (2015), the National Women's Law Center and NAACP (2014), and Georgetown Law School (Epstein et al., 2017), the girls' voices are present as a result of focus groups and listening sessions conducted by researchers. In the Girls for Gender Equity report, the girls took on the role of researchers through employing a youth participatory action research methodology (Cammarota & Fine, 2010), in which they interviewed and conducted focus groups with their Black girl classmates.

Though these reports did not specifically focus on emotions, by having the voices of the girls at the center, these reports help us begin to understand the emotional dimensions of Black girls' lives in schools. Across all of the reports, Black girls express the emotions of fear and anger in response to the interactions they have with school policies and authority figures who enforce the often restrictive policies. Fear and anger took the form of questioning the overt presence of surveillance within their schools through the use of metal detectors and school resource officers (security guards), which, instead of making them feel safe, made them feel as though they were "criminals" or being targeted for no reason (Girls for Gender Equity, 2017). Moments of fear and anger also stemmed from how experiences within their classrooms, in school hallways, and other areas of their school communicated a priority of discipline and order rather than academic and social-emotional growth (Crenshaw et al., 2015). Across the reports, the girls displayed their understandable and well-justified anger that they deserve better schools and educations than they were currently experiencing.

Another dominant emotion in these girls' narratives is a sense of resignation that their schools will never change enough to support their academic and emotional needs. As Monique Morris (2016) described through the concept of being "pushed out" from school, these feelings of resignation are evident in how Black girls gradually become disengaged in class and disconnected from school. Lastly, but perhaps most importantly, the girls also express emotions of determination and confidence through their recommendations and visions for how schools can work to support and care for Black girls. Recommendations centered on teacher training, curriculum revisions, and discipline policy reviews all speak to Black girls' confidence in knowing how they deserve to be treated and what rights they have to demand a better environment within their schools (Crenshaw et al., 2015; Girls for Gender Equity, 2017).

Significantly, the findings from Rebecca Epstein, Jamilia Blake, and Thalia Gonzalez's (2017) report on the experiences of Black girls in schools offer a contextual lens through which to understand Black girls' emotional lives, which is by highlighting biases that adults, particularly those in positions of authority, have about Black girls and Black girlhood. In their report, the authors describe the phenomenon of how Black girls are "adultified" (p. 1), in that they are often viewed as more adult than their White peers, beginning at the age of 5. Adults enact this process of adultification through assumptions that Black girls need less nurturing, protection, and support, and that they are more independent than their White peers. In schools, these assumptions can then translate into behaviors of teachers and school leaders focusing more on correcting the social behavior of Black girls rather than their academic progress, and not taking Black girls' emotions seriously (Epstein et al., 2017; E. Morris, 2007). Based on these interactions with adults in schools, it is no wonder that Black girls experience emotions of fear and anger, relying on emotions of determination and confidence in order to navigate their school lives, according to what the girls share with us through their reports focusing on their school lives (Crenshaw et al. 2015; Girls for Gender Equity, 2017; Jacobs, 2020).

Taken together, the slow shift in attitudes about the importance of emotions in schools, and a renewed focus on the experiences of Black girls in schools through their own voices, provides a solid backdrop through which to further analyze Black girls' emotional lives in schools.

Theoretical Framework

This chapter uses the concepts of Black girl critical literacies (BGCL) and armoring in order to better understand how the social identifiers of race, gender, and age intersect with the white supremacist norms of society and schools create a unique experience for Black girls in terms of their emotions. Both concepts highlight the developmental trajectories and socializing experiences that define the emotional lives of Black girls in schools.

Black Girl Critical Literacies

BGCL is a preliminary concept that draws on the theoretical frameworks of Black girlhood (Brown, 2013) and racial literacy (Stevenson, 2014) to understand how Black girls process the daily raced, gendered, and classed encounters in their lives. Specifically, I define BGCL as *the phenomenon in which Black girls use particular competencies to recognize, process, and respond to messages that they receive connected to their status as Black adolescent girls in U.S. society while simultaneously crafting their own sense of their Black girl identities.* An essential stance of BGCL is that it not only highlights *what* the experiences of Black girls are but also *how* Black girls understand and critically view their experiences. BGCL is composed of three different components: a developing critical consciousness, emotional literacy, and agency and activism (see Figure 4.1). For the purposes of this chapter, I will focus on the emotional literacy component of the framework.

Drawing on the concept of Paulo Freire's (2011) critical consciousness, Patricia Hill Collins's (2009) notion of Black female standpoint, and Gholdy Muhammad and Marcelle Haddix's (2016) conceptualization of Black girl literacies in the classroom, I argue that Black girls are required to develop a particular *emotional literacy* that operates on both an internal and external level in order to navigate their school lives. On an internal level, this concept describes the awareness that Black girls have of their own emotions and the decisions they make to display those emotions. Being able to trace the origins of their

Figure 4.1. A preliminary theory of Black girl critical literacies.

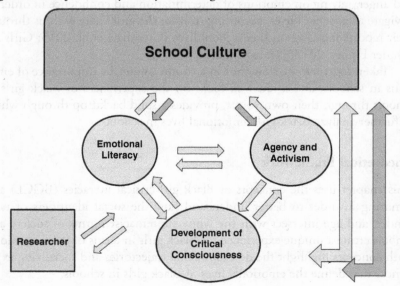

emotions during a particular encounter and developing the skills to manage their emotions is critical to an emerging literacy about one's own emotions.

On an external level, similar to critical consciousness, this concept reflects Black girls' awareness of how their emotions might be viewed by others because of the stereotypes associated with Black girls and women, and the current status that Black girls and women have in U.S. society. Emotional literacy also requires that Black girls are able to read others' emotions. This aspect of emotional literacy is particularly important as Black girls make decisions about when and how to respond to encounters of race, gender, and class within the context of their school culture, which has its own rules and norms about which emotions are allowed to be made visible and how they are allowed to be enacted.

Armoring

Conceptualized through the work of Tamara Beauboeuf-Lafontant (2007) and Ella Edmondson Bell and Stella Nkomo (1998), the phenomenon of *armoring* describes a process in which "a girl child acquires the cultural attitudes, preferences, and social behaviors for two cultural contexts. Armoring is also a 'political strategy for self-protection' whereby a girl develops a 'psychological resistance' to defy racism and sexism" (Edmondson Bell & Nkomo, 1998, citing Rogers, 1991, p. 38). Situated within the field of psychology, armoring highlights the ways in which Black girls (who later grow into Black women) are socialized at an early age to prepare for harmful and painful experiences of racism and sexism. Typically, this socialization occurs through the messages, conversations, and modeling behavior from Black girls' mothers, grandmothers, or other adult Black women role models in their lives.

In preadolescent and adolescent girls, armoring presents itself in two almost contradictory ways—one is through what Beauboeuf-Lafontant (2007) called the "silencing paradigm" (p. 29), and the other is an overt demonstration of self-reliance and confidence (Edmondson Bell & Nkomo, 1998). In the "silencing paradigm," Black girls engage in self-silencing through not being vocal about their own needs and desires, and often instead focus on supporting the needs of others. Beauboeuf-Lafontant (2007) describes how at a young age, Black girls begin to internalize the controlling image of the "strong Black woman" (p. 31) through appearing stoic in times of emotional or physical stress or struggle. Another outcome of armoring that Beauboeuf-Lafontant describes is how Black girls demonstrate confidence and self-reliance by navigating through their daily lives on a rather individual and isolated level, focusing on the fact that they are successfully able to do things on their own and with their own minds.

Although within the field of psychotherapy armoring is described as a coping mechanism (Edmondson Bell & Nkomo, 1998), in the long-term sense, it is not an effective one. Suppressing or repressing one's emotions can lead to feelings of anxiety and depression (Beauboeuf-Lafontant, 2007; Belgrave, 2009). Additionally, the constant action of putting everyone else's needs before one's own and not asking for help means that Black girls and women are often operating in environments where they receive little emotional or psychological support (Beauboeuf-Lafontant, 2007). Relatedly, because armoring requires that Black girls and women literally shield their feelings from others, using it as a coping mechanism can also influence the quality and level of intimacy of relationships that Black girls and women are a part of.

The concepts of emotional literacy and armoring come together to create a framework through which to understand Black girls' and women's emotional experiences and interactions in both internal and external arenas. These concepts present a framework that not only reveals how Black girls and women are socialized around emotional expression, but also the agency that they employ when making decisions about how to navigate different encounters. The remainder of this chapter will illustrate how the concepts of emotional literacy and armoring function for Black girls within the context of school.

Methods

The preliminary concept of BGCL has emerged from my research with adolescent Black girls in different educational contexts, my former experiences as a seventh-grade humanities teacher and executive director of a nonprofit focused on girls' rights, and my own experience as a Black girl navigating through different educational institutions. The narratives for this chapter emerge from a research study that I conducted with Black girls in grades 9–12 at two different elite predominantly White independent school[1] sites located just outside of an urban center in the northeastern part of the United States. What made these schools elite is that on average the tuition for schools of this type is $27,950 per year, with an average of 26.7% of students who attend these types of independent schools receiving financial assistance from the school (NAIS, 2020), meaning that on average more than three quarters of the student body is able to pay full tuition to attend. Another aspect of the elite nature of these schools is that students are selected to attend the schools through a specific admissions process that often includes a review of an application form, a writing sample, standardized test scores, teacher recommendations, and a campus interview (Howard & Gaztambide-Fernández, 2010).

Grace School was a coed school and the Olympia School (both pseudonyms) was an all-girls school. There were 10 to 15 girls at each site who self-selected to be a part of the study, representing a wide range of experiences based on the number of years they had attended their school (a third had been in the school since kindergarten, a third entered in middle school, and a third entered in high school), socioeconomic background, and academic standing.

Over a period of 4 months, the girls participated in a weekly discussion group where they talked about their experiences as Black girls in their school, in their communities, and in larger society. The weekly discussion groups contained prompts that drew on themes of Black feminism (Collins, 2009), intersectionality (Crenshaw, 1990), and critical pedagogy (Giroux, 1983). The weekly sessions also included activities such as identity mapping; watching videos and news clips connected to topics central to their lived experiences of being young, Black, and girls; and brainstorming sessions around changes the participants wanted to see in their schools.

In Their Own Voices: Black Girls' Emotional Lives in School

At both Grace School and the Olympia School, the themes that emerged related to Black girls' emotional experiences in schools operated at both micro and macro levels. At the micro level, narratives illustrated how Black girls demonstrated emotional literacy in managing their emotions through their daily interactions with their peers, teachers, and administrators in their schools by either choosing to publicly express or internally suppress their emotions. At the macro level, the girls' experiences highlight how the particular culture and structure of their schools contributed to a specific context connected to the norms and expectations of emotions and emotionality.

The Micro Level: Armoring and Making a Choice Between Expression and Suppression

This aspect of emotional literacy required the girls to balance acknowledging their own feelings as valid while at the same time fighting the internalization of deficit-oriented messages. When thinking about their emotional expression, one participant described herself as having "an attitude," being "rude" and "having a temper," to which she often tries to "make sure I'm . . . appropriate" because she feels like people are judging her. Relatedly, other girls also described the tensions between wanting to express their emotions but also being aware of the particular context in which they were being expressed:

> Um, I think our school—how I feel here is like that we are treated like so differently and like—I think we're kind of held to like a higher standard in some things, like we should be like more understanding, like, of the White students if they don't understand something about race. Or like if a White student like tweets something ignorant . . . or like the N-word or something, it's like we have to be the ones that are like understanding and like, "They didn't know better, and this or that." But if like something happens to us and we're like, if like, one of us tweets the N-word it's like World War III and like someone was taken in front of like a board [the disciplinary board] and it's called like "Black supremacy" and then like, what are you talking about because there's like 2 percent of us in this entire school? (Kendra, 11th grade)

Although the girls discussed how they were careful about how they chose to express their feelings of anger, frustration, and disappointment—knowing that these emotions could be read differently by their peers, teachers, and administrators, another emotion that schools monitored was joy. Our weekly girls' group space was not just a place for venting; it was also a place where we had a good time, laughing and enjoying the community of our space. At both schools, administrators and teachers consistently wanted to know what the girls had shared in the meeting, and at one of the schools White administrators (mostly men) would often be in the room at the start of our meeting and would linger, asking what was on the agenda for the day, or would poke their heads in the room after the session had already started to see what was going on. The fact that the girls were not allowed to have their own emotional space, even one that was specifically designated for them, illustrates the ways in which their emotional lives were confined within the hypervigilant behaviors enacted in their schools. A true emotional space for Black girls in these schools would have been a space where they could freely and authentically express their emotions to each other and to trusted adults within the room without having to worry about intrusions from outsiders to the space, who often viewed the space as something akin to an oddity or a spectacle.

The theme of emotional suppression stemmed from how some of the girls described hiding their feelings in some way from others. In sharing their identity maps and talking with the girls in one-on-one interviews, the impetus for emotional suppression was often feelings of embarrassment or not being sure that their emotions were appropriate according to others. In their identity maps one participant described "separating herself from people," and another participant wrote that one of the things that describes her is "shutting people out." This same participant wrote that she is known for "over exaggerating" and "taking things too seriously"—sentiments that communicate that she believes she is overreacting to certain experiences. Relatedly, other participants described themselves as being afraid to show that they were "sensitive" and whether it was okay for them consistently "taking things to heart."

Another aspect of emotional suppression was how the girls described the puzzle of figuring out how to move from a space where they were continually suppressing their emotions to a mental and emotional mindset where they felt able to communicate their emotions to others, and as a result, feel supported. Tanya, a 12th-grader and a lifer at her school, described her emotional trajectory from middle school to high school in this way:

> I hated middle school so much. I just hated everyone. Like that—those three years were like living hell, like, I just hated *everything* about middle school. And it's like, I don't know, like, keeping things bottled up like those three years . . . ninth grade it was so different. Like, it was so much free, like you were just free . . . so everything just [snaps] the little things, like set everything off. Oh, then I just like—maybe I got it all out of my system, or like I just—I may well like talk about things more like I just maybe I'm able to like communicate with other people about different situations better than I was.
>
> And I mean—like I have people here who like support me and I'm able to go and just talk to them about what's going on in my life and like what problems I'm having, and I'm just—I don't have to like sit and think about it all to myself.

Though Tanya and the other participants in this section display skills of emotional literacy by recognizing and making sense of their own emotions, they also demonstrate how structural and institutional norms around emotions are raced and gendered, leading them to make the choice to suppress their emotions rather than risk being hurt more by being in a place of vulnerability and then not getting the support they need from others. As a coping mechanism, suppressing one's emotions could lead to more challenges rather than productive development. Recent research highlights how "nearly half of all Black adolescent girls in the United States report experiencing severe and persistent feelings of sadness and hopelessness, which are consistent with symptoms of depression" (Stokes et al., 2020, p. 2175). Additionally, in 2017, Black girls were found to be the most likely subpopulation of youth to report attempting suicide (Stokes et al., 2020). These data alone point to the potentially severe outcomes if Black girls feel pressured to suppress rather than express their emotions.

The girls' engagement with armoring through the decision to either express or suppress their emotions demonstrates a form of what Margaret Beale Spencer and her colleagues (2003) termed a "reactive coping method" (p. 182). These coping methods can either be adaptive or maladaptive depending on the circumstances, with adaptive coping methods leading to "good health, positive relationships, and high self-esteem" (p. 182), and maladaptive coping methods leading to "poor health, incarceration, and self-destructive behaviors" (p. 182). Additionally, research has found that coping methods such as these could also lead to anxiety, depression, and disengagement in school (Beauboeuf-Lafontant, 2007; Belgrave, 2009).

In the case of the girls in this study, emotional expression gave them the opportunity to make sense of their emotions and then respond in a way that would align with who they believed themselves to be, and to communicate what outcomes they wanted from a particular interaction with peers, teachers, or administrators. Emotional suppression, however, functioned as a way for the girls to distance themselves not only from their emotions, but also from certain aspects of their identities that they felt were not valued or good. By engaging in maladaptive coping mechanisms, the girls were moving away from not only the acknowledgment of what they were feeling, but also being able to experience the connectedness and intimacy that is developed in relationships through experiences of reciprocal vulnerability.

The Macro Level: The Mythology of Emotionally Safe Spaces in Schools for Black Girls

In the study, the girls also discussed how their definitions and expectations of their school as a "safe space" differed from how their schools seemed to define "safe spaces." Based on the girls' assessment, their schools' approach toward creating a "safe space" meant maintaining a particular "culture of niceness" (Evans, 2012; Hoo, 2004) by only having superficial discussions about difference, identity, and status, or maintaining a general silence about difference in favor of focusing on everyone being a part of the same larger school community. In contrast, the girls identified safe spaces as being places or having a school culture that promoted students and teachers talking about issues and not just "skating over" them, and in doing so, everyone is "working to understand where the other is coming from." Patricia, a ninth-grader, described her vision for what she would want to have happen at her school, particularly when issues of race emerge in class discussions:

> I want people to feel like they [her White classmates] can still say what they want to say with me there, like I don't want people to feel like they're tiptoeing around everything because there's a Black person there. But, like, at the same time I think they need to see, like, view the Black perspective on all these issues because . . . they don't understand how—what it's like to be Black like every day.

Contrary to their vision of safe spaces, the girls described their schools as "sensitive," "timid," "worried," and "afraid." Many of their discussions focused on what their schools needed to do in order to move toward a culture that was safe for everyone, and not just protecting the emotions of White students, teachers, and administrators. In the following example, the girls at Grace School were having a discussion about an upper school assembly that they had attended where a Black male speaker talked about the legacy of race and racism in the United States and its connection to current events such as the shooting of Michael Brown in Ferguson, Missouri. As the discussion progressed, the girls analyzed the school culture at Grace in relation to having conversations about these issues. Renée, a 12th-grader, offered these points:

> My main issue with Grace is just that I think it's just like, too afraid. Like, it—like, we don't tackle certain subjects that we need to tackle, and like, everyone is just so timid and so worried about everything, and I think like, you're supposed to be uncomfortable at certain things. Like, you're not supposed to be comfortable when you talk about like, Ferguson or something. Even when we had that like, the speaker come in. . . . I mean like, he had good points . . . and you know when we came back to advisory just to talk about it, and everything, they [White students in her advisory] were like, "Oh, it just made me uncomfortable" like, you know, and it's just like we take that and then we're just like, "Ok, we're going to shut everything down." We should press into it—"Why did it make you uncomfortable?," you know, like . . . it made you uncomfortable, but it could have made someone else feel, like, comfortable or everything like that. But it's just like "no," as soon as you say "I'm uncomfortable" it just ends it, and I think that's the main problem, is that we're not kind of looking to everyone as a community.

Renée's reflection not only highlights what she thinks the school should do to foster a more inclusive community (by "pressing" into those who are resistant), but also demonstrates her skills of emotional literacy, in which she is able to point to how the institutional culture of her school, situated within prevailing emotions of fear and discomfort in the school community, stifle productive discussions, thereby communicating to the girls that White students' and teachers' feelings are more valued than those of Black girls.

Discussion

The findings in this chapter highlight how the emotional lives of Black girls in schools are dominated by an ever-present context of symbolic, institutional, and physical violence. Bourdieu (1979) describes symbolic violence as the everyday practices and policies in which members of a marginalized group are forced to adopt the habitus (mannerisms, behaviors, and perspectives) of the dominant group. In schools, the ongoing invisibility of Black girls' emotions is an act of symbolic violence. The fact that Black girls shared that they did not often feel safe fully expressing their emotions in school, did not feel as though they had trusted people in school who they could reach out to, is a form of symbolic violence in that Black girls receive the message that their emotions and emotional expression do not matter. Relatedly, when Black girls do choose to express their emotions and have made their needs known through acts of resistance such as truth telling, asking questions, or asking for support, they are often ignored, placated, or accused of being disrespectful or insubordinate. As Epstein et al. (2017) illustrated, educators' and adults' tendency to "adultify" Black girls by treating them and their emotional lives as they would adults rather than supporting them as they would other adolescents has the result of Black girls and their emotions not receiving the care and attention that they deserve. The reality is that Black girls are given very little latitude in what emotions they are allowed to express in school and how they are allowed to do so.

When Black girls express their emotions in ways that are not pleasing to their peers, adults, or other authority figures, the result is often psychological or physical violence against them. The findings of the reports discussed at the beginning of this chapter as well as current events illustrate how physical violence against Black girls' emotions manifests through Black girls being wrestled to the ground by school resource officers, physically restrained by teachers, and sexually harassed by people in positions of authority at school.

The impact of this symbolic, institutional, and psychological violence against Black girls and their emotional expression is evident in increased rates of Black girls suffering from anxiety and depression (Beauboeuf-Lafontant, 2007), as well an increase in recent years in the rate of Black girls taking their own lives in responses to school-related encounters, particularly situations where they were bullied at school or online by their peers (Branigan, 2018; Frederick, 2015; Walker, 2016).

In her book *Sing a Rhythm, Dance a Blues* (2019), Monique Morris illuminates the complexity of the status of Black girl emotions within the contexts of school and society by juxtaposing Black girls' experiences of "the blues"—"bearing witness to contradictions and then working through them to bring about critical, intellectually responsible thinking and action" (p. 7) and the need for schools to become places of emotional healing in order for Black girls to feel supported and enable them to learn. Morris's perspective offers a way for us not only to acknowledge and critique the ways in which schools and society limit Black girls' emotional expression, but also plants the seeds for how we can recognize and nurture Black girls' joy and healing.

Conclusion

The literature supporting this chapter and the particular findings illustrating how Black girls navigate their daily school lives through choices around emotional suppression or expression and experiencing both institutional and interpersonal violence speaks to the fact that emotional literacy development is a critical aspect of Black girl survival. In order for Black girls to be able to survive in their schools and in society, they need to be able to recognize and communicate their feelings to those who will support them and protect them. In schools, this requires an examination of school policies, practices, and programs for bias and the reinforcement of racism, sexism, and adultism. Additionally, echoing the recommendations from the girls in my study as well as those in the previously mentioned reports, ongoing training is needed for school administrators, teachers, and students around issues of racism, sexism, white supremacy, power, and dominance.

Scholars such as Ruth Nicole Brown, Aimee Cox, Kimberlé Crenshaw, Venus Evans-Winters, Monique Morris, and Maisha Winn have led the charge in producing research on the lives of Black girls, and critical conversations, research, and the exploration of the emotional lives of Black girls need to continue. Although much of the research that we currently have looks at the experiences of adolescent Black girls, another area that needs to be explored is the different facets of the school lives of younger Black girls, including their emotional lives. At the core of these conversations for adolescent and younger Black girls alike should be the question *What are the things that need to be put in place for Black girls to thrive emotionally?*

As researchers, scholars, policymakers, and practitioners, we owe it to our Black girls to continue to create and protect spaces where their voices can be heard and taken seriously, where their humanity is acknowledged and embraced, and where they are nurtured, tended to, and cared for like the precious, brilliant, and amazing beings that they are.

Suggestions for Policy, Practice, and Curriculum in Schools to Promote the Emotional Safety and Literacy of Black Girls

Policy

- Policymakers should review their policies using the lens of realist evaluation (INTRAC, 2017) by asking questions such as "What works about this policy for Black girls? What doesn't work for Black girls? In which circumstances does this policy work (or not?) How and why does this policy work for Black girls (or not)?"

Practice

- School leaders should review their current practices through a trauma-informed and healing-centered lens—what are the intents of current practices within schools (such as discipline practices, dress codes, accepted interactions between students and teachers, etc.) and what are the impacts of the practices on Black girls?
- School leaders should examine the mental health services and supports that are offered in their schools. Are mental health practitioners trained in intersectional and culturally responsive practices? Do they have experience with or have they attended professional development trainings geared specifically toward working with Black girls?
- School leaders, educators, and practitioners also need to leverage the knowledge that Black girls have about their own lived experiences in order to develop practices that actually support the needs of Black girls. Conducting listening sessions or developing spaces or methods through which Black girls can provide authentic feedback about their experiences in schools is a way to develop the reciprocal relationships that should exist between practitioners and students in creating a supportive, nurturing, and developmentally appropriate school environment.

Curriculum

- Curriculum should intentionally center the positive development of social-emotional learning through an intersectional and healing-centered lens. Educators should review their curriculum to look for opportunities to bring in discussions of emotions, students' experiences, and the teaching of positive coping strategies such as mindfulness practices, the development of self-care plans, and the identification of outside support networks.

- Centering Black girls in the curriculum requires that their voices and experiences are a key part of the curriculum. When reviewing their curriculum educators should ask themselves, "Who and whose experiences are represented in my curriculum and how? Whose experiences are missing?" This centering also requires educators to ask Black girls for feedback about what is working for them in the curriculum and what is not, and why.

Discussion Questions

1. What sorts of training do educators need to engage in to recognize their own biases and perceptions when it comes to interacting with Black girls and reading their emotions?
2. How can schools make space for Black girl joy and create places of healing within the classroom curriculum and school policies and programs?
3. What are the different ways that educators, policymakers, and researchers can continue to put the voices of Black girls at the center of their work?

Note

1 Independent schools, according to the National Association of Independent Schools (www.nais.org/), the accrediting body for over 1,400 independent schools in the United States, are "non-profit private schools that are independent in philosophy: each is driven by a unique mission. They are also independent in the way they are managed and financed: each is governed by an independent board of trustees and each is primarily supported through tuition payments and charitable contributions. They are accountable to their communities and are accredited by state-approving accrediting bodies" (NAIS website, 2021).

Further Reading

Collins, C. F. (2015). *Black girls and adolescents: Facing the challenges*. Praeger.
Cox, A. M. (2015). *Shapeshifters: Black girls and the choreography of citizenship*. Duke University Press.
Green, E. L., Walker, M., & Shapiro, E. (2020, October 1). A battle for the souls of black girls. *New York Times*. https://www.nytimes.com/2020/10/01/us/politics/black-girls-school-discipline.html
Kaler-Jones, C. (2020). *When SEL is used as another form of policing*. https://medium.com/@justschools/when-sel-is-used-as-another-form-of-policing-fa53cf85dce4

National Women's Law Center. (2018). *DRESS CODED: Black girls, bodies, and bias in D.C. schools*. https://nwlc.org/resources/dresscoded/
National Women's Law Center. (2019). *DRESS CODED II: Protest, progress and power in D.C. schools*. https://nwlc.org/resources/dresscoded-ii/

References

African American Policy Forum & Center for Intersectionality and Social Policy Studies. (2015). *Black girls matter: Pushed out, overpoliced and underprotected*. http://static1.squarespace.com/static/53f20d90e4b0b80451158d8c/t/54dcc1ece 4b001c03e323448/1423753708557/AAPF_BlackGirlsMatterReport.pdf
Beauboeuf-Lafontant, T. (2007). "You have to show strength": An exploration of gender, race, and depression. *Gender & Society, 21*(1), 28–51. https://doi .org/10.1177/0891243206294108
Belgrave, F. Z. (2009). *African American girls: Reframing perceptions and changing experiences*. Springer.
Bourdieu, P. (1979). Symbolic power. *Critique of Anthropology, 4*(13–14), 77–85. https://doi.org/10.1177/0308275X7900401307
Bowles, S., & Gintis, H. (1976). *Schooling in capitalist America*. Basic Books.
Branigin, A. (2018, January 24). Death at DC boarding school highlights the alarming increase of suicides among young black children. *The Root*. https://www.the-root.com/death-at-d-c-boarding-school-highlights-the-alarming-i-1822369943
Brown, R. N. (2013). *Hear our truths: The creative potential of black girlhood*. University of Illinois Press.
Cammarota, J., & Fine, M. (Eds.). (2010). *Revolutionizing education: Youth participatory action research in motion*. Routledge.
Collins, P. H. (1986). Learning from the outsider within: The sociological significance of Black feminist thought. *Social Problems, 33*(6), s14–s32. https://doi .org/10.2307/800672
Collins, P. H. (2009). *Black feminist thought: Knowledge, consciousness, and the politics of empowerment* (2nd ed.). Routledge.
Crenshaw, K. (1990). Mapping the margins: Intersectionality, identity politics, and violence against women of color. *Stan. L. Rev., 43*, 1241. https://heinonline.org/ HOL/LandingPage?handle=hein.journals/stflr43&div=52&id=&page=
Crenshaw, K., Ocen, P., & Nanda, J. (2015). *Black girls matter: Pushed out, overpoliced and underprotected*. African American Policy Forum & Center for Intersectionality and Social Policy Studies. http://static1.squarespace.com/ static/53f20d90e4b0b80451158d8c/t/54dcc1ece4b001c03e323448/ 1423753708557/AAPF_BlackGirlsMatterReport.pdf
Criss, D. (2017, April 10). New Jersey teen gets accepted by all 8 Ivy League schools. *CNN News*. https://www.cnn.com/2017/04/04/us/teen-ivy-league-trnd/index .html

Edmondson Bell, E. L. J., & Nkomo, S. M. (1998). Armoring: Learning to withstand racial oppression. *Journal of Comparative Family Studies, 29*(2), 285–295. https://doi.org/10.3138/jcfs.29.2.285

Epstein, R., Blake, J. J., & González, T. (2017). *Girlhood interrupted: The erasure of black girls' childhood.* Georgetown Law Center on Poverty and Inequality. http://www.law.georgetown.edu/academics/centers-institutes/poverty-inequality/upload/girlhood-interrupted.pdf

Evans, R. (2012). Getting to no: Building true collegiality in schools. *Independent School, 71*(2), 99–107. https://eric.ed.gov/?id=EJ972311

Frederick, A. (2015). Suicidality among gifted African American females attending elite schools: Impact of diminished community support. In C. F. Collins (Ed.), *Black girls and adolescents: Facing the challenges* (pp. 211–219). Praeger.

Freire, P. (2011). *Pedagogy of the oppressed* (30th anniversary ed.). Bloomsbury.

Girls for Gender Equity. (2017). *The school girls deserve.* https://www.ggenyc.org/wp-content/uploads/2017/11/GGE_school_girls_deserveDRAFT6FINALWEB.pdf

Giroux, H. A. (1983). *Theory and resistance in education: A pedagogy for the opposition.* Bergin & Garvey.

Gordon, T. (2006). Girls in education: Citizenship, agency, and emotions. *Gender and Education, 18*(1), 1–15. https://doi.org/10.1080/09540250500194880

Hargreaves, A. (2000). Mixed emotions: Teachers' perceptions of their interactions with students. *Teaching and Teacher Education, 16*, 811–826. https://doi.org/10.1016/S0742-051X(00)00028-7

Hoo, S. S. (2004). We change the world by doing nothing. *Teacher Education Quarterly, 31*(1), 199–211. https://www.jstor.org/stable/23478430

Howard, A., & Gaztambide-Fernandez, R. A. (Eds.). (2010). *Educating elites: Class privilege and educational advantage.* R&L Education.

Hull, G. T., Scott, P. B, & Smith, B. (1982). *All the women are white, all the blacks are men, but some of us are brave: Black women's studies.* Feminist Press.

International NGO Training and Research Centre for Civil Society. (2017). *Realist evaluation.* https://www.intrac.org/wpcms/wp-content/uploads/2017/01/Realist-evaluation.pdf

Jacobs, C. E. (2017). *The development of black girl critical literacies of race, gender, and class in independent schools: Awareness, agency, and emotion* [Doctoral dissertation, University of Pennsylvania]. Publicly Accessible Penn Dissertations 2356. https://repository.upenn.edu/edissertations/2356

Jacobs, C. E. (2018). Remember, black girls aren't doing "just fine": Supporting black girls in the classroom. In E. Moore Jr., M. Penick-Parks, & A. Michael (Eds.), *A guide for white women teaching black boys* (pp. 377–384). Corwin.

Jacobs, C. E. (2020). *Ready to lead: Leadership supports and barriers for black and Latinx girls* [Research study report]. Girls Leadership. https://girlsleadership.org/resources/research/black-and-latinx-girls-are-ready-to-lead/?fbclid=IwAR1O3NFXDDfQ1Q9ZRFQ-bPS4OXb2LwpReqHHGIcd9kZ4IvX31g0q7xEtL8I

Ladner, J. (1971). *Tomorrow's tomorrow: The black woman.* University of Nebraska Press.

Morris, E. W. (2007). "Ladies" or "loudies"? Perceptions and experiences of black girls in classrooms. *Youth & Society, 38*(4), 490–515. https://doi .org/10.1177/0044118X06296778

Morris, M. (2016). *Pushout: The criminalization of Black girls in schools.* The New Press.

Morris, M. (2019). *Sing a rhythm, dance a blues: Education for the liberation of Black and Brown girls.* The New Press.

Muhammad, G. E., & Haddix, M. (2016). Centering Black girls' literacies: A review of literature on the multiple ways of knowing of Black girls. *English Education, 48*(4), 299–336. https://www.jstor.org/stable/26492572

National Association of Independent Schools. (2020). *Facts at a glance 2020–21.* https://www.nais.org/getmedia/f24d0185-1218-4941-9f84-2a0b11707f46/ Facts-at-a-Glance-2020-2021-(NAIS-Members).pdf

National Women's Law Center & NAACP Legal Defense and Educational Fund. (2014). *Unlocking opportunity for African-American girls: A call to action for educational equity.* http://www.naacpldf.org/files/publications/Unlocking%20Opportunity%20for%20African%20American%20Girls_0.pdf

Orenstein, P. (2013). *Schoolgirls: Young women, self-esteem, and the confidence gap.* Anchor.

Osher, D., Kidron, Y., Brackett, M., Dymnicki, A., Jones, S., & Weissberg, R. P. (2016). Advancing the science and practice of social and emotional learning: Looking back and moving forward. *Review of Research in Education, 40,* 644–681. https://doi.org/10.3102/0091732X16673595

Pipher, M. B., & Gilliam, S. P. (1994/2019). *Reviving Ophelia: Saving the selves of adolescent girls.* Riverhead Books.

Roffey, S. (2008). Emotional literacy and the ecology of school wellbeing. *Educational and Child Psychology, 25*(2), 29–39. http://growinggreatschoolsworldwide. com/wp-content/uploads/2014/02/2008-EL-Ecology-Wellbeing.pdf

Spencer, M. B., Fegley, S. G., & Harpalani, V. (2003). A theoretical and empirical examination of identity as coping: Linking coping resources to the self processes of African American youth. In *Beyond the Self* (pp. 181–188). Routledge.

Stevenson. H. C. (2014). *Promoting racial literacy in schools: Differences that make a difference.* Teachers College Press.

Stokes, M. N., Hope, E. C., & Cryer-Coupet, Q. R. (2020). Black girl blues: The roles of racial socialization, gendered racial socialization, and racial identity on depressive symptoms among Black girls. *Journal of Youth and Adolescence, 49*(11), 2175–2189. https://link.springer.com/article/10.1007/s10964-020-01317-8

Walker, R. (2016, June 15). As suicide rates for black children rise, protecting emotional health is vital. *Ebony Magazine.* https://www.ebony.com/health/black-suicide-rates/

Ward, J. V., & Robinson-Wood, T. L. (2006). Room at the table: Racial and gendered realities in the schooling of black children. In C. Skelton, B. Francis, & L. Smulyan (Eds.), *The Sage handbook of gender and education* (pp. 325–338). Sage.

NAMING AND CHALLENGING THE VIOLENCE AND CRIMINALIZATION OF BLACK WOMEN AND GIRLS

PART TWO

NAMING AND CHALLENGING
THE VIOLENCE AND
CRIMINALIZATION OF BLACK
WOMEN AND GIRLS

5

THE MISEDUCATION
OF OUR SISTERS

Erin S. Corbett

Never has it been more important to invest in the education of Black women and girls. Despite evidence of increases in education and credential attainment for Black women, these rates of credential attainment are deceptively positive when not properly contextualized. Recent data from the National Center for Education Statistics (NCES) indicate that Black women constitute the majority of Black people awarded either an associate's, bachelor's, master's, or doctorate in 2016–2017 (NCES, 2020). However, when rates of degree attainment for Black women are compared to the total number of degrees awarded overall, we see that Black women comprise only 7% of awarded credentials (NCES, 2020). Further, when observing data around career trajectories from the Bureau of Labor Statistics, Black girls and women, aged 16 and older, are less represented in management, professional, and business fields but more represented in service-related fields than their white counterparts (U.S. Bureau of Labor Statistics, 2019).

These credential and career attainment gaps are illustrative of a number of factors, including racism and patriarchy embedded in the P–20 educational pipeline, but are also a byproduct of increasingly salient racism and misogynoir ingrained in the fabric of the United States criminal legal system and the ways that said system disproportionately impacts Black people, generally, and Black women and girls, specifically. Black women and girls, as a result of the interplay among these larger societal systems (education, legal, etc.), become particularly susceptible to constrained life outcomes related to career advancement and trajectories; as a result, it is incumbent upon practitioners and scholars to comprehensively understand how Black women and girls are mistreated and miseducated in a society that routinely forgets the uniqueness of their struggles.

Data around the epidemic of American mass incarceration are well known. As a nation we comprise 5% of the world's population yet are responsible for approximately 25% of the world's incarcerated population (Wagner & Bertram, 2020). These data and their implications, however, obscure the fact that when we disaggregate along lines of race/ethnicity and gender identity, more terrifying trends emerge when we examine the impact of the carceral system on Black women and girls. At year's end 2017, women were 7% of the total prison population (Bronson & Carson, 2019). And although there were twice as many white women imprisoned as Black women (49,100 vs. 19,600), the incarceration *rate* for Black women, at 92 per 100,000, was almost double that of their white counterparts, at 49 per 100,000 (Bronson & Carson, 2019), and this is even after recognizing that the incarceration rate for Black women dropped by 55% between 2000 and 2017 (Sentencing Project, 2019).

Looking even closer at incarceration, and disaggregating by age distribution, Black girls aged 18–19, who might otherwise be seamlessly transitioning to higher education credential opportunities, were 4.4 times more likely to be incarcerated than their white counterparts (Bronson & Carson, 2019). Even more disconcerting is that we can trace these enormous disparities to a school-to-prison pipeline that leads to girls occupying 15% of youth residential placements (Sentencing Project, 2019), many of which are a result of technical violations and/or offenses that are not even crimes, like truancy and running away; some allegations of offenses are entirely subjective, like incorrigibility, yet they still impact Black girls disproportionately (Sawyer & Wagner, 2019). So how does this happen? How do Black women and girls, who have the potential to be college students and graduates, flourishing in life, end up impacted by the carceral state? It begins with our earliest encounters with the educational system and the practical implementation and systemic normalization of the school-to-prison pipeline.

The Pushout of Black Girls

Morris (2016) penned the seminal text *Pushout*, a piece that painstakingly tells the "necessary and inspiring, infuriating and redeeming" (p. xvii) story of Black girls and the ways that schools criminalize them from the very beginning. She outlines how Black girls, in being labeled "not docile" (p. 59), do not conform to heteropatriarchal, presumptive expectations of how girls should behave and, thus, suffer the consequences that include increases in school discipline at rates that far outpace their white counterparts (Morris, 2016).

One of the posited theoretical underpinnings of the Black girl–focused school-to-prison pipeline is rooted in the concept of adultification, defined as "a social or cultural stereotype that is based on how adults perceive children in the absence of knowledge of children's behavior and verbalizations. This . . . form of adultification . . . is based in part on race" (Epstein et al. 2017, p. 4). The authors note that the disparities in treatment and, relevant for this analysis, punishment in school of youth of color are possibly rooted in a societal belief that Black children bear a higher burden of responsibility for their actions and behavior (Goff, 2014; Graham & Lowery, 2004; Morris, 2016; Rattan et al., 2012). Additionally, Epstein et al. (2017) found the following in the survey they conducted:

> Across all age ranges, participants viewed Black girls collectively as more adult than white girls. Responses revealed, in particular, that participants perceived Black girls as needing less protection and nurturing than white girls, and that Black girls were perceived to know more about adult topics and are more knowledgeable about sex than their white peers. The most significant differences were found in the age brackets that encompass mid-childhood and early adolescence—ages 5–9 and 10–14. (p. 8)

As many children begin their encounters with school around the age of 5 with enrollment in kindergarten, the impact of these perceptions about the maturity, exposure, and experience of Black girls becomes increasingly relevant. Although there is no documented, causal inference between perceptions of adultification and the disproportional doling out of school discipline, it does offer a conceptual framework within which to analyze evidence that highlights a profound disparity in punishment at the elementary and middle school level when it comes to Black girls and their white peers.

Smith and Harper (2015) found that, nationally, Black girls comprised 45% of the suspended girl population and 42% of the expelled girl population. This trend continued, as highlighted by the National Women's Law Center as cited in Epstein et al. (2017), and found that of all girls enrolled in K–12 in the 2013–2014 academic year, Black girls comprised 15.6% of that student population; however, they simultaneously comprised 36.6% of in-school suspensions, 41.6% of single suspensions, and 52% of those students with multiple suspensions (National Women's Law Center, 2017, as cited in Epstein et al., 2017). In that same year, Black girls comprised 28.2% of girls referred to law enforcement at school and 37.3% of girls arrested at school (National Women's Law Center, 2017, as cited in Epstein et al., 2017). Even more telling is what many of these Black girls were disciplined for. They were twice as likely to be disciplined for minor violations, like dress code or cell phone use. But they were two and a half times more likely to be disciplined for disobedience and three times more likely to be disciplined for disruptive behaviors, where the language of disobedience and disruptive behavior signals more, potentially, about school culture and race-based expectations of Black girl dispositions than it does about actual, objective behaviors (Morris, 2016).

Black Girls and Women and the Criminal Legal System

For those Black girls with increased exposure to school discipline and/or law enforcement at school, their continued experiences in and with the legal system are extensions of the disparate treatment they received in school. For Black girls, prosecutors are less likely to exercise discretion to dismiss cases (Taylor, 2006, as cited in Epstein et al., 2017), courts are less likely to offer diversion opportunities (DOJ, 2017, as cited in Epstein et al., 2017), Black girls are three times more likely to be removed from their homes (NWLC, 2009, as cited in Epstein et al., 2017), and they, overall, receive more harsh penalties "even after accounting for seriousness of the offense, prior record, and age" (Nanda, 2012, as cited in Epstein et al., 2017). The perpetuation of the trends that begin in elementary school far too often culminate in Black girls and women ending up mired in civil and municipal matters related to the legal system; locked up under municipal, state, or federal custody; and locked out of many of the educational opportunities that their white counterparts can take advantage of due to less harsh legal system decisions and fewer school discipline barriers.

Systemic patriarchy in the United States, as a substantial contributor to the overall epidemic of mass incarceration, has masked an obscene explosion in incarceration rates of women. Because women represent only 7% of the incarcerated population (Bronson & Carson, 2019), it is easy to overlook the unique space they occupy in the carceral state. However, it is precisely because of the fact that they are underrepresented in the total incarcerated population that we need to deliberately attend to the specific challenges that both land them in prison and govern their experiences while incarcerated. Over the past 40 years, the incarceration rate of women increased more than 834% (Sawyer & Bertram, 2018); that growth is double the growth of the incarceration rate of men during the same time period. In some states, the rise in incarceration rates of women has even counteracted decreases in the incarceration rates of men. In addition to the hypercriminalization of Black girls that begins in elementary and middle schools, this exponential growth of women in prisons in such a short time frame can be traced substantially, though certainly not completely, to the legislative changes that occurred during the 1970s, 1980s, and 1990s during the "war on drugs." This politically manufactured war began officially on June 17, 1971, when then president Richard Nixon leveraged a press conference to declare drugs as "public enemy #1" (Perry, 2018). Yet decades later, a former Nixon aide, John Ehrlichman, revealed what those on the receiving end of increased punishments that disproportionately impacted Black communities already knew:

> You want to know what this was really all about. The Nixon campaign in 1968, and the Nixon White House after that, had two enemies: the antiwar left and black people. You understand what I'm saying. We knew we couldn't make it illegal to be either against the war or black, but by getting the public to associate the hippies with marijuana and blacks with heroin, and then criminalizing both heavily, we could disrupt those communities. We could arrest their leaders, raid their homes, break up their meetings, and vilify them night after night on the evening news. Did we know we were lying about the drugs? Of course we did. (Drug Policy Alliance, n.d., para. 6)

From Nixon placing federal attention on drug laws to the passing of the excessively draconian Rockefeller drug laws of New York later in the decade, the drug war continued uninterrupted through the 1980s when President Ronald Reagan reemphasized a federal focus on drug legislation. The legislative component of this war culminated with the passage of the Violent Crimes Act (VCA) in 1994, an act that (re)defined mandatory minimums and truth in sentencing for those accused of federal charges and introduced the ban on Pell access by any person incarcerated in a state or federal correctional facility. As a result of the drug war, women were more likely than men to be incarcerated on drug-related offenses; more than 2 decades later, Black women continue to be incarcerated at higher rates than their white counterparts (Sentencing Project, 2019). With Black women and girls increasingly incarcerated, casualties of what all data outline is a failed drug war, and with limited access to education due to constraints on access to federal aid, educational attainment remains elusive for many.

How the Failed War on Drugs Impacted Black Women

Although the VCA was a federal law specifically governing those in federal custody, the act also provided extensive financial incentives for states to adopt similarly punitive policies and practices; those financial incentives led to the building of more prisons to house the increase of those in custody, and although the focus was on the men piled into these new facilities, women were also caught in the community wreckage. Women were caught in this drug war, many times convicted on accessory or possession charges relating to their partners/spouses/significant others. Many of these women were also in abusive relationships where they may have had little choice to not participate in related drug activity. Increasingly, as women began to seek freedom from these abusive relationships, more ended up incarcerated for violent offenses like assault or homicide related to an abusive partner, sexual assault assailant, or sex trafficker/pimp.

Overall, the war on drugs not only imprisoned entire communities of men but also removed many mothers from their homes. In altogether too many cases, interactions with the legal system ultimately removed both parents from the household and/or the neighboring community, leaving behind close to 2 million children (Sentencing Project, 2008). As of 2007, 744,200 incarcerated individuals were fathers; 65,600 were mothers, representing an increase in the incarceration rate of mothers of 122% since 1991 (Sentencing Project, 2008). Of the 65,600 mothers who were incarcerated, approximately 64% were the primary caregivers and/or custodial parent prior to incarceration; additionally, data from the same time frame highlight that 1 in 15 Black children had a parent in prison and that Black children were 7.5 times more likely to have a parent in prison (Sentencing Project, 2008).

In 2019, the Prison Policy Initiative estimated that of the women jailed (in local jails as opposed to state prisons) in the United States, approximately 80% were mothers (Sawyer & Wagner, 2019). In these scenarios, children are often left to either fend for themselves, sent to foster care or group homes, or raised by friends and/or family members while parents serve their sentences. The cycle, at this point, was complete where an interrupted K–12 experience, coupled with an increased likelihood of exposure to, and forensic interactions with, law enforcement, led to incarceration at various times before, during, or after the time wherein a Black girl or woman might find herself enrolling in a higher education institution.

Education and the Justice-Impacted Black Woman

Understanding the impact of interruptions of educational trajectories demands an understanding that such interruptions tend to yield credential attainment levels lower than the average household. This holds true when considering the credential attainment of Black women and girls prior to incarceration. At any given time during incarceration, a state-level facility has 38% of incarcerated parents who have less than a high school equivalency or secondary credential (Sentencing Project, 2008). Even more bleak is the fact that only 30% of incarcerated parents have had exposure to higher education courses, potentially falling into the "some college, no degree" categorization (Sentencing Project, 2008). Even fewer have completed an undergraduate degree and fewer, still, have an advanced degree or doctorate. And as jobs in the United States continue to require postsecondary credentials in order to be hired, this credential gap provides insight into how the school-to-prison pipeline, as a comprehensively disculterative phenomenon, continues to adversely and disproportionately impact Black women and girls.

As conversations around criminal justice reform have increased in frequency, both politically and socially, one of the topics of the conversation is the role of higher education in prison. With former president Barack Obama's focus on the Second Chance Act and the launch of the Second Chance Pell Pilot Program (Wexler, 2016), the intensity of the debate has reached the hallowed halls of the United States Congress, particularly in light of impending reauthorization of the Higher Education Act of 1965. Embedded in this conversation about the provision of higher education behind bars is an implicit question, at least on the part of conservative legislators, of whether incarcerated persons are deserving of receiving an education. However, that premise should be categorically rejected; access to education is a human right and, for Black girls and women, is often the critical bridge toward succeeding and thriving in life, despite circumstances. In some instances, incarcerated women have access to quality higher education programs. For many women, however, the educational programs to which they have access may not be of quality, if there are even programs available.

Liberal Arts or Home Ec? Gendered Responses to Educating Incarcerated (Black) Women

The availability of higher education programming is inconsistent, varying from state to state, facility to facility. Within this variation of availability is also variation in the amount, and type, of programs from which the women have to choose. For example, the state of Connecticut has one women's facility and the women there have access not only to adult basic education/GED courses, scaffolded by educational attainment at the time of intake, but to numerous postsecondary, credit-bearing programs offered by both community colleges and private, 4-year institutions like Three Rivers Community College and Wesleyan University, respectively. They also have a deep bench of volunteers who provide enrichment opportunities like writing workshops, dance opportunities, and access to tutors through partnership with Connecticut College. In other states, however, the options and opportunities are far fewer.

On the other end of the continuum is Texas, a state ranking in the top 10 for the highest rates of incarcerated women. where the incarcerated rate of women has increased 908% between 1980 and 2016, more than double the increase in incarceration rate of men at 396% (Texas Criminal Justice Coalition, 2018). Texas has very few educational opportunities available for women who have completed ABE/GED coursework, whereas incarcerated men have access to at least four postsecondary credentials and certifications in 21 professions, like cabinet making, advanced computer technology, and welding. Women only have access to one postsecondary credential and certificate in office administration and culinary arts/hospitality management. There are even disparities in secondary pursuits, where men have access to 48 courses while women only have access to 21. These discrepancies are exacerbated by the fact that 65% of surveyed incarcerated women had not completed a secondary credential, 35% completed less than 12th grade before being incarcerated, and 11% had not completed more than the eighth grade (Texas Criminal Justice Coalition, 2018). Additionally, like in Louisiana and Mississippi, the available educational offerings are stereotypically gendered, where women take home economics and culinary arts whereas men are able to access carpentry, machinist courses, or other vocational, skilled trades (Harris, 2018; Linder, 2018).

Black Women and Higher Education in Prison

For incarcerated Black women and girls, the availability of educational opportunities, especially higher education while they are incarcerated, has the potential to be transformative. Willingham (2017) conducted research on instructors who provided postsecondary-level English courses inside correctional facilities across the country and found that, across the board, instructors noted that their students responded favorably and energetically to the opportunity to engage their minds while they served their sentences. One instructor noted that students would "use their writing to cope with their experiences with violence and other traumatic life events," as a way, Willingham (2017) noted, "[to help] incarcerated women reclaim and define their power and identity" (p. 149).

But the ability to provide these programs in correctional facilities, especially accredited higher education programs that lead to a credential, is constrained due to financial limitations. Because the VCA banned Pell access for incarcerated students, affordability is a major barrier to accessing higher education, especially as state aid is inconsistently and infrequently available for incarcerated students. Additionally, amendments to the Higher Education Act of 1965 over the course of several reauthorizations further constrained higher education access for incarcerated learners. Not only did it remove federal financial assistance for students through banning Pell, but it also constrained higher education institutions that had long catered to the confined learner population. As a result, institutions with more than 25% incarcerated students were no longer eligible to receive federal aid and schools that offered more than 50% of their courses through correspondence were not eligible either. Although there were other amendments that constrained the incarcerated student, these two amendments did a substantial amount of damage, unreasonably forcing restrictions on students who specifically chose distance programs, or specialized programs, due to their residential circumstances.

And for women, the lack of educational opportunities is even more pronounced. Because there are far fewer women incarcerated than men in any given state, many times the women's facility is not in a highly traveled or accessible area. Therefore, access to the correctional facility by would-be instructors is often hampered by distance. Typically, in this scenario, prior to 1994, a woman could enroll in any number of correspondence courses but with the removal of federal aid, even the number of those programs decreased. Despite government interference that created both student-level financial barriers as well as institutional hurdles to content delivery, the importance of educational access for Black women remains intact.

Michelle Daniel Jones, Cyntoia Brown, and Syrita Steib

Michelle Daniel Jones, renowned history and justice scholar and doctoral candidate at New York University, often speaks about the education she received at the Indiana Women's Prison and continues to advocate for increasing higher education access for confined learners (Jones, 2019; Jones & Jones, 2019). She also recounts the devastation that swept the halls when the Pell ban was announced and implemented in 1994. For those women, Indiana state aid picked up to cover some of the cost, and programs were able to continue. However, in 2011, Indiana banned incarcerated people from accessing state aid, and program participation suffered. Although it is easy to think intellectually about what it means to lose access to education, or to a program, it is necessary to understand the individual-level impact that these decisions and legislative policies have on many people who have already been mistreated by the educational industrial complex, an increasingly elitist paradigm rooted in colonialism and white supremacy, and marginalized by the prison industrial complex, a system motivated by greed and rooted in racism, patriarchy, and the subjugation of one's humanity.

The impact of education on Black women and girls is substantive and it goes beyond the metrics that policymakers want to see—recidivism and employment. In fact, it must go beyond those metrics because research demonstrates that, overall, Black people with criminal records get called back to interview and are hired at lower rates than their white counterparts (Pager, 2007; Western, 2006), and women, overall, have lower labor force participation rates than men, 57.2% to 69.2%, respectively (U.S. Department of Labor, 2019). Although it is easy to intellectually understand that the attainment of a credential can positively impact myriad life circumstances of Black women and girls, it is important to remember that having college credits, or even a degree, does not always automatically mean that a formerly incarcerated or otherwise systems-impacted Black woman will find a job. Certainly, she will possess a more marketable portfolio, but sometimes the intersections of the systems of oppression that impact Black women's lives (racism, sexism, trans*phobia, etc.) have an even larger impact despite the best attempts to mitigate their influence.

As an example, in 2006 in Tennessee, Cyntoia Brown was sentenced as an adult, at age 16, for killing the man who raped her (Allyn, 2019). She was granted clemency and released from prison in August 2019. Part of her clemency appeal included an explanation of how she spent her time while incarcerated. Not only had she grown and matured into an adult who had earned the respect of her peers, but she enrolled in the Lipscomb University's LIFE Program and received her bachelor's degree. She says of her time in the Lipscomb learning environment inside the facility, "The power of education to come in and completely overhaul your sense of self and view of the world is incredible" (Ross, 2019, para. 10). Brown's case is unique, in that she is well known; celebrities like John Legend and Kim Kardashian advocated for her release and many grassroots activists put pressure on the Tennessee governor, Bill Haslam, to grant her clemency. Through it all, though, Brown remained poised and ready for any question asked, any decision rendered. Part of that growth, poise, and confidence comes with time and maturity, certainly, but a part of it is also embedded in what education can do for Black women and girls across the world.

For the incarcerated Black women and girls who will be released from custody, the struggle is not over. If their elementary and middle school lives were interrupted by interactions with law enforcement, gaining entry to higher education institutions is an additional challenge. Many institutions have either implicit or explicit policies that prohibit the admission of anyone with a criminal record. Many schools still have what is called "the box," a question or set of questions that inquire about a student's criminal justice involvement, either past or current. One survey found that 66% of responding colleges collect criminal background information; however, fewer than half of the schools that collect the information have written policies in place.

Even more disappointing is that only about 40% of the schools that collect criminal background data have even thought to train campus staff on how to properly interpret and contextualize the information collected (Center for Community Alternatives, 2010).

Syrita Steib often speaks about her challenges getting admitted into a higher education institution after her incarceration, noting that of the two applications she submitted to Louisiana State University, the only difference was that she checked the box on the first and was denied; she unchecked the box on the second and was accepted. This success encouraged her to take on the conservative Louisiana legislature to seek to ban the box on the admission applications of public, in-state institutions. She and her Operation Restoration cofounder, Annie Phoenix, wrote, rewrote, and amended legislation that ultimately passed in 2017, providing a pathway to, and model for, success that other states soon followed with similar legislation, like Maryland and Washington.

The legislative success of Louisiana, Maryland, and Washington stands not only as a testament to a changing societal narrative about what reentry and rehabilitation look like for formerly incarcerated, systems-impacted people, but also to the power of education in the lives of Black women and girls. Steib-Martin opined, "When you give people the opportunity to educate themselves, they start looking at things differently and assessing situations differently" (Edwards, 2019, para. 8), but that opportunity, in and of itself, is insufficient to effect long lasting change, said Steib:

> It's one thing to give someone an opportunity, but you have to be really invested in making sure that the person can take advantage of the opportunity, because just giving them the opportunity can still present a barrier because they don't have the things that they need to take advantage of the opportunity. (para. 19)

Conclusion

As we critically examine how Black women and girls are forced to navigate the intersection of education and justice/legal system involvement, it is clear that the challenges, by design, begin early. From the ways in which those who teach Black girls in elementary and middle school may inequitably dole out disciplinary infractions, and more serious consequences, based upon an unfounded belief that Black girls are more "grown" than they really are, to the ways that the legal system continues to mete out harsher sentences to young Black women who resist colonizing notions of respectability deference in middle and high school and face law enforcement interaction, to the way that incarceration irreparably disrupts the ability of many Black women to be present mothers and community members, Black women and girls are plagued on all proverbial sides. The role of education in alleviating even some of these circumstances is significant, though it is, by no means, a panacea. As we move forward in the work to center Black women and girls in educational pursuits, and higher education in particular, it is helpful to consider a four-pronged approach utilized by Operation Restoration, Steib's nonprofit.

First, we must provide educational access not only to our systems-impacted sisters, both inside and out, but we must do so for our sisters who are not systems-impacted. Finding ways to create proximity between those spaces (impacted/nonimpacted) requires genuine commitment on the part of policymakers, scholars, and activists, and demands the thoughtful, authentic, and compensated inclusion of directly impacted women in critical conversations. These women are not just their stories; their stories allow them the insight to interrogate our notions of justice, our notion of fairness and equity, our notion of sisterhood. We then, second, must foreground policy change connected to criminal justice inform. As Steib-Martin noted, providing opportunities is not enough, especially when systems continue to discriminate. Third, the provision of direct services for systems-impacted Black women and girls must become a priority, especially in the academy where, for some institutions, resources are plentiful. We must leverage those resources to provide tools to those who need them most. Fourth, and finally, we have to "put our money where our mouth is." The success of education programs, policy conversations, and other direct service programs requires financial support of programs doing the work. In particular it is necessary to ensure that Black women who are doing this work are not overlooked and dismissed in favor of larger resourced institutions or organizations, led by white women and/or men.

Investing in the education of Black women and girls benefits everyone; it benefits the women and girls, their families, and society as a whole. Our presence in these spaces, these research, policy, and practitioner spaces, is vital to the continued forward movement of elevating our role in redefining how we see ourselves and each other and the ways in which our sisterhood can be made manifest through the coordinated provision of educational opportunities, but also in remaining abreast of important research that emerges and employing decolonizing theoretical frameworks to identify how new findings impact Black women and girls. To that end, there are some resources that continue to provide current information about criminal justice and some, like the Prison Policy Initiative and the Sentencing Project, intentionally include disaggregated data to ensure that populations, like Black folks, like women, and like Black women, are not summarily dismissed, overlooked, or ignored. Many of these sources are in the chapter's references but bear mentioning in this context.

Further Resources

The Prison Policy Initiative
The Sentencing Project
The Marshall Project
National Inventory of Collateral Consequences of Conviction
The Katal Center for Health, Equity, and Justice

Discussion Questions

1. How can practitioners and researchers apply political pressure to change the educational and/or school-based policies that adversely impact Black women and girls?
2. To what degree are individual institutions responsible for the inequities they perpetuate? To what degree are the systems that govern these institutions responsible for said inequities?
3. How do we build structures for policy and practice accountability that emphasize and prioritize the voices of those directly impacted as well as the impacted communities from which those people hail? What is the role of oversight committees in ensuring that policies and practices do not disproportionately impact one portion of the population more than another?
4. What is the role of community organizing in ushering in change and how do practitioners and researchers provide support to community-based organizations currently doing work on the ground to change policy?

References

Allyn, B. (2019, August 7). Cyntoia Brown released after 15 years in prison for murder. *NPR.* https://www.npr.org/2019/08/07/749025458/cyntoia-brown-released-after-15-years-in-prison-for-murder

Bronson, J., & Carson, A. (2019). *Prisoners in 2017* (Report NCJ 252156). U.S. Department of Justice, Bureau of Justice Statistics.

Center for Community Alternatives. (2010). *The use of criminal history records in college admissions: Reconsidered.* http://www.communityalternatives.org/pdf/Reconsidered-criminal-hist-recs-in-college-admissions.pdf

Drug Policy Alliance. (n.d.). *A brief history of the drug war.* http://www.drugpolicy.org/issues/brief-history-drug-war

Edwards, B. (2019, May 10). She, the people: Syrita Steib-Martin, Operation Restoration and changing the system of mass incarceration one woman at a time. *Essence.* https://www.essence.com/feature/syrita-steib-martin-operation-restoration-art-for-justice/

Epstein, R., Blake, J. J., & González, T. (2017). *Girlhood interrupted: The erasure of Black girls' childhood.* Georgetown University Law School Center on Poverty and Inequality. https://papers.ssrn.com/sol3/papers.cfm?abstract_id=3000695

Goff, P. A., Jackson, M. C., Di Leone, B. A., Culotta, C. M., & DiTomasso, N. A. (2014). The essence of innocence: Consequences of dehumanizing Black children. *Journal of Personality and Social Psychology, 106*, 526–542.

Graham, S., & Lowery, B. S. (2004). Priming unconscious racial stereotypes about adolescent offenders. *Law & Human Behavior, 28*, 483–504. https://doi.org/10.1023/B:LAHU.0000046430.65485.1f

Harris, A. (2018, April 30). Women in prison take home economics, while men take carpentry. *Atlantic.* https://www.theatlantic.com/education/archive/2018/04/the-continuing-disparity-in-womens-prison-education/559274/

Jones, M. (2019). Do what makes sense: The value of higher education in prison. In G. Robinson & E. English (Eds.), *Student voices of education for liberation: The politics of promise and reform inside and beyond America's prisons.* Rowman & Littlefield.

Jones, M., & Jones, T. (2019, March 4). *The case for college behind bars.* Future ED. https://www.future-ed.org/the-case-for-college-behind-bars/

Linder, L. (2018, April). *An unsupported population: The treatment of women in Texas' criminal justice system* [Report]. Texas Criminal Justice Coalition.

Morris, M. W. (2016). *Pushout: The criminalization of Black girls in schools.* The New Press.

National Center for Education Statistics. (2020). *Bachelor's degrees conferred by postsecondary institutions, by race/ethnicity and sex of student: Selected years, 1976–77 through 2017–18.* https://nces.ed.gov/fastfacts/display.asp?id=72

Pager, D. (2007). *Marked: Race, crime, and finding work in an era of mass incarceration.* The University of Chicago Press.

Perry, M. J. (2018, June 14). *The shocking story behind Richard Nixon's "War on Drugs" that targeted Blacks and anti-war activists.* http://www.aei.org/publication/the-shocking-and-sickening-story-behind-nixons-war-on-drugs-that-targeted-blacks-and-anti-war-activists/

Rattan, A., Levine. C. S., Dweck, C. S., & Eberhardt, J. L. (2012). Race and the fragility of the legal distinction between juveniles and adults. *PLoS ONE, 7*(5), e36680. https://doi.org/10.1371/journal.pone.0036680

Ross, B. (2019, January). *Cyntoia Brown: Lipscomb University "changed my life."* https://christianchronicle.org/cyntoia-brown-lipscomb-university-changed-my-life/

Sawyer, W., & Bertram, W. (2018). *Briefings: Mother's Day.* Prison Policy Initiative. https://www.prisonpolicy.org/blog/2018/05/13/mothers-day-2018/

Sawyer, W., & Wagner, P. (2019, March 19). *Mass incarceration: The whole pie, 2019.* Prison Policy Initiative. https://www.prisonpolicy.org/reports/pie2019.html

Sentencing Project. (2008). *Fact sheet.* https://www.sentencingproject.org/wp-content/uploads/2016/01/Parents-in-Prison.pdf

Sentencing Project. (2019, June). *Fact sheet: Incarcerated women and girls 2019.* https://www.sentencingproject.org/publications/incarcerated-women-and-girls/

Smith, E. J., & Harper, S. R. (2015). *Disproportionate impact of K–12 school suspension and expulsion on Black students in southern states.* University of Pennsylvania, Center for the Study of Race and Equity in Education.

Texas Criminal Justice Coalition. (2018). https://www.texascjc.org/

U.S. Bureau of Labor Statistics. (2019). *Labor force statistics from the Current Population Survey: Demographics.* https://www.bls.gov/cps/demographics.htm

U.S. Department of Labor, Women's Bureau. (2019). *Facts over time. Labor force status of women and men.* https://www.dol.gov/wb/widget/

Wagner, P., & Bertram, W. (2020). *What percent of the U.S. is incarcerated? (And other ways to measure mass incarceration).* Prison Policy Initiative. https://www.prisonpolicy.org/blog/2020/01/16/percent-incarcerated/

Western, B. (2006). *Punishment and inequality in America.* Russell Sage Foundation.

Wexler, E. (2016, June 24). Prisoners to get 'second chance Pell'. *Inside Higher Ed.* http.//www.insidehighered.com

Willingham, B. (2017). It's a way to get out of prison: Writing and teaching in women's prisons. In E. R. Haden & T. R. Jach (Eds.), *Incarcerated women: A history of struggles, oppression and resistance in American prisons* (pp. 147–165). Lexington Books.

6

UNPROTECTED AND LEFT FOR DEAD

Educational Policy and the "Nobodyness" of Black Girls Disciplined Through Suspension and School-Related Arrests

Venus E. Evans-Winters and Dorothy E. Hines

Black girls are often overlooked and undertheorized in educational policy discourse analysis. Their stories are subsumed under racial narratives or erased from gender narratives. Black girls, essentially, are nobodies. In *Nobody: Casualties of America's War on the Vulnerable, From Ferguson to Flint*, Lamont Hill (2017) explained that to be a *Nobody* in the 21st century is to be "vulnerable . . . subjected to State violence . . . confront systems of State violence . . . to be abandoned . . . and to be disposable" (pp. xiii–xxi). Recent documentation suggests that Black girls are just as abandoned and disposable within and across school contexts (Carter Andrews et al., 2019; Hines-Datiri & Carter Andrews, 2017).

Outside of school spaces, Black women and girls continue to be victims of police brutality, as seen with Mya Hall and Alexia Christian, who were both executed by law enforcement only 1 month apart, in 2015 (Lindsey, 2015; Towns, 2016). For younger Black women state-sanctioned violence also looks like housing discrimination, lower pay in the workplace, over-representation in the criminal justice system, and risk of sexual victimization in prison (National Coalition on Black Civic Participation, 2016). Black women and girls are made vulnerable in society and being "nobodies" permeates the Pk–12 education system.

For instance, Black girls represent 14% of youth in the United States, but make up 33% of girls arrested and transferred into juvenile justice institutions (Chesney-Lind & Shelden, 2013; National Coalition on Black Civic Participation, 2016). As early as preschool, Black girls are criminalized and face higher rates of suspension and expulsion at the age of 5 (Civil Rights Data Collection, 2013). As Black females enter into the middle grades and high school they are more susceptible to outside-of-school suspensions (OSS) and expulsions (Slate et al., 2016). Unfortunately, while Black boys' schooling is considered by many educational reformists to be in a "state of emergency," Black girls are "invisible" in school (Patton et al., 2016). Consequently, Black female students' experiences with hyperpunishment are left out of educational policy discourse while, at the same time, their intersectional identities are being erased from national and statewide statistical analysis and educational data altogether.

In this chapter, we impenitently argue that Black girls are treated as *Nobodies* in educational policy discourse on school discipline, and asseverate that their identities as young women are seen within their singularity (i.e., separately as Black and girl) rather than through an intersectional and antiessentialist analysis. Using U.S. Department of Education (USDE) Civil Rights Data (CDR) (2013–2014) and critical race feminism as an interpretive lens, (a) we illuminate Black girls' overrepresentation in school-based punishments, and (b) we bring attention to the manner that they are disproportionately sanctioned through the use of OSS and school-related arrests. We spotlight OSS and school-related arrests, because when students are removed from school through suspension or by police apprehension, then they become more likely to enter into the criminal justice system (Mowen & Brent, 2016; Shollenberger, 2015). Given this consideration, it is now crucial for educational policymakers, educators, and schools to analyze Black girls' experiences on a national scale so that school reform efforts can focus on eradicating racial and gender disproportionality in punishments.

Critical Race Feminism

Critical race feminism (CRF) is a theoretical frame for understanding the experiences of Black girls as Nobodies in Pk–12 schools, and it provides an analytical lens for examining their disciplinary outcomes. Emerging from critical legal studies, critical race theory (CRT), and framed by feminist legal studies, CRF examines the multiple marginalities and intersectional identities that women and girls of color have in society (Evans-Winters, 2016; Wing, 1997, 2015). CRT was introduced in the field of education by Ladson-Billings and Tate (1995), who deepened the exploration of racism as a normalized component of society. The tenets of CRT (Delgado & Stefancic, 2017) include the following concepts and ideas:

1. racism as normal in society
2. White ideologies of race being neutral, race as race-less, and objectivity
3. interest convergence
4. counterstory-telling as truth-telling
5. interdisciplinarity in stance

Critical race scholars including Derrick Bell (2008) adamantly conveyed that racism is a "permanent part of the American landscape" (p. 92) and it invades every aspect of American life, including schools. Given that racism is embedded within the fabric of society, it is no surprise why women of color are placed at the *bottom of the well*. CRT has been used by educational researchers to examine racism as aberrant in society and identity at its intersections (DeCuir-Gunby et al., 2018; Dixson & Rousseau Anderson, 2018; Young & Hines, 2018). In our analysis we focus on two of the five tenets: (a) racism as aberrant and (b) colorblindness. We use these two tenets to expound upon how the experiences of Black girls operate within a larger framework of being Nobodies that is rooted in anti-Black racism and colorblindness that has historically framed federal educational policies as being race-neutral.

In "Mapping the Margins," Crenshaw (1990) introduced the term *inter-sectionality* to describe the ways in which women of color exist at the intersections of two or more socially constructed identities and become one distinct set of categories. For example, Crenshaw discussed how violence is enacted against women of color and how race and gender must also include multiple forms of identity, including social class. The intersectional forms of violence that women of color face are often disguised as an either/or race conversation that omits the need for examining identity as a mosaic. CRF seeks to attend to the intersectional identities of women of color and decenters traditional feminists' privileging of White women at the expense and marginalization of women of color. CRF uses counterstory-telling, is multidisciplinary, and sees Black women as valued and valid sources of knowledge.

The CRF approach is the necessary lens for understanding Black girls' experiences as Nobodies in educational policy discourse and analysis. CRF allows identity to be multidimensional and moves beyond singular stories (Berry, 2010). Black girls' cultural backgrounds and experiences are from across the diaspora, and to limit their racial and ethnic identity is to deny all of their racial and ethnic identity. In addition, Evans-Winters (2017) reminded us that the experiences of Black girls and girls of color are "undertheorized," not only in race-based scholarship but also in feminist analysis of girlhood experiences inside and outside of schools. We hope in this analysis to add to the growing body of literature that examines Black girls as having agency, brilliance, and strength—attributes that are underutilized in schools. In this chapter we also discuss how education policy discourse and analysis impacts the educational experiences of Black female students. We now use CRF as an analytical framework to examine federal law, we consider how Black girls have been treated as Nobodies in educational policy, and we reflect on how such an erasure impacts their disciplinary outcomes.

Nobodyness of Black Girls in Educational Policy Discourse

To recognize the relationship between racialized gender bias in schools, researchers and practitioners have to understand the relationship between national policy and policing of the "other," foreigners, and criminalized bodies. Black girls and other girls of color in schools are casualties of larger socio-historical and political wars. Like other minoritized public school pupils, Black girls are deemed disposable in urban war zones. Black girls education and schooling are comprised as a part of larger policy agendas.

The Gun Free Schools Act (1984)

The passage of the Gun Free Schools Act of 1984 under former president Bill Clinton redirected federal funding and policies to safeguard public schools from extreme acts of violence that threatened the safety and well-being of students and school staff. The Gun Free Schools Act, later known as "zero tolerance," mandated 1-year suspensions for students who carried weapons and/or who committed criminal offenses on school campuses (Hines-Datiri & Carter Andrews, 2017). However, as noted by numerous research studies, zero tolerance policies have disproportionally been used by educators to hyperpunish students of color and, in particular, Black students. Incidents of gun violence across the country have mostly been conducted by White male assailants, yet students of color remain the most targeted group through the use of such policies (Triplett et al., 2014). Middle-class White students are often seen as nonthreatening or not aggressive and are less susceptible to being a part of the school-to-prison pipeline.

In comparison, there has been an increase in racial and gender dispro-portionality in school punishments for Black and Brown students for minor issues, and many schools that these children attend have become prisons themselves. The *school–prison nexus* criminalizes students even before they enter into school, when schools are created, organized, and executed as prisonlike environments (Stovall, 2018). This includes bars on classroom windows (if there are even windows at all), police departments in school buildings, and high-tech security features (Wun, 2016). Black female students' Nobodyness is a function of an educational system where they face multiplicative forms of abandonment and rejection from schools who do not carry their interests or needs in mind, or see their identities as valuable and necessary in schooling spaces.

Under zero tolerance policies, Black girls, in some states including South Carolina and cities such as Chicago, can be disciplined under the notion of "willful disobedience," which results in disproportionate outcomes (Morris, 2016). "Willful disobedience" is a catchall phrase for any behavior, including more subjective behaviors like attitude and disposition, that are considered to be disrespectful to authority. The continuing narrative that Black girls are punished for valid reasons of insubordination and "misbehavior" have been shown to be, in part, based on how the teacher engages with Black female students and is influenced by the teachers' own standards of femininity and understanding of race (Haynes et al., 2016), not to mention age-old racialized, gendered tropes like Jezebel and Sapphire.

Black girls cannot be educated in a classroom space that hates Black girlhood. Nor can they enter into teaching environments where their behaviors are coded as "willful," but educators who engage in acts of racialized violence through their teaching practices, curriculum, and beliefs about Black girls are seen as being "unaware" or acting due to a "misunderstanding." Too many Black girls are being disposed of in the process. Consequently, such policies as zero tolerance have contributed to the school–prison nexus, discipline disparities, and overpunishment of Black girls. When Black female students are punished as Nobodies, then they will also be made invisible even after they return to school.

Additionally, when Black girls do not have a sense of belonging in school, then the treatment that they receive from educators will only be further compounded with their criminalization. Although neighborhoods, parents, and Black girls shape their schooling experiences, given that there is limited research on how education policy has addressed the interconnectedness of these issues, it further underscores the need for a critical analysis of not only the intent of educational policies but also the actual outcomes that they have on Black girls.

No Child Left Behind as an Anti–Black Girl Policy

In 2001 former president George Bush Jr. signed the No Child Left Behind (NCLB) law into legislation as a means for equalizing educational opportunity in the U.S. public school system. NCLB was designed to implement standards-based reform coupled with high academic goals established through annual yearly progress (AYP) goals. NCLB "requires states to: (a) Raise the percentage of students who are proficient in reading and mathematics; and (b) Narrow the achievement gap between advantaged and disadvantaged students" (Harrison-Jones, 2007, p. 346). However, despite a policy that included AYP, Black students still have not received equitable opportunities in the public school system as compared to White students. The policy encouraged the disaggregation of data by race and gender, which only helped to expose inequitable educational outcomes that the Black community and Black schools knew had already existed. In terms of Black students, NCLB appears to have further pathologized Black children. Wun (2014) argued that NCLB was an anti-Black policy, and although it was presumed to support all students and "one designed to ensure accountability to historically marginalized youth, it is undergirded by an anti-Black fetishization—one that renders Black bodies as perennially deficient" (p. 469). From an intersectional perspective, Black girls are caught in the nexus of racism, sexism, and classism in educational institutions.

With intersectionality in mind, NCLB being an anti-Black policy, we contend that NCLB was a policy that sacrificed the education of Black girl students. Dumas (2016) suggested that educational policies are created within an anti-Black logic and declared that for schools and policymakers "any incisive analysis of racial(ized) discourse and policy processes in education must grapple with cultural disregard for and disgust with blackness" (p. 12). In *The Anti-Black Order of No Child Left Behind* (2014), Wun went on to further contend that "NCLB is a means by which antiblackness is written into law" (p. 472). It is clear that if NCLB's main objective was to raise proficiency and "narrow gaps," then actually eradicating these gaps was never its actual intention in the first place.

After the passage of NCLB in 2001 Black girls still were underrepresented in gifted education classes, yet overrepresented in special education (Evans-Winters, 2016; Young et al., 2017). Black girls still are disciplined at higher rates than other girls of color and White female students (Hines-Datiri & Carter Andrews, 2017). Black girls fall through the cracks in most discussions on inequities in advance placement, special education, and discipline policies, nothwithstanding that, for Black female students who are academically successful in school, they more often than not have to present themselves as being "race-less" and have to "deny who they are and adopt the characteristics of the majority culture" (Ricks, 2014, p. 14). Simply put, Black girls are no more further along than they were before the passage of NCLB, and for those who were able to persist, despite NCLB being an anti-Black policy, then we have to ask: At what costs?

Black Girl Students, OSS, and School-Related Arrests

Black girl students enter schools as individuals and as members of a larger sociocultural group. They enter schools with multiple identities as students, adolescents, and girls who are a part of larger racial and cultural groups. The complexities of their identities have left them simultaneously vulnerable and protected.

Out-of-School Suspensions

Black girls are seen as being bad, combative, sexualized, and angry (Evans-Winters, 2005; Morris, 2016; Muhammad & McArthur, 2015), which further underscores their Nobodyness in schools. Black women and girls are *presumed* to be violent and *presumed not to be in need of protection* (from state actors like teachers, police officers, and policymakers). In schools, this presumption of violence and aggressiveness is perpetuated by a Nobody framework that they are seen as operating within. It is no wonder why Black girls who are weaponless in school are disproportionately given OSS or arrested at school and sent to juvenile justice institutions and in many cases to the penitentiary. A Black girl aesthetic itself is under surveillance and "under fire" in school environments. For instance, OSS has been used as one of the main tools for adjudicating Black students from school for minor incidents that would have normally been handled by an adult at school (Hines-Datiri, 2015).

The National Center for Education Statistics (2019) defines *suspension* as follows:

> An out-of-school suspension is an instance in which a student is temporarily removed from his or her regular school for disciplinary purposes for at least half a day (but less than the remainder of the school year) to another setting (e.g., home or behavior center). This does not include students who served their suspension in the school.

Black girls who are suspended from school are not only excluded from being on school grounds, but they often do not have access to classwork or other materials—which hinders learning. Black female students represent the largest increase (of all girls) in placements in out-of-school suspension (Morris, 2013). Not only do teacher–student interactions and perceptions of White femininity affect Black girls' disciplinary experiences, but they can also be sent to OSS for having natural hair in box braids in addition to being policed for their bodily attire (Esposito & Edwards, 2018). Sadly, states and school districts often depend on OSS (Gregory & Fergus, 2017) as a system for legally removing students for minor issues, which speaks to a larger issue of teacher pedagogy and lack of culturally inclusive ways to teach Black children. White teachers represent the highest percentage of educators from Pk–12, and they are often unqualified to educate racially and culturally diverse students (Whitaker & Hines-Datiri, 2018).

In comparison to OSS, school-related arrests have been used to physically, and often violently, remove Black girls from school grounds. In Table 6.1 we present national data on OSS. As evident in Table 6.1, Black female students without disabilities accounted for over 1.2 million OSSs (across categories) during the 2013–2014 school year. Black girls are overrepresented in disciplinary punishments across the stated OSS categories (one suspension, one or more suspensions, and more than one suspension). For school-related arrests, Black girls have higher percentages of being arrested on school grounds. Within disciplinary punishments (OSS and school-related arrests), Black girls are hyperpunished.

During the 2013–2014 school year approximately 614,597 Black young women students received either OSS (across categories) or were arrested at school and accounted for about 49% of disciplinary punishments for OSS

TABLE 6.1
Girls of Color in K–12 by Out-of-School Suspension Categories (2013–2014)

Demographic Category	% One OSS**	% One or More OSS**	% More Than One OSS**	Total Number Disciplined
Race				
Black Girls	43.3	47.5	57.4	609,181
White	28.3	25.9	21.8	332,833
Latina	22.8	20.9	18.5	268,828
Asian	1 to 3[a]	0.8	0.5	10,074
American Indian/ Alaskan Native	1.5	1.5	1.4	19,056
Female				
Total Population	393,198	619,959	226,815	1,230,972

[a] 1 to 3 means data has been suppressed due to sample size (n) being too low.

Note. From U.S. Department of Education, Office for Civil Rights Data Collection (2013–2014), https://www2.ed.gov/about/offices/list/ocr/docs/crdc-2013-14.html.

** ELL students are listed as a racial group in dataset; total may not equal 100%.

(across categories) and school-related arrests. It is important, however, to antiessentialize Black girls' OSS as influenced by colorism. Although *all* Black girls remain at risk of disciplinary punishments, for Black female students who have lighter complexions, their disciplinary experiences differ from dark-skinned Black girls.

Hannon et al. (2013) found that lighter skin complexion or racial ambiguity can lead to an ideology of superiority or others extending forgiveness or benefit of the doubt that may not be granted to darker skinned girls. Such forgiveness or second chances may be disproportionate school punishment for those with darker skin. Darker skinned girls were not only penalized more, but such treatments could be perceived as being justifiable. There are various factors that impact OSS for Black young girls that can lead to the beliefs by which they are seen as Nobodies. Despite their academic achievement or assertiveness in the classroom, if educators see their intellect as unwanted then these students will continue to be academically abandoned and their disposability will continue to be second nature.

School-Related Arrests

The use of school resource officers (SROs), security guards, or police in schools is not a new phenomenon. Public schools have used SROs since the 1950s and "school-based policing is the fastest growing area of law enforcement" (Theriot, 2009, p. 281). Although SROs and police have become active agents in schools across the country, their hypervisibility in urban schools is no coincidence and their policing of students of color is often influenced by law enforcement's perception of crime in majority non-White areas. Research indicates that people of color more often than not have negative, pessimistic perceptions and attitudes about police (Chaney & Robertson, 2015; Hill, 2018). This is often a result of overpolicing, criminalization, and policies such as "broken window" and zero tolerance policing in Black and Brown communities.

There are persistent racial disparities in policing that exist in society and in schools. Given this, potential and actual interactions with law enforcement can lead to "excessive force including homicide" (Carbado, 2017, p. 128) that are committed by police officers. Carbado contended that there are "circuits of violence" that make Black people at risk of "ongoing police surveillance and contact . . . [leading to] serious bodily injury and death" (p. 128). Such circuits of violence also exist in schools across the country. Black women and girls have been the subject of #SayHerName to call attention to repeated acts of police brutality that go unpunished inside and outside of school environments (Baylor, 2016).

In schools, this equates to Black girls being seen as adults despite the verity that they are developmentally children and adolescents (Epstein et al., 2017). Along with being seen as older than they are, Black girls also can be harassed by SROs in school. In Watson's (2016) study of Black girls attending an urban school, the author found that security guards would harass the girls, and as a result the students would not feel safe or did not feel "mentally healthy" (p. 243). The mere presence of these "school safety agents" largely did not make the girls feel safe, and in many cases, the security guards patrolled them and conducted unsolicited bodily checks for illegal substances. The presence of SROs and not the absence of them has been correlated with more minor crimes (Morris, 2016). In many cases, such increased crime levels may be associated with increased surveillance where law enforcement is simply looking for offenses to punish. Not to mention, many of these young women are survivors of domestic violence and street harassment, only to go to school, where they are further victimized by those in authority.

As noted in Table 6.2, Black girls have higher rates of school-related arrests than other girls, and their effects are disproportionate to the percentage of Black female students enrolled in the public school system. When an incident ensues, educators and school staff often have to make quick decisions

TABLE 6.2
Girls of Color in K–12 School-Related Arrests (2013–2014)

Demographic Category	Percentage of School-Related Arrests*	Total Number School-Related Arrests	Total Number Disciplined (both tables combined)
Race			
Black Girls	39.5	39.5	614,597
White	29.6	4,056	336,889
Latina	24.0	3,294	272,122
Asian	1.5	204	10,278
American Indian/ Alaskan Native	1.7	231	19,287
Female			
Total Population		13,201	1,253,173

Note. From U.S. Department of Education Office for Civil Rights Data Collection (2013–2014), https://www2.ed.gov/about/offices/list/ocr/docs/crdc-2013-14.html.

*ELL students are listed as a racial group in dataset; total may not equal 100%.

regarding the use of police that may cause emotional trauma or result in altercations with Black girls, who are often unarmed and ill-equipped to physically defend themselves against adults. These moments of "quick decisions" (and in some case it is an explicit decision) that are rooted in racial biases (Gupta-Kagan, 2017) will result in more harmful outcomes for Black girls who are seen as criminal even before they walk into the classroom door.

From the Every Student Succeeds Act to Secretary Betsy DeVos

Former president Obama signed the Every Student Succeeds Act into law in 2015 to address the academic needs of students of color who have traditionally been excluded and marginalized from and within the public school system. The Every Student Succeeds Act (ESSA) seeks to improve the schooling conditions and educational outcomes of children of color by focusing on improving graduation rates, closing achievement gaps, and serving the needs of students from low-income and impoverished communities. Components of ESSA require the following:

1. Academic achievement as measured by proficiency on annual assessments in English language arts and math (in each of grades 3–8, plus one grade in high school);
2. Another "valid and reliable statewide academic indicator" for elementary and middle schools, which can be a measure of student growth;
3. The four-year adjusted cohort graduation rate for high schools (states may add an extended year adjusted cohort graduation rate if they choose);
4. A measure of progress in English language proficiency for English language learners (in each of grades 3–8, plus one grade in high school); and
5. At least one measure of school quality or student success that is valid, reliable, and comparable across the state and allows for meaningful differentiation in school performance. These measures may include student engagement, student access to advanced coursework, postsecondary readiness, school climate and safety, or other measures. (Darling-Hammond et al., 2016, p. 5)

ESSA has various indicators that are used to determine the effectiveness of state and school districts' plans to foster student achievement. However, despite this policy's effort to outline different gaps in student performance that should be closed, states still have autonomy in creating and implementing programs. In addition, ESSA calls for school districts to review their disciplinary outcomes. Given that federal policies have not served the academic needs of Black girls even with additional provisions to NCLB, there are no guarantees that Black female students will benefit from such policies if policy actors (educators, administrators, guidance counselors, SROs, and school staff) are implementing them in racially biased and prejudiced ways. For instance, ESSA outlines additional measures for ensuring that school districts reduce discipline disparities by prohibiting the overuse of such policies. However, with policies implemented on the ground level, it is difficult to define what educators who may hold racist views about Black girls will consider to be an "overuse" and not "justifiable use" of discipline policies.

With Betsy DeVos as the Secretary of Education (2017–2021), the question was whether the administration would eliminate components of ESSA that, in part, sought to make states and school districts develop interventions for discipline disparities. As DeVos occupied the position, and as her efforts to expand charter schools continued, Black girls needed to be centered in discussions on school choice and how it could affect current discipline disparities. DeVos and Attorney General Jeff Sessions held two powerful positions in the U.S. government that could turn the tide on how discrimination suits were defined and punished, and how discipline disparities, in terms of civil rights, could be addressed by the courts (Quinn, 2017). We called for educational reform efforts and data reports that considered both race and gender as categories.

Conclusion: From Nobodies to Humanbodies

Black girls are not being adequately served by the public school system, and they continue to face disproportionate rates of OSS punishments and school-related arrests. Black girls' bodies are not only positioned in schools to be criminalized, but Brown and Young (2017) contended that when Black girls take ownership of their bodies they are put at higher risk of policing and punishment. When schools take away Black girls' "ownership" of their bodies, they normalize the treatment and disciplinary punishment of Black female students as Nobodies. The inhumanity of the Black body makes it a site for dehumanization and subsequently its erasure. Educational policymakers, schools, and educators must address the antiessentialist needs of Black girls while collaboratively working to eradicate discipline gaps.

We posit that it is not enough for school districts and teachers to incorporate more so-called multicultural curriculum, if and when Black students get to school they are adjudicated through OSS or arrested on school grounds. How can schools claim to be inclusive and/or multicultural if the majority of the Black girl students are pushed out of schools? As federal educational policies continue to negate the experiential knowledge and experiences of Black girls, policy initiatives will further miseducate, debase, and muffle the intellectual and cultural capital that Black young women bring with them to school.

As Secretary DeVos looked to implement new educational policies and federal regulations it became important for educational advocates to contest antiblackness as policy, and we must continue to challenge policy that directly or indirectly causes Black girls to experience racial and gender violence as a set of harsh discipline policies, dehumanizing practices, and school pushout factors. What is the role of educational practitioners, researchers, and policy-makers in challenging biased disciplinary policies and practices in ensuring that Black girls will not continue to be unprotected, seen as Nobodies, and left for dead? Our role is to expose the ways in which Black girls fall through the cracks and become invisible in educational discourse and practice. In sum, we call for education policy analysis and theories that present Black girls and women as a unique social group in need of a distinct social category in analysis methodologies. In other words, list Black girl students as a unique educational category in need of federal, state, and local protection (and advocacy) against racism, sexism, and classism in education settings.

Discussion Questions

1. How can school policies better serve the academic and socioemotional needs of Black girls who fall through the cracks of educational discourse?
2. What role can school support staff have (guidance counselors and social workers) in fostering a racially and culturally inclusive schooling context for Black girls throughout the continuum?
3. How can school SROs and police departments partner with communities of color and develop racial and gender bias curriculums and training that promote effective and measurable outcomes?

Resources

African American Policy Forum. https://aapf.org/publications
Georgetown University Law School. https://www.law.georgetown.edu/news/research-confirms-that-black-girls-feel-the-sting-of-adultification-bias-identified-in-earlier-georgetown-law-study/
National Black Women's Justice Institute. https://www.nbwji.org/
National Women's Law Center. https://www.nwlc.org

References

Baylor, A. (2016). *# SayHerName captured: Using video to challenge law enforcement violence against women.* American Bar Association.

Bell, D. (2008). *Faces at the bottom of the well: The permanence of racism.* Basic Books.

Berry, T. R. (2010). Engaged pedagogy and critical race feminism. *The Journal of Educational Foundations, 24*(3/4), 19. https://eric.ed.gov/?id=EJ902670

Brown, N. E., & Young, L. (2017). Ratchet politics: Moving beyond Black women's bodies to indict institutions and structures. In M. Mitchell & D. Covin (Eds.), *Broadening the contours in the study of black politics: Citizenship and popular culture* (p. 45). Transaction.

Carbado, D. W. (2017). From stopping black people to killing black people: The Fourth Amendment pathways to police violence. *Calif. L. Rev., 105*, 125.

Carter Andrews, D. J., Brown, T., Castro, E., & Id-Deen, E. (2019). The impossibility of being "perfect and white": Black girls' racialized and gendered schooling experiences. *American Educational Research Journal, 56*(6), 2531–2572. https://doi.org/10.3102/0002831219849392

Chaney, C., & Robertson, R. V. (2015). Armed and dangerous? An examination of fatal shootings of unarmed black people by police. *Journal of Pan African Studies, 8*(4), 45–78.

Chesney-Lind, M., & Shelden, R. G. (2013). *Girls, delinquency, and juvenile justice.* Wiley.

Civil Rights Data Collection. (2013). *A first look.* https://ocrdata.ed.gov/assets/downloads/2013-14-first-look.pdf

Crenshaw, K. (1990). Mapping the margins: Intersectionality, identity politics, and violence against women of color. *Stan. L. Rev., 43*, 1241–1299.

Darling-Hammond, L., Bae, S., Cook-Harvey, C. M., Lam, L., Mercer, C., Podolsky, A., & Stosich, E. L. (2016). *Pathways to new accountability through the Every Student Succeeds Act.* Learning Policy Institute. https://learningpolicyinstitute.org/wp-content/uploads/2016/04/Pathways_New-Accountability_Through_Every_Student_Succeeds_Act_04202016.pdf

DeCuir-Gunby, J. T., Chapman, T. K., & Schutz, P. A. (2018). Critical race theory, racial justice, and education. In J. T. DeCuir-Gunby, T. K. Chapman, & P. A. Schutz (Eds.), *Understanding critical race research methods and methodologies: Lessons from the field.* Routledge.

Delgado, R., & Stefancic, J. (2017). *Critical race theory: An introduction.* NYU Press.

Dixson, A. D., & Rousseau Anderson, C. (2018). Where are we? Critical race theory in education 20 years later. *Peabody Journal of Education, 93*(1), 121–131. https://doi.org/10.1080/0161956X.2017.1403194

Dumas, M. J. (2016). Against the dark: Antiblackness in education policy and discourse. *Theory Into Practice, 55*(1), 11–19. https://doi.org/10.1080/00405841.2016.1116852

Epstein, R., Blake, J., & González, T. (2017). *Girlhood interrupted: The erasure of Black girls' childhood.* Georgetown Law Center on Poverty and Inequality. http://dx.doi.org/10.2139/ssrn.3000695

Esposito, J., & Edwards, E. B. (2018). When Black girls fight: Interrogating, interrupting, and (re) imagining dangerous scripts of femininity in urban classrooms. *Education and Urban Society, 50*(1), 87–107. https://doi.org/10.1177/0013124517729206

Evans-Winters, V. E. (2005). *Teaching black girls: Resiliency in urban classrooms.* Peter Lang.

Evans-Winters, V. E. (2016). Schooling at the liminal: Black girls and special education. *The Wisconsin English Journal, 58*(2), 140–153.

Evans-Winters, V. E. (with Girls for Gender Equity). (2017). Flipping the script: The dangerous bodies of girls of color. *Cultural Studies ↔ Critical Methodologies, 17*(5), 415–423. https://doi.org/10.1177/1532708616684867

Gregory, A., & Fergus, E. (2017). *Social and emotional learning and equity in school discipline.* The Future of Children. https://www.researchgate.net/profile/Edward-Fergus/publication/319482587_Social_and_Emotional_Learning_and_Equity_in_School_Discipline/links/5a455615a6fdcce1971a59f8/Social-and-Emotional-Learning-and-Equity-in-School-Discipline.pdf

Gupta-Kagan, J. (2017). The school-to-prison pipeline's legal architecture: Lessons from the Spring Valley incident and its aftermath. *Fordham Urban Law Journal, 45*, 83.

Hannon, L., DeFina, R., & Bruch, S. (2013). The relationship between skin tone and school suspension for African Americans. *Race and Social Problems, 5*(4), 281–295. https://link.springer.com/article/10.1007%2Fs12552-013-9104-z

Harrison-Jones, L. (2007). No Child Left Behind and implications for Black students. *The Journal of Negro Education, 76*(3), 346–356. http://www.jstor.org/stable/40034577

Haynes, C., Stewart, S., & Allen, E. (2016). Three paths, one struggle: Black women and girls battling invisibility in US classrooms. *The Journal of Negro Education, 85*(3), 380–391. https://doi.org/10.7709/jnegroeducation.85.3.0380

Hill, M. L. (2017). *Nobody: Casualties of America's war on the vulnerable, from Ferguson to Flint and beyond.* Simon and Schuster.

Hill, M. L. (2018). "Thank you, Black twitter": State violence, digital counterpublics, and pedagogies of resistance. *Urban Education, 53*(2), 286–302. https://doi.org/10.1177/0042085917747124.

Hines-Datiri, D. (2015). When police intervene: Race, gender, and discipline of Black male students at an urban high school. *Journal of Cases in Educational Leadership, 18*(2), 122–133.

Hines-Datiri, D., & Carter Andrews, D. J. (2017). The effects of zero tolerance policies on Black girls: Using critical race feminism and figured worlds to examine school discipline. *Urban Education, 55*(10), 1419–1440. https://doi.org/10.1177/0042085917690204

Ladson-Billings, G., & Tate, W. (1995). Toward a critical race theory of education. *Teachers College Record, 97*(1), 48–68.

Lindsey, T. B. (2015). A love letter to black feminism. *The Black Scholar, 45*(4), 1–6. https://doi.org/10.1080/00064246.2015.1080911

Morris, M. (2013). Education and the caged bird: Black girls, school pushout and the juvenile court school. *Poverty & Race, 22*(6), 5–7.

Morris, M. (2016). *Pushout: The criminalization of Black girls.* The New Press.

Mowen, T., & Brent, J. (2016). School discipline as a turning point: The cumulative effect of suspension on arrest. *Journal of Research in Crime and Delinquency, 53*(5), 628–653. https://doi.org/10.1177/0022427816643135

Muhammad, G. E., & McArthur, S. A. (2015). "Styled by their perceptions": Black adolescent girls interpret representations of Black females in popular culture. *Multicultural Perspectives, 17*(3), 133–140. https://doi.org/10.1080/15210960.2015.1048340

National Center for Educational Statistics. (2019). *Status and trends in the education of racial and ethnic groups.* https://nces.ed.gov/programs/raceindicators/indicator_rda.asp

National Coalition on Black Civic Participation. (2016). *Black women in the United States: Power of the sister vote.* Black Women's Roundtable. https://www.ncbcp.org/news/releases/5Black_Women_in_the_US_2016.pdf

Patton, L. D., Crenshaw, K., Haynes, C., & Watson, T. N. (2016). Why we can't wait: (Re)examining the opportunities and challenges for Black women and girls in education [Guest Editorial]. *The Journal of Negro Education, 85*(3), 194–198. https://doi.org/10.7709/jnegroeducation.85.3.0194

Quinn, D. J. (2017). School discipline disparities: Lessons and suggestions. *Mid-Western Educational Researcher, 29*(3), 291.

Ricks, S. A. (2014). Falling through the cracks: Black girls and education. *Interdisciplinary Journal of Teaching and Learning, 4*(1), 10–21. https://eric.ed.gov/?id=EJ1063223

Shollenberger, T. L. (2015). Racial disparities in school suspension and subsequent outcomes. In D. J. Losen (Ed.), *Closing the school discipline gap: Equitable remedies for excessive exclusion* (pp. 31–44). Teachers College Press.

Slate, J. R., Gray, P. L., & Jones, B. (2016). A clear lack of equity in disciplinary consequences for Black girls in Texas: A statewide examination. *The Journal of Negro Education, 85*(3), 250–260. https://doi.org/10.7709/jnegroeducation.85.3.0250

Stovall, D. (2018). Are we ready for "school" abolition? Thoughts and practices of radical imaginary in education. *Taboo: The Journal of Culture and Education, 17*(1), 6. https://doi.org/10.31390/taboo.17.1.06

Theriot, M. T. (2009). School resource officers and the criminalization of student behavior. *Journal of Criminal Justice, 37*(3), 280–287. https://doi.org/10.1016/j.jcrimjus.2009.04.008

Towns, A. R. (2016). Geographies of pain: #SayHerName and the fear of black women's mobility. *Women's Studies in Communication, 39*(2), 122–126. https://doi.org/10.1080/07491409.2016.1176807

Triplett, N. P., Allen, A., & Lewis, C. W. (2014). Zero tolerance, school shootings, and the post-Brown quest for equity in discipline policy: An examination of how urban minorities are punished for white suburban violence. *The Journal of Negro*

Education, 83(3), 352–370. https://www.jstor.org/stable/10.7709/jnegroeducation.83.3.0352

U.S. Department of Education, Office for Civil Rights Data Collection (2013–2014). https://www2.ed.gov/about/offices/list/ocr/docs/crdc-2013-14.html

Watson, T. N. (2016). "Talking back": The perceptions and experiences of black girls who attend City High School. *The Journal of Negro Education, 85*(3), 239–249. https://doi.org/10.7709/jnegroeducation.85.3.0239

Whitaker, M. C., & Hines-Datiri, D. (2018). Teaching what we don't know: Community-based learning as a tool for implementing Critical Race Praxis. In T. D. Meidl & M.-M. Sulentic Dowell (Eds.), *Handbook of research on service-learning initiatives in teacher education programs* (pp. 315–332). IGI Global.

Wing, A. K. (2015). Critical race feminism. In K. Murji and J. Solomos (Eds.), *Theories of race and ethnicity: Contemporary debates and perspectives* (p. 162). Cambridge University Press.

Wun, C. (2014). The anti-Black order of No Child Left Behind: Using Lacanian psychoanalysis and critical race theory to examine NCLB. *Educational Philosophy and Theory, 46*(5), 462–474. https://doi.org/10.1080/00131857.2012.732011

Wun, C. (2016). Against captivity: Black girls and school discipline policies in the afterlife of slavery. *Educational Policy, 30*(1), 171–196. https://doi.org/10.1177/0895904815615439

Young, J. L., & Hines, D. E. (2018). Killing my spirit, renewing my soul: Black female professors' critical reflections on spirit killings while teaching. *Women, Gender, and Families of Color, 6*(1), 18–25. https://doi.org/10.5406/womgenfamcol.6.1.0018

Young, J. L., Young, J. R., & Ford, D. Y. (2017). Standing in the gaps: Examining the effects of early gifted education on Black girl achievement in STEM. *Journal of Advanced Academics, 28*(4), 290–312. https://doi.org/10.1177/1932202X17730549

7

"STAYING OUT THE WAY"

Connecting Black Girls' Experiences With School Discipline to Collegiate Experiences

Tiffany L. Steele

B lack girls and women have battled with the experiences of disposability within the education system. On the one hand, statistics demonstrate triumph in terms of educational attainment for Black girls and women at astonishing rates in comparison to their Black male counterparts (Banks, 2009; Muhammad & Dixson, 2008; O'Connor, 2002; Schwartz & Washington, 1999). However, these statistics are typically weaponized to justify the little to no attention given to the lived experiences that Black girls and women encounter during their educational journeys. With closer examination, one would uncover the harsh treatment and difficult occurrences Black girls and women are exposed to while accessing the fundamental right of education. Of these occurrences, the issue of disciplinary sanctioning[1] in K–12 education is one of great importance to explore.

Most current literature around external outcomes of disciplinary sanctioning translates into a discussion on the school-to-prison pipeline for Black boys, and interventions are then created in order to begin alleviating this prevalent problem. First, this approach invalidates Black girls' experience with the school-to-prison pipeline. In addition, it perpetuates Black girls' existence and experiences only being recognized in comparison to Black boys. Researchers such as Monique Morris (2016) have served as trailblazers to illuminate how discipline influences the life trajectories of Black girls by calling out institutions of education for the ways they "push out" Black girls from schools by criminalization. According to Morris (2013), "Black girls represent the fastest growing population in residential placement and secure confinement and have experienced the greatest increase in the rate of exclusionary discipline" (p. 5). With an increased presence of law enforcement within public schools, students who are reprimanded for behavioral issues or class disruptions also can be arrested on school property (Smith-Evans et al., 2014). Dependent upon the level of offense, students can be brought into the juvenile court system and, unfortunately, removed from the classroom and learning environment entirely (Smith-Evans et al., 2014).

Through a case study analysis of Black girls in Northern California, Morris (2013) found that 88% of the Black girls interviewed from juvenile court schools were consistently reprimanded in school through suspension and 65% of the girls faced expulsion within their districts. Of these girls, educational aspirations and experiences were limited to the juvenile court schools that, similar to issues shared by Black girls in public schools, housed underprepared teachers and curricula that were not comparable to district high schools where the students hoped to transfer (M. Morris, 2013). Additional research shows that "girls who are suspended face a significantly greater likelihood of dropping out of school" (Crenshaw et al., 2015, p. 24). Although extreme, this example of Black girls subjected to harsh disciplinary action highlights the limited educational opportunities provided to them, leading to more limited academic experiences, aspirations, and, unfortunately, potentially exiting the realm of education entirely.

Therefore, more research is needed, specifically in the K–12 literature, about the overarching experiences of Black girls in education and their experiences with discipline while also understanding what it takes for Black girls to be successful in school (Neal-Jackson, 2018). In addition, the negative residual effects of these experiences for Black girls and women are not only detrimental during their K–12 experiences but can also influence their collegiate experiences, which warrants more understanding and research. As such, the purpose of this chapter is to elucidate the ways in which disciplinary sanctions inform how Black college women navigate higher education. Based on a larger research study examining the connections between high school sanctioning and collegiate experiences among 1st-year Black women, this chapter will highlight two key findings: disengagement from educational environments and lack of trust in authority figures. The following section explores the dearth of literature on the experiences Black girls have with discipline in the K–12 system. Next, findings are shared from my research to illustrate connections between high school discipline and collegiate experiences of Black women. Lastly, implications for secondary and higher education are shared.

Black Girls' Experiences With K–12 Discipline

The oppressiveness of K–12 education is evident in the maltreatment of Black girls through experiences and forms of discipline such as silencing in the classroom, exclusion from knowledge, structural barriers to resources, and preconceived notions held about their level of intelligence (Neal-Jackson, 2018). Essentially, they are judged before they can act through consistent surveillance, yet, ironically, ignored for their exceptional academic performance and engagement (Crenshaw et al., 2015; Smith-Evans et al., 2014). Researchers are beginning to acknowledge how previous studies admire Black girls for their resilient nature in such daunting spaces without ever holding institutions accountable for their inequitable structures that trigger a mode of survival (O'Connor, 1997; Williams & Bryan, 2013).

When discussing issues of discipline, it must begin with admitting that Black girls are overrepresented among the population of K–12 students who are disciplined (Crenshaw et al., 2015). More specifically, Black girls represent a small percentage of students in the K–12 educational system and yet 43% of Black girls have experienced a school-related arrest (Wun, 2016). Neal-Jackson (2018) captured the role of K–12 education systems and officials in relation to validation used to discipline Black girls:

> Overall the school officials' accounts of their Black female students personified negative dominant narratives about Black girls and women by positioning them as undisciplined in their academic habits and unequivocally misaligned with school norms. School officials suggested they were unapproachable, unteachable, and ultimately fully responsible for the limited academic opportunities they experienced. (p. 515)

This statement evokes a certain notion of the "need" for correction or discipline in the lives of Black girls in order to make them adhere to societal norms and teach them to become anything other than themselves.

In addition, research shows that the presence and perspectives of teachers and school officials are pertinent to the development and educational experiences of students (Neal-Jackson, 2018). Within the foundational education period of K–12 studies, students begin to develop attitudes about learning, their potential as individuals, and their abilities to excel in the classroom (Darling-Hammond & Cook-Harvey, 2018). Therefore, teachers and school officials, particularly guidance counselors, play a critical role in the shaping of behaviors and thoughts about students succeeding in educational spaces and the opportunities they have access to in order to grow. Unfortunately, most investigations of the experiences of Black girls expose unfavorable and discouraging interactions with teachers or guidance counselors during their educational journeys (Archer-Banks & Behar-Horenstein, 2012; Evans-Winters, 2005; E. Morris, 2007; Murphy et al., 2013).

Specifically, teachers were found to hold negative perceptions of Black girls in the classroom that impacted their interactions and approach to engaging Black girls in the learning environment (Brickhouse et al., 2000; Francis, 2012; West-Olatunji et al., 2010). To begin, the manner in which Black girls engage with teachers and the classroom environment sometimes differs from the expectations of teachers in terms of appropriate behavior, which is often aligned with white, middle-class, feminine norms. Being direct, consistently speaking in regard to class topics, and answering questions posed by the teacher seemed to be met with adverse reactions from teachers when Black girls performed these acts (E. Morris, 2007). Morris depicted this portrayal in his observation of a teacher threatening to punish a classroom due to the consistent participation of a Black female student in her class. Filled with embarrassment, the female student placed her head down on her desk and disengaged from classroom activities for the rest of the period (E. Morris, 2007). Stories such as these are spread far and wide through K–12 classrooms, as some teachers misinterpret the classroom engagement of Black girls as disrespectful behavior.

Much of the research also focuses on how teachers, mostly white female teachers, can feel threatened by Black girls in class because the practice of their femininity does not mirror dominant white norms on traditional displays of femininity. Essentially, teachers are described as trying to socialize Black girls into "acceptable" behaviors young women should display, such as modesty, quietness, and being less authoritative (Neal-Jackson, 2018). The method in which Black girls engage the educational space is viewed as domineering, causing teachers to use their authority toward Black girls whom they feel are challenging their control (E. Morris, 2007). However, this idea of children challenging and controlling the space is more limited to Black girls, based on their "adultification" by others (Ferguson, 2000).

Adultification in relation to Black girls simply put means that Black girls are viewed as more socially mature than peers and, therefore, treated differently from other students or viewed and treated as adult women (E. Morris, 2007). Although teachers do not directly describe Black girls as adults, the descriptions of their behaviors such as controlling, loud, dominating, or "thinking they are adults too" highlight a parallel to the authority actual adults, and teachers specifically, feel that they should hold in educational spaces (E. Morris, 2007; M. Morris, 2013). The adultification of Black girls can lead to negative instances in their educational development because they become viewed as independent, self-sufficient, and undeserving of help and support, and ultimately, easy targets of discipline (Brickhouse et al., 2000).

Moreover, although other students may be sanctioned for more concrete offenses, research shows that Black girls are found to be punished far more subjectively for things such as being disrespectful, loud, or defiant, all loosely determined at the discretion of those in authority. Classroom management practices of teachers in the K–12 system may not include culturally relevant pedagogy on engaging and interacting with students of color, particularly Black girls, leading to misinterpretations of actions (Neal-Jackson, 2018). Such lack of practices leave space for Black girls to become commonly misunderstood and susceptible to unwarranted discipline. To cope and survive within their academic environments, Black girls and women develop tactics such as interacting less with teachers and school officials or disengaging from the learning environment (Crenshaw et al., 2015; E. Morris, 2007; Neal-Jackson, 2018). However, mechanisms such as this contradict what higher education identifies as necessary tools for college success.

The methodology of portraiture was imperative in the exploration of this topic in order to develop an authentic foundation for this new space in research. Portraiture methodology (Lawrence-Lightfoot & Davis, 1997) was used to guide this study's focus on the influence of disciplinary action and policing on the views and experiences of Black 1st-year college women. Under the guidance of a critical-constructivist epistemology, I conducted two individual interviews and one focus group interview of five participants. Participant-driven photo elicitation was used as an activity to guide the content explored within the focus group interview. Data provided was analyzed to illuminate the shared and contrasting experiences across participants' stories in addition to the development of portraits.

Connecting Experiences With Discipline to Collegiate Journeys

Participants in the larger research study, situated within the higher education context, shared the ways in which they choose to navigate their educational environments as a result of unpleasant experiences with discipline. Of those ways, disengaging from the school environment and not trusting authority had the most direct connection to their navigation of higher education (Steele, 2020).

Disengaging From the School Environment

As discussed in the literature, participants in the larger research study provided countless examples of how disengaging from their school environment was beneficial to their survival. Disengaging from their school environment for participants was a form of self-silencing in which they no longer participated in their normal extracurricular activities, spoke less in class, and appeared as disengaged or defensive, or they opted for class schedules that afforded them the least amount of time in school (Steele, 2020). All of the measures, on the surface, could be viewed as extreme, but for participants in the study, they were necessary actions to complete their high school education and move forward. The need to disengage also relates to previous literature exploration of the unsafe schooling environments Black girls traverse. Black girls who were already reprimanded for their behavior felt pressure and anxiety due to consistent monitoring from teachers and school officials (Crenshaw et al., 2015; Neal-Jackson, 2018). Students felt that the main interactions they experienced with teachers were negative, based on only being addressed when in trouble. From this excessive monitoring, students expressed feeling limited in their academic success.

When describing the elements of disengagement in school environments, participants simultaneously expressed feelings of isolation as an outcome of this decision. Although some forms of discipline experienced were physical isolation from peers within the classroom, in terms of coping, participants described a feeling of loneliness. Not being able to engage with peers due to a fear of more trouble, while also limiting extracurricular activities, left participants to navigate their educational journey alone at times. As participants entered college, the idea of disengagement followed as a result of the ongoing feelings of isolation they felt previously in high school. In addition to their college campus being larger than their high school environments, participants also felt isolated based on the limited number of Black students present and visible at their predominantly white institution. The polarizing racial environment participants experienced caused them to feel othered as they looked for affirming spaces or peer groups to join for solidarity and support. However, participants' isolation continued as there were limited spaces or campus groups that specifically centered the experiences of Black college women. The lack of representation among campus resources and organizations supported participants' decision to be less socially engaged on campus.

In addition to isolation, the collegiate environments participants explored left them feeling susceptible to racially driven targeting. In a short period of time, participants had witnessed countless instances where their Black peers were targeted on campus by other students, staff, and campus police. Many mentioned that these experiences reminded them of various news stories about other Black girls who were targeted in school and harmed by school safety officers. With the thought of potentially being disciplined on the collegiate level, and also implicated by campus police wrongfully due to race, participants also found this to be reason enough to be less involved on campus and "stay out the way" of possible trouble (Steele, 2020). What is concerning about this method of coping is that it differs from what higher education researchers espouse as foundational factors for student retention and collegiate success in terms of the importance of social engagement (Astin, 1999; Pascarella & Terenzini, 2005; Tinto, 1993). Therefore, the current idea of collegiate success does not consider both the positive and negative external factors that form the lens that Black collegiate women use to navigate their environments. Unfortunately, the lack of trust in educational environments for Black girls and women also includes a lack of trust toward authority figures who inhabit the environments as well.

Lack of Trust in Authority

As discussed in the literature, authority figures such as teachers, administrators, and other school officials play a huge role in the subjective discipline Black girls experience. Participants also expressed how their experiences with discipline, particularly instances that seemed excessive or unnecessary, left them not trusting of most teachers or administrators. Specifically, the disciplinary actions taken against students by administrators and teachers caused participants to then question their behaviors and motives going forward (Steele, 2020). As supported by current literature, in line with the experiences of subjective discipline toward Black girls in school, participants lacked trust toward those in authority due to minimal communication about the reasons they were experiencing discipline or reprimands in school. When participants tried to engage in dialogue or ask questions about the discipline they were experiencing, those in authority typically viewed this as a challenge to their status, leaving students with no response. With confusion around reasoning for discipline and no answers in sight, participants expressed feeling a sense of betrayal and a need to protect themselves from more trouble by no longer engaging with authority figures at school. There was an assumption by participants that teachers and administrators who consistently targeted them for discipline had no interest in understanding them as people or the circumstances that may have led to their actions.

When entering college, the practice of distancing from authority figures was present in the way participants chose to interact with faculty. Although participants were assertive in asking for help from faculty when experiencing difficulties in class, they were not interested in developing relationships with faculty members. From their experience in high school with others in authority, there was a clear assumption that faculty may have no interest in getting to know them personally beyond the scope of a class. This approach, although informed by prior experience with teachers, also does not align with the collegiate factor of faculty engagement and/or mentorship to aid in the development of student success and access to academic opportunities (Astin, 1999; Tinto, 1993). This experience left participants to rely on other students or staff with whom they had a trusted relationship to learn more about opportunities to positively supplement their academic experience.

In relation to the concern of being targeted on their college campus, participants also expressed a lack of trust toward those in authority with whom they did not have relationships. Staff members such as hall directors or campus police officers were viewed as untrustworthy due to the witnessing of or personal experiences participants had with collegiate discipline. Similar to the presence of race in polarizing environments, participants described the implicit bias they witnessed in which staff members were eligible to enact sanctioning/conduct and which behavior campus officers displayed when deciding "who" should be disciplined and the severity of their discipline. When describing personal instances of experiences with discipline, participants, as Black women on a predominantly white campus, were painted as a threat to others and guilty of wrongdoing. Therefore, in addition to not trusting those in authority, the continuation of isolation and "staying out the way" as they navigated campus environments such as classrooms, student spaces, and residence halls continued.

Summary

Although participants in the study developed similar patterns for navigating their environments based in their experiences with high school discipline, we must acknowledge that these actions were born out of a lack of individual and institutional care. A lack of individual care on the part of teachers, administrators, or school officials who perceived Black girls as "unapproachable" or "unteachable" had further impacts beyond the high school environment for participants in this study. A lack of institutional care as a result of ambiguous disciplinary policies continues to empower those in authority to wrongfully discipline Black girls and treat them as disposable while ultimately influencing their perceptions of higher education. The message of disposability is depicted through literature and the findings of this study as both K–12 and collegiate environments continuously excluded, separated, and targeted Black girls and women in comparison to their peers. The projected meaning of "you do not belong here" was the environmental norm and ultimately guided participants' perceptions of safety within educational spaces. Following this idea of othering, individuals and institutions who are exposing Black girls and women to maltreatment through discipline in education are not being held responsible for the emotional labor this population must exhibit to survive and navigate these volatile spaces. However, these institutions and their actors continue to explicitly display the lack of interest in the surviving or thriving of Black girls and women. The literature and experiences discussed in this chapter demonstrate that these instances are not siloed but rather connected to influence the choices Black girls and women make throughout their educational journeys.

Implications

The experiences explored in this chapter point to a larger issue around institutional responsibility for the care of Black girls and women. Educational institutions across the P–20 pipeline need to be held responsible for the lack of care and concern they bestow upon Black girls and women. The current lack of care has prolonged consequences for those who are rendered invisible and ignored while receiving education. When reflecting on the lack of responsibility attributed to institutions of higher education, Black girls and women are left with taking ownership of issues and struggles that they did not cause. This places the Black girl and women population in the position of fighting battles and, ultimately, surviving the setbacks placed before them by educational institutions rather than thriving within these educational spaces. However, their ability to succeed in these unfair instances calls forward researchers who identify the population as "resilient" or "persistent," nullifying the fact that the circumstances they are under should never be present in the first place.

Secondary Education

Based on the available literature and experiences of participants discussed in this chapter, there is much work to be done in relation to practice and policy when working with Black girls in high school:

1. The lack of clear communication between students, teachers, and administrators on the level of severity and intention of discipline needs to be addressed. Teachers should clearly communicate to students why they are being disciplined and what conduct policy they have violated.
2. More training is needed for teachers, staff, and administrators in the areas of classroom management styles that are culturally appropriate, trauma-informed, and responsive to the needs of students. This includes addressing implicit and explicit biases of teachers toward children of color and,

specifically, Black girls and their ways of knowing. A part of the training could consist of proper facilitation of dialogue between teachers and students to deescalate moments of conflict or heightened emotions.

3. Most importantly, teachers should attempt to engage all students and develop genuine relationships with their students. The act of developing student relationships invites students to open up and also allows teachers to see students as humans. This understanding of the student may allow for teachers to also have a better understanding of the context the student comes from that influences their experiences in school.

4. Defining infractions and overarching disciplinary policies need to be reviewed through a critical lens at the district level to identify ways each policy oppresses and targets Black girls. This review should also address the level of ambiguity that leaves room for biased treatment toward Black girls through the use of said policies.

5. Lastly, there need to be clear repercussions for authority figures who misuse disciplinary policies to target Black girls. Without a clear system of checks and balances for the use of disciplinary policies across a district and within schools, Black girls will always be at risk of being overrepresented in the population of those disciplined.

Higher Education

Institutions of higher education are also capable of doing more to acknowledge the humanity of Black women on their campuses while also supporting their specific interests and needs as they transition to their new collegiate environment.

1. To facilitate genuine connection between Black women and faculty, more programmatic efforts need to be developed that center Black collegiate women, their needs, and their access to collegiate opportunities. Networking events specifically for Black collegiate women can catalyze the development of better student–faculty relationships and engagement in high-impact practices such as research, study abroad, and, overall, more campus engagement.

2. Similar to secondary education institutions, faculty, staff, administrators, and campus police officers need to experience in-depth screenings and training around their own implicit biases as they relate to their assumptions about Black collegiate women. In addition to screening and training, clear repercussions for those who misuse power should be developed and utilized to uphold an institutional standard of genuine care.

3. In terms of isolation and solidarity, Black collegiate women need more institutionally supported and provided organizations and spaces that allow them to find community among one another and aid in their unique transition to campus. For too long, Black collegiate women have taken it in their own hands to create spaces and support for each other. It is time for institutions to intentionally invest in support and nurturing under their own terms.

Discussion Questions

1. In what ways could you encourage the acknowledgment of Black girlhood in your field or area of expertise?
2. How would you create space for Black girls to explore their own ideas of femininity and how it shows up in educational spaces?
3. What alternatives exist to disciplinary sanctioning that would be conducive to learning for Black girls in education?
4. What could be done to address implicit bias of authority figures toward Black girls and women in educational spaces?
5. How would you prepare Black girls who have experienced disciplinary sanctioning for transitioning to collegiate environments?
6. How could institutions of higher education become better equipped to visibly acknowledge and support Black college women?

Notes

1. For the purposes of this chapter, *disciplinary sanctioning* is defined as punitive techniques such as "unpleasant verbal reprimands, 'the evil eye,' proximity control (i.e., standing near the student), and taking away privileges (e.g., recess) to much harsher forms such as suspension, expulsion, removal to an alternative education program, and corporal punishment" (Bear, 2010, p. 3).

Further Reading

Brown, R. N. (2009). *Black girlhood celebration: Toward a hip-hop feminist pedagogy.* Peter Lang.

Crenshaw, K., Ocen, P., & Nanda, J. (2015). *Black girls matter: Pushed out, overpoliced, and underprotected.* African American Policy Forum & Center for Intersectionality and Social Policy Studies. http://static1.squarespace.com/static/53f20d90e4b0b80451158d8c/t/54dcc1ece4b001c03e323448/1423753708557/AAPF_BlackGirlsMatterReport.pdf

Epstein, R., Blake, J., & González, T. (2017). *Girlhood interrupted: The erasure of Black girls' childhood.* Georgetown Law Center on Poverty and Inequality. http://www.law.georgetown.edu/academics/centers-institutes/poverty-inequality/upload/girlhood-interrupted.pdf

Francis, D. V. (2012). Sugar and spice and everything nice? Teacher perceptions of Black girls in the classroom. *The Review of Black Political Economy, 39*(3), 311–320. https://doi.org/10.1007/s12114-011-9098-y

Morris, M. (2016). *Pushout: The criminalization of Black girls in schools.* The New Press.

Morris, M. (2019). *Sing a rhythm, dance a blues: Education for the liberation of Black and Brown girls.* The New Press.

Neal-Jackson, A. (2018). A meta-ethnographic review of the experiences of African American girls and young women in K–12 education. *Review of Educational Research, 88*(4), 508–546. https://doi.org/10.3102/0034654318760785

Wun, C. (2016). Against captivity: Black girls and school discipline policies in the afterlife of slavery. *Educational Policy, 30*(1), 171–196. https://doi.org/10.1177/0895904815615439

References

Archer-Banks, D. A., & Behar-Horenstein, L. S. (2012). Ogbu revisited: Unpacking high achieving African American girls' high school experiences. *Urban Education, 47*, 198–223. https://doi.org/10.1177/0042085911427739

Astin, A. W. (1999). Student involvement: A developmental theory for higher education. *Journal of College Student Development, 40*(5), 518–529. https://psycnet.apa.org/record/1999-01418-006

Banks, C. A. (2009). *Black women undergraduates, cultural capital, and college success.* Peter Lang.

Bear, G. (2010). Discipline: Effective school practices. *National Association of School Psychologists: Helping Children at Home and School, 3*, 1–5.

Brickhouse, N. W., Lowery, P., & Schultz, K. (2000). What kind of a girl does science? The construction of school science identities. *Journal of Research in Science Teaching, 37*, 441–458. https://doi.org/10.1002/(SICI)1098-2736(200005)37:5<441::AID-TEA4>3.0.CO;2-3

Crenshaw, K., Ocen, P., & Nanda, J. (2015). *Black girls matter: Pushed out, overpoliced, and underprotected.* Center for Intersectionality and Social Policy Studies, Columbia University. http://static1.squarespace.com/static/53f20d90e4b0b80451158d8c/t/54dcc1ece4b001c03e323448/1423753708557/AAPF_BlackGirlsMatterReport.pdf

Darling-Hammond, L., & Cook-Harvey, C. M. (2018). *Educating the whole child: Improving school climate to support student success.* Learning Policy Institute.

Evans-Winters, V. E. (2005). *Teaching black girls: Resiliency in urban classrooms.* Peter Lang.

Ferguson, A. A. (2000). *Bad boys: Public schools in the making of Black masculinity.* University of Michigan Press.

Francis, D. V. (2012). Sugar and spice and everything nice? Teacher perceptions of Black girls in the classroom. *The Review of Black Political Economy, 39*(3), 311–320. https://doi.org/10.1007/s12114-011-9098-y

Lawrence-Lightfoot, S., & Davis, J. H. (1997). *The art and science of portraiture.* Jossey-Bass.

Morris, E. W. (2007). "Ladies" or "loudies"? Perceptions and experiences of Black girls in classrooms. *Youth and Society, 38*, 490–515. https://doi.org/10.1177/0044118X06296778

Morris, M. W. (2013). Education and the caged bird: Black girls, school pushout and the juvenile court school. *Poverty & Race, 22*(6), 5–7. https://www.academia.edu/7871608/Education_and_The_Caged_Bird_Black_Girls_School_Pushout_and_the_Juvenile_Court_School

Morris, M. W. (2016). *Pushout: The criminalization of Black girls in schools.* The New Press.

Muhammad, C. G., & Dixson, A. D. (2008). Black females in high school: A statistical educational profile. *Negro Educational Review, 59*(3/4), 163. https://www.proquest.com/openview/78508e3666c4fb15cfae0b865bb16e5f/1?pq-origsite=gscholar&cbl=46710

Murphy, A. S., Acosta, M. A., & Kennedy-Lewis, B. L. (2013). "I'm not running around with my pants sagging, so how am I not acting like a lady?" Intersections of race and gender in the experiences of female middle school troublemakers. *Urban Review, 45*, 586–610. https://doi.org/10.1007/s11256-013-0236-7

Neal-Jackson, A. (2018). A meta-ethnographic review of the experiences of African American girls and young women in K–12 education. *Review of Educational Research, 88*(4), 508–546. https://doi.org/10.3102/0034654318760785

O'Connor, C. (1997). Dispositions toward (collective) struggle and educational resilience in the inner city: A case analysis of six African-American high school students. *American Educational Research Journal, 34*(4), 593–629. https://doi.org/10.3102/00028312034004593

O'Connor, C. (2002). Black women beating the odds from one generation to the next: How the changing dynamics of constraint and opportunity affect the process of educational resilience. *American Educational Research Journal, 39*(4), 855–903. https://doi.org/10.3102/00028312039004855

Pascarella, E. T., & Terenzini, P. T. (2005). *How college affects students: A third decade of research* (Vol. 2). Jossey-Bass.

Schwartz, R. A., & Washington, C. M. (1999). Predicting academic success and retention for African-American women in college. *Journal of College Student Retention: Research, Theory & Practice, 1*(2), 177–191. https://doi.org/10.2190/R6GT-NH93-MB0N-TJD2

Smith-Evans, L., George, J., Graves, F. G., Kaufmann, L. S., & Frohlich, L. (2014). *Unlocking opportunity for African American girls: A call to action for educational equity.* National Women's Law Center.

Steele, T. L. (2020). *Disciplinary disruption: Exploring the connection between high school sanctioning and Black collegiate women's experiences* [Unpublished doctoral dissertation]. The Ohio State University.

Tinto, V. (1993). *Leaving college: Rethinking the causes and cures of student attrition.* University of Chicago Press.

West-Olatunji, C., Shure, L., Pringle, R., Adams, T., Lewis, D., & Cholewa, B. (2010). Exploring how school counselors position low-income African American girls as mathematics and science learners. *Professional School Counseling, 13*(3), 184–195. https://doi.org/10.1177/2156759X1001300306

Williams, J. M., & Bryan, J. (2013). Overcoming adversity: High-achieving African American youth's perspectives on educational resilience. *Journal of Counseling & Development, 91*(3), 291–300. https://doi.org/10.1002/j.1556-6676 .2013.00097.x

Wun, C. (2016). Against captivity: Black girls and school discipline policies in the afterlife of slavery. *Educational Policy, 30*(1), 171–196. https://doi.org/ 10.1177/0895904815615439

8

VISIBLE AND VALUABLE

(Re)imagining Title IX's Interpretations to Create
Hostile-Free Racially Gendered Educational
Environments for Blackgirls and Blackwomyn

LaWanda W.M. Ward, Ayana T. Hardaway, and Nadrea R. Njoku

In the United States Blackgirls[1] and Blackwomyn have and continue to
persist against racially gendered discrimination, at times in the form of
sexual harassment, in their quest to participate in educational institutions.
Historically, lawsuits have served as one way to combat Blacks' exclusion
from education. Exemplars include 9-year-old Linda Brown's well-known
U.S. Supreme Court case, *Brown v. Board of Education* (1954), and before
Brown, then recent Langston University graduate Ada Lois Sipuel Fisher sued
the University of Oklahoma's law school (*Sipuel v. Board of Regents of the
University of Oklahoma*, 1948). Despite a Supreme Court ruling in Sipuel
Fisher's favor for admission to the law school, she encountered racially gen-
dered discrimination on her 1st day.

In her autobiography, Sipuel Fisher (1996) recalls being the only Black
person, as well as the only womyon, in her classes when she started in the
summer of 1949. Her classmates were 300 white men. In the last row of a
theatre-style classroom, Sipuel Fisher was required to sit in a seat roped off
and with a "colored" sign on it. Her hostile educational environment (Fox-
Davis, 2009) was intensified with a white man constitutional law professor
who also represented the law school in Sipuel Fisher's lawsuit. The legacy
continues of law professors advancing racially gendered and exclusionary ideologies in U.S. law schools (Chotiner, 2019; Fox-Davis, 2009; Raben, 2019)
that promote and normalize legal rationales that Blackwomyn are undeserving of respect and human dignity–affirming experiences. These harmful legal
logics are used to create laws and educational policies that disproportionately

and negatively impact Blackgirls and Blackwomyn across the K–20 spectrum (Crenshaw et al., 2015; Patton & Ward, 2016).

In addition to educators using curricula and policies to inflict harm on Blackgirls and Blackwomyn, they endure harassment in various forms including unwanted sexual advances carried out through verbal and physical expressions. Specifically, Blackgirls and Blackwomyn are subjected to boys and men, across races, targeting them for sexual and domination gratification. When Blackgirls and Blackwomyn seek legal redress to address sexual harassment in educational settings, it is typically because they have exhausted all the nonlegal avenues available that are supposed to ensure that they are learning in harm-free spaces. In short, Blackgirls and Blackwomyn report their distressing experiences to administrators who deliver no or inadequate responses. As a last resort, Blackgirls and Blackwomyn turn to the legal[2] system to rectify situations. To center, render visible, and affirm Blackgirls and Blackwomyn in education, we use critical race feminism as our guiding lens to explore how Title IX interpretations in K–12 and higher education lacking an intersectional sensibility (Collins, 1990; Crenshaw, 1989) do more harm to Blackgirls and Blackwomyn than help them with hostile-free and harassment-free educational experiences. We suggest how policy formation and legal interpretations should be catalysts in (re)shaping educational environments that support Blackgirls and Blackwomyn in their educational pursuits.

Theoretical Framework: Critical Race Feminism

Critical race feminism (CRF) is a theoretical framework that reflects the intersection of race, gender, sexual orientation, and other inextricable identities that distinguish lived experiences. Hence, CRF is useful in exploring and making meaning of Blackgirls' and Blackwomyn's educational journeys. CRF also critiques systems and structures that do not engage an intersectional approach to institutional decision-making and legal interpretations (Collins, 2007; Crenshaw, 1991; Wing, 2003). Additionally, CRF refutes and disrupts essentialism (the erroneous maxim that one person's experiences reflects an entire group's truths). In the educational context, single-axis analyses of obstacles are flawed because they fail to yield solutions that serve more than privileged white, cisgender, heterosexual, and able-bodied white women. Our adoption of CRF provided an opportunity to engage in a more nuanced and heightened sense of intersecting power-affected identities of Blackgirls and Blackwomyn as they combat harassment experiences in education.

Patton and Ward (2016) conducted an exploratory study about missing undergraduate Blackwomyn guided by a CRF sensibility and employed

CRF methodologies (CRFM). Their approach, in which theory and process aligned, exceeded asking new questions and engaging only traditional artifacts such as books and research articles for answers. The authors intentionally conducted research informed by three undergirding tenets. First, a recognition that since Blackgirls and Blackwomyn were captured and enslaved, their existence, bodies, and lived realities in the United States are invisible and relegated in all societal institutions, including law and education. An exemplar of invisibility is how foundational case law for Title IX involved Blackgirl Lashonda Davis, yet she is often not acknowledged as a Blackgirl plaintiff in the case or nuances of the situation such as her suicide note due to administrators' neglect. Only the expansion of the legal test "deliberate indifference" from Lashonda's case to determine if educational entities can be held responsible for peer-to-peer sexual harassment is deemed significant. To avoid positioning Blackgirls in the background of matters, CRFM begin with centering Blackgirls and Blackwomyn in research and legal inquiries.

A second tenet of CRFM commands naming challenges. Hence, the harassment and sexual violence against Blackgirls and Blackwomyn must be identified and labeled with emphasis on Title IX's role in their educational experiences. Balance is key in recognizing similar experiences while also not categorizing Blackgirls and Blackwomyn into monolithic groups because of their shared racially gendered identities. Adherents of CRFM are cognizant of not presenting Blackgirls' and Blackwomyn's sexual violence experiences as a comparison to other womyn. Additionally, it is understood that various educational experiences require exploring institutional types in order to properly contextualize influential environmental factors. For example, Blackwomyn who attend historically white institutions (HWIs) may experience Title IX interpretations differently from Blackwomyn at historically Black colleges and universities (HBCUs).

A third tenet is that intersectional sensibilities are needed to not only recognize sociodemographic identities but also the power-infused structures of law and educational processes. Power has a prominent role in ensuring that Blackgirls and Blackwomyn are ignored and silenced when they assert Title IX violations. Further, when their claims are investigated, Title IX interpretations absent a nuanced understanding of Blackgirls' and Blackwomyn's lived experiences push them further into the margins and compromise effective harassment and sexual violence prevention solutions. We are committed to interrogating and complicating discourses around harassment and violence experienced by Blackgirls and Blackwomyn in education with the goal of pulling their realities from the margins.

Crenshaw (1991) offered a tripartite sensibility—structural intersectionality, political intersectionality, and representational intersectionality—that can aid in not only viewing experiences of Blackgirls and Blackwomyn narrowly but also allows for a more nuanced analysis. First, *structural intersectionality* involves understanding how social identities converge to form, and at times result in, oppressive situations (Crenshaw, 1991). Using structural intersectionality aids in thinking about how educational systems are rooted in white, cisgender, heteronormative logics that make it difficult for Blackgirls and Blackwomyn to be viewed as deserving attention when they report harm.

Second, *political intersectionality* is a critical reminder that social identities are always relevant in agenda setting, and one's access to power determines their ability or lack thereof to negotiate for resources (Crenshaw, 1991). Because societal barriers continue to exist disproportionately for the Black community, Blackgirls and Blackwomyn are at an automatic disadvantage when requesting culturally relevant interventions. Furthermore, political intersectionality probes Blackwomyn's cultural construction (Crenshaw, 1991). This sensibility considers societal stereotypes and tropes about Blackgirls and Blackwomyn in ways that can obscure their actual, real-life experiences. Specifically, in the context of violence against womyn, shortcomings within the legal system, policy development for survivors of violence, and biases associated with penalties for perpetrators of violence can all be examined through political intersectionality.

And third, *representational intersectionality* delves into the cultural construction of Blackwomyn (Crenshaw, 1991). The data overwhelmingly suggest that Blackgirls are subject to more severe punishments in educational contexts, which can be attributed to racially gendered biases and stereotypes (Crenshaw et al., 2015; Epstein et al., 2017). According to Smith-Evans et al. (2014), Blackgirls are framed as being louder and more disorderly than their White peers (Epstein et al., 2017; Smith-Evans et al., 2014). So-called behavioral issues warrant Blackgirls being reprimanded and labeled insubordinate. Subsequently, they are more likely to be reprimanded for talking back to teachers than other groups of girls. In the collegiate setting, Blackwomyn's stress management due to racially gendered discriminatory practices has also been explored (Shorter-Gooden, 2004). Study results conveyed that Blackwomyn are subjected to perceived racially gendered sexual harassment, slurs, and stereotypes. Negative constructions of Blackwomyn have a historical context that has yet to be eradicated, and as a result, Blackwomynhood remains a target for disrespect, hostility, and erasure. Conducting inquires with the tripartite sensibility of intersectionality can produce transformative ways of understanding Title IX violations that Blackgirls and Blackwomyn encounter as well as (re)formulating supportive policies.

The fourth tenet of CRFM is to rely on data in multiple forms because knowledge is not considered exclusive to academics, especially because ways of knowing created by Blackgirls and Blackwomyn exceed formal theoretical sources. CRFM allow researchers, especially Blackwomyn researchers, "to grapple with visibility and the lack of frames available to fully comprehend the complexities that arise when attempting to name a problem or context that remains unnamed" (Patton & Ward, 2016, p. 344). Law's role in shaping Blackgirls' and Blackwomyn's educational experiences is worthy of exploration because legal interpretations of federal policies and laws along with court opinions are vital to how Blackgirls and Blackwomyn are positioned in and experience educational contexts. Title IX interpretations with an intersectional sensibility are critical for ensuring harms are not only named but critiqued and (re)formulated to support Blackgirls and Blackwomyn. In the next section we discuss the historical legacy of sexual violence that haunts Blackgirls in their higher education pursuits.

The Persisting Legacy of Sexual Violence Against Blackgirls and Blackwomyn

Beyond the P–12 educational context, enduring stereotypes about Blackwomyn's sexuality and controlling images, such as the Jezebel, are also prevalent in college settings. Collins (1990) maintained that the Jezebel image originated in slavery through elite white male images of Blackwomynhood. Such an image maintains that Blackwomyn are sexually promiscuous and further complicates collegiate Blackwomyn's educational experiences by adding challenges of dealing with sexual assault and harassment challenges (Hardaway et al., 2019). For example, on-campus sexual assault incidents continue to be a pervasive issue for Blackwomyn. Although college womyn aged 18–24 are three times more likely than all womyn to experience sexual violence, Blackwomyn experience relationship violence at a rate 35% higher than their whitewomyn peers (Acker, 2017). Alarming and stymying to sexual violence reporting, the Jezebel stereotype has been found to influence perceptions of rape survivors (West, 2008). As noted by West (2008), Blackwomyn survivors reported having internalized beliefs consistent with the Jezebel image, which led to their own victim blaming. Additionally, researchers on campus rape of Blackwomyn have contended that "racial history and rape myths thus make African American womyn more vulnerable to forced sexual encounters while simultaneously making accusations of rape more difficult for them" (Foley et al., 1995, p. 15). If educational stakeholders begin to acknowledge the impermeable influence of such images on the physical and mental health of Blackwomyn survivors, only then can we begin to address barriers to reporting the sexual violence exacted against them. The work of Blackwomyn researchers aids in explaining how rape's historical context influences if and how Blackwomyn disclose sexual violence (White, 2001; Wyatt, 1992).

Historically, sexual violence against Blackwomyn without punishment was commonplace (Omolade, 1989). The combination of racially gendered stereotypes and systemic oppression made convicting white men of raping a Blackwomon virtually impossible. CRF legal scholar Kimberlé Crenshaw (1989) stated:

> When Black women were raped by white males, they were being raped not as women generally, but as Black women specifically: Their femaleness made them sexually vulnerable to racist domination, while their Blackness effectively denied them any protection. This white male power was rein-forced by a judicial system in which the successful conviction of a white man for raping a Black woman was virtually unthinkable. (pp. 158–159)

What Crenshaw spoke of is the invisibility of Blackwomyn within the legal system. A failure to attend to the intersectional obstacles facing Blackwomyn renders them invisible in law and policy. This invisibility extends to Title IX as its interpretations have mainly centered around whitewomyn's experiences and not those of Blackwomyn in higher education (Harris & Linder, 2016).

Currently, there is a dearth of literature explicating sexual violence against Blackwomyn at predominantly white institutions (PWIs) as most of the data is focused on whitewomyn's experiences. Empirical studies involving HBCUs are scant at best and, of the literature that does exist, are not entirely produced mainly by Black scholars. For example, a study team composed of a white man, two whitewomyn, and three Blackwomyn as the last three authors (Krebs et al., 2011) conducted a study of 3,951 Blackwomyn at four HBCUs. They found that 14% of participants expe-rienced an attempted or completed sexual violent encounter since entering college. The data collected from this study was compared to non-HBCU Blackwomyn. In another study that included the same white scholars but with one additional whitewomyn and two different Blackwomyn as fourth and sixth authors (Linquist et al., 2013), they explored the context of sexual violence experienced by participants. Their findings demonstrate correlations between alcohol consumption and violence, with most victims reporting they were acquainted with their assailants. Analysis also showed that most victims of sexual violence reported the incident to a close friend or confidant (69.3% of physically forced sexual violence; 55.7% of incapaci-tated sexual violence). Less than 14% sought medical attention and an even lower percentage of participants reported the incident to law enforcement. Blackwomyn scholars who study Blackwomyn's experiences illuminate why reporting differences exist as well as therapeutic interventions created with Blackwomyn at the center (Donovan & Williams, 2002).

Although these studies provide statistical information on violence, reporting, and the context surrounding the incidents, through using CRFM as a lens, we concluded that these studies did not use an intersectional approach to the research. Specifically, we did not see evidence of an intersectional lens demonstrated in their methodology, nor did the authors' scholarship reflect a consideration for the nuances of Black college environments. Additionally, in comparing HBCU and HWI womyn, the authors did not take into consideration relevant cultural factors which influence how Blackwomyn study participants viewed the sexual violence, made their choice and timing to report, and understood their institutional support needs (Bent-Goodley, 2009; Donovan & Williams, 2002; Harris & Linder, 2016; Taylor, 2000). Our CRFM perspective interpreted study implications to reflect the use of a "white gaze" (Morrison, 1994) to understand difficulties involving collegiate Blackwomyn. Morrison describes the white gaze as ways in which whites take notice of and have a visual interest in observing, and at times policing, the lives of Black people. This outlook explains how what was learned from studying Blackwomyn by mostly white researchers who lacked an intersectional lens serves to mainly benefit whitewomyn.

Current critical reflections of Blackwomyn scholars on Blackwomyn and their susceptibility to racially gendered dangers, particularly acts that occur on a college campus, assert that for equitable research and policy changes to occur, we must center Blackwomyn (Patton & Haynes, 2018; Patton & Ward, 2016). Centering them includes considering their voices as primary knowledge sources, foregrounding the historical context that impacts their positionality, and using methodologies that speak to their ways of knowing and living. Harris and Linder (2016) opined that CRF centers the experiences of womyn of color who are sexual violence survivors by rethinking how power is studied. Power, privilege, and patriarchal domination require a nuanced analysis to reveal the ways in which the tripartite sensibility operates as a normal phenomenon in societal institutions such as higher education. When Blackgirls and Blackwomyn attempt to address racially gendered sexual violence in education settings, Title IX's interpretations do not consistently reflect an understanding of their experiences.

Title IX

On June 23, 1972, Title IX became a federal law that prohibited discrimination in educational programs based on sex (Chambers, 2017). Although the law does not contain the phrase "sexual harassment," legal scholars have persuasively argued that based on Title IX's legislative history and stated purposes, it is intended to address sexual harassment in educational settings. Language to support such assertions includes "women with solid legal protection from persistent, pernicious discrimination which is serving to perpetuate second-class citizenship for American women" (Bayh, 1972, p. 5804). Even more compelling is that the U.S. Supreme Court decided in *Franklin v. Gwinnett County Public Schools* (1992) that Title IX is applicable to sexual harassment claims and schools can be held monetarily liable if the law is violated. Eight years after *Franklin*, Blackwomon attorney Williams represented 10-year-old Blackgirl Lashonda Davis in a peer-to-peer sexual harassment lawsuit. The U.S. Supreme Court in a 5–4 decision ruled in Davis's favor after she had complained to no avail to her teacher and the principal about a white boy classmate's constant sexual innuendos that occurred over a time period of approximately 5 months. The close division of the Supreme Court's decision coupled with the dissenting opinions reflect a chasm in judicial philosophies, as well as embedded sexism and heternormativity in law and discourse around supposed *normal growing pains* for boys. The justices who disagreed give credence to deviant behavior being a legitimate way to interact with Blackgirls. Collegiate environments also reflect sexual harassment and violence allowances for men toward collegiate Blackwomyn when administrators and police pose questions rooted in victim blaming discourse. Davis's case is important in Title IX's interpretation because her case added the peer-to-peer harassment component to the Supreme Court's established "deliberately indifferent" standard for teacher–student harassment in *Gebser v. Lago Vista School Independent School District* (1998) that all educational institutions are held to in evaluating their actions once students have complained of sexual harassment. In other words, a court will analyze accusations of inaction by school administrators who were informed of unwelcomed words and actions of a sexual nature by peers and/or adult personnel to determine if administrators did or did not address Title IX complaints. Debates about what language and action qualify as sexual harassment remain in flux as our society, educators, and members of the U.S. Supreme Court believe societal gender ideas such as "boys will be boys" should be tolerated in educational settings. When these sexual violence–supporting beliefs are validated and unaddressed in K–12, students embrace them and carry them out in collegiate environments.

Existing literature on Blackwomyn collegians and sexual violence in various higher education institutions is burgeoning with a need for more scholarship. Although Blackwomyn's experiences are centered within some scholarship, their experiences are scant and a critical analysis of why they should be centered is not always offered (Barrick et al., 2013; Krebs et al.,

2011; Lindquist et al., 2013). Despite the ever-evolving nature of federal policy, including sweeping changes implemented by the Trump administration, we aim to demonstrate how continued analyses that do not account for racially gendered experiences can disproportionately leave Blackwomyn without adequate care and assistance in critical and sensitive times. We care about how policy changes impact their educational opportunities and provide a platform for voices that have virtually been muted. It is this forced silence we hope to eradicate so that Blackwomyn's narratives may serve as influential scholarship for future policy creation. In the next section we share our interpretation of a lawsuit filed by a Black mother, LaTanya Thomas, after her 19-year-old daughter and 1st-year student at Peru State College (PSC), Tyler Thomas, went missing from an HWI. We use this lawsuit as a case to focus on how a narrow Title IX interpretation communicates to Blackgirls and Blackwomyn that they do not deserve protection from sexual violence and demise in their educational pursuits.

Devalued by Narrow Interpretations of the Deliberate Indifference Standard

On December 3, 2010, Tyler disappeared. A security camera captured Tyler's last sighting at 1:30 a.m. leaving an off-campus party headed toward her residence hall. Joshua Keadle, a 29-year-old white man and PSC student, was questioned by the police about Tyler. He initially denied being alone with her on December 3rd and avoided answering additional questions until several days later when he admitted to picking Tyler up and driving her to a remote area (Hammel, 2017). Three years after Tyler went missing, a Nebraska court declared her deceased without her whereabouts being located. In the interim, two complaints were lodged against Keadle, one in 2010 and the other in 2012. In 2010, an 18-year-old whitewomyn enrolled at PSC reported that Keadle took her to the same remote area as Tyler where he threatened to throw the white woman in the Missouri River if she did not perform a sex act. Keadle was charged with several felonies that were eventually dropped. In 2012, while Keadle was a student at Midland College, he was arrested for first-degree sexual assault of a 15-year-old white girl and sentenced to 15–20 years. On October 17, 2017, the Omaha attorney general filed first-degree murder charges against Keadle for Tyler's death. Her family suffered from grief and no justice for almost 7 years. Hardaway et al. (2019) argued the allegations involving whitewomyn accusers resulted in timely charges against Keadle, whereas his arrest for Tyler's death lingered far too long, especially when early in the investigation, local authorities held suspicions of his involvement in Tyler's disappearance.

LaTanya Thomas, Tyler's mother, filed a Title IX lawsuit, *Thomas v. Nebraska State Colleges* (2017) because she believed PSC had enough information about Keadle's past behaviors to expel him and therefore he would not have interacted with Tyler as he may likely have been responsible for her demise. Title IX is applicable in this case because the U.S. Supreme Court's decision for Davis's case determined that private citizens who allege peer-to-peer sexual harassment in an educational setting would receive a particular legal analysis. The legal approach entails determining if

> the funding recipient is *deliberately indifferent* [emphasis added] to sexual harassment, of which the recipient has actual knowledge, and that harassment is so severe, pervasive, and objectively offensive that it can be said to deprive the victims of access to the educational opportunities or benefits provided by the school. (*Davis v. Monroe Board of Education*, 1999, p. 629)

To obtain success with the Title IX claim, the court stated Tyler's mother had to demonstrate

> that the Board [of Trustees of Nebraska State Colleges] had actual knowledge that Keadle posed a substantial risk of harm to Tyler, and that the Board, through deliberate indifference, exposed Tyler to that harm. It is not enough for Thomas to show that the Board could, or should, have done more to discipline Keadle or to protect Tyler and other young women at PSC. Rather, the law requires Thomas to show that the Board disregarded a known or obvious risk. (*Thomas*, 2017, p. 733)

A CRFM sensibility critiques the court's perspective that did not consider relevant facts enough to establish deliberate indifference—specifically, reducing the importance of PSC officials who knew about Keadle's other instances of being accused of sexual assault prior to Tyler's abduction and presumed death, and Keadle's failure to initially complete his sanction of 10 hours of community service and an online education module after he admitted to one of the instances. Concluding that these situations were inadequate evidence to connect Keadle to Tyler's death sends a message of devaluation for Blackgirls and Blackwomyn in educational settings. When courts take a narrow view of disappearances in collegiate settings without recognizing the ways racially gendered incidents are treated by university officials and police, the "Missing White Girl Syndrome," a concept coined by the late Blackwomyn news anchor Gwen Ifill, dominates legal interpretations without consideration of Blackgirls, Blackwomyn, and other womyn of color. Ultimately, Tyler's Title IX lawsuit was dismissed. The court's ahistorical and acontextual assessment of harm to Tyler left her and other collegiate Blackwomyn vulnerable to inadequate legal interpretations used to determine institutional liability. This approach by the courts will more times than not yield a decision that renders Blackwomyn's realities silenced in lieu of an unequal privileging of white accounts of malfeasance and no justice for mourning Black families (Hardaway et al., 2019).

Implications and Suggestions

Daily, Blackgirls and Blackwomyn in educational settings must contend with more than coursework. They reject and report unwanted sexual advances from peers and those in power positions. Although Congress passed Title IX to eradicate gender-based discrimination and the Supreme Court expanded its scope to include addressing sexual harassment, Blackgirls and Blackwomyn remain vulnerable to legal interpretations. Legal rationales that do not hold officials responsible for ensuring individuals with patterns and prior records of sexual harassment and sexual violence are held accountable reinforce a historical message that in the eyes of the law, Blackgirls and Blackwomyn are unworthy of protection from unwanted attention and behaviors.

Mental health scholarship on collegiate Blackwomyn is an additional reason for K–12 school and higher education administrators to elevate their awareness of the harms that result from sexual harassment and sexual violence (Jones & Pritchett-Johnson, 2018; West et al., 2016). Studies show that to persist and thrive in HWIs, Blackwomyn engage in debilitating strategies to cope such as embodying the "Strong Black Woman Stereotype" (Jones & Pritchett-Johnson, 2018; West et al., 2016). In order to relieve the perceived necessity to invest additional energy into withstanding harmful actions in educational settings, we suggest two policy-oriented solutions. One, require professional development for Title IX coordinators across the educational spectrum on problematic investments in systemic and structural biases that silence Blackgirls in reporting Title IX violations. Trainings should include scholarship that illuminates Blackgirls' and Blackwomyn's experiences in ways that draw attention to flawed policies and their interpretations that create hostile learning environments.

And two, we agree with other Blackwomyn higher education scholars (Patton & Haynes, 2018) who urge institutional leaders to engage in transformational change and advocate for Title IX coordinators to use an intersectional approach to incidents which contextualizes the sociodemographic identities of all involved as well as the power dynamics. When lawsuits are filed for Title IX claims, educational leaders, students, and those who support them invest a lot of energy, money, and time attempting to explain what happened and who should be responsible. Despite the sexual harassment and assault experiences of Blackwomyn and their peers disrupting their learning environments, courts tend to side with educational institutions, like Peru State College, if no evidence of egregious neglect is presented. Unfortunately, judges do not feel compelled to consider historical and contemporary targeted violence against Blackgirls and Blackwomyn in deciding legal claims brought about and for them. Therefore, because courts tend to take a narrow perspective on what evidence is compelling to establish institutional liability, as CRFM adherents view, working toward transformational institutional reform of policies to address racially gendered complaints and concerns before matters become litigious is better for improving the educational experiences of Blackgirls and Blackwomyn as well as showing an investment in all students' success.

Discussion Questions

1. How does including Blackwomyn's historical experiences of sexual violence (re)shape conversations about Blackgirls' and Blackwomyn's experiences in various educational settings?
2. What future studies can CRFM be engaged with to illuminate and explore Blackgirls' and Blackwomyn's educational experiences?

Notes

1. We use *Black* as an umbrella term for girls and womyn of African descent. We use the words *womon* and *womyn* to reject the erasure of Blackwomyn due to a societal perspective that perpetuates *Black men* and *Black people* as proxies for *Blackwomyn*. Also, we model Black critical race feminist scholar Cheryl Harris's (1992) practice of joining *Black* with *wom[y]n* and *girls* as a political social identity rationale to emphasize their inextricable unity. Overall, the intentional couplings are a form of liberatory resistance against societal pressure to privilege one social identity over the other and to deessentialize the assumed ways of being and knowing of Blackgirls and Blackwomyn. College-attending Blackwomyn are the demographic of this writing.

2. Mogul et al. (2011) intentionally used the phrase "criminal legal system" instead of "criminal justice system" to bring attention to the lack of fairness realized for minoritized and marginalized populations. Similarly, we use "legal system" instead of "justice system" to illuminate law as a formal process but not one that necessarily results in humanity-affirming redress for Blackgirls and Blackwomyn.

Further Reading

Harrison, L. (2017). Redefining intersectionality theory through the lens of African American young adolescent girls' racialized experiences. *Youth & Society, 49*(8), 1023–1039.

Moss, J. L. (2019). The forgotten victims of missing white woman syndrome: An examination of legal measures that contribute to the lack of search and recovery of missing black girls and women. *William and Mary Journal of Race, Gender & Society, 25*(3), 737–762.

References

Acker, L. (2017). *Faces in the crowd: A narrative inquiry of relationship violence of four Black college women* [Unpublished doctoral dissertation]. Iowa State University.

Barrick, K., Krebs, C. P., & Lindquist, C. H. (2013). Intimate partner violence victimization among undergraduate women at historically black colleges and universities (HBCUs). *Violence against women, 19*(8), 1014–1033. https://doi .org/10.1177/1077801213499243

Bayh, E. (1972). 118 Cong. Rec. 5804.

Bent-Goodley, T. B. (2009). A black experience-based approach to gender-based violence. *Social Work, 54*(3), 262–269. https://doi.org/10.1093/sw/54.3.262

Brown v. Board of Education, 347 U.S. 483 (1954).

Chambers, C. R. (2017). *Law and social justice in higher education.* Routledge. https://doi.org/10.4324/9781315777931

Chotiner, J. (2019, August 23). A Penn law professor wants to make America white again. *New Yorker.* https://www.newyorker.com/news/q-and-a/a-penn-law-professor-wants-to-make-america-white-again

Collins, P. H. (1990). *Black feminist thought: Knowledge, consciousness, and the politics of empowerment.* Routledge.

Collins, P. H. (2007). Black Feminist Epistemology [1990]. In Craig J. Calhoun (Ed.), *Contemporary Sociological Theory.* Blackwell.

Crenshaw, K. (1989). Demarginalizing the intersection of race and sex: A Black feminist critique of antidiscrimination doctrine, feminist theory, and anti-racist politics. *University of Chicago Legal Forum, 139*, 139–164. https://doi .org/10.4324/9780429500480-5

Crenshaw, K. (1991). Mapping the margins: Intersectionality, identity politics, and violence against women of color. *Stanford Law Review, 43*(6), 1241–1299. https://doi.org/10.2307/1229039

Crenshaw, K., Ocen, P., & Nanda, J. (2015). *Black girls matter: Pushed out, overpoliced, and underprotected.* African American Policy Forum & Center for Intersectionality and Social Policy Studies. https://static1.squarespace. com/static/53f20d90e4b0b80451158d8c/t/54d2d37ce4b024b41443b 0ba/1423102844010/BlackGirlsMatter_Report.pdf

Davis v. Monroe Board of Education, 526 U.S. 629 (1999).

Donovan, R., & Williams, M. (2002). Living at the intersection. *Women & Therapy*, *25*(3–4), 95–105. https://doi.org/10.1300/j015v25n03_07

Epstein, R., Blake, J., & González, T. (2017). *Girlhood interrupted. The erasure of Black girls' childhood*. Georgetown Law Center on Poverty and Inequality. https://doi.org/10.2139/ssrn.3000695 or https://www.law.georgetown.edu/poverty-ine-quality-center/wp-content/uploads/sites/14/2017/08/girlhood-interrupted.pdf

Fisher, A. L. S. (1996). *A matter of Black and White: The autobiography of Ada Lois Sipuel Fisher*. University of Oklahoma Press. https://doi.org/10.2307/40027872

Foley, L. A., Evanic, C., Karnik, K., King, J., & Parks, A. (1995). Date rape: Effects of race assailant and victim and gender of subjects on perceptions. *Journal of Black Studies*, *32*, 6–18. https://doi.org/10.1177/009579849502211002

Fox-Davis, K. (2009). A badge of inferiority: One law student's story of a racially hostile educational environment. *National Black Law Journal*, *23*(1), 98–120.

Franklin v. Gwinnett County Public Schools, 503 U.S. 60 (1992).

Gebser v. Lago Vista School Independent School District, 524 U.S. 274 (1998).

Hammel, P. (2017, October 19). Joshua Keadle charged with murder in disappear-ance of Tyler Thomas, a Peru State student from Omaha. *Omaha World-Herald*. https://www.omaha.com/news/crime/joshua-keadle-charged-with-murder-in-disappearance-of-tyler-thomas/article_6dfaaf46-b369-11e7-8a37-9b2b7e1dc5e0.html

Hardaway, A. T., Ward, L. M., & Howell, D. (2019). Black girls and womyn mat-ter: Using Black feminist thought to examine violence and erasure in education. *Urban Education Research and Policy*, *6*(1), 31–46.

Harris, C. I. (1992). Law professors of color and the academy: Of poets and kings. *Chicago-Kent Law Review*, *68*(1), 331–352.

Harris, J. C., & Linder, C. (Eds.). (2016). *Intersections of identity and sexual violence on campus: Centering minoritized students' experiences*. Stylus.

Jones, M. K., & Pritchett-Johnson, B. (2018). "Invincible Black women": Group therapy for Black college women. *The Journal of Specialists in Group Work*, *43*(4), 349–375.

Krebs, C. P., Barrick, K., Lindquist, C. H., Crosby, C. M., Boyd, C., & Bogan, Y. (2011). The sexual assault of undergraduate women at Historically Black Colleges and Universities (HBCUs). *Journal of Interpersonal Violence*, *26*(18), 3640–3666. https://doi.org/10.1177/0886260511403759

Lindquist, C. H., Barrick, K., Krebs, C. P., Crosby, C. M., Lockart, A. J., & Sanders-Phillips, K. (2013). The context and consequences of sexual assault at Histori-cally Black Colleges and Universities (HBCUs). *Journal of Interpersonal Violence*, *28*(12), 2437–2461. https://doi.org/10.1177/0886260513479032

Mogul, J. L., Ritchie, A. J., & Whitlock, K. (2011). *Queer (in)justice: The criminali-zation of LGBT people in the United States*. Beacon Press.

Morrison, T. (1994). *The bluest eye*. Plume.

Omolade, B. (1989). Black women, black men, and Tawana Brawley: The shared condition. *Harvard Women's Law Journal*, *12*(3), 11–23.

Patton, L. D., & Haynes, C. (2018). Hidden in plain sight: The Black Women's Blueprint for institutional transformation in higher education. *Teachers College Record*, *120*(4), 1–18.

Patton, L. D., & Ward, L. W. (2016). Missing Black undergraduate women and the politics of disposability: A critical race feminist perspective [Special issue]. *The Journal of Negro Education*, *85*(3), 330–349. https://doi.org/10.7709/jnegroeducation.85.3.0330

Raben, D. (2019, March 5). Racism thrives at the law school. *The Chicago Maroon*. https://www.chicagomaroon.com/article/2019/3/5/racism-thrives-law-school/

Shorter-Gooden, K. (2004). Multiple resistance strategies: How African American women cope with racism and sexism. *Journal of Black Psychology*, *30(3)*, 406–425. https://doi.org/10.1177/0095798404266050

Sipuel v. Board of Regents of the University of Oklahoma, 332 U.S. 631 (1948).

Smith-Evans, L., George, J., Graves, F. G., Kaufmann, L. S., & Frohlich, L. (2014). *Unlocking opportunity for African American girls: A call to action for educational equity*. NAACP Legal Defense Fund & National Women's Law Center.

Taylor, J. Y. (2000). Sisters of the yam: African American women's healing and self-recovery from intimate male partner violence. *Issues in Mental Health Nursing*, *21*(5), 515–531. https://doi.org/10.1080/01612840050044267

Thomas v. Board of Trustees of Nebraska State Colleges, 296 Neb. 726 (Nebraska Supreme Court 2017).

West, C. (2008). Mammy, Jezebel, Sapphire, and their homegirls: Developing an "oppositional gaze" toward the images of Black women. In J. Chrisler, C. Golden, & P. Rozee (Eds.), *Lectures on the Psychology of Women* (4th ed., pp. 287–286). McGraw Hill.

West, L. M., Donovan, R. A., & Daniel, A. R. (2016). The price of strength: Black college women's perspectives on the strong black woman stereotype. *Women & Therapy*, *39* (3–4), 390–412. https://doi.org/10.1080/02703149.2016.1116871

White, A. M. (2001). I am because we are: Combined race and gender political consciousness among African American women and men anti-rape activists. *Women's Studies International Forum*, *24*(1), 11–24. https://doi.org/10.1016/s0277-5395(00)00167-9

Wing, A. (Ed.). (2003). *Critical race feminism: A reader* (2nd ed.). New York University Press.

Wyatt, G. E. (1992). The sociocultural context of African American and white American women's rape. *Journal of Social Issues*, *48*(1), 77–91. https://doi.org/10.1111/j.1540-4560.1992.tb01158.x

PART THREE

NAVIGATING POLITICS AND
THE POLITICIZATION OF
BLACK WOMEN AND GIRLS IN
HIGHER EDUCATION

9

BLACK WOMEN UNDERGRADUATES' REFLECTIONS ON THE PATHWAY TO COLLEGE

Naming and Challenging Structural Disinvestments

Lori D. Patton, Keeley Copridge, and Sacha Sharp

Black women were historically relegated to a low position in the United States, precipitated by enslavement. Despite the horrors of enslavement, Black women "inherited self-sufficiency" (Noble, 1957, p. 18), a characteristic that would be vital for their preservation. This same self-sufficiency would become the driver for their educational aspirations. Over 200 years have passed since women were allowed to pursue higher education. Prior to the early 1800s, the possibility of receiving a college education was nonexistent for them. According to Sanford-Harris (1990), it was a widely held belief that women should not be educated in the same way as men. The education of Black women, in particular, was not a priority, nor were investments in their education. When Oberlin College opened its doors in 1833, women were accepted as students into the coeducational institution (Evans, 2008). More importantly, the opening of Oberlin ushered in the first significant presence of Black women in the academy. Yet there was very little concern about providing Black women with educational opportunities beyond courses promoting morality and domesticity (Evans, 2008; Perkins, 2015).

According to Rusher (1996), "The early beginnings of education for African American women were highly dependent upon the educational opportunity for African American men and white women" (p. 16). Evans (2008) chronicled Black women's access to higher education during 1865–1910. In reference to college access, Evans shared:

> Between the end of the Civil War and the beginning of World War I, many black women blossomed in fertile academic ground. . . . This growth, though significant, was qualified; black women were admitted to schools but not always to the college department. (p. 36)

Not only were Black women denied more academically rigorous courses, they were also limited in choosing which institutions they could access. Noble (1957) noted, "To be sure, Negro women were entering college at a time when there was great controversy concerning the abilities and mental fitness of Negroes and women" (p. 17). Furthermore, they had to contend with not only societal disinvestments in their education but also disinvestments by Black men. In *A Voice From the South* noted educator and leader Anna Julia Cooper (1892) addressed the phenomenon of disinvestment, stating:

> It seems hardly a gracious thing to say, but it strikes me as true, that while our men seem thoroughly abreast of the times on almost every other subject, when they strike the woman question they drop back into sixteenth century logic. . . . I fear the majority of colored men do not yet think it worthwhile that women aspire to higher education. (p. 75)

She continued further, explaining:

> Let us insist then on special encouragement for the education of our women and special care in their training. Let our girls feel that we expect something more of them than that they merely look pretty . . . let money be raised and scholarships be founded in our colleges and universities for self-supporting, worthy young women. (pp. 78–79)

In contemporary times, Black women's postsecondary options are far more robust. Technically speaking, Black women now have the option to choose the institutions they wish to attend, which significantly differs from the aforementioned time period in which they were purposefully subjected to exclusionary practices prohibiting them from pursuing college. Yet the college choice literature has not substantively focused on Black women, nor has the literature emphasized the extent to which investments have been made toward Black women's educational pathways to college, save the presence of Bennett and Spelman College (Guy-Sheftall, 1982; Thomas & Jackson, 2007). Evans-Winters and Esposito (2010) noted:

> Very few research studies examine positive adaptation and school resilience among African American women students, perhaps because not many scholars are aware of the large proportions of Black girls who succeed in school despite social imposition, such as poor social and economic conditions impeding in the lives of their families and school communities. (p. 14)

The absence of this line of research is especially intriguing given news headlines indicating Black women are "the most educated group in the U.S." (Rogers, 2016, p. 1), that they "enroll in college more than any race and gender" (Morton, 2013, p. 1), and that Black women "far outnumber Black men at the nation's highest-ranked universities" ("Black Women," n.d., p. 1).

Currently, there is no significant literature base for examining how and why Black women undergraduates ultimately pursue college. Although we know the structural barriers Black women undergraduates face while accessing college, more exploration is needed to learn about investments in their educational success. What is clear, however, is that a large number of Black women access college and do so by attending for-profit and community colleges (Iloh & Toldson, 2013). Enrollment of racially minoritized students at these types of open-access institutions is not uncommon. Overall, Black students comprise 12.65% of the total undergraduate student population across U.S. institutions (Hussar et al., 2020). Although this number currently remains fairly consistent across all institutional types, this consistency is due to a new drop in Black student undergraduate enrollment (Hussar et al., 2020). Until recently, the percentage of Black students at 4-year colleges and universities, both public and private, remained lower than that of the overall Black student population across institutions (Arbeit & Horn, 2017). What remains unchanged is the overall enrollment of Black students in higher education being largely situated at community colleges and for-profits (Hussar et al., 2020; Iloh & Toldson, 2013). They comprise 28–29% of students at for-profit institutions (Hussar et al., 2020). However, given that Black women's college enrollment outpaces Black men and other racially minoritized/underrepresented groups, their attendance at these institutions is particularly pronounced.

In addition to attending for-profits and community colleges, both of which are considered less selective institutions, there is a tendency among Black women to undermatch as they explore options for postsecondary institutions. Bastedo and Jaquette (2011) explained, "The undermatching hypothesis suggests that there is a significant pool of low-socioeconomic-status (SES) students who are attending colleges that are less selective than the ones they could have attended based on their academic preparation" (p. 318). Black women's decisions to attend college, and certain types of institutions in particular, can be linked to a range of circumstances. For example, Black women from low socioeconomic backgrounds may attend less selective institutions due to perceived affordability. First-generation Black women may undermatch or choose less selective institutions due to limited access to formalized information and resources to facilitate thorough research on college options (Perkins, 2015). Black women may also believe that attending less selective institutions will offer more flexibility if they have children or are working to support themselves and other family members (Iloh & Toldson, 2013). Moreover, less selective institutions may factor into Black women's research process as a last resort for actually accessing college.

If more Black women are attending less selective institutions, then it would logically follow that fewer are attending highly selective schools. A recent analysis by the *New York Times* indicated that the number of Black 1st-year students at elite schools had not changed since 1980, with the exception of gains made at a few selective liberal arts colleges (Ashkenas et al., 2017). Bielby et al.'s (2014) study offers one solid explanation for why the majority of Black women are in less selective institutions. They explored why women, broadly speaking, were underrepresented at elite colleges. The findings indicated that the low representation was less about women's decision-making and choice process, and more about issues of access. In other words, the admissions structures and norms—namely, the reliance on standardized test scores—are designed to privilege White men who apply and ultimately gain access. In this instance, the structure in and of itself represents a ready-made disinvestment in Black women. In addition to structures that prohibit Black women from accessing elite institutions, research has shown gendered differences in factors affecting Black women's college aspirations. For example, Hubbard (1999) examined college aspirations among high-achieving, low-income Black high school students. She noticed that the men desired college as an avenue to pursue athletics and often experienced disappointment in not receiving the needed scholarships to afford college. The women, however, aspired to pursue particular career avenues. They viewed solid grades and receiving academic scholarships as their pathway to college.

The introduction to this chapter reveals the long road that Black women have faced in terms of accessing a college education due to structures (e.g., enslavement, societal positioning, perceived incompetence) that prohibited them at every turn. These structures force Black women to survive and thrive in the absence of resources that might have otherwise promoted access and smooth transition into earning an education. Black women's educational histories and access to college reveal narratives of their overwhelming success (i.e., outcomes) despite the odds. Yet the same narratives do not necessarily match the resources and opportunities afforded them (i.e., inputs), aside from their own desires and investments in themselves (with the exception of Black women's colleges).

Theorizing (Dis)Investments in Black Women's College Pathways

Borrowing from Giroux (2006), Patton and Ward (2016) wrote about disposability politics in reference to Black women collegians who had gone missing. Such disposability, they noted, is "deeply rooted in the confluence of historical, political, educational, cultural, and social systems and structures that regardless of circumstance either locate Black women at the bottom, position them on the margins, or dispose of them altogether" (p. 334). At the heart of disposability is the reality that we live in a society that fundamentally disregards Black women and girls regardless of sector. For the purposes of offering a conceptual frame for this chapter, we propose that disposability shows up in particular ways when considering Black women and college. For example, multiple scholars (Chavous & Cogburn, 2007; Gholson, 2016; Sesko & Biernat, 2010) have discussed the invisibility shrouding Black women and girls. Such invisibility does not exist in a vacuum, but rather is a logical extension of a larger politics of disposability, where it is difficult to see them. As Crenshaw (1989) noted, society lacks the proper framing through which our visibility would become more palatable.

Similarly, disinvestment and/or failure to invest in Black women extends from disposability politics. For example, in the 2016 presidential race, the overwhelming majority of Black people who voted for presidential hopeful Hillary Clinton were women (94%; Williams, 2016). However, there was no aspect of Clinton's campaign that spoke to Black women, nor was there any particular investment in addressing Black women's concerns, yet their votes mattered (Jackson, 2016). Fast forward to the 2017 election in Alabama, where Black women represented the largest voter turnout (98%), ultimately leading to the victory of Doug Jones, who would become the first Democratic U.S. senator from that state (Duster & Tuakli, 2017; Pearson, 2018). News headlines circulated and lauded Black women, but never grappled with how Black women's investment in these respective campaigns was not mirrored in the agenda of these candidates, and still are not in most campaigns, despite the critical importance of their collective vote. Inarguably, there is a clear disinvestment in Black women within the political sector, signaling their disposability.

Within education, Black women's pathways, particularly their postsecondary opportunities, are deeply connected to disposability politics. Given Black women's educational histories noted earlier, the common thread in terms of accessing college is that they are not simply afforded an opportunity to attend college and choose the schools where they desire to pursue education. Instead, they are positioned last in the larger narrative related to college-going processes, and are required to fend for themselves, searching for resources that are not readily available at the outset. Black women have historically and in present contexts been waymakers for themselves and others, but this waymaking can come at a particular cost because it is fueled by disinvestment. One way to characterize this process is by what Shaw (2017) referred to as struggling successfully. Shaw stated:

> Black women are being overlooked as a distinct population worthy of support—not because Black women are not struggling to succeed in college, but because they are struggling more successfully than their counterparts. . . . Black women's educational achievements at the postsecondary level seems to occur in spite of, and not because of, institutional support. (p. 204)

Struggling successfully, an implication of disinvestment, further maintains systemic oppression and harms Black women and girls. The harm is not produced by their educational successes. Conversely, the harm is promulgated by the presumption that Black women and girls are unicorns and somehow magical because they invested in themselves, while the larger educational system failed to mirror that same investment. Their accomplishment of getting to and through college is celebrated within larger discourses where their actual labor is dismissed, their struggles are not acknowledged, or their experiences are subsumed under or equated with all students. Ultimately, the realities of their experiences are overshadowed. This process fuels Black women's disposability because if they are deemed successful, then institutions presume they are doing just fine and can succeed without resources that would actually reduce the struggle in the first place. Black women are celebrated for succeeding and overcoming odds that would not have existed had the educational system invested in them. This framing is what we used to understand the college pathways of Black women undergraduates as they reflected on their experiences.

Learning From Our Data

We designed a critical qualitative study designed to examine the experiences of undergraduate Black women. We recruited and conducted semistructured interviews with 13 Black women 18–25 years old. These women were at various levels of their undergraduate careers and pursued majors ranging from journalism, fashion and interior design, and business to social work and marketing (see Table 9.1).

In listening to the Black women's stories, notions of disinvestment were clear, as they themselves primarily paved their own way to college. Although what we present here stems from a larger data corpus, we focus on participants' reflections on college choice processes, particularly their individual investments in attending college. The women relied on their personal strengths and self-investments to navigate the college decision process. Most participants had already decided they were attending college, based upon comments they shared. For example, Shach, a college sophomore, said,

> I just feel like it is one of those things that when you grow up and you know that college is a thing, there was no other option in my mind. You know what I mean? That is just what I've known.

For Shach, college becoming a "thing" was largely influenced by observing her mother go to college when she was younger. Her mother, a single parent, became a role model and a source of motivation for her. Shach shared,

TABLE 9.1
Participant Demographics

Pseudonym	Major	Rank	Age	Hometown
Cece	Biology	Junior	21	Chicago, IL
Jordan	Broadcast Journalism and English	Junior	20	Louisville, KY
Tasha	Mathematics	Senior	22	Detroit, MI
Ari	Marketing, Business Analytics	Sophomore	18	Merrillville, IN
Jazz	Arts Management	Sophomore	25	Gary, IN
Shach	Biology	Sophomore	19	Evansville, IN
Fport	Human Development and Family Studies	Junior	21	Chicago, IL
Des	Business Management	Sophomore	19	Gary, IN
Clare	Political Science	Junior	20	Fishers, IN
Taylor	Social Work	Senior	21	Hoffman Estates, IL
Lexy	Fashion Design	Sophomore	20	Kokomo, IN
Boni	Psychology	Sophomore	20	Indianapolis, IN
Ana	Broadcast Journalism	Sophomore	19	Chicago, IL

> She [her mother] went to college throughout my younger years. She [her mother] went back and got her degree. So maybe like seeing her go to school when I was younger. . . . My mom isn't using her degree but like the fact that she went to college and did well for herself compared to everybody else I guess is just set in my mind.

Ari, a college sophomore, expressed, "For me it was the next thing to do. I feel like if I have this opportunity, I might as well do it." Ari had the ability of seeing the opportunity in college for herself, and therefore felt like it was something she had to pursue.

Other Black undergraduate women expressed how college was presented as an opportunity for them to leave their hometown. For example, Des, a college sophomore, asserted, "But I think I kind of like motivated myself to go to college because I knew I didn't want to be like stuck in Gary for the rest of my life." Similarly, Ana, a college sophomore, explained, "I just kind of knew that I was going to college. I just knew that that was the next step after. I couldn't imagine being at home after high school."

Given their plans to attend college, participants invested their efforts toward earning solid grades and high academic achievement. Most of the women in this study excelled in school, and because of grades and involvement in extracurricular activities, participants felt college was the natural next step. Lexy, a college sophomore, shared,

> Ok, so I was a straight A student during elementary, middle and high school. Just kind of you get to the end of high school and you try to figure out what you want to do with your life and where you want to go. So, college for me was always a must. I don't not want to go to college. I'm going to college.

Des expressed how her involvement in extracurricular activities helped direct her path to college by stating,

> I mean it was like, I was like an honor student most of the time I was there. All of high school you could say I was an honor student. I was in honor society. I was in student council, volleyball. I was a cheerleader. We made a club called Random Acts of Kindness club. I was very involved in high school.

Lexy discussed how she invested in her grades in an effort to stand out from her peers by saying,

> If I mess up I was like no, I don't want any B's or A−'s. I want only A+. And so, for me it was just kind of my own decision like, where did I want to be at. How did I want to set myself apart from my other counterparts in Kokomo, Indiana?

Ultimately, students realized they did not want all of their achievement in secondary school to go to waste, which could be summed up by Tasha, a college senior, who said, "One of the things that pushed me was the fact that I always put in 200%, so by the time I got to my senior year I was like if I don't go to college why did I put in 200%?"

In addition to their efforts to get to college, participants acknowledged how their parents supported their decision to go to college and even expected them to attend college. However, the process of applying to these colleges was largely self-motivated. Outside of college preparation programs, participants created their own access to resources. When asked about an individual who assisted her in applying for college, Boni, a college sophomore, stated:

> To be honest, I went to a school with 1,800 people and one counselor. I had about 450 people in my graduating class, so it was kind of like favoritism with the college counselor. I was in the top 1% of my class so she never really said, "Oh, you should go to college" or "You shouldn't go to college." If I needed something from her, I got it, but it was never like "I'm going to motivate you." Motivation usually went to everyone who was below me.

Being cognizant of the limited resources available to her, Jazz, a college sophomore, started early with researching college:

> I had the college counselor like give me free application waivers but to be very honest, not to sound boastful, but I did do it all myself. I started learning about college when I was in 6th grade. I was plotting on college for 6 years. Like, I said there was no direct person saying "you better go to college." It was just like, oh, university my mom keeps talking about and then from there I started researching things. And then by the time my senior year came, my parents said you know October came and I had applied to 17 different schools without telling them. I'm a very autonomous person so like I did a lot of stuff without my parents knowing.

In another instance, a participant discussed how her school lacked the educational resources needed for success, yet that participant rejected those who said she could not achieve her goals of attending college. Cece, a college junior, stated:

> Back home in Chicago, I was in a pretty urban area so I'm not sure if this identifies the same way Indiana does. I went to a Title I school. A vast majority of my classmates received free or reduced lunch. So, with that also came a lack of educational resources. A lack of things that maybe more

upper-class type schools had. Despite that I was a pretty high achieving student. I graduated with a 4.3 GPA. As far as like things that were given to me to allow me to go to college, I had some people in my ear but not many. I had more tell me I couldn't rather than I could.

Cece illustrated her ability to perform above average even when she was not exposed to essential resources. Doing this allowed her to reject naysayers and aspire to college. Another participant shared the benefits of attending college for gaining knowledge and resources that would benefit her in her future career. Ari said:

I think that education is an amazing thing. You can learn so many different things from like social experience and volunteering. You gain humanities. I think that a formal education is something that will propel you in your human capital as well as teach you things about yourself that you do not know in any other context. So, I make it a mission to reach for something that is outside of my major program. Something that is just for me because there are so many different things you can learn from all these experts here. I need to capitalize on the opportunity because in 5 years I am never going to be in a place like this again. Probably not.

Considerations

Based on the stories shared by the Black women undergraduates we learned they were motivated to attend college early and relied on self-investments to pursue their college goals. For the women, college was a necessary next step based on their academic achievements in the K–12 setting. Their desire to achieve their career goals and follow their dreams so they "could be somebody" and they wouldn't be "stuck" is symptomatic of disinvestments within larger societal structures that can be confining for some Black women and girls (Patton & Ward, 2016). These disinvestments are emblematic of an educational system that has historically undervalued Black women and their potential. Further, the desire to be somebody could signal that these women were already experiencing invisibility, requiring them to be self-sufficient when it came to college matriculation. College may have been viewed as an opportunity to feel a greater sense of validation and to flourish in ways not possible at their high school or in their home life.

Although family members somewhat influenced Black women undergraduates' decisions to attend college, the Black women's career goals and academic accomplishments were ultimate drivers for their research about attending college. These women participated in various college-going literacy activities to assist them in pursuing their postsecondary education. The women would utilize school counseling services in order to access college vouchers, while also noting that their success was not prioritized by those counselors. Participants who had limited resources to assist them used their personal capital in the form of self-motivation and efficacy to conduct activities for themselves, such as doing their own research on potential colleges. In spite of the limited resources available to them, the women were able to successfully matriculate to college. This finding is consistent with the concept of struggling successfully (Shaw, 2017), and the fact that societal structures force Black women to do more with less. Therefore, Black women have learned to fend for themselves and in doing so successfully, are typically neglected or ignored.

Overall, we examined how Black women made sense of attending-college processes despite existing disinvestment barriers. The participants were goal oriented and expected to go to college. In other words, college was not simply an option; for most it was their only option. These findings support research by Patton and Ward (2016) pertaining to disposability politics and the disinvestment of Black women. Moreover, we learned that the women in this study showed signs of struggling successfully (Shaw, 2017) prior to even attending college.

Implications and Recommendations

We concluded that Black women use self-motivation skills to create college pathways for themselves. Although self-motivation is important for college choice and matriculation, self-motivation may be driven by the participants' sense that they are on their own rather than supported in the college-going process. We recommend educational practitioners do more to encourage college attendance among Black women by designing college-going pathways that are unique to the needs of those women. This would entail practitioners investing in Black women by learning about their experiences and their reasons for attending or wanting to attend college. We learned some Black women attend college to escape hometown settings or as a necessary next step to high achievement. Educational practitioners should be mindful of factors within these settings that might prove limiting for Black women with college aspirations. Asking them intentional questions, learning about their experiences, or meeting with them to assess their needs are all strategies that center Black women and allow their voices to be heard. However, more research is needed to discover other reasons for college attendance among Black women, aside from a desire to escape. Once those reasons are identified, practitioners can incorporate this information into programming, school counseling, and resources geared toward widening college pathways for Black women.

Although family members set expectations for Black women to attend college, more research should be done to better understand the extent to which these expectations shape the college research and choice process. Our research findings suggest Black women are often left to fend for themselves when it comes to the college-going process, but more information is warranted to confirm the impact of family expectations on college attendance for Black women. Moreover, research on Black women and college attendance should be explored in depth beyond family to examine the impact friends, peers, or sister circles have on their college pathways. We also recommend high school guidance counselors and university admissions officers do more to partner with one another to engage family members in discussions about college attendance. Because families affect college choice outcomes for Black women, including them in the process could be the type of investment needed to encourage college going.

This research speaks to the importance of supporting Black women who aspire to be college graduates by examining the various entities that support and hinder their postsecondary education. The postsecondary education of Black girls matters. Thus, as Black women scholars who reflected on our own process of learning about college and later attending college, we encourage practice as well as research designed to create a more equitable college choice process for Black women.

Discussion Questions

1. How can colleges better support Black women matriculants given college attendance is seen as a gateway to opportunity?
2. What type of investments can K–12 practitioners make in Black women to assist with the college-going process?
3. What are ways to disrupt the concept of struggling successfully for Black women in both K–12 and college settings?

Resource

Black Girl on Campus. https://www.blackgirloncampus.com/

Further Reading

Commodore, F., Baker, D. J., & Arroyo, A. T. (2018). *Black women college students: A guide to student success in higher education*. Routledge. https://doi .org/10.4324/9781315620244

Patton, L. D., & Croom, N. N. (Eds.). (2017). *Critical perspectives on Black women and college success*. Taylor & Francis. https://doi.org/10.4324/9781315744421

Zamani-Gallaher, E. M., & Polite, V. C. (Eds.). (2013). *African American females: Addressing challenges and nurturing the future*. MSU Press. https://www.jstor.org/stable/10.14321/j.ctt7zt8z0

References

Arbeit, C. A., & Horn, L. (2017). *A profile of the enrollment patterns and demographic characteristics of undergraduates at for-profit institutions* (NCES Statistics in Brief No. 2017416). National Center for Education Statistics. https://nces.ed.gov/pubsearch/pubsinfo.asp?pubid=2017416

Ashkenas, J., Park, H., & Pierce, A. (2017, August 24). Even with affirmative action, Blacks and Hispanics are more underrepresented at top colleges than 35 years ago. *New York Times*. https://www.nytimes.com/interactive/2017/08/24/us/affirmative-action.html

Bastedo, M. N., & Jaquette, O. (2011). Running in place: Low-income students and the dynamics of higher education stratification. *Educational Evaluation and Policy Analysis, 33*(3), 318–339. https://doi.org/10.3102/0162373711406718

Bielby, R., Posselt, J. R., Jaquette, O., & Bastedo, M. N. (2014). Why are women underrepresented in elite colleges and universities? A non-linear decomposition analysis. *Research in Higher Education, 55*(8), 735–760. https://doi.org/10.1007/s11162-014-9334-y

Black women students far outnumber Black men at the nation's highest-ranked universities. (n.d). *Journal of Blacks in Higher Education*. https://www.jbhe.com/news_views/51_gendergap_universities.html

Chavous, T., & Cogburn, C. D. (2007). Superinvisible women: Black girls and women in education. *Black Women, Gender & Families, 1*(2), 24–51. https://www.jstor.org/stable/10.5406/blacwomegendfami.1.2.0024

Cooper, A. J. (1892). *A voice from the South*. Aldine.

Crenshaw, K. (1989). Demarginalizing the intersection of race and sex: A black feminist critique of antidiscrimination doctrine, feminist theory and antiracist politics. *University of Chicago Legal Forum, 1989*, 139–168. https://chicagounbound.uchicago.edu/uclf/vol1989/iss1/8

Duster, C. R., & Tuakli, F. (2017, December 13). *Why black women voters showed up for Doug Jones*. NBC News. https://www.nbcnews.com/news/nbcblk/why-black-women-showed-vote-doug-jones-n829411

Evans, S. Y. (2008). *Black women in the ivory tower, 1850–1954: An intellectual history*. University Press of Florida.

Evans-Winters, V. E., & Esposito, J. (2010). Other people's daughters: Critical race feminism and Black girls' education. *Educational Foundations, 24*(1/2), 11–24. https://eric.ed.gov/?id=EJ885912

Gholson, M. L. (2016). Clean corners and algebra: A critical examination of the constructed invisibility of Black girls and women in mathematics. *The Journal of Negro Education, 85*(3), 290–301. https://doi.org/10.7709/jnegroeducation .85.3.0290

Giroux, H. (2006, September 1). *The politics of disposability.* Dissident Voice. http:// www.dissidentvoice.org/Sept06/Giroux01.htm

Guy-Sheftall, B. (1982). Black women and higher education: Spelman and Bennett colleges revisited. *The Journal of Negro Education, 51*(3), 278–287. https://doi .org/10.2307/2294695

Hubbard, L. (1999). College aspirations among low-income African American high school students: Gendered strategies for success. *Anthropology & Education Quarterly, 30*(3), 363–383. https://doi.org/10.1525/aeq.1999.30.3.363

Hussar, B., Zhang, J., Hein, S., Wang, K., Roberts, A., Cui, J., Smith, M., Bullock Mann, F., Barmer, A., & Dilig, R. (2020). *The condition of education 2020* (NCES 2020-144). National Center for Education Statistics. https://nces.ed.gov/ pubs2020/2020144.pdf

Iloh, C., & Toldson, I. A. (2013). Black students in 21st century higher education: A closer look at for-profit and community colleges. *The Journal of Negro Education, 82*(3), 205–212. https://doi.org/10.7709/jnegroeducation.82.3.0205

Jackson, S. J. (2016). (Re) imagining intersectional democracy from Black feminism to hashtag activism. *Women's Studies in Communication, 39*(4), 375–379. https:// doi.org/10.1080/07491409.2016.1226654

Morton, J. (2013, June 5). *Good news: Black women enroll in college more than any race and gender* [Web log post]. http://naturallymoi.com/2013/06/good-news-black-women-have-highest-college-enrollment-than-any-race/

Noble, J. L. (1957). Negro women today and their education. *The Journal of Negro Education, 26*(1), 15–21. https://doi.org/10.2307/2293318

Patton, L. D., & Ward, L. W. (2016). Missing Black undergraduate women and the politics of disposability: A critical race feminist perspective. *The Journal of Negro Education, 85*(3), 330–349. https://doi.org/10.7709/jnegroeducation.85.3.0330

Pearson, R. (2018, April 12). In Chicago speech, Clinton hails Black women voters for leading "hope and resilience" during Trump era. *Chicago Tribune.* https:// www.chicagotribune.com/politics/ct-met-hillary-clinton-chicago-speech-20180412-story.html

Perkins, L. M. (2015). "Bound to them by a common sorrow": African American women, higher education, and collective advancement. *Journal of African American History, 100*(4), 721–747. https://doi.org/10.5323/jafriamerhist.100.4.0721

Rogers, J. D. (2016). *Black women are the most educated group in the U.S.* Madame Noire. https://madamenoire.com/700338/black-women-are-the-most-educated/

Rusher, A. W. (1996). *African American women administrators.* University Press of America.

Sanford-Harris, J. (1990). *A profile of Black women college presidents and chief executive officers* [Unpublished doctoral dissertation]. Boston College.

Sesko, A. K., & Biernat, M. (2010). Prototypes of race and gender: The invisibility of Black women. *Journal of Experimental Social Psychology, 46*(2), 356–360. https://doi.org/10.1016/j.jesp.2009.10.016

Shaw, M. D. (2017). Supporting students who struggle successfully: Developing and institutionalizing support for Black undergraduate women. In L. D. Patton & N. N. Croom (Eds.), *Critical perspectives on Black women and college success* (pp. 200–212). Routledge.

Thomas, V. G., & Jackson, J. A. (2007). The education of African American girls and women: Past to present. *The Journal of Negro Education, 76*(3), 357–372. https://www.jstor.org/stable/40034578

Williams, V. (2016). Black women—Hillary Clinton's most reliable voting bloc—look beyond defeat. *Washington Post.* https://www.washingtonpost.com/politics/black-women--hillary-clintons-most-reliable-voting-bloc--look-beyond-defeat/2016/11/12/86d9182a-a845-11e6-ba59-a7d93165c6d4_story.html

KINKS, CURLS, AND BRAIDS

Untangling the Hidden Hair Politics of Undergraduate Black Women Student Leaders at Historically Black Colleges and Universities

Jamila L. Lee-Johnson

I keep a Blazer, a Wig, and a pair of Heels in my car, just in case I am called into a meeting.

—Kayla B., SGA vice president

From Afro Puffs to hair weaves, sisterlocks, relaxers, or even rocking hair in its natural state, hair has always been something that Black girls and women have constantly felt pressures from society about and dealt with in regard to their identity (Bellinger, 2007; Brownmiller, 1984; Byrd & Tharps, 2001; Patton, 2006; White, 2005). Utilizing social comparison theory (Thompson, 2009) and Black feminist thought (Collins, 2002), this chapter explores the experiences of four undergraduate Black women student leaders (Ziya, Jessie J., Kayla B., and Missy) as they navigate the politics of wearing their hair a certain way while being in the position of a student leader on a historically Black college and university (HBCU) campus.

Since slavery, Black women and men have found and tried various ways to alter or texture their hair in order to make their hair straight (Banks, 2000). Hair texture alteration among Black women has held a tenacious hold on the culture, expectations, discrimination, oppression, and self-identity of Black women. Mercer (2000) suggested that "as an aesthetic practice inscribed in everyday life, all Black hairstyles are political in that they each articulate responses to the panoply of historical forces which have invested this element of the ethnic signifier with both symbolic meaning and significance" (p. 112). A modern Black woman may explain her hair by stating that she is not trying to conform to a "White" standard of beauty. An example of this is a Black woman straightening her hair before a job interview in order to be seen as professional. Often, we as Black women make decisions about our self-identity, self-acceptance, even job security due to European standards. Although the dialogue about hair has expanded and Black women can more readily name the pressure around particular hair styles as conformity to Eurocentric beauty standards, that does not relieve the pressures to conform, nor does it relieve the penalties and repercussions from society for nonconformity.

For Black women collectively, our hair defines us, but impacts us each differently. Every day Black women have to decide how to wear their hair in all spaces because racism, sexism, and discrimination permeate society (Ladson-Billings, 2009). The military, K–12 schools, colleges, and even workplaces have had discrimination policies about Black hair. Black girls and women wear their hair in various styles for numerous reasons; however, when some of these styles are not accepted by dominant culture, then it becomes a problem for Black women. For example, Bellinger (2007) found that at an early age, Black girls are socialized to adopt a more Eurocentric standard of beauty (such as straight hair). Furthermore, Banks (2000) discovered that Black children, specifically between the ages of 3 and 4, have a good understanding of what "good" hair means and the social hierarchy it can create for them. Having "good hair" is often a myth dictated by society, that in order to have "good hair" your hair should be of a straightened or loosely curly texture. Black children are taught at an early age that having nappy hair is shameful (Banks, 2000; Bellinger, 2007). Not only do Black girls and women experience discrimination about their hair from their families and communities, but they also experience it in schools and in the workplace.

Hair-Story1 of Discrimination Against Black Women

Although some may believe that hair straightening is a vestige of the past, it is actually still a phenomenon of the present. For Black girls and women, how they wear or style their hair is still a major topic of discussion when it comes to attending school or even going to work (Lee-Johnson & Henderson, 2019). Society's policing of Black women's hair (this includes but is not limited to family, friends, teachers, administrators, military, etc.) explains how visual presentation is only acceptable through narrow frames of White supremacy and its patriarchal and hegemonic order (hooks, 1984; Patton, 2017). Before there were campaigns like "Nappily Ever After"[2] or "My Black Is Beautiful"[3] that were centered around standards of beauty for Black women, activists like W.E.B. Du Bois and Booker T. Washington would often talk about Black women's hair subliminally in their speeches (Patton, 2017). For example, Booker T. Washington and other Black men activists worried that Black women straightening their hair would lead to the internalization of White standards of beauty (Patton, 2017). In Du Bois's "Damnation of Women" essay, he described hair as a mark of heritage and that Black women will be judged by Black men's White standard of beauty (Du Bois, 1995). Du Bois then acknowledged that he is not one of those Black men who judges Black women's beauty features. But the mere fact that he mentions hair is evidence that he is also interested in how Black women wear their hair.

The themes of Du Bois's discussion of women and their hair is also visible in present-day educational settings where men as leaders have dictated how girls and women are to wear their hair and what is deemed appropriate (Thompson, 2009). The judgment of Black women's hair often sits at the intersection of racism and sexism (C. Jacobs, personal communication, October, 2020). Du Bois's (1940; cited in Rabaka, 2003) and Washington's comments are examples of how sexism comes into play in regard to Black women. For example, if a Black man was to wear their hair or dress a certain way, they would not be criticized as much or as often as Black women (Lee-Johnson, 2019). That Du Bois and Washington were prominent Black male leaders who had and still have the ears of many Black and White people is significant in that their judgments about Black women and their hair could easily be adopted by others and seen as being the truth (C. Jacobs, personal communication, October, 2020).

K–12 and Black Hair Discrimination

In K–12 educational spaces, Black girls and women are confronted about their hair from their own race and about what dominant beauty ideals and their hair textures should look like from school policies. So much so that the federal government, the Department of Education, and school districts also have had a say in how we wear our hair. For example, in 2016, a public high school in Kentucky introduced a new dress code that included banning twists, dreadlocks, and Afros longer than 2 inches (Wilson, 2016). In 2018, a school leader in Louisiana asked an 11-year-old Black girl to leave class because her hair was braided with extensions. The school's policy wrote that only a student's natural hair was permitted and that extensions, wigs, and hair pieces of any kind were not allowed (Perry, 2019). When elementary and middle schools are attempting to regulate Black girls' hair through dress codes, these policies can have lasting effects that then create future leaders who enforce Eurocentric standards of beauty onto other Black women.

How Society Views Black Women Leaders

There is typically a double jeopardy when it comes to Black women's leadership (Jean-Marie et al., 2009). That double jeopardy is race and gender. Black women have a long history of leadership from slavery up through the Black Lives Matter movement and beyond (Garza, 2014). However, Black women have not always been given the recognition that they deserve regarding leadership. Myers's (2002) study of Black women in the academy illustrated how Black women at both predominantly Black and White institutions experience racism and sexism. For example, many women have experienced being silenced, not taken seriously, and have been even expected to take on a matronly role within the academy. Similar to Myers (2002), Bonner and Thomas (2001) found that Black women leaders at HBCUs face more sexism from their Black male counterparts than Black women at predominantly White institutions. Black women leaders continue to be ridiculed and policed based on their gender.

The Politics of Being a Black Woman Leader at an HBCU

For Black women, HBCUs are supposed to be places of refuge that provide a supportive environment (Davis, 2014; Njoku et al., 2017). However, since the beginning of their inception and creation, HBCUs have had certain standards for Black women that may not have always been the same for Black men. For example, being a "proper young lady" enrolled in an HBCU during the early years consisted of dressing appropriately, including hair being neat, and refraining from using profanity (Commodore et al., 2018). Although some of these ideals may have changed over time, many of them still apply at HBCUs. For example, at some HBCUs, Black women students and administrators are not encouraged to raise issues around gender on their college campuses (Njoku et al., 2017).

Although HBCUs often serve as places for Black women to thrive, they also have their challenges at these institutions. Situated in environments where Black men dominate, such as HBCU campuses, Black women struggle to assert themselves, which leads to decreased success (Fleming, 1984). An example of this is that when articles are written about HBCUs, they are often male-centered and portray Black women as if they were not even present (Gasman, 2007). In reality, Black women at HBCUs graduate in higher numbers than Black men, and according to the National Center for Education Statistics, Black women represent more than 61% of the student population at HBCUs (Nealy, 2008). Another example of Black women being forgotten is through student involvement. Harper et al. (2004) and Bond (2011) found that although Black women were as equally involved on HBCU campuses as Black men, they were less likely to receive as much attention as Black men because there are so few Black men enrolled on college campuses. However, I would argue that Black women's experiences in student leadership and participation in student organizations help prepare them for the realities of civil, political, and social life they will encounter after graduating from college.

Beauty Standards at HBCUs

HBCUs are not new to controversy regarding hair and dress, as they are often known for being very traditional and conservative and often adhere to mainstream society's views on gender and what is deemed respectable attire or looks for Black men and women (Grundy, 2012; Mobley & Johnson, 2019). Njoku and Patton (2017) and Harper and Gasman (2008) both emphasized that HBCUs can be very conservative in regard to attire and often have policies that require students to dress and look professional. For example, both Hampton University (in 2012) and Morehouse College (in 2009) implemented policies banning natural hairstyles and attire for men (Mobley & Johnson, 2019). In regard to hair and dress, HBCUs often have a constructed campus environment that shapes how Black women are viewed based on their identity (Njoku & Patton, 2017).

Social Comparison Theory, Black Feminist Thought, and Hair

The personal stories and the research on Black women mentioned earlier help to lay the foundation for the theoretical lenses through which to view this topic of navigating the politics of being a Black woman leader and their hair on campus. Social comparison theory (SCT) provides a measure to how and why people compare themselves to societal standards when assessing their own behaviors (Thompson, 2009). When thinking about Black women's hair, SCT and part of Collins's (2002) Black feminist thought (BFT) theory focused on how controlling images depicting Black women in U.S. society can provide a critical lens as to why undergraduate Black woman leaders make certain choices with their hair. BFT is a theory that is designed to center Black women's lived experiences. Controlling images about Black women have been around since the beginning of slavery and continue to have an impact on how Black women are portrayed (Collins, 2002). Skin color, facial features, and hair texture are a few examples of controlling images and how they derogate Black women (Collins, 2002). Some examples of controlled images of Black women are Mammy,[4] Aunt Jemima,[5] and Black women in beauty pageants who almost always are wearing their hair straight or have a wig—very few are seen with their hair in its natural state.

Methodology

The research presented in this chapter stems from a larger critical life stories project (Atkinson, 1998; Carspecken, 1996) that examined the experiences of 18 undergraduate Black women leaders from 15 public and private HBCUs across the United States and explored their leadership experiences from precollege through college. For the purpose of this study, "leaders" were defined as women who had been elected into student government–affiliated positions (i.e., student government president, their executive cabinet, or the university's campus queen). The data in this chapter are from four student leaders who were their universities' student government officers: SGA president, vice president, chief of staff, and campus queen (see Table 10.1). This study took place with undergraduate Black women leaders, and specifically dealt with college-aged Black women. I refer to them collectively as Black women leaders to be inclusive of the types of pressures that they have faced not only at the collegiate level but also since early childhood. Participants were interviewed twice: once when they were first elected and then after they had been in their positions for one full academic semester.

Table 10.1 shows more information about the four women in this chapter. Participants were all seniors in college and had recently been elected into their positions. Each participant participated in two 90-minute interviews. One key question that the participants were asked was "Do you wear your hair a certain way as a student leader?" Other questions participants were asked included the following:

1. Does the way I wear my hair make me a better leader?
2. Does the way I wear my hair make me look less professional?
3. Does the way I wear my hair offend other Black women?
4. Do I need to look a certain way to be a leader?

TABLE 10.1
Student Government Participants

Name	Public or Private HBCU	Student Leadership Position Title	Classification	Major
Ziya	Public	Campus queen	Senior	Chemistry
Missy	Private	Chief of staff	Senior	Psychology
Kayla B.	Private	SGA vice president	Senior	Nursing
Jess J.	Private	SGA president	Senior	Biochemistry

Participants described that they wear their hair in various styles such as wigs, sew-ins, Afros, or straightened as a student leader. Many of the women in this study revealed that they chose to wear a wig or maybe have their hair straightened for convenience and so that they won't receive questionable looks from faculty, staff, and peers at their schools. For the purposes of this chapter, I will focus on how Ziya, Missy, Kayla B., and Jess J.'s hair has shaped their experiences with leadership and how it has affected how they lead or feel that they are perceived as leaders on campus.

Findings

The findings of this study support BFT's controlling images narrative and revealed that social comparison theory (SCT) did exist in what these Black women thought of themselves as leaders. SCT exists when people compare themselves to what society has deemed as a standard, while still acknowledging their own behavior. SCT made the Black women leaders in this study have to focus more on how they looked than how they governed. There were two major findings from this study: *Sis, why are you discriminating on me and we have the same hair* and *Sometimes it didn't matter what I did; I was judged by my appearance first.*

Sis, Why Are You Discriminating on Me and We Have the Same Hair?

There is often a narrative regarding how others view Black women leaders, but there is no real understanding or statement from Black women themselves and how they view themselves or other Black women as leaders. As mentioned earlier, in society, men and those in power who are outside of Black women's culture often dictate how Black women should dress, act, and even wear their hair. However, sometimes it is not just men; it also can be other women who offer critique and reinforce harmful norms as well. The data that emerged from this study explored how the Black women leaders perceived how their hair should look as a leader on campus. Based on their responses, I compiled some of the participants' responses from their interviews and developed this chart based on how they felt their hair needed to be as a student leader. The words and phrases listed in the chart (see Table 10.2) have impacted these Black women leaders so much that many of them are not interested in wearing their hair in its natural state so that they can be taken seriously as a campus leader.

Based on the words listed in Table 10.2, the Black women leaders in this study self-internalized how they looked and in turn projected some of those

TABLE 10.2
Chronicles of Hair

As a student leader on campus, my hair has to be . . .	<ul><li>tamed</li><li>natural</li><li>straight</li><li>combed</li><li>curled</li><li>professional</li></ul>

same feelings of internalization onto other Black women leaders. For example, Ziya, a campus queen,[6] felt like she had to wear or have multiple wigs, because the previous campus queen had wigs in order to keep up with all the appearances she had to have in her position. This is a deficit approach and an attack on their ability to be leaders. It is as if how they wear their hair is not good enough, so therefore it has to be molded into something more acceptable and presentable.

Missy, SGA chief of staff, wore her hair natural, but she kept her Afro "tamed" and not all over the place (in her own words). Although many of the women in this study would argue that they are not trying to conform to a certain standard regarding their hair and leadership, they are. Altering their hair has had a major impact on how they view themselves as leaders or how others view them as a leader. In the following, Missy and Jess J. mention instances of being excluded by other Black women on their campuses just because of how they wore their hair:

> A lot of the time women tell me to tame my hair. Women. Black women. Tell me to tame my hair, because I have other students looking up to me, and I'm not understanding why my hair is an issue. The only reason why some of these women's hair is tamed because they have weaves, so, I'm really not getting it and that's something that really bothered me, because as Black women we're supposed to uplift other Black women. That's something that we're supposed to do and you're putting me down to tell me: "Oh, you need to change this, you need to change that about yourself, you don't need to be too boisterous, you need to be ladylike." That word bothers me. Like, you need to be ladylike and I'm, like, "What is ladylike?" Ladylike is conforming to what a man wants me to do and they're not in my shoes, so, I don't understand why I've got to perform to what the hell they want. I'm good. (Missy, SGA chief of staff)

Missy, who wears her hair in an Afro, was highly offended that other Black women (in this case faculty and administrators from her institution) told her she needed to tame her hair. As I spoke with Missy, she was very bothered that other Black women were conforming to society's standards of what a Black woman leader should be. This an example of BFT's controlling images and hegemonic domain of power. Hegemonic domains of power in the consciousness are the manipulations of ideas, images, and symbols (Collins, 2002). The faculty and administrators felt that because Missy was a student leader and other students were looking up to her, her hair needed to be a certain way. When the women brought up being "ladylike," it was an example of how society has placed a standard on them of what and how a woman should behave. Similar to Missy, Jess J. experienced not wanting to wear a certain hair style for fear of how others would view her while being SGA president.

> When I first began my presidency, I was way more self-conscious about what people would think of how I should wear my hair or stuff like that. I was always concerned about wearing box braids. I don't really see people in the professional realm wearing box braids, so maybe as SGA President I shouldn't wear them. . . . There came to a point, where I decided I didn't want to care. So, I gave one of my speeches with braids, and I got so many compliments even from administrators about it, and it made me feel good. (Jess J., SGA president)

For Black women, hair is a major component of who they are and a symbol of their identity (Thompson, 2009). Given that Jess J. was in a leadership role, at first she was uncomfortable with the idea of wearing box braids as a leader because she had not seen many other professional women wear them. Jess J. experienced uneasiness at being her authentic self simply because of a hairstyle. She experienced a form of prejudice that often, presumably, impacted her and other Black women on campus who do not feel comfortable being themselves because of how they wore their hair. For many participants in this study, the way they wore their hair or dressed played an important role in how they viewed themselves as student leaders. I found that participants reflected throughout this entire study on how often they were judged first by how they looked versus what came out of their mouths.

Sometimes It Didn't Matter What I Did, I Was Judged by My Looks First

One time, I was having a bad hair day, and I just did not have time to do my hair because I'd been up all night studying for a test. So, I put on one of the various wigs that I own, and a really cute hat to go and take my test. Before I could finish taking my test, my phone was buzzing off the hook. Someone had taken a picture of me in my hat, and sent to an upper level administrator. I got in trouble because I was told I did not look "regal or queenly" enough. After that I was told, I could not wear hats anymore. (Ziya, campus queen)

Ziya was a campus queen on her college campus. Similar to other women in this study, hair played a major role in leadership as the campus queen. After being reprimanded and being told that she was not regal enough, Ziya felt as if more emphasis was placed on her hair and looks versus who she was as a leader. Ziya experienced an example of a controlling image in relationship to BFT—she had to maintain a certain image as a campus queen that society (in this case her college campus) had placed on her. Ziya being reprimanded is also an example of how she felt she needed to conform to be like a previous leader was before her—SCT. For example, she felt that because the previous queen wore wigs and did everything correctly, she had to do similar things. Similar to Ziya, Kayla B. wore wigs in her student leadership role:

> I keep a blazer, a wig, and a pair of heels in my car, just in case I am called into a meeting and need to jazz it up. Being natural in Louisiana the humidity is not my friend at all so I am constantly recurling my hair, making sure that it's not all over my head or looking untamed. So it is just easier for me to wear a wig. I keep a wig with me, so that when I get to campus, and I get called into a meeting, I don't look crazy. I knew what I signed up for being SGA Vice-President, and I knew what image I needed to maintain to assure my student body that they elected the right woman for the job. (Kayla B., SGA vice president)

Kayla B. knew that she had a certain image to maintain in order for her peers to take her seriously. Yet the fact that she felt like she needed to carry a wig with her because she did not want to be "looking crazy" if she got called into a meeting is absurd. Kayla felt as if she would be judged first by her hair before even making an appearance. Kayla experienced SCT from her peers because she felt as if she had to maintain a certain look in order be taken seriously, versus her peers listening to what she had to say.

Missy, Kayla B., Ziya, and Jess J. experienced various forms of SCT and discrimination regarding their hair. We know that Black women's hair is often judged very differently than that of their peers, but these women almost have a triple standard going on: They have to be a student leader, a woman, and a student. With all of the things these women have going, the last issue that they should be worried about is how they are viewed because of their hair.

Discussion and Conclusion

In reflecting on Black women, controlling images, and hair, bell hooks (2001) wrote, "The reality is: straightened hair is linked historically and currently to a system of racial domination that impresses upon Black people, and especially Black women, that we are not acceptable as we are, that we are not beautiful" (p. 115). However, it cannot be assumed that a majority of Black women who choose to straighten their hair in order to achieve "good" hair status are practicing self-hatred. These ideas and images of having "good hair" or having to dress or look a certain way are not new to many of these women, because many of them have been experiencing this since girlhood, and many of the same messages they are receiving in college were also present in the K–12 environment.

When HBCUs or even faculty and administrators at these institutions place the emphasis that student leaders need to have straight or tamed hair, that causes a major problem. I would argue that institutions of higher education as a whole, including administrators, faculty, and peers, impose unfounded expectations and preconceived notions on Black women based on aesthetic features such as skin and hair and political ideologies associated with those features. One way that HBCUs in particular can address this issue is by deconstructing the aesthetics of what a Black woman leader should look like. When these women are running for office, they should be encouraged to truly be themselves and that should include how they look and dress. Women should not be encouraged to go out and spend money on beauty standards in order to just receive a vote or like. When HBCUs enforce beauty standards they are reinforcing White patriarchal standards of what Black girls and women should look like. These standards reinforce respectability politics, and I am calling on HBCU administrators to stop judging these Black girls and women so harshly. These women are students first before they become student leaders, and when certain respectability politics are forced on to them, it places a double standard on who they are as Black women and leaders. These Black women leaders want to be leaders who create systemic change on their campuses; how they wear their hair should not be a priority on the list. For Black girls and women, society already places a lot of expectations on us to be more than what we should be, and hair should not be our main concern.

Discussion Questions

1. What are some of the experiences of Black women concerning hair on your college campus?
2. What opportunities are there for leadership for Black women on your campus?
3. What kinds of support systems are there in place for Black women on your campus? What types of support systems are needed?
4. What does leadership look like for Black women (students, faculty, and administrators) on your campus?

Resources

Listen to Solange's *Don't Touch my Hair.*
www.thecrownact.com (A bill that was passed in the state of California that offers protection against employers and schools that instate rules requiring "race-neutral" hair styles).
Chris Rock's (2009) movie *Good Hair.*

Notes

1. *Hair-Story* is used to represent *history* in this chapter; this word was often cited in other articles describing Black women and their hair (e.g., Brisbown, 2007; Patton, 2017).

2. *Nappily Ever After* was a book written about a Black woman who finds freedom within herself after she cuts her hair and begins to wear it natural.

3. My Black is Beautiful is a campaign designed to celebrate African American women and encourage them to promote a beauty standard that is an authentic reflection of themselves.

4. Mammy is a domestic worker and servant who works at a White man's home catering to his wife and children. Mammy is often punished for not displaying a pleasant personality (Collins, 2002).

5. Aunt Jemima is based on the enslaved "Mammy" archetype. Aunt Jemima represents an example of exploitation during slavery of Black women who were the cooks.

6. Campus queens at HBCUs are often the face of the university. The queen has a platform that she creates that year for the university. She is typically voted on by her peers and will also represent the university at various philanthropic events.

Further Reading

Cooper, B. C. (2017). *Beyond respectability: The intellectual thought of race women.* University of Illinois Press. Cooper talks about the National Association of Colored Women and Club Movement; she describes how Mary Church Terrell reinforced respectability, such that she wanted Black women fighting for justice to be dignified in style of dress.

Cooper, B. (2018). *Eloquent rage: A Black feminist discovers her superpower.* St. Martin's Press. There is a chapter where Cooper mentions when she ran for SGA president at Howard University; she details issues around colorism, hair, and body image.

Ford, T. C. (2012). Soul generation: Radical fashion, beauty, and the transnational black liberation movement, 1954–1980. *Journal of Pan African Studies, 5*(1), 294–296. https://go.gale.com/ps/i.do?id=GALE%7CA306514728&sid=google Scholar&v=2.1&it=r&linkaccess=abs&issn=08886601&p=AONE&sw=w&userGroupName=anon%7E4bbf7776

Ford, T. C. (2015). *Liberated threads: Black women, style, and the global politics of soul.* UNC Press Books.

Harris, P. J. (2003). Gatekeeping and remaking: The politics of respectability in African American women's history and Black feminism. *Journal of Women's History, 15*(1), 212–220. https://muse.jhu.edu/article/43088/summary

Higginbotham, E. B. (1994). *Righteous discontent: The women's movement in the Black Baptist church, 1880–1920.* Harvard University Press.

References

Atkinson, R. (1998). *The life story interview.* Sage.

Banks, I. (2000). *Hair matters: Beauty, power, and Black women's consciousness.* New York University Press.

Bellinger, W. (2007). Why African American women try to obtain "good hair." *Sociological Viewpoints, 23,* 63. http://citeseerx.ist.psu.edu/viewdoc/download?doi=10.1.1.473.1938&rep=rep1&type=pdf

Bond, H. (2011). Black females in higher education at HBCUs: The paradox of success. In C. R. Chambers (Ed.), *Support systems and services for diverse populations: Considering the intersection of race, gender, and the needs of Black female undergraduates* (pp. 131–144). Emerald Group Publishing Limited.

Bonner, F. B., & Thomas, V. G. (2001). Introduction and overview: New and continuing challenges and opportunities for Black women in the academy. *The Journal of Negro Education, 70*(3), 121–123. https://doi.org/10.2307/3211204

Brownmiller, S. (1984). *Femininity.* Fawcett Columbine.

Byrd, A. D., & Tharps, L. L. (2001). *Hair story: Untangling the roots of black hair in America.* St. Martin's/Griffin.

Carspecken, P. F. (1996). *Critical ethnography in educational research: A theoretical and practical guide.* Psychology Press.

Collins, P. H. (2002). *Black feminist thought: Knowledge, consciousness, and the politics of empowerment.* Routledge.

Commodore, F., Baker, D. J., & Arroyo, A. T. (2018). *Black women college students: A guide to student success in higher education.* Routledge.

Davis, L. D. (2014). Preserving respectability or blatant disrespect: A critical discourse analysis of the Morehouse College Appropriate Attire Policy and implications for intersectional approaches to examining campus policies. *International Journal of Qualitative Studies in Education, 27*(6), 724–746. https://doi.org/10.1080/09518398.2014.901576

Du Bois, W. E. B. (1995). *WEB Du Bois: A reader.* Macmillan.

Fleming, J. (1984). *Blacks in college.* Jossey-Bass.

Garza, A. (2014). *A herstory of the Black Lives Matter movement.* The Feminist Wire. https://thefeministwire.com/2014/10/blacklivesmatter-2/

Gasman, M. (2007). Swept under the rug? A historiography of gender and Black colleges. *American Educational Research Journal, 44*(4), 760–805. https://doi.org/10.3102/0002831207308639

Grundy, S. (2012). "An air of expectancy": Class, crisis, and the making of manhood at a historically Black college for men. *Annals of the American Academy of Political and Social Science, 642*(1), 43–60. https://doi.org/10.1177/0002716212438203

Harper, S. R., & Gasman, M. (2008). Consequences of conservatism: Black male undergraduates and the politics of historically black colleges and universities. *The Journal of Negro Education, 77*, 336–351. https://www.jstor.org/stable/25608703

Harper, S. R., Karini, R. M., Bridges, B. K., & Hayek, J. C. (2004). Gender differences in student engagement among African American undergraduates at historically Black colleges and universities. *Journal of College Student Development, 45*(3), 271–284. https://muse.jhu.edu/article/171136/summary

hooks, b. (1984). *Feminist theory: From margin to center*. South End Press.

hooks, b. (2001). Straightening our hair. In J. Harris and P. Johnson (Eds.), *Tenderheaded: A comb-bending collection of hair stories* (pp. 111–115). Pocket Books.

Jean-Marie, G., Williams, V. A., & Sherman, S. L. (2009). Black women's leadership experiences: Examining the intersectionality of race and gender. *Advances in Developing Human Resources, 11*(5), 562–581. https://doi.org/10.1177/1523422309351836

Ladson-Billings, G. (2009). Critical race theory in education. In M. W. Apple, W. Au, & L. A. Gandin (Eds.), *The Routledge international handbook of critical education* (pp. 110–122). Routledge.

Lee-Johnson, J. L. (2019). *I am becoming: Understanding the experiences of undergraduate black women at historically black colleges and universities in elected student leadership positions* [Doctoral dissertation, University of Wisconsin-Madison]. ProQuest Dissertations Publishing 13900800.

Lee-Johnson, J., & Henderson, L. (2019) Using social media to (re)center Black women's voices in educational research. In R. Winkle-Wagner, J. Lee-Johnson, & A. Gaskew (Eds.), *Critical theory and qualitative data analysis in education* (pp. 223–235). Routledge.

Mercer, K. (2000). Black hair/style politics. In K. Owusu (Ed.), *Black British culture and society: A text reader* (pp. 111–121). Routledge.

Mobley, S. D., Jr., & Johnson, J. M. (2019). "No pumps allowed": The "problem" with gender expression and the Morehouse College "appropriate attire" policy. *Journal of Homosexuality, 66*(7), 867–895. https://doi.org/10.1080/00918369.2018.1486063

Myers, L. W. (2002). *A broken silence: Voices of African American women in the academy*. Greenwood Publishing.

Nealy, M. J. (2008, March 5). Status of black women and HBCUs: Focus of urban league report. *Diverse*. National Urban League. https://www.diverseeducation.com/leadership-policy/article/15086795/status-of-black-women-and-hbcus-focus-of-urban-league-report

Njoku, N., Butler, M., & Beatty, C. C. (2017). Reimagining the historically Black college and university (HBCU) environment: Exposing race secrets and the binding chains of respectability and othermothering. *International Journal of*

Qualitative Studies in Education, 30(8), 783–799. https://doi.org/10.1080/095 18398.2017.1350297

Njoku, N. R., & Patton, L. D. (2017). Explorations of respectability and resistance in constructions of Black womanhood at HBCUs. In L. D. Patton & N. N. Croom (Eds.), *Critical perspectives on Black women and college success* (pp. 143–157). Routledge.

Patton, T. O. (2006). Hey girl, am I more than my hair?: African American women and their struggles with beauty, body image, and hair. *NWSA journal, 18*(2), 24–51. https://www.jstor.org/stable/4317206

Patton, T. O. (2017). Hair, racism, and marginalization in the "equality state." In L. D. Patton & N. N. Croom (Eds.), *Critical perspectives on Black women and college success* (pp. 141–156). Routledge.

Perry, A. (2019, March 5). Schools are policing Black kids' hair, and Betsy DeVos needs to stop them. *Nation.* https://www.thenation.com/article/hair-school-education-betsy-devos/

Rabaka, R. (2003). WEB Du Bois and "The Damnation of Women": An essay on Africana anti-sexist critical social theory. *Journal of African American Studies, 7*(2), 37–60.

Thompson, C. (2009). Black women, beauty, and hair as a matter of being. *Women's Studies, 38*(8), 831–856. https://doi.org/10.1080/00497870903238463

White, S. B. (2005). Releasing the pursuit of bouncin' and behavin' hair: Natural hair as an Afrocentric feminist aesthetic for beauty. *International Journal of Media and Cultural Politics, 1*(3), 295–308. https://doi.org/10.1386/macp.1.3.295/1

Wilson, J. (2016, July 29). Kentucky high school's dress code "stinks of racism," bans dreadlocks, cornrows and braids. *Essence.* https://www.essence.com/hair/natural/kentucky-high-school-bans-natural-hairstyles-racism/

II

BLACK UNDERGRADUATE WOMEN NAVIGATING (MIS)REPRESENTATION, STRENGTH, AND STRATEGIES

An Analysis of Influences on Their Mental Wellness

Janice A. Byrd and Christa J. Porter

Much of the scholarship that focuses on Black undergraduate women (BUW) on college campuses discusses academic development (e.g., retention, academic performance and success, college acceptance Banks, 2009; Commodore et al., 2018; Patton & Croom, 2017), career trajectory (e.g., career pathways, STEM fields, graduate school preparation; Gibson & Espino, 2016; Porter et al., 2018; Storlie et al., 2018), and identity development (Hannon et al., 2016; Porter, 2017; Porter & Dean, 2015; Porter et al., 2020), but little on their social/emotional and mental wellness needs. Katz and Davison (2014) shared that undergraduate students generally experience psychological challenges such as stress, anxiety disorders, depression, trauma/crisis, and adjustment disorders. However, BUW face culturally specific mental health concerns beyond the common issues to include, but not limited to, gendered racism and trauma (Szymanski & Lewis, 2016), stereotyping (Donovan, 2011), and body image and beauty (Hesse-Biber et al., 2010). Collectively, the consequences of these concerns directly influence BUW's identity, academic, and career development and can cause psychological concerns over the course of their life span (Katz & Davison, 2014; Thomas et al., 2008).

These culturally specific issues are not merely a result of Black women's upbringing or caused by individual characteristics; they are a result of perpetuated systemic oppression, subjugation, and racial barbarity experienced over many centuries (Collins, 1990; Hernton, 1965; hooks, 1981). Black women's social location has been predicated by exploitation of their bodies, experiences, and their status of being invisible yet hypervisible at the same time while little concern is given to how they make meaning of, heal from, and develop despite these circumstances (Collins, 1990; Crenshaw, 2016; Mowatt et al., 2013).

Positionality of Researchers

We identify as Black, cisgender women with varied academic trajectories as students, educators, and faculty, as well as personal (and socially constructed) identities situated within both predominantly White and Black spaces. Our previous and current experiences as Black women guide our individual (and collective) research agendas; we center the experiences of Black women and girls across the educational pipeline and their trajectories and development into and within higher education. We consider ourselves critical qualitative researchers because we not only explore experiences but also examine the systems and structures that hinder and/or facilitate Black women's growth and development.

Theoretical Framework

Triple consciousness attends to the unique dynamics that undergird our understanding of BUW on college campuses by highlighting how they make meaning of their present context (e.g., person living in the United States), racialized identity, gendered identity, and their physical body and the connection to their ancestors (De Walt, 2013; Fanon, 1967). To examine these dynamics in depth, we employ intersectionality (Collins, 1990; Collins & Bilge, 2016; Crenshaw, 1989, 1991) as a theoretical framework to interrogate how research discusses the mental wellness of Black women on college campuses. Intersectionality honors how the intertwined nature of race, gender, class, and sexuality is important to consider when attempting to understand the unique experiences of Black women. Incomplete and inaccurate narratives are created when one assumes race and gender are exclusive of one another (Crenshaw, 1989). Crenshaw asserted to focus on race or gender solely as the reference point of discrimination "creates a distorted analysis of racism and sexism because the operative conceptions of race and sex become grounded in experiences that actually represent only a subset of a much more complex phenomenon" (p. 140). As a result, intersectionality extends the critical analyses of oppression, which is imperative considering Black women hold membership of multiple marginalized identities (e.g., race, gender, and social class) within larger systems and structures of oppression.

Critical Discourse Analysis

We performed a critical discourse analysis (CDA) to illuminate the ways Black women's experiences in college have been discussed throughout recent published articles. Critical discourse analysis uses language to mediate relationships between privilege and power in bodies of knowledge or institutions; it moves beyond simple description to articulate various versions of the social world (Foucault, 1969/1972; Wodak, 2001). CDA assesses the reproduction and repetition of ideology in language without a particular focus on frameworks or theories (Fairclough, 1992). The following three dimensions of analysis represent Fairclough's (1989) CDA model: (a) the object of analysis (e.g., visual, verbal, or both texts); (b) how the object is received or produced (e.g., speaking, writing); and (c) the social and historical conditions through which the processes are governed. Additionally, each dimension necessitates a particular type of analysis—descriptive, interpretation or processing, and explanation. Everett and Croom (2017) conducted a CDA to examine the ways Black women's experiences were narrated across higher education and student affairs journals. They extended Fairclough's model by specifically naming their interpretations as the following three constructions: Black women as race plus gender, persistence in the face of diversity, and preeminence of interdependent relationships.

Data Collection

We reviewed journal articles across disciplines—journals specific to both counseling and higher education and any academic journal/article both relevant to our conditions and published between 2008 and 2018. Our analysis was limited to a 10-year time frame so we could deeply explore how more recent scholarship situated conversations about Black women. We collected data in four parts in order to narrow our initial list of 1,764 published articles to our final list of 35. First, we identified articles in all databases available to us through our institutional library (e.g., ERIC, APA PsycInfo, Academic Search Complete, Education Research Complete, ProjectMUSE, Scopus, and JSTOR) by using the keywords "Black women or African American women" AND "undergraduate or college" OR "Black females or African American females." We specified conditions on age by including only "young adulthood (18–29)" and "adulthood (18 or older)" as well as articles in scholarly journals and academic journals during 2008–2018. Second, we read each title and abstract to eliminate any studies not focused specifically on BUW; we eliminated research on Black girls and any study that compared Black women to White men, Black men, and/or other women of color. This second step collapsed our initial set of 1,764 to 68 articles and we then created an Excel spreadsheet with information on each article (e.g., title, year, author, citation, journal, link to article, and abstract). Third, we cross-checked the list against our discipline-specific journals (e.g., higher education, student affairs, and counseling) and refereed journals unavailable through our institution library (e.g., *Journal of College Counseling* and *The Journal of Negro Education*). We reviewed each journal's website for every volume and issue from 2008–2018 and found 10 additional articles. Finally, we read all 78 articles and focused on Black women's experiences in relation to success and identity development in college. Keywords that assisted us narrowing down the 78 to 35 included the following: *identity, development, self-concept, success, achievement, persistence*, and/or *sense of belonging*.

Data Analysis

We used Fairclough's (1989) CDA dimensions to guide our analysis of the 35 articles. How Black women's experiences in higher education were discussed was the object of our analysis. Our first analysis yielded the following nine descriptive topical areas across the 35 articles: interpersonal relationships (one article), family (two articles), group support (two articles), leadership (two articles), spirituality (two articles), mental and physical well-being (five articles), the intersection of race and gender (five articles), science, engineering, technology, and mathematics (STEM; five articles), and institutional environment (11 articles). Our next analysis included the process or interpretation of how the object is produced; by reviewing article findings, discussion, and implications sections, we examined how authors made meaning of Black women's experiences. We identified 102 total categorical interpretations across the 35 articles. Third, we analyzed sociohistorical factors that influenced Black women's experiences in college. In alignment with Everett and Croom's (2017) previous CDA study, we identified these 11 explanations or influences as constructions.

Discussion of Findings

Our interdisciplinary data collection and analysis of published articles within the past 10 years examined how the narratives of Black women's experiences in college were constructed in the literature. Chapter findings focused on the following four of the 11 total constructions: (a) being a Black woman as not a monolithic experience, (b) the cost(s) of being strong, (c) wellness threats and strategies, and (d) maintaining relationships and roles.

Being a Black Woman Is Not a Monolithic Experience

Black women not only have diverse identities among each other but they also experience and make meaning of these identities differently depending on various factors—for example, institutional context, precollegiate socialization and upbringing, identity saliency and intersections, and understanding of their social location(s) within systems of oppression (Corbin et al., 2018; Howard-Hamilton, 2003; Njoku & Patton, 2017; Porter & Maddox, 2014). "Today, there are many fantasies about Black women in higher education that must be critically interrogated and examined to illuminate the complexities of our experiences across the higher education landscape" (Patton & Croom, 2017, p. 1). Historically, Black women's experiences and narratives have been told from the "perceptions and agendas of members from the dominant society" (Howard-Hamilton, 2003, p. 20). More recently, researchers and scholars have centered the unique experiences, persons, and systems that influence(d) Black women's diverse identities, socialization processes, and trajectories into and through respective collegiate environments (Bonner et al., 2015; Gibson & Espino, 2016; Jackson, 2013; McGuire et al., 2016).

We interpreted our first construction of Black women's experiences concerning monolithism because we found it necessary to affirm the various identities highlighted by authors. Example categories for this construction included the intersection of being Black, woman, and Muslim in college (McGuire et al., 2016); a "one size fits all" approach being insufficient when meeting the needs of diverse student populations (Bonner et al., 2015); expanding Black women's identity to include STEM culture (Jackson, 2013); and integrating into engineering (as an academic major) causing Black women to redefine their Black womanhood (Gibson & Espino, 2016). Collectively, these four articles addressed the varying needs and experiences of BUW and the heterogeneity among them. McGuire et al. (2016) highlighted the ways societal/systemic oppression (e.g., Islamophobia) influenced Black Muslim women's daily realities on and off campus. Bonner et al. (2015) examined the social integration experiences of BUW who were nontraditionally aged and enrolled at a Hispanic-serving institution. Jackson (2013) denoted the importance of community when developing a STEM identity among her BUW participants who were community college transfers to a historically Black college and university. BUW engineering majors identified themselves as double minorities and described the ways their two minority statuses influenced their interactions with fellow students and faculty (Gibson & Espino, 2016).

Cost(s) of Being Strong

Although researchers and scholars explicate and center Black women's unique experiences in relation to combating monolithism, the strong Black woman trope has continued to narrate a problematic discourse that stigmatizes Black women (Chavers, 2016; Patton & Croom, 2017). Chavers (2016) connected the recent hashtag #BlackGirlMagic with the older trope:

> The "strong, black woman" archetype, which also includes the mourning black woman who suffers in silence, is the idea that we can survive it all, that we can withstand it. That we are, in fact, superhuman. Black girl magic sounds to me like just another way of saying the same thing, and it is smothering and stunting. It is, above all, constricting rather than freeing. (para. 4)

Patton and Croom (2017) challenged us to reflect on the psychological toll these stigmas place on Black women, particularly how they influence the diverse narratives of BUW (whether created by Black women or used against Black women). Example categories for this second construction in our analysis of Black women's experiences included strong Black woman being triggered as a coping response (Corbin et al., 2018); Black women's use of the term *strong* as racial self-identification and all-encompassing (Winkle-Wagner, 2008); Black women being required to be resilient in the face of adversity (Brown et al., 2017); and the implications of strength on Black women's development (West et al., 2016). Authors discussed the ways predominantly and historically White educational spaces influenced Black women's navigation between strong Black woman and angry Black woman archetypes (Corbin et al., 2018), how strength represented both empowerment and a liability on campus (Winkle-Wagner, 2008), messages BUW received as part of their gendered-racial socialization as Black women (Brown et al., 2017), and how the internalization of strength was related to mental wellness, problems, and strategies (West et al., 2016).

Wellness Threats and Strategies

Black women, broadly, are receptive and open to engage in counseling on college campuses to attend to their mental health concerns, but are still apprehensive as they fear counselors will not be sensitive to their cultural needs (CCMH, 2016; Harris, 2012) or may not engage due to how they were socialized to view mental health services. This understanding is not merely rooted in a lack of knowledge of mental health services but a mistrust of providers and in consideration that Black people were historically not allowed to receive these services. Black people have experienced mistrust of White medical and service providers as there is a documented history of subjugation and a long legacy of exploitation and discrimination due to being forced, without consent, to participate in medical examinations (Brandt, 1978), being pathologized for attempting to escape enslavement (Logan & Denby, 2013), and not receiving comparable treatment for mental health diagnoses (Whaley, 2001). Even though BUW may not be aware of this historical legacy, the feelings of mistrust are salient among the collective community consciousness (Whaley, 2001). As a result, BUW often suffer in silence when contending with threats to their mental well-being.

Despite mistrust or lack of mental health services, Black people have historically leaned on or created resources within their community to heal individually and collectively. BUW often engage in Black women collectives that operate as support groups providing counterspaces to collectively illuminate the structural and systemic discrimination they face and to connect by engaging in similar cultural practices (Croom et al., 2017; Patton et al., 2017). Examples of such spaces are sister circles and sororities, which have been very influential in Black women's identity development and success in college (Croom et al., 2017; Greyerbiehl & Mitchell, 2014).

Example categories for this third construction included the use of intersectionality in all facets of the counseling process (Szymanski & Lewis, 2016), awareness of unique adjustment issues (Jones, 2009), impact of racial identity on perceptions of body image (Hesse-Biber et al., 2010), and culturally sensitive strategies to maintain mental wellness (Jones, 2009; Jones & Sam, 2018). Szymanski and Lewis (2016) focused on exploring the ways in which BUW coped after experiencing discrimination; they determined that coping can result in negative consequences like disengagement, which can disrupt academic success. Similar to Jones (2009), they stressed the importance of counselors incorporating intersectionality in understanding BUW experiences, but also infusing it in treatment approaches. Jones and Sam (2018) added that an Afrocentric worldview infused within counseling group interventions, individual counseling, and shared coping strategies led to positive outcomes.

An intersectionality framework would also help counselors understand the varying cultural (and systemic) layers that inform how BUW have developed views of themselves (e.g., self-image, self-concept, self-esteem). Much of BUW's racial identity has been developed and informed by their socialization processes, K–12 school, neighborhood, peer groups, and other life relationships, events, and environments before they enter college (Hesse-Biber et al., 2010; Porter, 2017). Hesse-Biber et al. (2010) argued that how BUW conceptualize their racial identity influences their satisfaction with their body image and that broadly for participants in their study, "the extent to which they were at risk for developing body image issues was dependent on the ideals to which they ascribe" and that these ideals were most often formed in early developmental stages (p. 711). For BUW who ascribe to White standards of beauty when forming an understanding of themselves, there are lifelong psychological repercussions and feelings of not being enough. The participants in Hesse-Biber et al. (2010) who voiced a stronger cultural identity described more positively their self-image and discussed a self-esteem rooted in Black consciousness, influencing pride, positive self-worth, and an awareness of psychological threats to Black bodies and thoughts (e.g., racism). These findings support the previous discussion emphasizing the importance of including an Afrocentric worldview throughout the counseling process.

Maintaining Relationships and Roles

Black people are culturally collective and relational, so maintaining familial, friendship, and community connections is a value that many BUW feel instinctively compelled to preserve while in college. However, this desire, if materialized, can either help support or disrupt their development depending on whether the relationship or role is healthy. Example categories for this fourth construction included familial connections (Kennedy & Winkle-Wagner, 2014), mothering while in school (Sealey-Ruiz, 2013), and experiences of homelessness while in school (Winkle-Wagner, 2009). Kennedy and Winkle-Wagner (2014) explored how Black women earn and maintain autonomy while protecting family ties and determined that these connections are crucial and inextricably tied to BUW academic success. The authors noted that even as BUW gained autonomy, they did not sever ties but leaned on their families to cope with new situations, make important decisions, and as a source of motivation (Kennedy & Winkle-Wagner, 2014). However, if relationships with families were contentious, this desire to maintain connection could pose a threat to well-being and success. Winkle-Wagner (2009) explored the experiences of Black women in college who described tense relationships with family members. Some of the participants expressed not feeling comfortable going home and, in many ways, felt it was akin to being homeless. Others experienced internal conflict when debating if they should cease communication with family and community to focus on attaining academic success.

Commitment to family was also true of reentry mothers represented in the Sealey-Ruiz (2013) study. BUW in this study were older than traditional college students and broadly viewed college enrollment as an integral part of defining themselves and viewed education as an act of resistance to stereotypical thoughts about Black mothers. In addition to combating stereotypes, they experienced their roles as mothers not being understood by faculty and peers, which created barriers while navigating these spaces to attain success.

Implications for Practice and Research

As part of a CDA, we interpreted four constructions of Black women's experiences in the past decade of literature: (a) being a Black woman as not a monolithic experience, (b) the cost(s) of being strong, (c) wellness threats and strategies, and (d) maintaining relationships and roles. These constructions not only acknowledged the diversity among BUW but also illustrated the ways they encountered micro- and macro-level systems of oppression on their respective campuses and society in general (e.g., monolithism and (mis) representation, stigmatization of strength, coping mechanisms and strategies, gendered-racial battle fatigue, negotiation of roles). We offer implications for practice specific to those working with/alongside Black women as college counselors, administrators, staff, and faculty in higher education. We offer future areas of research for those interested in continuing to center their experiences by contributing to and advancing this body of scholarship.

College Counselors

Broadly, the findings from the articles explored in this CDA provide three broad recommendations for college counselors working with Black women on campuses. One, become aware of the lens of intersectionality (e.g., specifically in relation to the ways oppressive structures influence procedure) and infuse this understanding throughout the entire counseling process (e.g., client intake, case conceptualization, theoretical orientation, and theories/ techniques employed). Intersectionality has been integrated in the cultural . competencies of fields such as counseling (Ratts et al., 2015) and psychology (American Psychological Association, 2017). Scholars have also discussed how intersectionality could be used throughout the therapeutic process (Adames et al., 2018; Ali & Lee, 2019). This awareness forces counselors to acknowledge that being a Black woman is not a monolithic experience as discussed previously. Therefore, approaches and techniques employed should be tailored to the individual and not informed by stereotypical thinking that suggests that all Black women are alike. Two, become aware of the tenets of an Afrocentric worldview and introduce techniques informed by this worldview to clients as possible treatment avenues. Afrocentric worldview is a strengths-based perspective that asserts "individuals and groups have strengths that can be enhanced; that individual problems are often structural in origin; that differences between individuals and groups are assumed and accepted; and that collective identity supersedes the individual" (Beckett & Lee, 2004, p. 103). An Afrocentric worldview used in the counseling process is believed to be more effective than Eurocentric approaches and can be accessible to Black women representing the African diaspora (Akbar, 1991; Jones, 2009). Three, in addition to revising counseling approaches to make them culturally sensitive, it is imperative that college counselors are culturally responsive. This includes being aware of their own bias, having an increased level of knowledge of the needs of Black women, and feeling comfortable employing culturally specific treatment approaches to increase effectiveness with Black women. Culturally responsive also includes using specific techniques like broaching. Day-Vines et al. (2007) defined *broaching* as follows:

> The counselor's ability to consider how sociopolitical factors such as race influence the client's counseling concerns. The counselor must learn to recognize the cultural meaning clients attach to phenomena and to subsequently translate that cultural knowledge into meaningful practice that facilitates client empowerment, strengthens the therapeutic alliance, and enhances counseling outcomes. (p. 401)

This technique allows the counselor to adopt a disposition that welcomes an ongoing conversation about diversity with the client and not feel fearful of discussing cultural differences within the session.

College counselors must understand that Black women are one of the largest minoritized groups served on college campuses (CCMH, 2014) and counselors have an ethical responsibility to be prepared to attend to their unique cultural needs and understand how they form and maintain connections (Jones & Sam, 2018). Broadly these three suggestions can lead to creating a more welcoming environment for BUW that can impact their feelings of belongingness, academic achievement, and career success.

Higher Education Administrators, Staff, and Faculty

Administrators, staff, and faculty must recognize that Black women have unique relationships with their multiple marginalized (and privileged) identities and enter their respective collegiate environments with varied understandings of systemic oppression, socialization, identity saliency, and articulation of who they are and what they need. Although there are similarities and shared experiences, Black undergraduate women are not the same and "one size fits all" approaches minimize and invalidate their unique experiences (Bonner et al., 2015; Howard-Hamilton, 2003). Second, those working with and alongside Black women must disrupt preconceived notions, assumptions, and stigmatization of Black women they serve. Reflecting on the four constructions, and specifically the cost(s) of being strong, assuming that Black women "have it all together" and are not in need of support is both detrimental to their academic success and damaging to their overall wellness and well-being. Administrators, staff, and faculty working in respective units/offices within both divisions of academic affairs and student affairs have a responsibility to serve and support Black women in and outside the classroom. Representation matters; recruiting and retaining Black women with varied life experiences and trajectories across the institution's organizational chart is necessary for BUW to see themselves, develop strategies, and matriculate at the institution. Although support may look different depending on one's identities, skills, relationships, trust, and understanding of experiences, none of these should preclude any person from the responsibility to serve and support BUW (Porter & Dean, 2015). Third, individual connections with (e.g., one-on-one mentoring relationships) and relationship building (e.g., group therapy, sister circles, leadership retreats; Croom et al., 2017) among Black women are critical to their development. Ask BUW what they need and support them accordingly.

Future Research

The experiences of Black women in college have been increasingly examined over the past decade (Banks, 2009; Chambers & Sharpe, 2012; Commodore et al., 2018; Patton & Croom, 2017; Patton et al., 2017; Porter, 2017); however, very few of these articles explore the psychological challenges and experiences of these women in their quest to become academically successful. Across the literature represented within this CDA, the authors of the articles noted there is a dearth of research that explores the challenges Black women face in college. These challenges add to their existing level of stress and disrupt their capacity to cope with gender- and/or race-related threats (and systems of oppression within their academic disciplines) to their mental well-being, college engagement, and academic performance. As a result, future research should explore the lifelong impact of these psychological threats, the experiences of Black women who seek help from mental health providers on college campuses, barriers to seeking help, and how counselors are trained to help Black women. Additionally, examining the unique experiences of Black women at varied institutional types—predominantly White, historically Black, and Hispanic-serving colleges and universities—would increase understanding of similarities and differences among BUW and provide strategies for those working with and alongside these students at their respective campuses. Future research should mirror the variations of experiences to avoid a "one size fits all" approach to appropriately serving and supporting the needs of BUW.

Conclusion

The present CDA explores how researchers make meaning of Black women's experiences in college. This exploration resulted in four constructions of these experiences: (a) being a Black woman as not a monolithic experience, (b) cost(s) of being strong, (c) wellness threats and strategies, and (d) maintaining relationships and roles. Across these constructions, Black women's experiences were influenced by societal, institutional, familial, and individual factors that impact (mis)representations of their unique identities, mental wellness, and connections with others. These influences can pose both disruptions and catalysts to their academic achievement and lifelong mental health. Analyzing the discourse of the experiences of Black women in college reinforces that their experiences and social locations often render them invisible and hypervisible at the same time. This study contributes to the larger body of scholarship on Black undergraduate women and implicates future research that continues to explore their psychological and mental wellness concerns.

Discussion Questions

1. What are the ways we can better address the varied wellness (e.g., mental and physical) and academic needs of BUW at differing institutional types?
2. What types of institutional support systems/initiatives can we create and/ or enhance that would foster collaboration, sustainability, and necessary resources (financial and human) to better serve and assist BUW?
3. What types of training for college administration, staff, and counselors would make them better equipped to attend to the systemic challenges/ oppressive structures that can influence mental health and wellness of BUW?
4. What higher education policies, practices, and structures enhance or disrupt the development of BUW? If disruptive, what strategies can be employed to interrupt these barriers?

Further Reading

Commodore, F., Baker, D. J., & Arroyo, A. T. (2018). *Black women college students: A guide to student success in higher education*. Routledge.

Evans, S. Y., Bell, K., & Burton, N. K. (2017). *Black women's mental health: Balancing strength and vulnerability*. SUNY Press.

hooks, b. (1993). *Sisters of the yam: Black women and self-recovery*. South End Press.

Patton, L. D., & Croom, N. N. (Eds.). (2017). *Critical perspectives on Black women and college success*. Routledge.

Walker-Barnes, C. (2014). *Too heavy a yoke: Black women and the burden of strength*. Wipf and Stock.

References

Adames, H. Y., Chavez-Dueñas, N. Y., Sharma, S., & La Roche, M. J. (2018). Intersectionality in psychotherapy: The experiences of an AfroLatinx queer immigrant. *Psychotherapy*, *55*(1), 73–79. https://doi.org/10.1037/pst0000152

Akbar, N. I. (1991). The evolution of human psychology for African Americans. In R. L. Jones (Ed.), *Black psychology* (pp. 99–123). Cobb & Henry.

Ali, S., & Lee, C. C. (2019). Using creativity to explore intersectionality in counseling. *Journal of Creativity in Mental Health*, *14*(4), 510–519. https://doi.org/10.1080/15401383.2019.1632767

American Psychological Association. (2017). *Multicultural guidelines: An ecological approach to context, identity, and intersectionality*. http://www.apa.org/about/policy/multicultural-guidelines.pdf

Banks, C. A. (2009). *Black women undergraduates, cultural capital, and college success*. Peter Lang.

Beckett, J. O., & Lee, N. L. (2004). Informing the future of child welfare practices with African American families. In J. E. Everett, S. P. Chipungu, & B. R. Leashore (Eds.), *Child welfare revisited: An Afrocentric perspective* (pp. 93–123). Rutgers University Press.

Bonner, F. A., II, Marbley, A. F., Evans, M. P., & Robinson, P. (2015). Triple jeopardy: A qualitative investigation of the experiences of nontraditional African American female students in one Hispanic-serving institution. *Journal of African American Studies*, *19*, 36–51. https://doi.org/10.1007/s12111-014-9287-4

Brandt, A. M. (1978). Racism and research: The case of the Tuskegee Syphilis Study. *Hastings Center Report*, *8*(6), 21–29. http://nrs.harvard.edu/urn-3:HUL.InstRepos:3372911

Brown, D. L., Blackmon, S., Rosnick, C. B., Griffin-Fennell, F. D., & White-Johnson, R. L. (2017). Initial development of a gendered-racial socialization scale for African American college women. *Sex Roles*, *77*, 178–193. https://doi.org/10.1007/s11199-016-0707-x

Center for Collegiate Mental Health. (2014, January). *2013 annual report* (Publication No. STA 14-43; ERIC database: ED572759).

Center for Collegiate Mental Health. (2016, January). *2015 annual report* (Publication No. STA 15-108). Pennsylvania State University.

Chambers, C. R., & Sharpe, R. V. (2012). *Black female undergraduates on campus: Successes and challenges.* Emerald Group.

Chavers, L. (2016, January 13). Here's my problem with #BlackGirlMagic: Black girls aren't magical, we're human. *Elle.* https://www.elle.com/life-love/a33180/why-i-dont-love-blackgirlmagic/

Collins, P. H. (1990). *Black feminist thought: Knowledge, consciousness, and the politics of empowerment.* Routledge.

Collins, P. H., & Bilge, S. (2016). *Intersectionality.* Polity Press.

Commodore, F., Baker, D. J., & Arroyo, A. T. (2018). *Black women college students: A guide to student success in higher education.* Routledge.

Corbin, N. A., Smith, W. A., & Garcia, J. R. (2018). Trapped between justified anger and being the strong Black woman: Black college women coping with racial battle fatigue at historically and predominantly White institutions. *International Journal of Qualitative Studies in Education, 31*(7), 626–643. https://doi.org/10.1080/09518398.2018.1468045

Crenshaw, K. (1989). Demarginalizing the intersection of race and sex: A Black feminist critique of antidiscrimination doctrine, feminist theory, and antiracist politics. *University of Chicago Legal Forum, 1989*(1), 139–167. https://is.muni.cz/el/fss/podzim2016/GEN505/um/Crenshaw_Black_Feminist_Critique_of_Antidiscrimination_Law.pdf

Crenshaw, K. (1991). Mapping the margins: Intersectionality, identity politics, and violence against women of color. *Stanford Law Review, 43*(6), 1241–1299. https://heinonline.org/HOL/LandingPage?handle=hein.journals/stflr43&div=52&id=&page=

Crenshaw, K. (2016). *The urgency of intersectionality.* https://www.ted.com/talks/kimberle_crenshaw_the_urgency_of_intersectionality

Croom, N. N., Beatty, C. C., Acker, L. D., & Butler, M. (2017). Exploring undergraduate Black womyn's motivations for engaging in "sister circle" organizations. *NASPA Journal About Women in Higher Education, 10*(2), 216–228. https://doi.org/10.1080/19407882.2017.1328694

Day-Vines, N. L., Wood, S. M., Grothaus, T., Craigen, L., Holman, A., Dotson-Blake, K., & Douglass, M. J. (2007). Broaching the subjects of race, ethnicity, and culture during the counseling process. *Journal of Counseling & Development, 85*(4), 401–409. https://doi.org/10.1002/j.1556-6678.2007.tb00608.x

De Walt, P. S. (2013). Discourse on African American/Black identity: Engaging the expanded nigrescence theory with a diasporic consciousness. *SpringerPlus, 2*(1), 233–243.

Donovan, R. A. (2011). Tough or tender (dis)similarities in White college students' perceptions of Black and White women. *Psychology of Women Quarterly, 35*, 458–468. https://doi.org/10.1177/0361684311406874

Everett, K. D., & Croom, N. N. (2017). From discourse to practice: Making discourses about Black undergraduate womyn visible in higher education journals and student affairs practice. In L. D. Patton and N. N. Croom (Eds.), *Critical perspectives on Black women and college success* (pp. 75–87). Routledge.

Fairclough, N. (1989). *Language and power*. Pearson Education.

Fairclough, N. (1992). *Discourse and social change*. Polity Press.

Fanon, F. (1967). *Black skin, white masks* (R. Philcox, Trans.). Grove Press.

Foucault, M. (1969/1972). Préface à la transgression (en hommage à Georges Bataille). In D. Defert & F. Ewald (Eds.), *Dits et* écrits (Vol. 1). Gallimard.

Gibson, S. L., & Espino, M. M. (2016). Uncovering Black womanhood in engineering. *NASPA Journal About Women in Higher Education, 9*(1), 56–73. https://doi.org/10.1080/19407882.2016.1143377

Greyerbiehl, L., & Mitchell, D., Jr. (2014). An intersectional social capital analysis of the influence of historically Black sororities on African American women's college experiences at a predominantly White institution. *Journal of Diversity in Higher Education, 7*(4), 282–294. https://doi.org/10.1037/a0037605

Hannon, C. R., Woodside, M., Pollard, B. L., & Roman, J. (2016). The meaning of African American college women's experiences attending a predominantly White institution: A phenomenological study. *Journal of College Student Development, 57*(6), 652–666. https://doi.org/10.1353/csd.2016.0036

Harris, A. L. (2012). *Barriers to group psychotherapy for African-American college students* [Doctoral dissertation, Wright State University]. CORE Scholar Theses and Dissertations. http://corescholar.libraries.wright.edu/etd_all/669/

Hernton, C. C. (1965). *Sex and racism in America*. Doubleday.

Hesse-Biber, S., Livingstone, S., Ramirez, D., Barko, E. B., & Johnson, A. L. (2010). Racial identity and body image among Black female college students attending predominantly White colleges. *Sex Roles, 63*(9–10), 697–711. https://doi.org/10.1007/s11199-010-9862-7

hooks, b. (1981). *Ain't I a woman?* South End Press.

Howard-Hamilton, M. (2003). Theoretical frameworks for African American women. In M. Howard-Hamilton (Ed.), *Meeting the needs of African American women* (New Directions for Student Services, no. 104, pp. 19–27). Jossey-Bass. https://doi.org/10.1002/ss.104

Jackson, D. L. (2013). A balancing act: Impacting and initiating the success of African American female community college transfer students in STEM into the HBCU environment. *The Journal of Negro Education, 82*(3), 255–271. https://doi.org/10.7709/jnegroeducation.82.3.0255

Jones, L. V. (2009). Claiming your connections: A psychosocial group intervention study of Black college women. *Social Work Research, 33*(3), 159–171. https://doi.org/10.1093/swr/33.3.159

Jones, M. K., & Sam, T. S. (2018). Cultural connections: An ethnocultural counseling intervention for Black women in college. *Journal of College Counseling, 21*(1), 73–86. https://doi.org/10.1002/jocc.12088

Katz, D. S., & Davison, K. (2014). Community college student mental health: A comparative analysis. *Community College Review*, *42*(4), 307–326. https://doi.org/10.1177/0091552114535466

Kennedy, S., & Winkle-Wagner, R. (2014). Earning autonomy while maintaining family ties: Black women's reflections on the transition into college. *NASPA Journal About Women in Higher Education*, *7*(2), 133–152. https://doi.org/10.1515/njawhe-2014-0011

Logan, S., & Denby, R. (2013). African-American mental health: A historical perspective. In S. Logan, R. Denby, & P. A. Gibson (Eds.), *Mental health care in the African-American community* (pp. 33–44). Routledge.

McGuire, K. M., Casanova, S., & Davis, C. H. F., III. (2016). I'm a Black female who happens to be Muslim: Multiple marginalities of an immigrant Black Muslim woman on a predominately White campus. *The Journal of Negro Education*, *85*(3), 316–329. https://doi.org/10.7709/jnegroeducation.85.3.0316

Mowatt, R. A., French, B. H., & Malebranche, D. A. (2013). Black/female/body hypervisibility and invisibility: A Black feminist augmentation of feminist leisure research. *Journal of Leisure Research*, *45*(5), 644–660. https://doi.org/10.18666/jlr-2013-v45-i5-4367

Njoku, N. R., & Patton, L. D. (2017). Explorations of respectability and resistance in constructions of Black womanhood at HBCUs. In L. D. Patton and N. N. Croom (Eds.), *Critical perspectives on Black women and college success* (pp. 143–157). Routledge.

Patton, L. D., & Croom, N. N. (Eds.). (2017). *Critical perspectives on Black women and college success*. Routledge.

Patton, L. D., Haynes, C., & Croom, N. N. (2017). Centering the diverse experiences of Black women undergraduates. *NASPA Journal About Women in Higher Education*, *10*(2), 141–143. https://doi.org/10.1080/19407882.2017.1331627

Porter, C. J. (2017). Articulation of identity in Black undergraduate women: Influences, interactions, and intersections. In L. D. Patton & N. N. Croom (Eds.), *Critical perspectives on Black women and college success* (pp. 88–100). Routledge.

Porter, C. J., & Dean, L. A. (2015). Making meaning: Identity development of Black undergraduate women. *NASPA Journal About Women in Higher Education*, *8*(2), 125–139. https://doi.org/10.1080/19407882.2015.1057164

Porter, C. J., Green, Q., Daniels, M., & Smola, M. (2020). Black women's socialization and identity development in college: Advancing Black feminist thought. *Journal of Student Affairs Research and Practice*, *57*(3), 253–265. https://doi.org/10.1080/19496591.2019.1683021

Porter, C. J., & Maddox, C. E. (2014). Using critical race theory and intersectionality to explore a Black lesbian's life in college: An analysis of Skye's narrative. *NASAP Journal*, *15*(2), 25–40. https://www.nasap.net/wp-content/uploads/2014/02/NASAP-Journal-Special-Edition-March-2014.pdf

Porter, C. J., Mlambo, Y. A., Hannibal, J., & Karunaratne, N. (2018). (Re)Defining student success: A qualitative study of Black undergraduate women pursuing veterinary medicine. *Journal of Women and Minorities in Science and Engineering*, *24*(1), 61–80. https://doi.org/10.1615/JWomenMinorScienEng.2017016952

Ratts, M. J., Singh, A. A., Nassar-McMillan, S., Butler, S. K., & McCullough, J. R. (2015). *Multicultural and social justice counseling competencies.* https://www.counseling.org/docs/default-source/competencies/multicultural-and-social-justice-counseling-competencies.pdf?sfvrsn=20

Sealey-Ruiz, Y. (2013). Learning to resist: Educational counter-narratives of Black college reentry mothers. *Teachers College Record, 115*(4), 1–31. https://www.tcrecord.org/library/abstract.asp?contentid=16911

Storlie, C. A., Hilton, T. L., Duenyas, D., Archer, R., & Glavin, K. (2018). Career narratives of African American female college students: Insights for college counselors. *Journal of College Counseling, 21,* 29–42. https://doi.org/10.1002/jocc.12085

Szymanski, D. M., & Lewis, J. A. (2016). Gendered racism, coping, identity centrality, and African American college women's psychological distress. *Psychology of Women Quarterly, 40*(2), 229–243. https://doi.org/10.1177/0361684315616113

Thomas, A. J., Witherspoon, K. M., & Speight, S. L. (2008). Gendered racism, psychological distress, and coping styles of African American women. *Cultural Diversity and Ethnic Minority Psychology, 14,* 307–314. https://doi.org/10.1037/1099-9809.14.4.307

West, L. M., Donovan, R. A., & Daniel, A. R. (2016). The price of strength: Black college women's perspectives on the strong Black woman stereotype. *Women & Therapy, 39,* 390–411. https://doi.org/10.1080/02703149.2016.1116871

Whaley, A. L. (2001). Cultural mistrust and mental health services for African Americans: A review and meta-analysis. *The Counseling Psychologist, 29*(4), 513–531. https://doi.org/10.1177/0011000001294003

Winkle-Wagner, R. (2008). Not feminist but strong: Black women's reflections of race and gender in college. *The Negro Educational Review, 59*(3–4), 181–195.

Winkle-Wagner, R. (2009). The perpetual homelessness of college experiences: Tensions between home and campus for African American women. *The Review of Higher Education, 33*(1), 1–36. https://doi.org/10.1353/rhe.0.0116

Wodak, R. (2001). The discourse-historical approach. *Methods of Critical Discourse Analysis, 1,* 63–95.

BLACK WOMEN'S TRANSITIONS AND EDUCATION AT (MY) INTERSECTIONS OF RACE, DIS/ABILITY, AND ABLEISM

Mercedes Adell Cannon

Drawing from critical race theory (CRT), disability studies in education (DSE), and womanist/Black feminist tenets, this chapter centers the voices and counternarratives of Black[1] women with dis/abilities[2] (BWD), including my own, as assets—useful and valuable to self, community, and broader society (Givens, 1999). Listening to the counternarratives of BWD and featuring their perspectives as assets allows us to focus on the voices that (re)present BWD culture situated within individual and community heritage, faith, spirituality, and rhetoric, notwithstanding various other strengths of BWD. In addition, Black women's assets, including self-definition, self-determination, and self-advocacy, are essential tools for building up individuals in ways that also give back to community assets—for example, poetry, pictures, prayer, meditation (Hill Collins, 2000). Concentrating and bringing these three concepts of *voice/counternarratives/assets* together is useful for building a restorative conscientious consciousness (hooks, 2000) can effectually decenter deficit thinking (Davis & Museus, 2019) and dominant narratives. To illustrate,

> Healing requires a critical consciousness, a way of understanding the social world through political resistance that prepares [Black] youth to confront racism and other forms of oppression . . . healing fosters a collective

optimism and a transformation of spirit that, over time, contributes to healthy, vibrant community life. (Ginwright, 2011, pp. 36–37)

Restorative consciousness is healing the mind, soul, and spirit of Black people, and, in particular, BWD (K. Cannon, 1988; M. Cannon, 2019; Hill Collins, 2003; Mishler, 2004; Myers, 2013).

This chapter is a part of a larger body of research (i.e., M. Cannon, 2019). In the study, I explored the intersections of race, gender, and dis/ability of BWD and their transitions and educational experiences from high school to college (Menchetti, 2008). In return, the narratives as *expert knowledge bearers* (Cannon, 2019; Cannon & Thorius, 2013). The voices/counternarratives/assets of BWDs (including my own) about their transitions and educational experiences at the intersection of race, ableism, and dis/ability and in their interrelationships decenter the master narrative of others. For example, dominant institutions who attribute deficit and ableist views upon this group further result in their pathologization, disablement, and erasure. *Pathologization* characterizes healthy or behavioral conditions from a medical model with a deficit (broken–suffering–abnormal) lens, and can result in disablement. *Disablement* refers to actions, attitudes, and harmful treatment of dis/abled individuals or those with dis/ability by others, resulting in environments that are more disabling than disabled folks' impairments. Finally, *exclusion* refers to the disabled person as alienated, segregated, and disconnected from opportunities that are open to all other students, which results in experiencing transition and education erasure.

Transition and Education

Within education, a dominant group's (e.g., white folks) perspective typically structures the understanding and practice of transition[3] education and planning. Transition education is a complex system that refers to multiple paths planned for disabled students' movement from high school to adulthood (Trainor, 2017). In addition, research (such as the National Longitudinal Transition Study 1 & 2) has not always reflected the paths of historically marginalized students (e.g., Black and Brown) with dis/abilities, especially at multiple intersections of oppression, in their trajectory to adulthood (Trainor, 2017). For example, the NLTS 1 & 2 reported steady improvement in high school completion rates for students with disabilities (Trainor, 2017). Still these percentages were not disaggregated by race to identify the location of an increase. Therefore, if we cannot identify who these students are, we cannot identify differences in gaining access to higher education along racial lines from within the reported percentages of students with disabilities completing high school. Consequently, this chapter highlights the need to understand *who is valued, by whom, and to what end* (King, 2009; Waitoller & Thorius, 2016) in education and transition education. To do so, we must listen to the voices of BWD. They counter deficit views of pathologization, disablement, and exclusion (in their experiences with teachers/professors, family, and peers), *pathologization,* deficit thinking, and alienation practices of others toward BWD resulting in self-doubt (M. Cannon, 2019). For example, Diana[4] stated:

> I had an IEP when I was about in second grade; my mother had to have a meeting with my teachers. They were saying I needed to be there because I was kind of behind; the level of reading wasn't at the same level as the other children. So, they put me in there from my second grade all the way up to my senior year in high school. [In] the last semester [of high school] I passed three out of my five classes, and two of them was A and B, but I did not pass the other two. It's hard, I was like, well, is it me? Am I not as smart as others? So, it's hard but I try—I did not know the answer and somewhat that others did. White people ask me about African Americans not being the smartest. We are not as smart, and you know being in college as an African American and surrounded by different races, Caucasian, Mexican, and Puerto Rican is not easy at all.

Diana's narrative of her ability from second grade through high school alerts her consciousness to wonder if it's her thinking she is not as smart as others, which results in her self-doubt to compete with her white peers. The beliefs, attitudes, and practices of others that marginalize, oppress, alienate, and isolate individuals with dis/abilities or disabilities (e.g., BWD) do not happen in a vacuum but rather via the disablement of environments. Such disabling practices subsequently lead to pathologization. Diana's narrative illustrates disablement in both the educational and physical environments. Master narratives and ableist practices support the exclusion of dis/abled individuals—those with dis/abilities or disabilities—from positive forward progression, and apart from marginalizing and disadvantaging them via institutionalized systems of oppression (Hernández-Saca, 2016; Reid & Knight, 2006).

Therefore, it is imperative that we reconceptualize transition education by centering the perspective of a marginalized and oppressed group of individuals transitioning to postsecondary education. According to Trainor (2017), the trajectory to postsecondary education has marked-out paths for the dominant group, but this is not true for other groups. Artiles (2019) suggests educators must trouble power relations and racial disparities and consider the sociohistorical context of students of color at various intersections of identities, because they experience differential treatment in general in and special education in comparison to white upper-middle-class children.

Intersections: Race and Gender, Disability and Ableism

Crenshaw's (1989) intersectionality theory reveals historical interlocking systems of oppression for Black women. She argues that Black women could not claim discrimination based on race because Black men were advancing in the workforce, nor claim discrimination based on gender because white women were being promoted in the workforce (Annamma et al., 2018). Thus, the concept of intersectionality is significant for critical awareness and a greater understanding of the complexity of separate intersecting identities and their effects on the lives of Black women (Crenshaw, 1991; McCall, 2005). The African American Policy Forum (2012) drew attention to the fact that "an intersectional approach extends the conventional analysis. The result is focus attention on injuries that otherwise might not be recognized (i.e., social problems, effective interventions; and the promotion of inclusive coalitional advocacy)" (p. 3). This circumstance reveals how Black women's intersections are ignored in society. Treatment or behavioral programs and educational contexts do not often mirror who they are holistically or how Black women view their well-being (Holcomb-McCoy & Moore-Thomas, 2001; Nabors & Pettee, 2003).

A focus on intersectionality is also promising for the dismantling of racist and ableist practices within education. Several scholars report the importance of counteracting the effects of transition education experienced by Black, Latino/a, and other Black Indigenous People of Color (BIPOC) subgroups of students that are pathologized (Annamma et al., 2013; M. Cannon, 2019; Ferri & Connor, 2010; Hernández-Saca, 2016; Petersen, 2009; Taylor, 2018). Intersectionality addresses various oppressions and inequalities at the intersection of multiple identities that perpetuate discriminatory practices and pathologization of BIPOC's physical bodies. This adds to existing deficit thinking and theorization of their differences (Annamma & Morrison, 2018; Baglieri et al., 2011; Bell, 2011; Davis & Museus, 2019; Erevelles, 2000; Smith, 2008).

Road Map to the Rest of the Chapter

This chapter provides a window into the perspectives and consciousness of Black women with disabilities and centers the voices of nine participants from five research studies.[5] I also explore my positionality to Black women with dis/abilities (Givens, 1999). Next, I present the transition and educational experiences of two participants (Cannon, 2019). First, I focus on their *voices/counternarratives/assets* in the context of race, ableism, and disability or dis/ability. Second, I present both sets of participants' (i.e., the BWD in the three studies reviewed and the BWD in the dissertation study) assets intertwined with their voices and/or as they countered master narrative views about transition processes from secondary to postsecondary education (M. Cannon, 2019; Delgado, 1989; Ferri & Connor, 2010; Petersen, 2009; Trainor, 2007). Third, I account for how research itself is a situated cultural practice (Arzubiaga et al., 2008). Next, I llustrate how transition education needs to be more inclusive of BWD's *cultural practices* through the lens of Trainor's (2017) work, which suggests that transition education should include cultural practices. Finally, in this chapter's discussion/implications section, I focus on strategies (i.e., subverted truths) and suggest ways transition education could be more inclusive of Black scholars' pedagogy, which would center those directly impacted by transitions and education at intersections of racism and ableism.

Perspectives and Consciousness of BWD

The stories of BWD aid in understanding *who is valued, by whom, and to what end* in transition planning and transition from secondary to postsecondary education. Transition planning under the Individuals with Disabilities Education Act (IDEA, 2004) is required within secondary education in order to prepare students for their transition to postsecondary education (Menchetti, 2008; Sitlington, 2003). Accordingly, individualized education plans (IEPs) for students with disabilities include a choice to transition after high school to one of three potential domains: (a) postsecondary education, (b) residential (housing), or (c) vocational (employment; Thoma et al., 2001). However, some BWD do not understand the meaning of transition planning and education post–high school means. To illustrate:

> Clarissa, a 16-year-old Black girl whose educational goals were to be an entrepreneur, lived by herself and with friends, did not know what it meant to have a transition plan or what is involved in the process. She said, "I didn't have that in my [IEP meeting] yet . . . they wasn't doin' all that. . . . Basically they focus on what I done did" (Trainor, 2007, p. 38). Tanya (an 18-year-old Black girl) added, "And when they say that . . . something about going to college after school it goes over my head" (Trainer, 2007, p. 38).

In centering these BWD's voices and listening to their stories of transition education and how each one encountered or countered deficit views attributed to them by teachers, family members, and peers, we hear their voices and self-perception of what an IEP is or how to access college. It is essential to center BWD's stories about their education to illuminate how they contribute to knowledge production and frame inequities in access, participation, and outcomes in higher education. Pairing their view of inequalities with the dearth of literature on the educational experiences of Black women at intersections of differences underscores the salience of their stories.

Similarly, Ferri and Connor's (2010) study explored the educational experiences of young urban working-class females of color with dis/abilities and what they had to say about life in and out of schools. Two participants from their study were Black females, 19-year-old Channell and 20-year-old Precious, who had received special education services in K–12 schools. The authors emphasized how all of the women of color understood and countered intersections of oppression as a result of the special education label. To illustrate, Channell stated,

> I remember . . . I was talking to this boy; he was in regular ed. . . . He didn't know I was in special ed. He would ask me am I in that class? I would say "Hell, no!" . . . But he would see me sit down; I'd move back, trying to hide . . . if he know, he know, and as long as he don't come out with it . . . we're all trying to hide something. (Ferri & Connor, 2010, p. 108)

Channell clashes with the boy's norm of ability as an attendee of regular education classes and the deflection of her dis/ability as an attendee of special education classes. Channell's story highlights her need to protect—keep secret her negative consciousness about her dis/ability label as it affected her academic ability and social identity in comparison to her peer. Relatedly, Precious states,

> [I]f you have money, you can like do practically anything. . . . You can hire a tutor to go to your house, you can hire somebody—shit! You can even pay somebody to do your tests for you! So nobody really know if you have a learning disability or not because . . . you're always hiring somebody to do things for you. (Ferri & Connor, 2010, p. 115)

Both Channell and Precious address intersectional oppressions that perpetuate inequitable practices specific to disability/ableism oppression. Pathologization alienates, excludes, and oppresses Blacks (e.g., BWD) through social systems that support white supremacy, which subjugates Black consciousness and results in the falsification of Black consciousness (Wilson, 1993). For girls of color, pathologization manifests in negative psychoemotional well-being (Annamma et al., 2016).

From three studies, the BWD framed their experiences in connection to race-based oppressions and identified how power structures contributed to their educational experiences. The researchers had a person-centered *and* an intersectional focus on each woman's lived experiences (Ferri & Connor, 2010; Petersen, 2009; Trainor, 2007). By *person-centered* I mean placing the person who is the most affected by transition and education in the center of the planning and processes (Thoma et al., 2001). Because IDEA requires compliance in transitioning students with disabilities from high school to adulthood, centering the goals and desires of disabled students or individuals with dis/abilities in the planning and processes underscores their human agency. Relatedly, through an emancipatory and critical praxis (i.e., voice/counternarrative) BWD's voices/stories centered in the transition and education planning should highlight their knowledge as assets to the academy.

Black Women With Dis/Abilities' Voices/Counternarratives/Assets

Guided by an interdisciplinary conceptual framework based on CRT and the theoretical lens of womanist/Black feminist studies and DSE and their tenets of voice and counternarrative, I ask: How do Black women with dis/abilities describe their transition and postsecondary educational experiences though the use of their voices/counternarratives/assets? Each interdisciplinary theoretical lens identifies the gaps, breaks, and silences in the scholarship about the intellect of Black women and provides a way of understanding the importance of marginalized identities' (i.e., BWD's) *voices* and conscientious experiences (hooks, 2000). The sharing of stories by individuals of color about themselves and their experiences is a way to counter (i.e., talk back, reject, subvert, etc.) the negative social constructions of differences that result from hierarchical subjugation (M. Cannon, 2019; Jackson & Penrose, 1994). This framework presents a critical analysis of counternarratives in contrast to master narratives (Hernández-Saca, 2016; Matsuda, 1991; Solorzano & Bernal, 2001) at intersecting identities of race, gender, and dis/ability. The use of CRT's *counternarrative* addresses and centers BWD's viewpoints within the field of transition education. Additionally, the DS/DSE and womanist/feminist tenet of *voice* "is a grassroots representation of the day-to-day dealings of ordinary people's daily lives, explains [community] and cares about the collective well-being and people's humanity" (M.

Cannon, 2019, p. 25). Voice is also appropriate for focusing on the subjectivity and the making of self-identity in the BWD stories (Ladson-Billings & Tate, 1995; Linton, 1998; Philips, 2006; Taylor, 2018; Thomas, 1999; Titchkosky & Michalko, 2012). These theoretical tools (i.e., counternarrative and voice) allow me to center their stories and "recognize the legitimacy and power of counternarrative" (Delgado & Stefancic, 2012, p. 52) and, I argue, voice and asset.

Researcher's Positionality

I too identify as a Black woman with a dis/ability label—speech and language impediment (SLI). This position provides me with an insider/outsider association with BWD voices/counternarratives/assets and their individual and collective transition and education experiences. In addition, I present myself as a *walking subversion*, meaning my life does not corroborate with characteristic traits that society attributes to an individual with an SLI identity label (i.e., speech). However, my story is reflexive of my dis/ability label of SLI. For example, when I was 4 years old, I experienced the unexpected death of my mother and stopped speaking for well over a year. In elementary school, I was pulled out of general education classes to work with a speech pathologist. The effect of my speech disruptions manifested itself in my incorrect enunciation of syllables, words, and sounds and revealed itself in my written communication (i.e., syntax). Thus, the opportunity to learn phonetically while I was a child affected my accent as an adult and my verbal and written communication.

Therefore, I critically analyzed not only the voices of five BWD in my study (Cannon, 2019), but I also reviewed the voices of seven BWD within the literature review to examine from their perspective how they perceived and discussed their dis/ability as they interacted with their professors, family members, and peers.

Subverted Truths: Race and Ability

Within Cannon (2019), I identified *truth themes* (i.e., pathology, disablement, and exclusion) and revealed the terrible, sticky truths associated with these themes that explicate a master narrative about acceptable norms that are found in racialized systems of oppression (e.g., schools and universities) that leave a negative residue in the psyche of BWD. Terrible and sticky truths are truth themes carried out (i.e., enacted) by nondisabled people. For example,

Alice, a BWD participant in my study, who dreamed about her future working in the postsecondary field, said:

> This man [who] has basically laughed in my face when I asked him, well, how long do I have to wait before I can apply for my record to be expunged here in [this state]. [Professor] "It'll be on your record for 99 years." You have to wait 99 years. And I was like, wow, really? You know, because I knew he was being smart alecky.

After Alice heard this, she was discouraged and contemplated not showing up as the guest speaker at a women's prison. She continues, "You know, honestly, I did not feel like going, to be very honest with you." The deficit thoughts, attitudes, and treatments of nondisabled people, whether intentionally or nonintentionally, left a sticky residue on her psyche.

My findings about how BWD described their transition and postsecondary educational experiences suggest that they did so through the use of their voices countering those terrible and sticky truths—and through subverted truths they (re)defined identities and radical love, (re)placed competence and knowledge, and (re)defined sisterhood and community. The BWD reconfigured, resisted, reauthored, and talked back to the terrible sticky truths that they experienced in social and educational settings. To illustrate with Karen and Alice's words from their third interview question about meaning-making, Karen argued, "I'm Black, in college, I'm a woman with a disability. I mean, just sometimes labels harm people—they label you but they don't be thinking like, okay, labels come with you but I have to live my life." Relatedly, Alice argued,

> Because nine times out of 10, well, probably 10 out of 10, no doubt I already checked my information. I'm going to use the same sources you would use, or maybe better sources because I have to make sure that when I say something that it is accurate and true. Because I know that, you would like it very much if the only Black person in this class were absolutely wrong about her information. It's not that I want them to think that I'm criticizing everything, but I want them to know that I have to look to make sure because they're fallible just like I am. So, I can make mistakes, but so can they.

Alice's spirit displays a Black woman's desire for human dignity, which goes beyond respect for their intellectual thought as raced women (Cooper, 2017). Here, I illustrate how (re)defined identity and radical love reveal these women's assets (e.g., spirit, heritage, and rhetoric) in relation to how they counter, acknowledge, and validate their transitions and educational experiences and in the context of terrible and sticky truths (M. Cannon, 2019). By *(re)defined identity*, I mean the representation of complex identities within sociocultural and historical contexts that acknowledge and validate BWD intersectional identities in contrast to other imposed social identities. By *radical love*, I mean rethinking how we value people's differences by going against structures and institutions that profit from sorting individuals' differences and respecting one's own worth to radically perceive and love others (Taylor, 2018).

In particular, these women's voices/counternarratives/assets, illustrated through the subverted truth of (re)defined identities and radical love, are what emerge from the excerpts of the BWD interviews. They challenge us to consider the multiple identities that individuals develop in connection to sociocultural and historical contexts. These socially constructed identities (e.g., deficit labels) are "baggage" that is "too heavy to carry" (Gold & Richards, 2012, p. 144) and require something greater to assist—an asset such as radical love. Accordingly, radical love goes against structures and institutions that sort individuals by differences (e.g., race, gender, disability, etc.). Instead it is steadfast, unwavering, and daringly defies dominant reasoning (Dotson, 2013; Taylor, 2018). I argue that it is even more:

> Love the Lord your God with all your heart and with all your soul and with all your strength and with all your mind. . . . Love your neighbor as yourself (*New American Standard Bible*, Luke 10:27).

This kind of love is unconditional—it is *agape*—originated by God, extended toward others, and is benevolent with sharing authentic confidence in one's worth in the sight of God. This concept has been valued among the Black women/community and is empowering when coupled with faith. Agape love undergirds one of the most radical love actions possible (Cannon & Morton, 2015; Morton & Cannon, 2020). Thus, the constructed identities of BWD subverted by the voices/counternarratives/assets of BWD about transitions and education is evidence of their legitimacy—their expert knowledge of and experiences with racism and ableism with the *ability* to (re)interpret the truth themes. The processes of redefining, supporting, and validating BWD experiences stem from their unique perspective in the world (Annamma et al., 2016), as illustrated in the next paragraph.

Tammy is a Black woman with cerebral palsy. As an adult woman, Tammy recalled a painful, disabling experience during her childhood when she was rendered powerless (Hollins & Sinason, 2000). Her mobility was restricted by a caregiver's disapproval of her crawling.

> I used to be able to crawl on the floor and I used to be very mobile crawling on the floor. But in foster care, I had a foster parent who did not like for me to crawl on the dirty floor, well she seen a family surgeon where I can get surgery and did not have to crawl on the floor. Now I cannot even crawl on the floor anymore due to the surgery. (M. Cannon, 2019, p. 121)

Tammy's parents did not value her perspective of her mobility, and her narrative demonstrates grief and some guilt. This "guilt" was socially engendered via psychoemotional disablism (Hernández-Saca & Cannon, 2019; Petersen, 2006; Reeve, 2002, 2019; Thomas, 1999). Yet, through the subverted truth of (re)defined identity and radical love, she stated, "I know why God put me in here. Not because I know I can't get up . . . but it is to encourage people that are in a wheelchair" (M. Cannon, 2019, p. 134).

Ableism, like disablement, is an understanding of disability whereby society disables the individual and/or body (Taylor, 2018) and impacts the perceptions and cultural arrangements in the context of trying to understand what dis/ability and identity mean (Annamma et al., 2016; Shakespeare, 1996; Wolbring, 2012). Furthermore, being made "unfit" and disabled due to disability diagnoses, structures, and environments mostly dominated by nondisabled people is disabling of those who are disabled (Davis, 2013). For example, Alice is a Black woman with comorbid diagnoses:

> I've been diagnosed with a compulsive disorder, also, obsessive-compulsive disorder, and bipolar disorder. You know, when I was about 12 or 13, the symptoms were just way out of control, mother was like, "I cannot take this." Black parents, they're not so in tune. . . . You don't hear about these things in the Black society because you're just acting out. . . . Blacks do not attribute the children's behavior as a mental illness. (M. Cannon, 2019, p. 114)

Alice argued that the medication she took resulted in overmedication that presumed her intellectual inferiority, which warranted her self-advocacy and determination to redefine her identity. It is important to process this reidentifying through the lens of a radical love that advocated for a restorative consciousness. Alice (re)claimed her right to define herself-for-herself as *the* authority on her mental illness. She also lovingly countered current perceptions of Black parents that normalize their children's behaviors as "acting out" instead of symptoms from mental health stresses. These encounters and their effects on her life and education interconnect to ways racism and ableism are normalized by hegemonic influences and power over those on the margins or at intersections of oppression.

Discussion

Through the use of DS/DSE, CRT, and womanist/Black feminist theories, tenets, counternarrative, and voice, this chapter highlights the intersections of race, dis/ability, and ableism practices in transition and education for BWD and, furthermore, the importance of privileging, listening to, and challenging dominant views about BWD and BIPOC folks with disabilities who are pathologized, disabled, and excluded in school and broader society is emphasized. The protests and growing self-advocacy in the 1970s of ordinary people treated differently because of their disabilities are foundational to DS (Fine & Asch, 1988; McDermott & Varenne, 1995). Yet we see that years later in schools throughout the United States the understanding of how disability is linked to intersections of oppression and other markers of differences has ignored disability and intersectionality in its analysis (Artiles, 2013; Ferri, 2010; Hernández-Saca et al., 2018).

Disability studies have reflected the efforts of scholars with dis/abilities (and nondisabled colleagues) to conceptualize and interpret the common complaints about the different treatment of people (i.e., Blacks, other groups, and those with dis/abilities) and their families (Lynn & Dixson, 2013; Shapiro, 1994). Artiles (1998) argued for including the perspectives of investigators and people of color within research in order to contextualize and appropriately respond to differences in schools (see Patton, 1998). However, up until recently, the focus on disability from the perspective of Black folks did not exist. Reflecting on the development of Black disability studies, the director of the National Black Disability Coalition (NBDC) emphasized "authenticity and commitment" in the work of helping "one another learn what we need to know to assist students in their discovery" (Durhamn et al., 2015, para. 6).

The structures of inequitable schools, the lack of resources, racism, and other challenges in institutions of learning, special education, and classroom practices are normalizing practices (Patton, 1998; Thorius & Stephenson, 2012; Thorius & Waitoller, 2017; Waitoller & Thorius, 2016). However, as with the movements for civil rights (Hernández-Saca et al., 2018) and disability rights, disability culture continues to have trouble reaching people who have little access to resources or higher education. In secondary education settings, disability is treated via practices that disconnect and marginalize disabled students and their parents. It is mostly systemic segregation, seclusion, and restraints that separate disabled students from other students (Vega et al., 2015). This is problematic for Blacks, Latinos/as, and other subgroups when our school structures and our pedagogical practices exclude, racially segregate, and lack resources for students to succeed. It is germane that critical discussions among DS scholars and CRT scholars involve educators and policymakers who are the decision-makers regarding operations of schools and colleges (Durhamn et al., 2015; Waitoller & Thorius, 2016).

Special education scholars are increasingly addressing the pathology of students of color with dis/abilities and those receiving special education services (e.g., Artiles, 2011; Artiles et al., 2010; Danforth & Taff, 2004). A growing group of critical special education, DSE, and CRT scholars are taking to task special education for pathologizing youth of color and those with dis/abilities (Annamma et al., 2013; Artiles, 2015; Blanchett, 2006, 2010; Connor, 2013; Ferri, 2010; Solórzano & Yosso, 2002; Tate, 1997; Waitoller & Thorius, 2016). Some of these scholars operate at the borders of DS and CRT communities to disrupt and deconstruct oppression in schools for students of color with dis/abilities (Valenzuela, 2010), including the support of their access to college and equitable postsecondary outcomes (Castellanos et al., 2016; Hutcheon & Wolbring, 2012; King, 2009).

In my previous research, the centering of voices and counternarratives of BWD transitions and education as assets have honored each woman's description of self, their self-naming, self-definition, and self-advocacy praxis that led these women to a restorative consciousness (King & Swartz, 2015; Wilson, 1993). This restorative consciousness also allowed each of the BWD the dignity and humanization that she deserved.

> Dignity highlights how each woman conceptualized her unique experience as a Black woman with dis/abilities. Movement from deficit-minded findings to living life from an emancipatory perspective require[d] re-envisioning dis/ability as an asset. In other words, *pausing* the taking in of pathological ideologies that permeate our broader society about Black women, [countering] the varied needs and preferences of BWD and *replacing* them with a sense of agency to conceptualize who they are above the imposed identity marker they are assigned. (M. Cannon, 2019, p. 60)

Voices and counternarratives are a catalyst for each BWD's ability to draw on her assets in postsecondary education in order to assist her in subverting the master narratives (M. Cannon, 2019). This chapter centered BWD in society as well as scholarship (e.g., white disability studies [Bell, 2011]) through continual subversion of dominant views that pathologize, disable, and exclude them from research. BWD are often written about, and such approaches fail to feature their voices/counternarratives/assets appropriately.

Implications

Similarly, concerning subverting dominant views of those on the margins, members of underrepresented and diverse groups, and/or those racialized and disabled by others, K–12 schools, or postsecondary education have scholars whose pedagogies/praxis examine and addresses the impact of inequitable educational systems and practices. For example, Waitoller and Thorius's (2016) scholarship extended that of Paris and Alim's (2012) culturally sustaining pedagogy (CSP) and Rose and Meyer's (2002) universal design for learning (UDL) via their cross-pollination of *loving critiques* of two asset pedagogies. One (i.e., UDL) provides students and teachers several pathways to "engage in a meaningful interrogation of ableism and racism" connected to BWD and BIPOC communities identified at multiple intersections of differences seeking knowledge (Waitoller & Thorius 2016, p. 374). There is a need for BIPOC scholars to discuss and produce scholarship and access asset pedagogies from a BIPOC perspective such as the Black disability studies (Black DS) approach. For example, the NBDC work, which focuses on the United States and the African diaspora (Durhamn et al., 2015), is promising for DS and DSE. The NBDC's mission is to "create a space for inquiry within universities that brings together faculty and students [. . .] to consider Black disability issues within broad-based social, cultural and historical contexts" (Durhamn et al., 2015, para. 1). The imminent development of Black DS is a charge to incorporate knowledge of DS within Black/Africana studies. The prospect of a Black DS is relevant to the need to develop a Black/Africana pedagogy that addresses race *and* ableism and produces dialogues and antiracist trainings from those directly impacted. Additionally, this work would continue to counter Eurocentric racism and white supremacy practices in education and their falsification of Black consciousness (Wilson, 1993, 1998).

Discussion Questions

1. In what other ways does racism and ableism's pathologization of Black and Brown bodies give us a window to whose voices matter in the discussion about racism and ableism?

2. In what ways would an ongoing dialogue between DS and CRT (Bell, 2011; Ferri, 2010) demystify racism and ableism practices for those who are directly impacted?

3. How could transition education scholars intentionally highlight institutional systemic hierarchies and dichotomies between white students and those of color and those labeled abled and disabled?

4. In what ways could a Black DS contribute to current DS or DSE literature in the area of deconstructing, disrupting, and subverting the structural inequities experienced by marginalized individuals (e.g., Black and Brown women) and those with dis/abilities navigating educational spaces?

Acknowledgments

This chapter acknowledges Kathleen King Thorius, my dissertation chair, and the five Black women with dis/abilities (BWD) who participated in my research study and final dissertation (*Because I Am Human: Centering Black Women With Dis/Abilities in Transition Planning From High School to College*), where I explored BWD stories at the intersections of their race, gender, and dis/ability, and privileged their narratives as knowledge (Cannon & Thorius, 2013). The dominant views that pathologized, disabled, and excluded these five BWD's voices, structures, practices, theory, and philosophical and ethical approaches to education that happen through social processes and imposed truths were countered and subverted by the perspectives of these women. This chapter also extends the body of knowledge from my dissertation and its importance in privileging, listening to, and challenging dominant views about Black and Brown folks with disabilities.

Notes

1. *Black* here specifically means African women/girls of African descent. In this chapter, "I capitalize 'Black' because 'Blacks,' and 'African Americans,' Latinos, and other 'minorities,' constitute a specific cultural group and, as such, require denotation as a proper noun" (M. Cannon, 2019, p. 1). Following Crenshaw's (1991) work, I "do not capitalize 'white,' which is not a proper noun since 'whites' do not constitute a specific cultural group. For the same reason, I do not capitalize 'women of color'" (p. 1241).

2. I use the terms *dis/abled, dis/ability*, or *dis/abilities* throughout the this chapter to delineate the idea that "dis/ability and ability differences are social constructions" (Kozleski & Thorius, 2013, p. 9). I also use *disability* without the slash between "dis" and "ability" to indicate the existence of disability as an impairment or a real predicament (Shakespeare, 1996).

3. The term *transition* by itself represents what Halpern (1994) defined as a "period of floundering that occurs for at least the first several years [post] leaving school as adolescents attempt to assume a variety of adult roles in their communities" (p. 203). I would add that it is also a time of discovery and growth in the area of identity and human development post high school and in preparation for the next transition (postsecondary, vocation, or residential living).

4. Diana, a BWD, was a participant in the dissertation study. Please note all participants' names are pseudonyms.

5. In this chapter's literature review, I only consider the voices of the Black women with disabilities participants within four of the five research studies reviewed in the larger study (i.e., Ferri & Connor, 2010; Petersen, 2006, 2009; Trainor, 2007), and only include three of their voices/stories (i.e., Clarissa, Tanya, Shana).

References

African American Policy Forum. (2012). *A primer on intersectionality.* Columbia Law School.

Annamma, S. A., Connor, D., & Ferri, B. (2013). Dis/ability critical race studies (DisCrit): Theorizing at the intersections of race and dis/ability. *Race Ethnicity and Education, 16*(1), 1–31. https://doi.org/10.1080/13613324.2012.730511

Annamma, S. A., Connor, D., & Ferri, B. (2016). Touchstone text: Disability critical race studies (DisCrit): Theorizing at the intersections of race and disa/bility. In D. Connor, B. Ferri, & S. A. Annamma (Eds.), *DisCrit: Disability studies and critical race theory in education* (pp. 9–34). Teachers College.

Annamma, S., Ferri, B. A., & Connor, D. J. (2018). Cultivating and expanding disability critical race theory (DisCrit). In K. Ellis, R. Garland-Thomson, M. Kent, & R. Robertson (Eds.), *Manifestos for the future of critical disability studies: Volume 1* (pp. 230–238). Routledge.

Annamma, S. A., & Morrison, D. (2018). DisCrit classroom ecology: Using praxis to dismantle dysfunctional education ecologies. *Teaching and Teacher Education, 73,* 70–80. https://doi.org/10.1016/j.tate.2018.03.008

Artiles, A. J. (1998). The dilemma of difference: Enriching the disproportionality discourse with theory and context. *The Journal of Special Education, 32*(1), 32–36. https://doi.org/10.1177/002246699803200105

Artiles, A. J. (2011). Toward an interdisciplinary understanding of educational equity and difference: The case of the racialization of ability. *Educational Researcher, 40*(9), 431–445. https://doi.org/10.3102/0013189X11429391

Artiles, A. J. (2013). Untangling the racialization of disabilities: An intersectionality critique across disability models. *Du Bois Review, 10,* 329–347. http://www.blackwomenrhetproject.com/uploads/2/5/5/9/25595205/artiles.untangling_the_racialization_of_disabilities.pdf

Artiles, A. J. (2015). Beyond responsiveness to identity badges: Future research on culture in disability and implications for response to intervention. *Educational Review, 67*(1), 1–22. https://doi.org/10.1080/00131911.2014.934322

Artiles, A. J. (2019). Fourteenth annual Brown lecture in educational research: Re-envisioning equity research: Disability identification disparities as a case in point. *Educational Researcher, 48*(6), 325–335. https://doi.org/10.3102%2F0013189X19871949

Artiles, A. J., Kozleski, E. B., Trent, S. C., Osher, D., & Ortiz, A. (2010). Justifying and explaining disproportionality, 1968–2008: A critique of underlying views of culture. *Exceptional Children, 76*(3), 279–299. https://doi.org/10.1177/001440291007600303

Arzubiaga, A. E., Artiles, A. J., King, K. A., & Harris-Murri, N. (2008). Beyond research on cultural minorities: Challenges and implications of research as situated cultural practice. *Exceptional Children, 74*(3), 309–327. https://doi.org/10.1177/001440290807400303

Baglieri, S., Bejoian, L. M., Broderick, A. A., Connor, D. J., & Valle, J. (2011). [Re] Claiming. *Teachers College Record, 113*(10), 2122–2154.

Bell, C. M. (2011). *Blackness and disability: Critical examinations and cultural interventions.* LIT Verlag Münster.

Blanchett, W. J. (2006). Disproportionate representation of African American students in special education: Acknowledging the role of white privilege and racism. *Educational Researcher, 35*(6), 24–28. https://doi.org/10.3102/0013189X035006024

Blanchett, W. J. (2010). Telling it like it is: The role of race, class, & culture in the perpetuation of learning disability as a privileged category for the White middle class. *Disability Studies Quarterly, 30*(2), 1234–1287. http://dsq-sds.org/article/view/

Cannon, K. (1988). *Black womanist ethics.* Scholars Press.

Cannon, M. A. (2019). *Because I am human: Centering Black women with dis/abilities in transition planning from high school to college* [Unpublished doctoral dissertation]. Indiana University-Purdue University Indianapolis.

Cannon, M. A., & Morton, C. (2015). God consciousness enacted: Living, moving, and having my being in Him. *Western Journal of Higher Education, 39*(2), 147–156. https://www.proquest.com/openview/bad5753ae4a70a662f6b45af546047 77/1?pq-origsite=gscholar&cbl=47709

Cannon, M. A., & Thorius, K. A. K. (2013, August). *Educational experiences of African American women with label with dis/ability.* [Paper presentation]. CRSEA Conference at Vanderbilt University Law School, Nashville, TN, United States.

Castellanos, J., Gloria, A. M., Besson, D., & Harvey, L. O. C. (2016). Mentoring matters: Racial ethnic minority undergraduates' cultural fit, mentorship, and college and life satisfaction. *Journal of College Reading and Learning, 46*(2), 81–98. https://doi.org/10.1080/10790195.2015.1121792

Connor, D. (2013). Social justice in education for students with disabilities. In L. Florian (Ed.), *The SAGE handbook of special education* (Vol. 1, pp. 111–128). SAGE. https://doi.org/10.4135/9781446282236.n9

Cooper, B. C. (2017). *Beyond respectability: The intellectual thought of race women.* University of Illinois Press.

Crenshaw, K. (1989). Demarginalizing the intersection of race and sex: A black feminist critique of antidiscrimination doctrine, feminist theory and antiracist politics. *University of Chicago Legal Feminist Press, 8*(1), 139–167.

Crenshaw, K. W. (1991). Mapping the margins: Intersectionality, identity politics, and violence against women of color. In K. Crenshaw, N. Gotanda, G. Peller, & K. Thomas (Eds.), *Critical race theory: Key writings that formed the movement* (pp. 357–383). The New Press.

Danforth, S., & Taff, S. D. (2004). Examining the practical implications of special education paradigms of social thought. In S. Danforth & S. D. Taff (Eds.), *Crucial readings in special education* (pp. 1–14). Prentice Hall.

Davis, L. J. (2013). The end of identity politics: On disability as an unstable category. In L. J. David (Ed.), *The disability studies reader* (4th ed., pp. 263–278). Routledge.

Davis, L. P., & Museus, S. (2019). What is deficit thinking? An analysis of conceptualizations of deficit thinking and implications for scholarly research. *Currents,*
1(1), 117–130. http://dx.doi.org/10.3998/currents.17387731.0001.110

Delgado, R. (1989). Storytelling for oppositionists and others: A plea for narrative.
Michigan Law Review, 87(8), 2411–2441.

Delgado, R., & Stefancic, J. (2012). *Critical race theory: An introduction.* New York
University Press.

Dotson, K. (2013). Radical love: Black philosophy as deliberate acts of inheritance.
The Black Scholar, 43(4), 38–45. https://doi.org/10.5816/blackscholar.43.4.0038

Durhamn, J., Harris, J., Jarrett, S., Moore, L., Nishida, A., Price, M., & Schalk, S.
(2015). Developing and reflecting on a Black disability studies pedagogy: Work
from the National Black Disability Coalition. *Disability Studies Quarterly, 35*(2).
http://dx.doi.org/10.18061/dsq.v35i2.4637

Ferri, B. A. (2010). A dialogue we've yet to have: Race and disability studies. In
C. Dudley-Marling & A. Gurn (Eds.), *The myth of the normal curve* (Vol. 11,
pp. 139–150). Peter Lang.

Ferri, B. A., & Connor, D. J. (2010). "I was the special ed. girl": Urban working
class young women of colour. *Gender and Education, 22*(1), 105–121. https://
doi.org/10.1080/09540250802612688

Fine, M., & Asch, A. (1988). Disability beyond stigma: Social interaction,
discrimination, and activism. *Journal of Social Issues, 44*(1), 3–21. https://doi
.org/10.1111/j.1540-4560.1988.tb02045.x

Ginwright, S. (2011). Hope, healing, and care: Pushing the boundaries of civic
engagement for African American youth. *Liberal Education, 97*(2), 34–39. http://
www.sbh4all.org/wp-content/uploads/2016/08/hope-healing-care-article.pdf

Givens, G. (1999). Writing self within the text: The impact of an educational narrative in the life of the researcher. *Educational Foundations, 13*(1), 41–60.

Gold, M. E., & Richards, H. (2012). To label or not to label: The special education
question for African Americans. *Educational Foundations, 26*, 143–156. https://
eric.ed.gov/?id=EJ968822

González, N., Moll, L. C., & Amanti, C. (Eds.). (2006). *Funds of knowledge: Theorizing practices in households, communities, and classrooms.* Routledge.

Halpern, A. S. (1994). Quality of life for students with disabilities in transition
from school to adulthood. *Social Indicators Research, 33*, 193–236. https://doi
.org/10.1007/BF01078962

Hernández-Saca, D. (2016). *Re-framing the master narratives of Dis/ability through an*
emotion lens: Voices of Latina/o students with learning dis/abilities [Doctoral dissertation,
Indiana University-Purdue University Indianapolis]. Order No. 10143698. ProQuest
Dissertations & Theses Global (1812960986). http://ulib.iupui.edu/cgi-bin/proxy.
pl?url=http://search.proquest.com/docview/1812960986?accountid=7398

Hernández-Saca, D. I., & Cannon, M. A. (2016, July 23). Disability as psycho-
emotional disablism: A theoretical and philosophical review of education
theory and practice. *Encyclopedia of Educational Philosophy and Theory.* https://
doi.org/10.1007/978-981-287-532-7_456-1

Hernández-Saca, D. I., & Cannon, M. A. (2019). Interrogating disability epistemologies: Towards collective dis/ability intersectional emotional, affective and spiritual autoethnographies for healing. *International Journal of Qualitative Studies in Education, 32*(3), 243–262. https://doi.org/10.1080/09518398.2019.1576944

Hernández-Saca, D. I., Gutmann Kahn, L., & Cannon, M. A. (2018). Intersectionality dis/ability research: How dis/ability research in education engages intersectionality to uncover the multidimensional construction of dis/abled experiences. *Review of Research in Education, 42*(1), 286–311. http://www.jstor.org/stable/41068619

Hill Collins, P. H. (2000). *Black feminist thought: Knowledge, consciousness, and the politics of empowerment* (2nd ed.). Routledge.

Hill Collins, P. H. (2003). Some group matters: Intersectionality, situated standpoint, and black feminist thought. In T. L. Lott and J. P. Pittman (Eds.), *A companion to African American philosophy* (pp. 205–229). Blackwell.

Holcomb-McCoy, C. C., & Moore-Thomas, C. (2001). Empowering African-American adolescent females. *Professional School Counseling, 5*(1), 19–27.

Hollins, S., & Sinason, V. (2000). Psychotherapy, learning disabilities and trauma: New perspectives. *The British Journal of Psychiatry, 176*(1), 32–36. https://www.cambridge.org/core/journals/the-british-journal-of-psychiatry/article/psychotherapy-learning-disabilities-and-trauma-new-perspectives/E3A14B7A0C1C290A35A19034A630949D

hooks, b. (2000). *Feminist theory: From margin to center.* Routledge.

Hutcheon, E. J., & Wolbring, G. (2012). Voices of "disabled" postsecondary students: Examining higher education "disability" policy using an ableism lens. *Journal of Diversity in Higher Education, 5*(1), 39. https://psycnet.apa.org/buy/2012-02768-001

Individuals with Dis/abilities Education Improvement Act of 2004, U.S.C. & 614 *et seq.* (2004).

Jackson, P., & Penrose, J. (Eds.). (1994). *Constructions of race, place, and nation.* University of Minnesota Press.

King, J. E., & Swartz, E. E. (2015). *The Afrocentric praxis of teaching for freedom: Connecting culture to learning.* Routledge.

King, K. A. (2009). A review of programs that promote higher education access for underrepresented students. *Journal of Diversity in Higher Education, 2*(1), 1–15. https://doi.org/10.1037/a0014327

Kozleski, E. B., & Thorius, K. K. (Eds.). (2013). *Ability, equity, and culture: Sustaining inclusive urban education reform.* Teachers College Press.

Ladson-Billings, G., & Tate, W. F. (1995). Toward a critical race theory of education. *Teachers College Record, 97*(1), 47–68.

Linton, S. (1998). *Claiming disability: Knowledge and identity.* NYU Press.

Lynn, M., & Dixson, A. D. (Eds.). (2013). *Handbook of critical race theory in education.* Routledge.

Matsuda, M. J. (1991). Voices of America: Accent, antidiscrimination law, and a jurisprudence for the last reconstruction. *Yale Law Journal, 100,* 1329–1407.

McCall, L. (2005). The complexity of intersectionality. *Signs*, *30*(3), 1771–1800. https://www.journals.uchicago.edu/doi/abs/10.1086/426800

McDermott, R., & Varenne, H. (1995). Culture as disability. *Anthropology & Education Quarterly*, *26*(3), 324–348. https://doi.org/10.1525/aeq.1995.26.3.05x0936z

Menchetti, M. B. (2008). Transition assessment: Emerging guidelines and promising practices. In F. Rusch (Ed.), *Beyond high school: Preparing adolescents for tomorrow's challenges* (pp. 178–199). Pearson Prentice Hall.

Mishler, E. (2004). Historian of the self: Restorying lives, revisiting identities. *Research in Human Development*, *1*(1–2), 102–121. https://doi.org/10.1080/154 27609.2004.9683331

Morton, C., & Cannon, M. A. (2020). Negotiating troubled waters through "Spiritual Sistering." In R. Jeffries (Ed.), *Queen mothers: Articulating the spirit of Black women teacher-leaders*. Information Age.

Myers, L. J. (2013). Restoration of spirit: An African-centered communal health model. *Journal of Black Psychology*, *39*(3), 257–260. https://doi.org/ 10.1177/0095798413478080

Nabors, N. A., & Pettee, M. F. (2003). Womanist therapy with African American women with dis/abilities. *Women & Therapy*, *26*(3–4), 331–341. https://doi .org/10.1300/J015v26n03_10

Paris, D., & Alim, H. S. (2014). What are we seeking to sustain through culturally sustaining pedagogy? A loving critique forward. *Harvard Educational Review*, *84*(1), 85–100. https://doi.org/10.17763/haer.84.1.982l873k2ht16m77

Patton, M. J. (1998). The disproportionate representation of African Americans in special education: Looking behind the curtain for understanding and solutions. *The Journal of Special Education*, *32*(1), 25–31.

Petersen, J. A. (2006). An African-American woman with dis/abilities: The intersection of gender, race, and disability. *Disability & Society*, *21*(7), 721–734. https://doi .org/10.1080/09687590600995345

Petersen, J. A. (2009). Shana's story: The struggles, quandaries and pitfalls surrounding self-determination. *Disability Studies Quarterly*, *29*(2), 2–20. http://www .dsq-sds.org/article/view/922/1097

Phillips, L. (Ed.). (2006). *The womanist reader*. Taylor & Francis.

Reeve, D. (2002). Negotiating psycho-emotional dimensions of disability and their influence on identity constructions. *Disability & Society*, *17*(5), 493–508. https:// doi.org/10.1080/09687590220148487

Reeve, D. (2020). Psycho-emotional disablism: The missing link?. In N. Watson & S. Vehmas (Eds.), *Routledge handbook of disability studies* (pp. 102–116). Routledge.

Reid, D. K., & Knight, M. G. (2006). Disability justifies exclusion of minority students: A critical history grounded in disability studies. *Educational Researcher*, *35*(6), 18–23. https://doi.org/10.3102/0013189X035006018

Rose, D. H., & Meyer, A. (2002). *Teaching every student in the digital age: Universal design for learning*. Association for Supervision and Curriculum Development.

Shakespeare, T. (1996). Disability, identity and difference. In C. Barnes & G. Mercer (Eds.), *Exploring the divide* (pp. 94–113). The Disability Press.

Shapiro, J. P. (1994). *No pity: People with disabilities forging a new civil rights movement*. Three Rivers Press.

Sitlington, P. L. (2003). Postsecondary education: The other transition. *Exceptionality, 11*(2), 103–113. https://doi.org/10.1207/S15327035EX1102_05

Smith, P. (2008). Cartographies of eugenics and special education: A history of the (ab) normal. In S. L. Gabel & S. Danforth (Eds.), *Disability and the politics of education: An international reader* (pp. 417–432). Peter Lang.

Solorzano, D. G., & Bernal, D. D. (2001). Examining transformational resistance through a critical race and LatCrit theory framework: Chicana and Chicano students in an urban context. *Urban Education, 36*(3), 308–342. https://doi.org/10.1177/0042085901363002

Solórzano, D. G., & Yosso, T. J. (2002). Critical race methodology: Counterstorytelling as an analytical framework for education research. *Qualitative Inquiry, 8*(1), 23–44. https://doi.org/10.1177/107780040200800103

Tate, W. F., IV. (1997). Critical race theory and education: History, theory, and implications. *Review of Research in Education, 22*(1), 195–247. https://doi.org/10.3102/0091732X022001195

Taylor, S. R. (2018). *The body is not an apology: The power of radical self-love*. Berrett-Koehler Publishers.

Thoma, C. A., Rogan, P., & Baker, S. R. (2001). Student involvement in transition planning: Unheard voices. *Education and Training in Mental Retardation and Developmental Disabilities, 36*(1), 16–29.

Thomas, C. (1999). *Female forms: Experiencing and understanding disability*. Open University Press.

Thorius, K. A., & Waitoller, F. R. (2017). Strategic coalitions against exclusion at the intersection of race and disability—A rejoinder. *Harvard Educational Review, 87*(2), 251–257. https://doi.org/10.17763/1943-5045-87.2.251

Thorius, K. A. K., & Stephenson, J. (2012). Racial and ethnic disproportionality in special education. In A. L. Noltemeyer & C. McLoughlin (Eds.), *Disproportionality in education and special education: A guide to creating more equitable learning environments* (pp. 25–44).

Titchkosky, T., & Michalko, R. (2012). The body as the problem of individuality: A phenomenological dis/ability studies approach. In D. Goodley, B. Hughes, & L. Davis (Eds.), *Dis/ability and Social Theory* (pp. 127–142). https://doi.org/10.1057/9781137023001_8

Trainor, A. (2007). Perceptions of adolescent girls with LD regarding self-determination and postsecondary transition planning. *Learning Disability Quarterly, 30*, 31–45. https://doi.org/10.2307/30035514

Trainor, A. (2017). *Transition by design: Improving equity and outcomes for adolescents with dis/abilities*. Teachers College.

Valenzuela, A. (2010). *Subtractive schooling: US-Mexican youth and the politics of caring*. SUNY Press.

Vega, D., Moore, J. L., III, & Miranda, A. H. (2015). Who really cares? Urban youths' perceptions of parental and programmatic support. *School Community Journal, 25*(1), 53–72. https://eric.ed.gov/?id=EJ1066219

Waitoller, F. R., & Thorius, K. A. (2016). Cross-pollinating culturally sustaining pedagogy and universal design for learning: Toward an inclusive pedagogy that accounts for dis/ability. *Harvard Educational Review, 86*(3), 366–389. https://doi.org/10.17763/1943-5045-86.3.366

Wilson, A. N. (1993). *The falsification of Afrikan consciousness: Eurocentric history, psychiatry, and the politics of white supremacy.* Afrikan World InfoSystems.

Wilson, A. N. (1998). *Blueprint for Black power: A moral, political, and economic imperative for the twenty-first century.* Afrikan World InfoSystems.

Wolbring, G. (2012). Expanding ableism: Taking down the ghettoization of impact of disability studies scholars. *Societies, 2*(3), 75–83. http://dx.doi.org/10.3390/soc2030075

13

THE MISTRESS AND THE MASTER'S HOUSE

Revisiting Lorde's Speech to the New York University Institute for the Humanities

Mildred Boveda

> *Survival is not an academic skill. It is learning how to stand alone, unpopular and sometimes reviled, and how to make common cause with those others identified as outside the structures in order to define and seek a world in which we can all flourish. It is learning how to take our differences and make them strengths. (Lorde, 1979, p. 99)*

I am the U.S.-born daughter of a Black Dominican woman who spent her youth serving people who were more White, more affluent, and held more power than her. Or were they *really* less Black, less poor, and less subordinated? The legacy of colonialism, anti-Haitianism, imperialism, and anti-Blackness in the Dominican Republic troubles these simple Black/White, rich/poor dichotomies. Regardless of whether the framing is that they were whiter than my mother, or less Black than her, the exploitative dynamic and power differential she experienced are undeniable. In this chapter, I center my understanding of my mother's childhood experiences to situate myself within the greater history of Black women in the United States who, like Audre Lorde, Angela Davis, and bell hooks, considered the interconnectivity of our issues in this country with the oppressions affecting multiple-minoritized people around the world. Contextualizing how the global colonial project is intertwined with my current role as a U.S.-based educational researcher, I revisit Audre Lorde's (1979) speech, "The Master's Tools Will Never Dismantle the Master's House," given at the New York University Institute for the Humanities, to examine the educational experiences of Black women and girls in relation to "the master," his house, and also his "mistress."

Mami: The Source of My Ontoepistemic Orientation

My mother, Mami, was once an unpaid servant. Even today, she maintains a relationship with the family that, approximately 60 years ago, first entangled her into their lives. At the age of 11, Mami desired to go to school. Doña Clara, the wife of a town official, promised my grandmother that she would pay for Mami's education during a time and place where access to public schools was not available—especially not for the daughter of two *campesinos* who themselves never learned to read or write. Unfortunately, Mami was never paid nor sent to school.

Doña Clara's and Mami's relationship began in the 1940s when Mami's mother became a widow. At that time, she could not even afford to buy her children shoes. Although working as a servant in Doña Clara's house meant that Mami was subjected to the housekeeping demands of strangers, in her mistress's home, she had access to greater comforts than what her mother was able to provide. For example, my grandmother Rosa lived at the margins of a rural town, in a two-room wooden shack covered with a tin roof; the family my mother served lived near the town plaza, in a house made of brick and mortar. She also knew that, by living with Doña Clara, she was alleviating a burden for her mother (Boveda, 2021). Mami was the fourth child of Rosa's eight surviving children, and her mother had to attend to the needs of the younger children. As such, Mami continued to live at Doña Clara's house for 7 years in a servant quarter that housed two beds. During her time there, she learned many skills and was exposed to a different life than her mother experienced. Other Black girls were recruited to help Mami tend to Doña Clara, her mistress's husband, and their daughter and son who were about the same age as Mami. Few girls stayed as long as she did, primarily because they did not meet Doña Clara's expectations.

Growing up, hearing these and other stories about how Mami navigated a world that was sexist, classist, and anti-Black situated my understanding of who I am (Boveda, 2017) and helped me forge an ontoepistemology that informs my research and theorizing about education and schooling (Boveda, 2019; Boveda & Bhattacharya, 2019). By *ontoepistemology*, I refer to an interconnected way of being and knowing that I rely on to make sense of my lived experiences, including my experiences as a Black woman in the academy. This ontoepistemic lens reveals the impossibility of separating the ways we generate knowledge from our material realities (Evans-Winter, 2021). Reflecting on my mother's socialization and its influence on my own upbringing and educational development, I address two questions. First, what are Black women in higher education's responsibilities to the Black girls who will eventually come through these "sacred halls"? Relatedly, when considering how we invest in the educational success of Black girls and women, what are the challenges and opportunities of Black women building coalitions with non-Black and White women? In asking these questions, I center girls in the United States and around the world who, like Mami, aspire(d) to reach higher levels of formalized education, but instead found themselves living in the master's house—recruited by his mistress, no less.

A Mami-Informed De/Colonial Analysis of the Mistress and the Master's House

The 1492 landing of Christopher Columbus on the islands of the Caribbean precipitated the colonization of Indigenous lands, enslavement and subjugation of non-Europeans, the persecution and marginalization of women and their ways of knowing (i.e., witch hunts, accusations of hysterics), and the plundering of resources throughout the world—all of which are linked to the development of universities in the modern and contemporary era (Grosfoguel, 2013). The exploitation of what came to be known as the Americas, coupled with the transatlantic trade of kidnapped and enslaved African people, precipitated and funded the establishment of these institutions of higher education (de Sousa Santos, 2015; Wilder, 2013), the Westernization of universities throughout the globe (Grosfoguel, 2013), and the eventual privileging of epistemologies of White men from five countries of the Global North: the United States, the United Kingdom, France, Germany, and to a lesser extent Italy (de Sousa Santos, 2010; Wilder, 2013).

The legacy of these colonial histories intersects with the type of access Black girls have to schooling and the academy. Black women faculty operate within a space established through the explicit exploitation and exclusion of Black women (Evans, 2008; Evans-Winters, 2019; White, 2009). As an Afro-Latina who is included among the Latina and Black women who make up 3% and 4%, respectively, of the full-time assistant professors in the country (National Center for Education Statistics, 2019), I continually reflect on what my responsibilities are in clarifying my resistance to the epistemological domination of the Westernized academy—even as I write in English, am employed by a U.S. institution, and publish my ideas about equity and justice in Western journals. I thus use the slash in *de/colonization* to indicate how as I attempt to disrupt inequities, I am also implicated in existing educational structures (Boveda & Bhattacharya, 2019).

Those of us engaged in equity-based education research and Black feminist theories may come across Audre Lorde's (1979) phrase "the master's tools will never dismantle the master's house" to, for example, discuss the methodological (im)possibilities of researching racial inequalities. Given my understanding of my mother's experiences as a youth—and the role the academy has in the hegemonic structures that led to her exclusion from formalized schooling—when engaging with the notion of the master's house I am reminded of her time in Doña Clara's house.

Mami literally lived in a master's house. Although Doña Clara would give Mami orders, Mami witnessed how Doña Clara had to answer to her husband, thus maintaining the patriarchal order that elevated his authority in their home. This was in sharp contrast to the decision-making partnership that Mami saw between her parents before her father died (Boveda, 2021). Furthermore, the irony of Doña Clara's name illustrates how the vestiges of slavery, patriarchy, colonialism, and other oppressions lingered over 100 years after Haitian revolutionaries ended the institutions of slavery on the island. The title translates from Spanish to English as "Mistress Claire"; its etymological translation is "light-skinned owner." When my mother sought to access formalized education, she was instead redirected to serve the needs of Doña Clara and her family. Today in U.S. schools, Black girls' and young women's initial entry to public schooling is most often ushered by teachers who are White women (Love, 2019). In analysis of relationships then and today, there is a need to look not only at the masters but also at their mistresses to understand their role in imparting the ways of knowing (epistemologies) and ways of being (ontologies) most privileged in Westernized educational systems.

What Mami and Lorde Teach Me About the Master's House

> Women of today are still being called upon to stretch across the gap of male ignorance and to educate men as to our existence and our needs. This is an old and primary tool of all oppressors to keep the oppressed occupied with the master's concerns. Now we hear that it is the task of Black and third world women to educate white women—in the face of tremendous resistance— as to our existence, our differences, our relative roles in our joint survival. This is a diversion of energies and a tragic repetition of racist patriarchal thought. (Lorde, 1979, p. 100)

Although not the space of formal schooling she desired, Doña Clara's house imparted lessons to Mami that permitted her the ability to make sense of what her options were in a world where imprints of enslavement lingered in people's minds and on their bodies. That is, being in proximity to Doña Clara furthered opened my mother's eyes to the realities of her family's situation. My mother's experiences may resonate with other Black women in the academy whose relatives served as "domestics" or servants in other (White) people's homes. These mothers, daughters, aunts, and grandmothers used the lessons learned in those houses to the benefit of their Black children and future generations.

Although she did not receive the formal education she desired, working in the master's house gave Mami more de/colonial, liberating possibilities than had she stayed living with her mother. Why? Because through hoarding of power and resources, not only were the master's tools found there, but also other resources Mami should have always had access to. What happens when you go from the rugged mountainside of a country in the Global South (or from the 'hood in the United States) and into the master's house? Often you realize that the house was built and decorated by materials that were yours and your ancestors' to begin with. The realization comes late in life, because your people were systematically barred from that house with the exception of the very few.

Keeping Mami's experience in mind, I now turn to Audre Lorde's speech. She first made her oft-quoted allusion within a very specific context. When she referenced the "master's house," she described the patriarchy, racism, heterosexism, ageism, and classism present in the academy. She admonished a group of White feminist academics for waiting until the last minute to invite the non-White women to the conference.

> And what does it mean in personal and political terms when even the two Black women who did present here were literally found at the last hour? What does it mean when the tools of a racist patriarchy are used to examine the fruits of that same patriarchy? It means that only the most narrow parameters of change are possible and allowable. (Lorde, 1979, p. 98)

Instead of feigning feeling honored by the last-minute invitation, Lorde admonished the conference organizers for their narrow focus on White, well-educated women's experiences as juxtaposed to men. "This is an old and primary tool of all oppressors to keep the oppressed occupied with the master's concerns" (p. 100). In addition, Lorde is critical of analytical tools used by those academics, "tools of a racist patriarchy," to supposedly examine social injustices. She urged her audience to instead think of the great wealth of knowledge there is within the diversity of women's experience, especially when examining structural inequities.

Examining the lives of women like my mother and grandmother have helped me locate other tools than those given to me by Westernized training (Boveda, 2019). Despite Doña Clara's exploitative intentions, Mami made the most out of their dynamic. Moreover, she not only considered her own desires but also her mother's needs and the opportunities that exposure to more privileged experiences could afford her. Mami worked without a wage and for her freedom as she mitigated oppressive realities and longings for an improved existence. There were several times that in her need for a reprieve from the indignities experienced while serving her mistress's family that Mami ran away to return to her siblings and mother. Each time Mami left, however, Doña Clara or her husband would find and convince her of the benefits of working in their home. If she would have stayed with my grandmother, Mami would have burdened an already poor family and been forced to work in harsher environments than that of Doña Clara's home. She therefore persisted until she was in a better position to improve her situation.

Lorde's emphasis on coalition building and joint survival was also evident in Mami's story. In addition to her time with her mother, Mami also gained strength and encouragement from working with the other girls who came to live in Doña Clara's house. An autodidact, Mami saved tips given by Doña Clara's acquaintances—along with earnings she and the network of girls garnered through their entrepreneurial efforts. Mami eventually was able to build her own home. She returned to the mountainside to bring her mother and siblings out into the new home she created. To this day, her siblings recognize Mami as the one that took them out of poverty and a marginalized experience. And it was because she was able to endure living in the master's house then that I am able to pontificate about Lorde's meanings of the term today.

Similarly, Black women in the academy have established intra- and inter-institutional networks of support in response to academe's exploitative and exclusionary practices. From informal sister circles and mentoring networks (Evans-Winter & Esposito, 2018) to national organizations, Black faculty women have and continue to respond to the oppressive logics of the academy in ways that assist Black and non-Black faculty women of color alike (Evans-Winters, 2019).

Different Tools Can Build a Different House

Forty years after Lorde (1979) first uttered her famous words, I have repeatedly found myself in the same position she described (i.e., being one of maybe two Black women in gatherings predominantly centering White women). How to navigate such a space with integrity and dignity requires an understanding of how to best disrupt the function of women in the master's house. As Audre Lorde (1979) reminded her audience, the way to accomplish this task is not by centering the master's unquenchable desires, but rather through coalition with others with an emphasis on our "joint survivals." When discussing the parallels between my moves in the academy, my mother's early experiences in the Dominican Republic, and Lorde's admonishment, I came to understand that Mami's years working in the master's house as an unpaid servant were relevant to my understanding of how I made the best of my experiences in the Westernized academy (Boveda, 2019).

Like Mami, I found it necessary to leave the urban communities I grew up in to gain better opportunities for liberating myself from the often fetishized challenges within poor Black and Brown communities. I also find myself focused on how to share the opportunities and resources I gain with others from the transnational community I come from. "And this fact," Lorde's (1979) admonishment continues, "is only threatening to those women who still define the master's house as their only source of support" (p. 99). For me, working in the master's house means working within predominantly White institutions of higher education (IHEs), and reminding potential coconspirers of the limitations of what the Westernized academy offers. This analogy is fitting given the previously mentioned linkages with colonialism and given how slavery is entangled with the establishment of U.S. IHEs. Returning to Lorde's speech and Mami's moves within and outside of Doña Clara's house, I am able to remind myself of the limits of the supports I can find within these privileged institutions.

I continue to ask myself and other Black women academics I am in community with what is our relationship to the master's house and how does it shape our commitment to other Black women and girls? For one, we must be clear that the tools provided within IHEs—such as status under the White gaze, proximity to hoarded power, and access to Westernized hegemony—are insufficient to dismantle the imperialist White supremacist capitalist patriarchy (hooks, 1984) baked into their modern and contemporary existences. Like Mami, I understand that, though the master's house may be a means to an end for many of us, liberation comes from other sources of support. Second, it is clear both from Mami's lived experiences and Lorde's theorizing about intersectionally diverse women that relying exclusively on the master's house—no matter the comforts it contains—is incompatible with true liberation, because in those spaces Black women are often expected to serve and honor the existing structure.

Just as Mami was recruited by Doña Clara to work in service to the master, his wife, and his children, enslaved Black people and their descendants have been in a marginal and subjugated state at American universities since their inception (Watkins, 2001). The enslavement of Black people in the Americas, the intentional exclusions of Black women from participating in the U.S. academy, and the proliferation of careers of White academics in disciplines created and sustained through centuries of exploiting Black women and our children are all instructive (e.g., Roberts, 1999, 2009; Skloot, 2010). In writing (some of) what was first told to us by our foremothers—and inscribing what partially informs the expectations, consciousness, intuiting, and knowings that facilitate quick understandings between us—I highlight how institutional misfit and the awkward positioning of Black girls and women in spaces such as the one that Lorde (1979) critiques is a demonstrable and historical feature of the design of U.S. IHEs. As such, I seek community with women who push back against the institutionalized notion that our presence at IHEs is only to be in service to racist patriarchy and imperial/colonial knowledge structures.

Implications and Provocations for Coalition-Builders

Given the racist history, colonization, and imperial legacies of the United States and its IHEs, it is important to understand their implications for Black women with Black feminist and de/colonial understandings currently working in these institutions. It would be irresponsible and ahistorical to ignore how Black women are affected by these histories. In this essay, I considered my ties to the colonial enslavement of Africans and the exploitation of the Global South's most vulnerable girls, as I acknowledged how these ties influence my role as a U.S.-based educator in a university-based faculty. In conclusion, I offer the following provocations for Black women who are daughters of once-enslaved Africans, domestics, and caretakers, as we attempt to build coalitions with non-Black women of color and others who seek to understand and dismantle multiple marginality within IHEs.

Provocation A

As our foremothers were broken, raped, separated from kinfolk, demonized, and exploited, their ability to create networks with other women and to sustain themselves despite the whims of the more powerful were central to their/our survivance. The Westernized university was designed to fragment us—to disorder our minds from our bodies and then fragment us from our histories and each other (Boveda et al., 2019). In collaborating with others, how do we reclaim that we are not fragmented beings, while acknowledging that IHEs have been built on our brokenness?

Provocation B

To effectively build coalitions with other women of color, it is critical to begin by understanding the racist, misogynistic, and colonial history of IHEs, as well as the distinctive histories of Black and non-Black women of color in the Westernized academy. How do we acknowledge these histories without reinforcing the notion that our beginnings are in relation to the exploitative Eurocratic engagement with the world? How can we recognize that the foundations of the Westernized university were set to reinforce White supremacy while simultaneously encouraging interconnectivity and space-making for Black and other girls and women of color in universities?

Provocation C

Within IHEs and masters' houses around the world, there are materials, knowledges, artifacts, and understandings that either originally belonged to our ancestors or that were constructed on the backs of our foremothers. How do we salvage these aspects of the master's house while refusing its dominance?

Implications

I am in agreement with Audre Lorde that despite the distinctiveness of our histories, the master's tools were intended to pathologize, silence, and make deviant those who are different from who these academic spaces were originally designed to serve. Therefore, transcending disciplinary and sociocultural divides to build coalitions is a tool unknown to the master. I thus hope that these provocations and guiding questions will facilitate Black women in the academy and their efforts to build coalitions within/out IHEs to improve the liberatory possibilities for all, and especially to improve the lived realities of Black women and girls in this and other nations.

Discussion Questions

1. How is Boveda's reflection on her mother and foremothers disruptive of what Lorde (1979) describes as "tools of a racist patriarchy" that center "the master's concerns?"
2. Boveda credits both her mother and Audre Lorde for teaching her lessons about her work as a university professor. What are those lessons, and how are they useful to your efforts to advocate for Black women and girls?

Further Reading

Evans, S. Y. (2008). *Black women in the ivory tower, 1850–1954: An intellectual history.* University Press of Florida.

Figueroa-Vásquez, Y. (2020). *Decolonizing diasporas: Radical mappings of Afro-Atlantic literature.* Northwestern University Press.
Lorde, A. (1984). *Sister outsider Essays and speeches.* Crossing Press.

References

Boveda, M. (2017). Sancocho: How Mami's stories fed my curiosity and continue to sustain me. In D. Y. Ford, J. L. Davis, M. Trotman Scott, & Y. Sealey-Ruiz (Eds.), *Gumbo for the soul: Liberating stories and memoirs to inspire gifted females of color* (pp. 45–50). Information Age.

Boveda, M. (2019). An Afro-Latina's navigation of the academy: Tracings of audacious departures, re-entries, and intersectional consciousness. *Feminist Formations, 31,* 103–123. https://doi.org/10.1353/ff.2019.0011

Boveda, M. (2021). *Mamá Osa in the mountains: African Ascendientes' embodiments of fugitivity, freedom, and self-care in the Americas.* Unpublished manuscript.

Boveda, M., & Bhattacharya, K. (2019). Love as de/colonial onto-epistemology: A post-oppositional approach to educational research ethics. *The Urban Review, 51,* 5–25.

Boveda, M., Reyes, G., & Aronson, B. A. (2019). Disciplined to access the general education curriculum: Girls of color, disabilities, and specialized education programming. *Curriculum Inquiry 4*(4), 405–425. https://doi.org/10.1080/036 26784.2019.1652543

de Sousa Santos, B. (2010). *Epistemologias del sur.* Siglo XXI.

de Sousa Santos, B. (2015). *Epistemologies of the South: Justice against epistemicide.* Routledge.

Evans, S. Y. (2008). *Black women in the Ivory Tower, 1850–1954: An intellectual history.* University Press of Florida.

Evans-Winters, V. E. (2019). *Black feminism in qualitative inquiry: A mosaic for writing our daughter's body.* Routledge.

Evans-Winters, V. E. (2021). Black women improvisations: Shifting methodological (mis) understandings within and across boundaries. *International Journal of Qualitative Studies in Education, 34*(6), 481–485. https://doi.org/10.1080/09 518398.2021.1910747

Evans-Winters, V., & Esposito, J. (2018). Researching the bridge called our backs: The invisibility of "us" in qualitative communities. *International Journal of Qualitative Studies in Education, 31*(9), 863–876. https://doi.org/10.1080/095 18398.2018.1478152

Grosfoguel, R. (2013). The structure of knowledge in westernized universities: Epistemic racism/sexism and the four genocides/epistemicides of the long 16th century. *Human Architecture: Journal of the Sociology of Self-Knowledge, 1,* 73–90. https://scholarworks.umb.edu/humanarchitecture/vol11/iss1/8/

hooks, b. (1984). *Feminist theory: From margins to center.* South End Press.

Lorde, A. (1979). The master's tools will never dismantle the master's house. In C. Moraga & G. Anzaldua (Eds.), *This bridge called my back* (pp. 98–101). Kitchen Table Women of Colour Press.

Love, B. (2019, March 18). Dear white teachers: You can't love your black students if you don't know them. *Education Week*. https://www.edweek.org/ew/articles/2019/03/20/dear-white-teachers-you-cant-love-your.html

National Center for Education Statistics. (2019). *Fast facts: Race/ethnicity of college faculty*. https://nces.ed.gov/fastfacts/display.asp?id=61

Roberts, D. E. (1999). *Killing the black body: Race, reproduction, and the meaning of liberty*. Vintage Books.

Roberts, D. E. (2009). Race, gender, and genetic technologies: A new reproductive dystopia? *Signs: Journal of Women in Culture and Society, 34*(4), 783–804.

Skloot, R. (2010). *The immortal life of Henrietta Lacks*. Broadway Press.

Watkins, W. H. (2001). *The White architects of Black education: Ideology and power in America, 1865–1954*. Teachers College Press.

White, D. G. (Ed.). (2009). *Telling histories: Black women historians in the ivory tower*. University of North Carolina Press.

Wilder, C. S. (2013). *Ebony and ivy: Race, slavery, and the troubled history of America's universities*. Bloomsbury.

PART FOUR

STILL WE RISE: BLACK WOMEN AND GIRLS LIFTING AND LOVING BLACK WOMEN AND GIRLS

14

PARADIGM SHIFTING
FOR BLACK GIRLS

Toward a Futures Matter Stance

Maisha T. Winn

In the opening of *War Girls*, Tochi Onyebuchi's character Onyii is detaching her arm—a practice that other girl soldiers in her camp often engage in before embarking on sleep. It is April in the year 2172 in southeastern Nigeria and Onyii, her sister, and other former child soldiers and orphaned girls are surviving in a camp with some imaginable and unimaginable technologies. "Other War Girls have gotten used to sleeping without their arms and legs. But Onyii's phantom limb haunts her in her sleep. In her dreams, she has all her arms and legs and can run. She can run far and fast and away from whatever is chasing her" (Onyebuchi, 2019, p. 3). When I first began to examine the intersectionality of youth justice and education, one of my first studies—a multisited ethnography—followed young playwrights or student artists aged 14–18 who learned the art of playmaking and performance in the context of youth detention centers or jails for children. I argued the student artists in my studies—African American girls, many of whom were incarcerated for status offenses[1]—lived "betwixt and between" lives that simultaneously straddled confinement and freedom (Winn, 2010a, 2010b). Like Onyii, these girls had dreams of running "far and fast and away" from whatever was chasing them. They wanted to run away from miseducation in their schools, lack of resources in their communities, and self-doubt while running toward more desirable lives where they could live with dignity and take care of themselves.

The purpose of this chapter is to revisit my work focused on supporting the educational needs and desires of Black girls to argue for a transformative justice education. A transformative justice teacher education and thus transformative justice framework is guided by the question "How do we teach in the age of hyperincarceration and the ongoing criminalization of multiply marginalized children and their families?" A transformative justice framework leverages restorative justice theory and practice to reimagine the teaching of science (Patterson & Gray, 2019), mathematics (Bullock & Meiners, 2019; Gholson & Robinson, 2019), history/social studies (Kohli et al., 2019), English/language arts (de los Rios et al., 2019), and digital media arts (Degand, 2019) as more than disciplines but opportunities for robust intellectual engagement through building community and shared commitments (Souto-Manning & Winn, 2019). Elsewhere, I argue that there are four pedagogical stances that educators must engage in order to practice justice in education contexts, including *history matters*, *race matters*, *justice matters*, and *language matters* (Winn, 2018). Most recently, I developed a fifth pedagogical stance, *futures matter*, which is informed by Afrofuturist and futurist theories and historiographies of Black education (Fisher, 2009). In this chapter, I provide a brief discussion of scholars who have fought to keep Black girls' voices and experiences in schools central. Next, I give an overview of restorative justice theory to contextualize the transformative justice education framework. And finally, I consider how the *futures matter* pedagogical stance (Winn, forthcoming), in particular, is key when thinking about how to engage Black girls' full humanity through working with Black girls who experienced confinement as a result of overpolicing and zero tolerance policies in schools and communities and my recent work with Black girls who experience particular freedoms in their restorative justice circle keeping work.

Listening, Hearing, and Getting It Right

Ruth Nicole Brown's (2009, 2013) groundbreaking work with Black girls provided a road map for futures work with Black girls. Arguing that there are a wealth of programs available to Black girls, Brown (2009) underscored that Black girls needed power more so than programming. Recognizing the diversity of Black girlhood, scholars have also examined intersectional identities. Muhammad (2015) examined how girls who identified as Black and Muslim leveraged knowledge of Islam in building literate identities. There have also been efforts to examine themes of resilience (Evans-Winters, 2005, 2011) and thriving as opposed to merely surviving (Love, 2019). A common theme exists in education research literature focusing on the lived experiences of Black girls: People are not listening to Black girls or challenging their own stereotypes and fixed ideas about who these girls are, where they come from, and what they desire and deserve. This strikes me as not only a missed opportunity but also as a form of neglect, which is unspeakable for any of our children.

Drawing from the "usable pasts" of Black women speakers, writers, and doers of the 19th century, I sought to understand the literary contributions of aforementioned student artists and playwrights in a larger history of Black women writers, readers, speakers, and "doers" of literacy (Fisher, 2009). Expanding Madison's (2005) notion of liminality or "a state of being neither here nor there—neither completely inside nor outside a given situation, structure or mindset" (p. 158), student artists, in my study, performed literacy to actively disrupt monolithic stories of who they were, what they valued, and the lives they desired (Winn, 2012; Winn & Jackson, 2011). At times they used this platform to speak back to institutions of power and at other times their work acquiesced to these institutions.

At the time there was a dearth of literature focused on the needs of Black girls in education contexts. In fact, I was often challenged to justify a need for this work when there was an explicit focus on "the trouble with Black boys" (Noguera, 2008). Many of us, however, were asking why we should wait until there was a so-called crisis with Black girls much like the crisis declared for the state of their male peers (Evans-Winters, 2005; Morris, 2016). Unfortunately, when the Office for Civil Rights released a "Data Snapshot" of school discipline in U.S. schools asserting that Black girls were being disproportionately suspended from schools, some of us were not surprised given the tensions Black girls were experiencing in classroom and school communities (U.S. Department of Education, 2014). In their report on the "erasure" of Black girls' childhoods, Epstein et al. (2017) asserted that Black girls are subjected to an adultification process rendering them void of the protections of childhood.

It was in this "betwixt and between" space where I engaged in a line of inquiry around restorative justice that seemed to be missing in this conversation about Black girls and education. Pursuing questions about restorative justice as part of my program of research in examining the relationships between justice and schools was initiated by my ethnography of the Girl Time playmaking program and my efforts to try to listen to and hear what girls needed and wanted (Winn, 2010a, 2010b, 2012; Winn & Behizadeh, 2011; Winn & Jackson, 2011). As I got to know girls, or student artists, in the Girl Time program, they shared their stories about getting in "trouble" once they entered middle school and high school after relatively uneventful elementary school careers. Some student artists expected to attend school and return home at the end of the day but found themselves detained in a regional youth detention center (RYDC) when school staff and administration called police to the school when wrongdoing occurred. Students were seldom, if ever, allowed to call parents or guardians before these transactions. I wondered what systems of accountability were in place for adults at their schools to ensure safety for children. I wanted to know how adults in schools justify sending students directly to law enforcement for nonviolent and nondrug-related harms. I wanted to know if there could be a process to mediate the relationship between schools and juvenile detention facilities. Some student artists reported teachers who knew them and not only believed in them but also disagreed with the punishment they were receiving from the administration; however, they were rendered powerless to this larger system of inequity and injustice.

From Restorative to Transformative: Paradigm Shifting for Black Girls

In order to understand the school discipline, relationship/community-building continuum, I immersed myself in the lives and activities of restorative justice practitioners in school, criminal justice, and community contexts. I wish to underscore the notion of continuum here as these activity systems are often presented as dichotomous when, in fact, school discipline policies and practices are often enacted without giving attention to healthy relationships with students, their families, and the larger community that schools serve. Discipline is not a bad thing, yet it has become synonymous with punishment in most U.S. schools (see Yang, 2009).

Restorative justice is a paradigm shift that privileges relationships, building community, and consensus over punishment and shame. However, it often looks like another branch on the discipline/punishment tree as it is used after harm has taken place as an alternative to suspensions and expulsions. Fidelity to the restorative justice process would mean that schools would spend a significant amount of time building community prior to introducing restorative justice to repair harm or address wrongdoing. Among the practitioners I spent time with—attorneys, nonprofit organization workers, classroom teachers, administrators, coaches—I learned the most from students trained as restorative justice circle keepers as a response to disproportionality in school suspensions and expulsions in one high school community (Winn, 2018). Part of this work included a critical participant ethnography in one high school community, Kennedy High School (KHS). KHS was housed in a school district that invested significant resources in training students to be restorative justice circle keepers. Restorative justice is a paradigm shift from a retributive approach to wrongdoing that is focused away from those who harmed and what to "do" with them to a restorative approach that focuses on who has been harmed, their needs, and whose obligation it is to meet these needs. Restorative justice circle processes are one tool in a restorative justice paradigm employed to invite stakeholders who harmed or experienced harm as well as their advocates to build consensus toward a viable response to the harm. In sum, restorative justice is accountability at the highest level in that it forces those who harmed to face the person or people they hurt and, in the best cases, try to get to the heart of why they are harming others so that they can make things right. Circle keepers, then, have the explicit role of holding space for a group of stakeholders gathered to engage in building sustainable communities where relationships are cultivated through shared values and guidelines. However, restorative justice circles are currently being used as a tool to address wrongdoing after harm has taken place. Therefore, restorative justice often looks like another rung on the punishment ladder to students and, from the perspective of teachers, it can look like another way out for students to avoid so-called punishment.

I found Black girls somewhere in between these spaces. In the context of KHS, most of the students trained as student circle keepers (SCKs) identified as Black or African American. These girls varied in terms of their personalities, school experiences, socioeconomic backgrounds, and interests. However, they all considered their role as SCKs to serve Black peers whom they saw in restorative justice (RJ) circles more than White, Asian, and Latinx peers. The prevalence of Black girls as SCKs caused me to raise questions about the race-ing and gendering of RJ and circle keeping in particular (Winn, 2018). I also sought to understand who is restorative justice for? Why? And is it possible to restore relationships or build a sense of community that did not actually exist for all students and educators? And, perhaps most importantly, whose job is it to restore justice? However, I have argued that RJ has become women's work and the work of multiply minoritized people. Both criminalized at schools and revered for problem-solving and peacekeeping, I saw Black girls in an in-between state—valued for their work and also put into these positions to give them something to do as if only their labor made them worthy of citizenship and belonging in their school community. SCKs who identified as Black girls enjoyed their work as peacemakers/keepers, yet they carried a burden that should have been distributed equally throughout the school.

This is when I started learning about RJ. Something was missing in all of this so-called discipline. My first task was to learn the process from the inside-out. I began with going through the processes and facilitator trainings. When I began my work in a school community that trained students as RJ facilitators, it felt like a stark contrast to how student artists in Girl Time experienced schools. Black girl SCKs were both advocates to their schoolmates and advisers to the staff and administration. Black girls in the role of SCKs were recognized as a reliable resource of wisdom, insight, and fairness. In their capacity as SCKs, they felt as if their ideas mattered. This was not without problems—which is beyond the scope of this chapter—but I found the RJ paradigm—the involvement of students or having students be a part of the solution—was a powerful tool to practice justice in schools.

What's Restorative Justice Got to Do With It?

Elsewhere I offer a conceptual framework for RJ and education. Initially I thought about this in English and literacy classrooms or what I referred to as a "Restorative English Education" (Winn, 2013). However, I learned that students and colleagues in math, social science, and science also needed to engage in this work. A restorative teacher education, then, asks how teachers across disciplines teach in the age of mass/hyperincarceration and the increased criminalization of multiply marginalized people. As I continued to learn with and from RJ practitioners, I discovered my omission of the word *justice* in these conceptual frameworks to be misleading and to undermine the work of practicing freedom and justice in schools.

The RJ community is currently challenging the notion of restoration; who or what is being restored? Why? And who gets to choose? RJ practitioners are also raising salient questions about whether or not schools in particular can be salvaged when these classrooms have never functioned as places of inspiration, rigor, and engaged citizenship for many children and Black girls in particular. Therefore, I have challenged my own thinking around the use of *transformative* as opposed to *restorative*.[2] Transformative justice in teacher education might help educators, teacher educators, and education researchers think about how one can teach math, English, social studies/history, science, and other disciplines so that people stop killing (Winn, 2016).[3] A transformative justice teacher education is a mindset that actively engages the idea that everyone is part of an "interrelated web" that requires everyone to care for each other and cultivate relationships to keep the web intact (Davis, 2016). A mindset must be cultivated and practiced as it is grounded in pedagogical stances that reflect a transformative and RJ ideology. In the next section, I offer brief descriptions of four pedagogical stances for paradigm shifting toward justice in the restoration and transformation process. A transformative justice teacher education framework is focused on what teachers need to do as opposed to what they need to do to children. This is a deeply reflective practice across disciplines that locates the work in cultivating pedagogy using the four pedagogical stances: *history matters, race matters, justice matters*, and *language matters* (Winn, 2018; Winn & Winn, 2019).

For example, a transformative justice science education focuses on a wholistic science pedagogy (WSP; Patterson & Gray, 2019), where science teachers ask what harm has been done in the name of science as well as who is responsible for this harm. In a sample lesson plan, Patterson and Gray demonstrated how the three questions in RJ—Who has been harmed? What are their needs? Whose obligations are these?—can be reframed to consider harm in science. Patterson and Gray demonstrated that building relationships is important and these relationships are leveraged to go deeper into the content and engage more rigorously than would otherwise be the case. Similarly, a transformative justice English education is primarily concerned with how educators might consider colonial harms in the teaching of English that teaching practices often engage sometimes willingly and unknowingly (de los Rios et al., 2019). In a transformative justice English education, ethnic studies is a tool to develop skills and disrupt racist ideas, especially using historical texts and primary source materials to extend and expand literary texts and offer context (de los Rios et al., 2019). Math scholars have repositioned Black child brilliance as the rule as opposed to the exception (Gholson et al., 2012) and provided new lenses to consider the often overlooked skills that Black girls bring to mathematics (Gholson & Martin, 2014; Joseph et al., 2017). A transformative justice mathematics education addresses harm and wrongdoing in mathematics education (Bullock & Meiners, 2019; Gholson & Robinson, 2019). Gholson and Robinson argued for a curricular approach—mathematics for justice, identity, and metacognition (MaJIC)—that moves away from memory and recall and toward embodying mathematics, whereas a transformative justice teacher education framework is even more vast and considers the intersectionality of race, gender, ability, and identity; these are some of the ways scholars are putting RJ theory and processes to work on behalf of multiply marginalized children and youth.

From Histories to Futures: Why We Need a Futures Matter Stance for Black Girls

RJ is a paradigm shift from punitive responses to those that focus on making wrongs right. Schools have borrowed elements of RJ from the criminal justice system in order to redress the disproportionate numbers of Black, Latinx, American Indian, and multiply marginalized children who are being isolated, suspended, and expelled in schools. However, as long as the adults in the building hold racist ideas that impede them from cultivating relationships with students, Black and Brown children will always be overrepresented in the school discipline data. I propose five pedagogical stances to engage in the important mindset work: *history matters, race matters, justice matters, language matters*, and *futures matter* (Winn, 2018, 2019a, 2019b; Winn & Winn, 2021). In this section I provide a brief overview of the first four pedagogical stances, as I have written about them extensively elsewhere, and provide context for the fifth stance, *futures matter*.

History Matters

In my aforementioned work on Black girl playwrights, I examined the historical context of Black women readers, writers, speakers, and "doers" of the word. Although this initially seemed like a divergence from my contemporary examination of incarcerated and formerly incarcerated Black girls who engaged in playwriting and performance with a group of committed women teaching artists, it was important to historicize the lives of these girls who found themselves translating their lived experiences and, in some cases, their humanity to others using playwriting as a tool. Using a sociocritical literacy framework (Gutierrez, 2008), I sought to understand how the Black girls' bodies had been subjugated through a history of being objectified and, thus, lacking humanity. If the enslavement of people of African descent was an act of dehumanization, the enslaved woman was denied both her gender identity and racial identity. Nia, who I write about in *Girl Time* (Winn, 2011) recounted her story of being searched by a male security guard at her high school. As a girl who, according to Nia, wore "boy clothes," the security staff determined that she did not deserve to be treated like other "girls." A *history matters* or *histories matter* stance challenges the ahistorical nature of schools and education—especially as it pertains to the devaluing of Black and Brown bodies that is tethered to racial terror in the United States. Nia's experience is part of a larger story of Black women's and girls' bodies rendered without agency and power.

Race Matters

The *race matters* pedagogical stance draws from Kendi's (2017) understanding that whereas racist ideas are learned, they can also be unlearned. For example, there are schools that have implemented RJ and, indeed, reduced suspensions and expulsions; however, racial disparities persist in their choices about who continues to experience these policies. Racist ideas impede good teaching; they determine how a child is understood before the child has an opportunity to present themselves.

Justice Matters

African American Policy Forum cofounder and executive director Kimberlé Crenshaw and her colleagues hosted the #SayHerName vigil to bring attention to Black women who were killed by police officers, yet whose names are often forgotten when people seek justice for victims of police brutality. In 2015, people gathered in New York City to "SayHerName," which the organizers described in this way:

> Building on the work of scholars and activists who have, over the past two decades, called for increased attention to Black women's experiences of policing, *Say Her Name* offers a number of stories that reveal ways gender, race, and sexuality can operate together to inform police abuse of Black women. (African American Policy Forum, 2015, p. 4)

Seeking justice for Black women and girls who are overpoliced in schools and communities has been difficult because their stories are often omitted from conversations about school discipline policies and police brutality. Crenshaw et al. (2015) collected the stories from Black girls throughout the country who have been rendered either invisible or hypervisible through a deficit lens.

Language Matters

Although the pedagogical stances were initially conceptualized as nested circles, I think of *language matters* at the center. The way educators speak to and about children and youth as well as their families and communities matters. When children and youth are assigned labels such as "loud," "having attitude," and even thinking about them as "troublemakers," a process of undermining their power and potential begins. These labels get passed from teacher to teacher and from grade level to grade level. In the case of Girl Time, student artists found that when they were referred to as "artists," "playwrights," "writers," and "performers," they felt more visible as opposed to labels they were used to hearing, such as "runaway," "promiscuous," and "delinquent."

Futures Matter

Opening this chapter with a scene from a science fiction story may have seemed like a departure from engaging research that centers Black girls in education. As I have imagined or reimagined Black girls' futures or the necessity of Black girls being able to access histories and futures for themselves, I have engaged Afrofuturism theory and products such as a growing collection of books of science fiction, speculative fiction, and fantasy where Black girls have a seat at the table. Like education, the aforementioned genres were not always accessible to Black girls and women, nor did they imagine Black girls like Onyii, with whom I opened this chapter, as central to any story.

In her essay that is a meditation on Janelle Monae as well as a critique of science fiction and fantasy genres, N.K. Jemison (2018) pondered, "Why did I have to travel to the margins of speculative fiction to see anything of myself? Why was it easier to find aliens and unicorns than people of color or realistic women?" In some ways, education has functioned like speculative fiction has by not acknowledging the many ways of knowing and being that Black girls have that are valuable across fields. A *futures matter* stance (Winn, Forthcoming) seeks to make futures more equitable or, as Gorbin (2016) posited, "People must see themselves as actors in the future. To do that, the abstract future must be made proximate and tangible" (para. 10).

There are intersectional realities for these stances and, one could argue, many more stances that matter. These five pedagogical stances are driven by 2 decades of research, including a multisited ethnography of RJ across education and criminal justice sites. These stances fuel the transformative justice teacher education framework by drawing from histories to provide opportunities for youth to imagine more agentive and nuanced futures.

Discussion Questions

These discussion questions are used at the Transformative Justice in Education (TJE) Center in the School of Education at the University of California, Davis, in some of the circle processes and trainings for students and educators. They are typically asked by an RJ circle keeper in "rounds."

1. What are some of your first memories of experiencing or witnessing racism?
2. If given an opportunity to revisit this incident, how would you engage? What language or vocabularies are available to you now that you may or may not have had in your possession at the time?
3. What are some of your first memories where you were aware of gender? How did this shape you?
4. Who were you as a thriving student? What did you have access to to help you thrive?
5. Who were you as a struggling student? What did you need?

Resource

Transformative Justice Teacher Education Framework. https://tje .ucdavis.edu/tjte-framework

Notes

1. Status offenses are considered noncriminal acts committed by minors, such as running away from home, truancy, underage drinking, and curfew violations (see OJJDP, 2015).

2. The restorative justice community is engaged in ongoing dialogue about whether the use of *restorative* goes far enough. Some have opted for *transformative* to signal the need for radical change.

3. Composition scholar Mary Rose O'Reilley revisits the question posed by one of her professors at the height of the Vietnam War ("How do we teach English so that people stop killing?") in her book *The Peaceable Classroom* (1993). I have written extensively about expanding this question to the other disciplines and why this question is worthy of reconsideration, as both physical and symbolic violence are hurting children in schools.

Further Reading

Annamma, S. A., Anyon, Y., Joseph, N., & Farrar, J. (2016, April). Black girls and school discipline: The complexities of being overrepresented and understudied. *Urban Education, 54*(2), 211–242. https://doi.org/10.1177/0042085916646610

Gholson, M. (2016). Clean comers in algebra: A critical examination of the construction of Black girls and women in mathematics. *The Journal of Negro Education, 85*(3), 290–301. https://doi.org/10.7709/jnegroeducation.85.3.0290

Jemisin, N. K. (2013). *How long 'til Black Future Month? The toxins of speculative fiction and the anecdote that is Janelle Monae.* http://nkjemisin.com/2013/09/how-long-til-black-future-month/

Joseph, N. (2016). Black female adolescents and racism in schools: Experiences in a colorblind society. *The High School Journal, 100*(1), 4–25. https://muse.jhu.edu/article/634277/summary

Muhammad, G. (2020). *Cultivating genius: An equity model for culturally and historically responsive literacy.* Scholastic.

Stickmon, J. (2019). *To Black parents visiting earth: Raising Black children in the 21st century.* Broken Shackle Publishing.

Sudbury, J. (2007). *Global lockdown: Race, gender, and the prison industrial complex.* Routledge.

References

African American Policy Forum. (2015). *Say her name: Resisting police brutality against black women.* Center for Intersectionality and Social Policy Studies, Columbia University. https://static1.squarespace.com/static/53f20d90e4b0b80451158d8c/t/560c068ee4b0af26f72741df/1443628686535/AAPF_SMN_Brief_Full_singles-min.pdf

Brown, R. N. (2009). *Black girlhood celebration: Toward a hip hop feminist pedagogy.* Peter Lang.

Brown, R. N. (2013). *Hear our truths: The creative potential of Black girlhood.* University of Illinois Press.

Bullock, E. C., & Meiners, E. R. (2019). Abolition by the numbers: Mathematics as a tool to dismantle the carceral state (and build alternatives). *Theory Into Practice, 58*(4), 338–346. https://doi.org/10.1080/00405841.2019.1626614

Crenshaw, K., Ocen, P., & Nanda, J. (2015). *Black girls matter: Pushed out, overpoliced and underprotected.* African American Policy Forum & Center for Intersectionality and Social Policy Studies.

Davis, F. (2016). This country needs a truth and reconciliation process on violence against African Americans right now. *Yes! Magazine.* https://www.yesmagazine .org/social-justice/2016/07/08/this-country-needs-a-truth-and-reconciliation-process-on-violence-against-african-americans/

Degand, D. (2019). Stereotypes vs. strategies for digital media artists: The case for culturally relevant media production. *Theory Into Practice, 58*(4), 368–376. https://doi.org/10.1080/00405841.2019.1626617

de los Rios, C. V., Martinez, D. C., Musser, A. D., Canady, A., Camangian, P., & Quijada, P. (2019). Upending colonial practices: Toward repairing harm in English education. *Theory Into Practice, 58*(4), 359–367. https://doi.org/10.1080/ 00405841.2019.1626615

Epstein, R., Blake, J. J., & González, T. (2017). *Girlhood interrupted: The erasure of Black girls' childhood.* Georgetown Law Center on Poverty and Inequality.

Evans-Winters, V. (2005). *Teaching Black girls: Resiliency in urban classrooms.* Peter Lang.

Evans-Winters, V. (2011). *Teaching Black girls: Resiliency in urban classrooms* (2nd ed.). Peter Lang.

Fisher, M. T. (2009). *Black literate lives: Historical and contemporary perspectives.* Routledge.

Gholson, M., Bullock, E. C., & Alexander, N. (2012). On the brilliance of Black children: A response to a Clarion Call. *Journal of Urban Mathematics Education, 5*(1), 1–7. https://doi.org/10.21423/jume-v5i1a180

Gholson, M., & Martin, D. B. (2014). Smart girls, Black girls, mean girls, and bullies: At the intersection of identities and the mediating role of young girls' social network in mathematics communities of practice. *Journal of Education, 194*(1), 19–33. https://doi.org/10.1177/002205741419400105

Gholson, M., & Robinson, D. (2019). Restoring mathematics identities of Black learners: A curricular approach. *Theory Into Practice, 58*(4), 347–358. https://doi .org/10.1080/00405841.2019.1626620

Gorbin, M. (2016). The future as a way of life: Alvin Toffler's unfinished business. *Medium.* https://medium.com/@mgorbis/the-future-as-a-way-of-life-4bc314ec97de

Gutierrez, K. (2008). Language and literacies as civil rights. In S. Greene (Ed.), *Literacy as a civil right: Reclaiming social justice in literacy teaching and learning* (pp. 169–184). Peter Lang.

Jemisin, N. K. (2018). *How long 'til Black Future Month?* Orbin Books. https://nkjemisin.com/2013/09/how-long-til-black-future-month/

Joseph, N., Hailu, M., & Boston, D. (2017). Black women's and girls' persistence in the P–20 mathematics pipeline: Two decades of children, youth, and adult education research. *Review of Research in Education, 41*(1), 203–227. https://doi.org/10.3102/0091732X16689045

Kendi, I. X. (2017). *Stamped from the beginning: The definitive history of racist ideas in America.* Perseus Books Group.

Kholi, R., Montaño, E., & Fisher, D. (2019). History matters: Challenging an a-historical approach to restorative justice in teacher education. *Theory Into Practice, 58*(4), 377–384. https://doi.org/10.1080/00405841.2019.1626613

Love, B. (2019). *We want to do more than survive: Abolitionist teaching and the pursuit of educational freedom.* Beacon Press.

Madison, D. S. (2005). *Critical ethnography: Method, ethics, and performance.* Sage.

Morris, M. (2016). *Pushout: The criminalization of Black girls in schools.* The New Press.

Muhammad, G. (2015). Iqra: African American Muslim girls reading and writing for social change. *Written Communication, 32*(3), 1–31. https://doi.org/10.1177/0741088315590136

Noguera, P. (2008). *The trouble with black boys . . . and other reflections on race, equity, and the future of public education.* Jossey-Bass.

Office for Juvenile Justice and Delinquency Prevention. (2015). *Literature review: Status offenders.* https://www.ojjdp.gov/mpg/litreviews/Status_Offenders.pdf

Onyebuchi, T. (2019). *War girls.* Razorbill.

Patterson, A., & Gray, S. (2019). Teaching to transform: (W)holistic science pedagogy. *Theory Into Practice, 58*(4), 328–337. https://doi.org/10.1080/00405841.2019.1626616

Souto-Manning, M., & Winn, L. T. (2019). Toward shared commitments for teacher educaton: Transformative justice as an ethical imperative. *Theory Into Practice, 58*(4), 308–317. https://doi.org/10.1080/00405841.2019.1626619

U.S. Department of Education Office for Civil Rights. (March 2014). *Data snapshot: School discipline.* Civil Rights Data Collection. https://ocrdata.ed.gov/assets/downloads/CRDC-School-Discipline-Snapshot.pdf.

Winn, M. T. (2010a, December). "Betwixt and between": Literacy, liminality, and the "celling" of Black girls. *Race Ethnicity and Education, 13*(4), 425–447. https://doi.org/10.1080/13613321003751601

Winn, M. T. (2010b, September). "Our side of the story": Moving incarcerated youth voices from margin to center. *Race Ethnicity and Education, 13*(3), 313–326. https://doi.org/10.1080/13613324.2010.500838

Winn, M. T. (2011). *Girl Time: Literacy, justice, and the school-to-prison pipeline.* Teachers College Press, Teaching for Social Justice Series.

Winn, M. T. (2012). The politics of desire and possibility in urban playwriting: (Re)reading and (re)writing the script. *Pedagogies: An International Journal, 7*(4), 317–332. https://doi.org/10.1080/1554480X.2012.715737

Winn, M. T. (2013). Toward a restorative English education. *Research in the Teaching of English, 48*(1), 126–135.

Winn, M. T. (2016). *Transforming justice. Transforming teacher education* [Working paper].University of Michigan.

Winn, M. T. (2018). *Justice on both sides: Transforming education through restorative justice.* Harvard Education Press.

Winn. M. T. (2019a, March 7). *Futures matter: Five pedagogical stances for shifting toward justice* [Lecture]. The Douglas Biklen Landscape of Urban Education Lecture Series, Syracuse, NY, United States.

Winn, M. T. (2019b). *Paradigm shifting toward justice in teacher education* [Working paper]. TeachingWorks, TeachingWorks. University of Michigan.

Winn, M. T. (Forthcoming). Futures matter: Creating just futures in this age of hyper-incarceration. *Peabody Journal.*

Winn, M. T., & Behizadeh, N. (2011). The right to be literate: Literacy, education, and the school-to-prison pipeline. *Review of Research in Education, 35*(1), 147–173. https://doi.org/10.3102/0091732X10387395

Winn, M. T., & Jackson, C. A. (2011, September–October). Toward a performance of possibilities: Resisting gendered (in)justice. *International Journal of Qualitative Studies in Education, 24*(5), 615–620. https://doi.org/10.1080/09518398.2011.600261

Winn, M. T., & Winn, L. T. (2019). This issue. *Theory Into Practice, 58*(4), 305–307.

Winn, M. T., & Winn, L. T. (2021). *Restorative justice in education: Transforming teaching and learning through the disciplines.* Harvard Education Press.

Yang, W. (2009). Discipline or punish: Some suggestions for school policy and teacher practice. *Language Arts, 87*(2), 49–61. https://www.jstor.org/stable/41484230

15

TOWARD A POLITICIZED ETHIC OF CARE ABOUT BLACK WOMEN AND GIRLS IN EDUCATION

Monique Lane

I am from early mornings and mama singin' the blues.
From kickbacks and cadillacs to breakin' all the rules.
Where I'm from, crooked cops make pit stops on boulevards of despair.
Police brutality is a grim reality—but I guess it ain't supposed to be fair.

Where I'm from, soldiers in camouflage pump black fists high, with pride.
The legacy of Malcolm and Assata behind every stride.
Revolution's the only solution, at least that's what they say.
Steady tryin' to break the cycle of self-hate impairing shorties around the way.

Cuz' see, I'm from "Aye aye baby what's yo' name?"
Bloodshot eyes gazing at me from behind, and he *know* he got game!
From bad-mouthed ballers, gold chains heavy like steel.
They are Kings in disguise. Humanity compromised. Genius concealed.

I am from *Queens* to *doodoo mamas, flips*, and *two-bit whores*.
And when we at school they call us fools, cuz' the Black woman is deplored.
Where I'm from, feminism is synonymous with lesbian or bitch.
But I'd rather be that, than a fuckin' door mat, and you can get wit' it or
be dismissed.

> See, I'm from a place u can't replicate,
> Ain't no science producing a clone.
> And although it's hood and we're misunderstood,
> This is the place I call home.
> —Lane (2014)

Black feminist discourse has historically upheld cultural memory as a fundamental category of epistemological importance that shapes African American women's expressive vernacular arts (Muhammad & Haddix, 2016; Richardson, 2002). Following in the tradition of countless Black women intellectual elders, I often turn to written expression to sharpen my ontological understanding of self in relation to the world around me. As Richardson (2013) asserted, "African American literacies include vernacular survival arts and cultural productions that carve out free spaces in oppressive locations" (p. 329). Hence, I have put pen to paper to celebrate love, sing Black girl songs, and salute the sun. To be candid, I also write to reckon with the horrifying truths and uneasy certainties tied to my subordination within intersecting oppressions of race, class, and gender (Collins, 2000). A common thread through much of my writing is the dialectic of African American women's subjugation and varied resistance strategies. To this end, written expression is a critical site of (re) humanization, which functions as my darkness and my peace.

I scribbled the opening poem on a piece of scratch paper during a half-hour writing session that I facilitated at King High School in South Los Angeles.[1] After earning my bachelor's degree from UCLA, I returned to my alma mater and taught high school English for 5 years. As I reflect on my tenure as a classroom practitioner, I have come to understand that poetry—more than any other genre of writing—inspired my Black and Brown students to speak out against socially toxic environments and stressors that impeded their ability to thrive as both students and human beings. Occasionally, I wrote *with* these young scholars to enrich our collective capacity for productive resistance and healing. It was in those shared moments of vulnerability that we accessed the temporal spaces of agency and possibility, and I connected most with the young people whom I had the pleasure of teaching.

The "Where I'm From" poem was a staple in my arsenal of community-building activities, and I generally facilitated the lesson in the 1st week of the fall semester. Each year, as I scribbled alongside my students, I reflected on the magic and misfortune of my selfhood and penned new life into my personal narrative. As former Black Panther and social activist Elaine Brown (1992) explained, "Memory seems a fragile spirit. It may be a river of reality that gathers dreams and desires and change in its flow" (p. xi). And for 5 consecutive years, I invented and reinvented myself in the "Where I'm From" poem through a hopeful and imagistic retelling of my life story. Although the people, places, and events varied in every draft, many of the same themes emerged. Each year, variations of racialized gender oppression, sexual harassment, hegemonic violence, and girlhood rebellion surfaced. As a young practitioner in my early 20s, the beauty and the terror of my life history as a Black woman had settled deep into my consciousness. Rearticulating my reality aloud—in front of an audience of attentive students no less—I shared a complex identity that was "distinct from, yet inclusive of the world around me" (hooks, 1996, p. xi).

Educational Injustice Against Black Women and Girls

A growing body of research has documented the long-standing, ubiquitous, and deep-seated violence against Black women and girls throughout American history (Harris-Perry, 2011; Roberts, 2017; White, 1985). Richardson (2013) reminded us that the

> system of brutal patriarchy and chattel slavery has been reduced and metamorphosed into present day forms of structural racism, sexism, and cultural hegemony and still powerfully influences the lives and futures of Black females, their families, and people around the world. (p. 329)

As Richardson suggested, societal disassociation with Black women is mirrored in U.S. institutions, and educative settings have prescribed African American women's subordination in especially pronounced ways. In fact, the poetry shared by the young Black women in the high school English classes I taught illuminated the insidious and cyclical nature of African American women's oppression, and the specific race–gender stigmatization that is unique to Black girlhood. The "Where I'm From" poem particularly exposed recurring acts of police brutality, underresourced and hypercriminalized schooling conditions, sexual abuse and harassment, and inequitable access to mental and physical health care. Although the young women unearthed a varied and diverse collective reality, their narratives hauntingly resembled my personal experiences as a Black girl adolescent. After this writing exercise and subsequent discussion, the air in our classroom sanctuary had become saturated with memories of triumph and tragedy. Sadly, most students' poetic musings highlighted the latter.

Even in the wake of current literature calling for radical interventions in educational policy, the disenfranchisement of Black girl learners is an ongoing concern. Recent scholarship by Crenshaw et al. (2015), Lane (2017), M. Morris (2016), and Sealey-Ruiz (2016) establishes with robust empiricism the ways in which Black women and girls are simultaneously *overlooked* and *hypervisible* in P–20 schools. These learners' heightened sense of invisibility is a consequence of educators' culturally irrelevant pedagogies and curricula, low expectations, and failure to recognize Black girls' intellectual promise and potential. Furthermore, Evans-Winters and Esposito (2010) maintained that when race and gender oppression combine with class inequities, Black girls face compounding disadvantages. Because these youth are more likely to live in economically dispossessed communities, the prolonged deprivation of critical resources in their school communities magnifies ongoing inequities. Grassroots organization Girls for Gender Equity's (2017) *Schools Girls Deserve* (SGD), a participatory action research project and policy report, underscores Evans-Winters and Esposito's claim. New York City girls of color aged 9 to 23 feel undervalued and pushed out of school because of the lack of social, cultural, emotional, and academic supports available to them. Listening sessions with over 120 young women participants illuminated the ways in which girls of color are denied the infrastructure and reinforcement to finish high school, including limited access to mental health services, restricted course offerings, and scarce extracurricular activities.

Notwithstanding Black women and girl learners' amplified sense of invisibility in educational settings, these students also expressed feelings of hypervisibility in U.S. schools. Reports published by the African American Policy Forum and the Center for Intersectionality and Social Policy Studies reveal that Black women and girls disproportionately experience institutional and interpersonal violence and are channeled into educational pathways that lead to criminalization (Crenshaw et al., 2015). For instance, in Boston and New York City, the relative rate of suspension is six times higher for young Black women than for White girls, and expulsion rates for African American young women are more than 10 times greater than for their White girl counterparts (Crenshaw et al., 2015). To note, Black girls' experiences with structural forms of violence within educational settings—including racism, sexism, cultural hegemony, and more—often overlap due to these youth's entangled social identities (Crenshaw, 1991). This is perhaps best evidenced by the reductive and myopic constructions of Black femininity in dominant educational discourses and popular media. Rhetoric that positions African American youth as welfare queens, irrationally hostile, sexually immoral, and ratchet[2] compromise these students' humanity and are an enduring threat to their budding identities (Fordham, 1993; Love, 2017; E. Morris, 2007; Sealey-Ruiz, 2007). These controlling and stereotypical images, moreover, also remain etched in the psyches of practitioners and other school personnel whose deficit ideologies about Black women and girls translate into culturally irresponsible and inhumane engagement with these youth.

Black Girl Learners' Educative and Life Outcomes

In Melissa Harris-Perry's (2011) book *Sister Citizen: Shame, Stereotypes, and Black Women in America*, she reminds us that the gaze of the powerful is "neither neutral nor benign" (p. 42): The misrecognition of Black women is inextricably tied to inequitable access to social, political, and economic goods, which hinders African American women's ability to fully participate as American citizens. Harris-Perry's assertion provides a space for educational researchers to consider the ramifications of systematic educational injustices imposed on Black girl students. Statistics maintained by the NAACP Legal Defense and Educational Fund and the National Women's Law Center (2014) revealed that in 2010, African American girls completed high school at lower rates than every other female racial group, with the exception of Native Americans. Sixty-six percent of Black girls graduated from high school, followed by Hispanic girls (71%), Whites (82%), and Asian/Pacific Islanders (83%). American Indian young women, however, had a much lower rate of 51%. The educational data that track women at the postsecondary level are similarly disenchanting. In 2013, only 24% of African American women aged 25 and over held a bachelor's degree or higher, compared with 35% of White women and 32% of all women. Numerous studies have confirmed that low rates of school completion among Black women and girl learners correlate with escalating rates of poverty and labor exploitation (Harris-Perry, 2011; M. Morris, 2016) and disproportionate percentages of incarceration (Civil Rights Data Collection, 2014).

In light of Black girl learners' ongoing struggle for greater equity and access in U.S. schools, there is an urgent need to illuminate pedagogical practices that affirm these learners' intersectional identities and facilitate more positive schooling behaviors. Amid a host of reform efforts that have sought to promote fairness and justice for learners from nondominant groups, one of the areas that is frequently overlooked is the importance of practitioner care. As such, this chapter introduces a *politicized ethic of care*, a teaching philosophy that is commonly rooted in the pedagogies of exemplary Black women teachers. In the following sections, I turn to relevant empirical and conceptual scholarship to elucidate Black women educators' politicized ethic of care and two key features of this framework: badassery and "for real love." The analyses draw from autoethnographic data from a 2-year study of a girls' empowerment program that I created as a classroom teacher at a large urban high school in California. Specifically, I will shed light on how the politicized ethic of care that I embodied as a high school teacher positively responded to the heightened sense of invisibility and hypervisibility that African American young women reported experiencing both inside and outside of classroom walls. I conclude with implications that may aid educators in promoting Black girl learners' construction of viable social identities and a more empowered orientation toward school.

Coconstructing a "Safe Place"

As a 2nd-year English teacher working at my alma mater, my understanding of Black young women's shifting social struggles had grown exponentially through our day-to-day interactions. Perhaps most notable was the revelation that traditional schooling environments inculcate in Black girls a general sense of isolation and fear of external analytic expression. In moments of quietude and self-reflexivity, I critiqued my own pedagogical praxis and my apparent participation in these young women's marginalization. I was particularly disturbed by my inability to consistently engage Black girls in critical class discussions about race–gender stigmatization *beyond* the "Where I'm From" poetry lesson. Through informal conversations with numerous students, I learned that many of the African American girls I taught refrained from verbal participation in these instances because they believed that their peers—particularly those who did not identify as Black girls—would not comprehend or appreciate their unique perspectives. After considerable reflection and the insight of a handful of student volunteers, I cocreated Black Girls United (BGU), a safe space for these young women that began in the fall 2005 semester and was sustained through the spring 2007 semester.

In developing the curricular and pedagogical structure of BGU, I relied on the scholarship of African American women practitioners such as bell hooks, Gloria Joseph, and other pioneers who explicitly situated their teaching practice within a Black feminist/womanist politic (e.g., Mary McLeod Bethune and Septima Clark). My (re)articulation of Black feminist pedagogy involved developing a framework that was heavily influenced by these women—although it also responded to the sensibilities of my distinct group of urban Black female youth and was informed by my personal experiences as an African American woman in a particular time, location, and sociopolitical context. Each week during lunch, members of BGU engaged in critical dialogue to investigate relevant historical and contemporary issues and celebrated the collective angle of vision that united them as young Black women (Collins, 2000). By prioritizing the sociocultural and academic concerns and empowerment of African American girl learners, this organization was uniquely poised to catalyze individual and collective changes that I hoped would yield sustainable improvements in how Black girls at King High experienced urban schooling.

After 2 years as BGU's faculty sponsor, I recognized three important, recurring phenomena: (a) Several students were developing an independent, self-defined standpoint; (b) African American girls generated and sustained individual and collective activism; and (c) many participants demonstrated a strong desire to engage in critical analytical discussions. BGU functioned as an alternative and unorthodox setting within our mainstream urban schooling context; young African American women were afforded the opportunity to *collectively* read the world (Freire, 1973) and move toward transforming their place within it. The success of the program inspired me to formally research, evaluate, and articulate the liberatory potential of Black feminist pedagogical practice in an urban educational context.

After returning to graduate school, I conducted a critical race feminist autoethnography to evaluate the success of the program and the effects of Black feminist pedagogy on the identity development of African American female students. Autoethnography is distinctive in that through the public exposure of personal narratives, the autobiographical and personal are linked to the cultural and social (Ellis, 2004). As an extension of critical race theory (Solorzano, 1997), critical race feminism complicates the practice of autobiographical storytelling within autoethnography by centering non-White racialized women's experiences (Delgado Bernal, 2002). Through an analysis of Black feminist curricula, in-class video footage, student artifacts, and interviews with former participants, the data revealed four key features of my Black feminist pedagogical practice (Lane, 2017): *critical feminist literature, positioning students as change agents,* a *politicized ethic of care,* and *collectivity.* The following section will elucidate how the politicized ethic of care that I espoused gave rise to educationally (re)dedicated and socially empowered young Black women participants.

Black Women's Politicized Ethic of Care: Badassery and For Real Love

A growing number of researchers have documented African American women educators' contributions to the immense story of the teaching profession (Case, 1997; Dixson & Dingus, 2008; Mogadime, 2000). Recently, scholars have introduced Black feminist pedagogy to delineate the teaching strategies of African American women educators, including those women who do not explicitly self-identify as feminist. Among the most insightful contemporary examinations are Beauboeuf-Lafontant (2002), Dixson and Dingus (2008), and Roseboro and Ross's (2009) investigations of Black women educators' entry into the profession and the distinctive ways in which these practitioners cultivate culturally empowering and academically rigorous classroom communities. Inquiries into Black women teachers' pedagogical practices have also emphasized the exceptional means by which these women express care—qualities that are central to their educational praxis. As noted by Gloria Joseph (1995), Black women teachers' caring pedagogies are rooted in an antideficit, antipathological stance that directly opposes historically oppressive educational policies and practices—and is informed by these women's race–gendered marginality and isolation.

Drawing on the work of the aforementioned scholars, as well as my former experience as a classroom practitioner, I use the term *politicized ethic of care* to capture African American women educators' political lucidity and deep emotional investment in the communities they serve. Black female teachers who espouse a politicized ethic of care have the capacity to draw from students' cultural frameworks, lived experiences, socioemotional needs, and diverse learning styles. These women are inherently *badass* because their embodiment of care operates as an activist response to African American students' prolonged subordination both inside and outside of U.S. schools. Furthermore, Black women's political lucidity is tied to their emotional attachment to the students they serve. Hence, the *for real love* exhibited by African American women practitioners is demonstrated through an authentic form of caring, which includes love for one's community, othermothering, and teaching the whole child.

Badassery

There is an abundance of scholarship in which researchers have conceptualized, reconceptualized, and extended our impressions of Black women educators' approaches to teaching (Beauboeuf-Lafontant, 2002; Case, 1997; Joseph, 1995; Lane, 2015). Despite myriad interpretations, scholars agree that Black women teachers exhibit sociopolitical clarity in their understanding that the practice of teaching for the purpose of liberation conflicts with the long-standing role of the institution as a vestige of bias and perpetuator of systems of social domination. In light of this political lucidity, Black women-identified practitioners maintain an acute awareness of their positionality and engage in practices that are steadily "at odds with the existing [oppressive] structure" (hooks, 1994, p. 135). Dixson and Dingus's (2008) analysis of findings from two separate studies on Black women teachers illuminated the unambiguous acknowledgment of the radical nature of teaching within Black women's educational praxis. The authors revealed that African American women teachers enter the profession "as part of a legacy of Black feminist activism that simultaneously prioritizes community uplift, youth's social and intellectual development, classroom management, and pedagogical skill" (p. 832).

My entry into the teaching profession mirrored the trajectories of numerous African American women educators who journeyed before me. The various adversities that I experienced as a Black girl adolescent growing up in a historically dispossessed community in Southern California informed my investment in the education of underserved student populations. Most influential, perhaps, was my high school experience. In one typical day, I occupied multiple spaces that each commingled race, class, and gender oppression. In my classes, well-meaning yet misguided educators trivialized my intelligence. In the hallways, teenage boys ogled and assaulted my maturing brown body via sexist epithets. Moreover, the ubiquity of reductive images of low-income African American women in the media—that positioned us as icons of cultural deviation and pathology—had me convinced that I was a social leper, linked to a group of naturally inferior people. Despite my efforts at negotiating these offenses, each interaction left an imprint of shame on my dignity; the collective effect was a powerful strike against my humanity.

When I returned to King High as an English teacher, my passion for education was visceral: I sought to become the type of educator I wished I had in high school. Like most Black women practitioners who identify as feminist, my chief objective was to engage in transformative, humanizing education for *all* students. Aligned with the luminaries before me, I believed that I was "*ethically and ethnically*" accountable for preparing youth of color to transcend social injustices—a philosophy heavily reflected in my pedagogical choices in BGU (Beauboeuf-Lafontant, 2002, p. 77). Indeed, the examination of interview quotes, video transcripts from former BGU classes, my Black feminist curriculum, field notes, and student artifacts revealed that my subversive methodology had assisted most individuals in crafting alternative and empowered understandings of their race, class, and gender identities.

For instance, I utilized an interdisciplinary approach to creating the curriculum. My classroom practice in BGU incorporated feminist epistemologies, cultural studies, and critical media literacy as tools to tap into participants' intellectual prowess and channel student resistance in the best interest of personal and social change. BGU participants developed a heightened consciousness of the sociopolitical location of African American women through group discussions of critical feminist literature and the sharing of students' multifaceted personal stories. Because we explored a variety of issues in the program, the young women were introduced to topics concerning Black women across the diaspora (e.g., female genital mutilation in Africa), as well as domestic phenomena that some individuals had not encountered in their own lives (e.g., adoption, child and domestic abuse, extreme poverty, and houselessness). As a former student named Tanya asserted during her interview, the learners in BGU "travelled down a path together," eventually reaching the conclusion that they are "similar *and* different at the same time" (Tanya, personal communication, December 22, 2012). Hence, as one significant outcome of my political consciousness and *badass* approach to my practice, students expanded their perspectives of Black women and their reimagining of, and ultimate opposition to, existing discourse around African American female inferiority.

For Real Love

> I knew you cared about us. Like really cared because you were always there to help us. We didn't even have to ask a lot of the time cuz, you'd be like, "You look tired [Tanya]. You hungry? You want some carrots?" And then you'd go to the fridge lookin' for some food. Or just, like, you'd see somebody just wasn't their usual self and you would step away from everybody and talk to that person separately. You know? You went out of your way. Or if somebody was havin' family drama you would ask about how they were doin'. Or even being nosey and asking about people's grades all the time. Just checkin' in with people all the damn time! It was about showin' concern. Like, you were uncomfortable when we were unhappy. It made you uncomfortable. Or, like, even if we came to you about a problem and you didn't have the answer we knew we could come to you anyway cuz you always connected us with whoever had the answer. (Tanya, Black Girls United Participant)

Through an analysis of Black feminist curricula, in-class video footage, student artifacts, and interviews with former participants, the students in BGU exposed the ways in which educators at King High School regularly displayed inauthentic forms of caring. From the students' perspectives, many of their teachers were emotionally disconnected and did not regard urban youth of color as a valuable investment of their time or worthy of sincere affection. Consequently, the behaviors of these alleged uncaring faculty contributed to the overwhelming sense of invisibility that the members of BGU commonly experienced at school. In contrast, my teaching practice in BGU was anchored by an authentic love and concern for the social and educational well-being of every student. In my second individual interview with a former member, Tanya described my disposition toward students in BGU as an "actual and for real love." When I asked Tanya to elaborate, she responded with the previous excerpt. From her perspective, my efforts to provide learners with the necessary supports to thrive in both their personal and educative lives (i.e., academic and emotional support, rides to school, home visits, feeding students, and frequent check-ins), was evidence that I "really cared" for the BGU participants.

Similar to other Black feminist educators, I exhibited care through the convention of othermothering (Collins, 2000). That is, I shared mothering responsibilities and exhibited authentic concern for students' holistic development beyond the bounds of the classroom. In my conversations with the participants of BGU, numerous individuals attributed their improved schooling behaviors, at least in part, to the "familiar and familial mother-child relationship" that I often exercised in my interactions with students (Beauboeuf-Lafontant, 2002, p. 74). In the following transcript, Ashanti recalled how my efforts to provide a wake-up call each morning improved her school attendance:

> I remember it was on a Friday cause I was like this lady ain't gon' call and wake me up, she gon' forget. And I remember that Monday morning you called at like 5 o'clock in the morning. I was pissed when my phone was going, I'm like what?! I'm like she really called my phone, like she really called my phone and woke me up! And it was like after that, everyday you called and woke me up and I was on time. Every single day after that I was on time. . . . Sometimes I just wanted to cut my phone off, but I'd be like I gotta go to school, I gotta go to school. . . . You took the time out of your busy mornin' to call me. Like, it kind of made me open my eyes a little more or kind of push me. Made me want to do better.

Calling Ashanti each morning provided the push she needed to attend her classes regularly and on time. I was not surprised by Ashanti's shift in behavior considering the disempowering schooling conditions that Black girls regularly confronted at King High School. The motherly love and daily wake-up calls that originated in my English class continued throughout the 2 years that Ashanti participated in BGU, which resulted in a lasting closeness between us.

In my individual interviews with a subsample of seven BGU members, participants described past experiences with other effective African American women teachers who also performed caring in ways that were strict, yet heartfelt. For instance, Black women practitioners characteristically went above and beyond the call of duty (i.e., providing rides to school, making home visits, and feeding students), and were often labeled as pushy and loving. A BGU member named Tanisha asserted that African American women educators stayed "on yo' head"—meaning, they frequently questioned students' whereabouts, monitored individuals' academic progress, and confronted youth who engaged in harmful social behaviors—thereby embodying a "no nonsense" motherly affection. In my own practice, I regularly jeopardized my "cool points" with BGU members, opting to engage the young women in difficult conversations that I hoped would evolve the limits of their abilities. As Duncan-Andrade (2009) acknowledged, educators who prioritize being liked often avoid unpleasant encounters with young people, and ultimately jeopardize their students' social and intellectual potential.

In sum, following the bold legacy of Black feminist educators—and countering the long-standing marginalization that Black girls at King High endured—I strategically performed caring with BGU youth by providing students the necessary tools to navigate personal and institutional barriers to their success. Hence, my politicized ethic of care was "infused with love, humility, passion, and power" (Roseboro & Ross, 2009, p. 36). Furthermore, the testimonies offered by the young women in BGU provide additional insight into African American women practitioners' *badassery* and *for real love*. We lead with a fiery embrace of the maternal, an obligation to transgress systemic injustice, and an eagerness to assist in the social and intellectual development of our students along the way.

Conclusion

A growing body of conceptual literature examines Black women teachers' multiple sites of consciousness at the crossroads of their roles as educators and community activists. Nevertheless, Dixson and Dingus (2008) challenged researchers "to make the tacit explicit" in our articulations and analyses of "good teaching," and consider "how best to illuminate the pedagogy of Black women teachers in a manner that informs the practices of *all* teachers" (p. 831). The ideas presented in this chapter respond to Dixson and Dingus's call to further conceptualize, interpret, and elucidate the pedagogy of exemplary African American women educators. However, I do not make the claim that all Black women educators teach from a liberatory standpoint. Moreover, I oppose the belief that African American women's caring pedagogies are a panacea to the widespread marginalization that Black girls encounter in schools across the nation.

Still, much scholarship corroborates the unique angle of vision that Black women bring to the practice of teaching and their enduring legacy of empowering subordinated student populations. Regretfully, we seldom find Black women's pedagogical practices highlighted within discourses of transformative education. Through this research, I hope to strengthen and advance current debates on "high-quality teaching" and "best practices" for our most vulnerable student populations, and Black girls, specifically. I maintain that African American women educators' politicized ethic of care is a necessary response to the marginality that Black girls endure in K–12 institutions and has striking implications for educators who struggle to engage the intellectual aptitude of these youth. Drawing on African American teachers' performance of care moves us through and beyond Black girls' historicized oppression and illuminates "imaginative responses" to the injustices burdening these learners (Collins, 2000, p. 12).

Bearing in mind the goal of this research—to inform future understandings of Black women educators' politicized ethic of care—it is critical to divulge the social, psychological, and physical consequences of embodying a pedagogy that is driven by a larger politic of social justice. Roseboro and Ross's (2009) hypotheses are instructive here:

> Care-sickness may stem from an imposed navigation of systemic oppression, inherited interpretive Black tradition(s), and an ideology of liberatory education that creates for Black women educators the responsibility of racial uplift. (p. 36)

Considering the well-documented propensity for burnout among Black women teachers specifically—and educators of color, in general—another aim of this chapter is to begin a fruitful dialogue that considers ways for practitioners to engage a politicized ethic of care healthfully and sustainably. Teachers of color with transformative goals routinely encounter threats of White supremacist backlash via prescribed curriculum, punitive policies, and administrative reprimand (Kohli et al., 2015; Roseboro & Ross, 2009). If respite is seldom granted to the teacher-activist, then future research investigations could provide a more in-depth focus on specific support structures that retain, develop, and reward justice-minded educators.

Acknowledgments

I am indebted to the Black Girls United participants for our extensive conversations, which sparked the ideas presented in this chapter.

Discussion Questions

1. The author maintains that BGU participants' positive responses to the politicized ethic of care that she espoused in the organization necessitates African American girl students' increased exposure to these practices. Explore the potential usefulness of a politicized ethic of care in conventional K–12 classroom settings.

2. Recent data indicate that Black women educators comprise less than
5% of the nation's public K–12 teachers, with White women making
up the majority of the teaching force (Feistritzer, 2011). In light of this
data, how might White women educators—who do not necessarily have
oppressed nationality people to orient themselves to—embody a politicized ethic of care (i.e., badassery and "for real love")?

Notes

1. Pseudonyms are used throughout this chapter to protect the confidentiality
of the institutions and individuals discussed.

2. Although there are various explanations of the term *ratchet*, the epithet
is commonly used in popular culture to debase low-income Black women who are
deemed loud, hostile, *and* reckless (Love, 2017).

Further Reading

Nyachae, T. (2016). Complicated contradictions amid Black feminism and millennial
Black women teachers creating curriculum for Black girls. *Gender and Education,
28*(6), 786–806. https://doi.org/10.1080/09540253.2016.1221896

Roberts, M. A. (2010). Toward a theory of culturally relevant critical teacher care:
African American teachers' definitions and perceptions of care for African
American students. *The Journal of Moral Education, 39*(4), 449–467. https://doi
.org/10.1080/03057241003754922

Sears, S. D. (2010). *Imagining Black womanhood: The negotiation of power and
identity within the Girls Empowerment Project*. SUNY Press.

Smith-Evans, L., George, J., Graves, F. G., Kaufmann, L. S., & Frohlich, L.
(2014). *Unlocking opportunity for African American girls: A call to action for
educational equity.* http://www.naacpldf.org/files/publications/Unlocking%20
Opportunity%20for%20African%20American%20Girls_0.pdf

References

Beauboeuf-Lafontant, T. (2002). A womanist experience of caring: Understanding
the pedagogy of exemplary Black women teachers. *The Urban Review, 34*(1),
71–86. https://doi.org/10.1023/A:1014497228517

Brown, E. (1992). *A taste of power*. Pantheon.

Case, K. I. (1997). African American othermothering in the urban elementary school.
The Urban Review, 29(1), 25–39. https://doi.org/10.1023/A:1024645710209

Civil Rights Data Collection. (2014, March). *Data snapshot: School discipline.* http://
www2.ed.gov/about/o ces/list/ocr/docs/crdc-disciplinesnapshot.pdf

Collins, P. H. (2000). *Black feminist thought: Knowledge, consciousness, and the politics of empowerment* (2nd ed.). Routledge.

Crenshaw, K. W. (1991). Mapping the margins: Intersectionality, identity politics, and violence against women of color. *Stanford Law Review, 43*(6), 1241–1299. https://doi.org/10.2307/1229039

Crenshaw, K. W., Ocen, P., & Nanda, J. (2015). *Black girls matter: Pushed out, overpoliced, and underprotected.* African American Policy Forum & Center for Intersectionality and Social Policy Studies. http://static1.squarespace.com/static/53f20d90e4b0b80451158d8c/t/54dcc1ece4b001c03e323448/1423753708557/AAPF_BlackGirlsMatterReport.pdf

Delgado Bernal, D. (2002). Critical race theory, Latino critical theory, and critical raced-gendered epistemologies: Recognizing students of color as holders and creators of knowledge. *Qualitative Inquiry, 8*(1), 105–126. https://doi.org/10.1177/107780040200800107

Dixson, A., & Dingus, J. (2008). In search of our mothers' gardens: Black women teachers and professional socialization. *Teachers College Record, 110*(4), 805–837. https://www.researchgate.net/publication/291857606_In_Search_of_Our_Mothers'_Gardens_Black_Women_Teachers_and_Professional_Socialization

Duncan-Adrade, J. M. R. (2009). Note to educators: Hope required when growing roses in concrete. *Harvard Educational Review, 79*(2), 1–13. https://www.sjsu.edu/people/marcos.pizarro/courses/185/s1/DuncanAndradeHOPE.pdf

Ellis, C. (2004). *The ethnographic I: A methodological novel about teaching and doing autoethnography.* AltaMira.

Evans-Winters, V. E., & Esposito, J. (2010). Other people's daughters: Critical race feminism and Black girls' education. *Educational Foundations, 24*(1/2), 11–24. https://files.eric.ed.gov/fulltext/EJ885912.pdf

Feistritzer, E. (2011). *Profile of teachers in the U.S. 2011.* http://www.edweek.org/media/pot2011final-blog.pdf

Fordham, S. (1993). "Those loud Black girls": (Black) women, silence, and gender "passing" in the academy. *Anthropology and Education Quarterly, 24*(1), 3–32. https://doi.org/10.1525/aeq.1993.24.1.05x1736t

Freire, P. (1973). *Pedagogy of the oppressed.* Continuum Press.

Girls for Gender Equity. (2017). *The school girls deserve.* http://www.ggenyc.org/the-schools-girls-deserve/

Harris-Perry, M. (2011). *Sister citizen: Shame, stereotypes, and Black women in America.* Yale University Press.

hooks, b. (1994). *Teaching to transgress: Education as the practice of freedom.* Routledge.

hooks, b. (1996). *Bone Black: Memories of girlhood.* Henry Holt.

Joseph, G. (1995). Black feminist pedagogy and schooling in White capitalist America. In B. Guy-Sheftall (Ed.), *Words of fire: An anthology of African-American feminist thought* (pp. 462–471). The New York Press.

Kohli, R., Picower, B., Martinez, A., & Ortiz, N. (2015). Critical professional development: Centering the social justice needs of teachers. *International*

Journal of Critical Pedagogy, 6(2), 7–24. http://libjournal.uncg.edu/ijcp/article/viewFile/1057/849

Lane, M. L. (2014). *Engendering sisterhood, solidarity, and self-love: Black feminist pedagogy and the identity formation of African-American girls* [Unpublished doctoral dissertation]. University of California, Los Angeles.

Lane, M. (2015). Black girl interrupted: A reflection on the challenges and possibilities in transitioning from the community to the academy. In V. Evans-Winters & B. Love (Eds.), *Black feminism in education: Black women speak back, up, & out* (pp. 163–172). Peter Lang.

Lane, M. (2017). Reclaiming our queendom: Black feminist pedagogy and the identity formation of African American girls. *Equity & Excellence in Education*, 50(1), 13–24. https://doi.org/10.1080/10665684.2016.1259025

Love, B. (2017). A ratchet lens: Black queer youth, agency, hip hop, and the Black ratchet imagination. *Educational Researcher*, 46(9), 539–547. https://doi.org/10.3102/0013189X17736520

Mogadime, D. (2000). Black girls/Black women-centered texts and Black teachers as othermothers. *Journal of the Association for the Research on Mothering*, 2(2), 222–233. https://citeseerx.ist.psu.edu/viewdoc/download?doi=10.1.1.867.1844&rep=rep1&type=pdf

Morris, E. W. (2007). "Ladies" or "loudies"? Perceptions and experiences of Black girls in classrooms. *Youth and Society*, 38(4), 490–515. https://doi.org/10.1177/0044118X06296778

Morris, M. (2016). *Pushout: The criminalization of Black girls in schools*. The New Press.

Muhammad, G. E., & Haddix, M. (2016). Centering Black girls' literacies: A review of literature on the multiple ways of knowing of Black girls. *English Education*, 48(4), 299–336. https://www.jstor.org/stable/26492572

NAACP Legal Defense and Educational Fund & The National Women's Law Center. (2014). *Unlocking opportunity for African American girls: A call to action for educational equity*. https://www.nwlc.org/sites/default/files/pdfs/unlocking_opportunity_for_african_american_girls_final.pdf

Richardson, E. (2002). "To protect and serve": African American female literacies. *College Composition and Communication*, 53(4), 675–704. https://doi.org/10.2307/1512121

Richardson, E. (2013). Developing critical hip hop feminist literacies: Centrality and subversion of sexuality in the lives of Black girls. *Equity & Excellence in Education*, 46(3), 327–341. https://doi.org/10.1080/10665684.2013.808095

Roberts, D. (2017). *Killing the Black body* (2nd ed.). Vintage.

Roseboro, D. L., & Ross, S. N. (2009). Care-sickness: Black women educators, care theory, and a hermeneutic of suspicion. *Educational Foundations*, 23(3/4), 19–40. https://files.eric.ed.gov/fulltext/EJ871546.pdf

Sealey-Ruiz, Y. (2007). Rising above reality: The voices of reentry Black mothers and their daughters. *Journal of Negro Education*, 76(2), 141–153. https://www.researchgate.net/publication/283614284_Rising_above_reality_The_voices_of_reentry_black_mothers_and_their_daughters

Sealey-Ruiz, Y. (2016). Why Black girls' literacies matter: New literacies for a new era. *English Education*, *48*(4), 290–298. https://www.jstor.org/stable/26492571

Solorzano, D. (1997). Images and words that wound: Critical race theory, racial stereotyping, and teacher education. *Teacher Education Quarterly*, *24*(3), 5–19. https://www.jstor.org/stable/23478088

White, D. G. (1985). *Ar'n't I a woman? Female slaves in the plantation South*. Norton.

16

STILL RETAINING
EACH OTHER

Black Women Building Community Through
Social Media and Other Digital Platforms

Tykeia Robinson and Brittany Williams

cademe can be an exclusionary, dehumanizing, and silencing space
for Black women (Henry, 2010; Patitu & Hinton, 2003; Patton &
Croom, 2017). Research suggests that only 2.86% of full professors are Black women (Croom & Patton Davis, 2011) whereas 10% of all
executive/administrative/managerial staff were Black women in 2011 (NCES,
2012). The percentage of Black women in leadership drops further at the
collegiate president level. Despite Black women's lower levels of professional
advancement in higher education, rates of degree completion continue in an
upward trajectory (NCES, 2012). In fact, Black women obtain a majority of
higher education degrees earned by *all* Black students, accounting for 68%
of associate's degrees, 66% of bachelor's degrees, 71% of master's degrees, and
65% percent of doctoral degrees (NCES, 2012). Despite increases in degree
attainment for Black women, disparities remain for Black women aspiring to
university leadership and tenured faculty roles.

The silencing and exclusion that Black women experience in academe
is not unique to higher education. In fact, the overpolicing and culminat-
ing suspensions, expulsions, and eventual pushout of Black girls on the
K–12 level directly connects to lower levels of Black women's advancement
in higher education. Morris's (2016) *Pushout* details how schools operate
as arbiters of violence against Black girls in the name of teaching them to
abide by rules. Ultimately, pushout functions as a way for schools to further
the school-to-prison pipeline (the same one that is most often talked about

regarding Black boys and men) by criminalizing Black womanhood through school dress code violations related to hair and through student reprimands for Black vernacular cultural language norms (Morris, 2016).

On the graduate level, Black women report feeling disproportionately underfunded and overworked (McCloud et al., n.d.; Patton, 2009), often expending labor on behalf of colleges and universities that would otherwise demand financial compensation (McCloud et al., n.d.). Despite institutional-level failures to meaningfully support Black women, and lack of compensation for Black women who do expend labor to help retain one another, Black women continue to develop tools and resources to facilitate one another's success in the name of sisterhood. This communal ethos is representative of a larger subculture within the academy where Black women, rather than the institutions we are a part of, engage retention work.

In this chapter, we explore how Black women in higher education offer support to one another and build community in digital spaces, often without formal institutional endorsement. Contextualized via the CiteASista, SisterPhD, and TeamTypingFast digital communities as well as the *Gettin' Grown* and *Schoolin Life* podcast platforms, this chapter illuminates mechanisms for the facilitation of community, accountability, and peer support by, for, and among Black women across higher education. We maintain that these spaces exemplify praxis from existing scholarship, namely Fries-Britt and Turner Kelly's (2005) work outlining the innovative ways that Black women retain each other in spaces that were neither designed for nor supportive of our experiences.

Theoretical Assumptions

Black women have historically and contemporarily worked tirelessly to help retain one another. Access to bidirectional friendships as well as mentoring and support from possibility models and peers are identified as critical contributors to the retention and academic and professional success of Black women in higher education (Henderson et al., 2010). Fries-Britt and Turner Kelly's (2005) example of a supportive relationship between Black women colleagues who are in close physical proximity guides future examinations of how these supportive relationships may be developed and sustained more broadly in virtual and digital contexts. This relationship between two Black women at divergent points of their professional trajectories in academe reveals conceptual tools that structure our exploration and understanding of if and how these relationships can be cultivated in other spaces and under other circumstances. Findings from this study underscore the key qualities of supportive relationships among Black women that ultimately lead to retaining and sustaining one another in academe.

Findings From Retaining Each Other

Narratives of two African American women in the academy characterize the key qualities of supportive relationships between Black women in three ways: (a) connecting as women of color, (b) living with vulnerability and establishing trust, and (c) maintaining motivation and momentum.

Connecting as Women of Color

Connecting as women of color emphasizes the value and importance of cultivating holistic connections and relationships that embrace and acknowledge the various dimensions of each woman's life and identity. Not only did the women connect as academics, they also connected as sisters, friends, spouses/life partners, mothers, daughters, and so on, and as women who experience a range of emotions, fears, and anxiety about their lives and professional trajectories (Patton, 2009). Relationships serve as discursive space where participants can process the experiences and challenges that are unique to Black women. These connections also afford women with possibility models and advisers who demonstrate and exemplify not only what one needs to do to survive and succeed in academe but also how to do what needs to be done (Patton, 2009; Patton & Harper, 2003). For example, "you modeled for me how to deal with racism and sexism in the academy" (Fries-Britt & Turner Kelly, 2005, p. 230). This is key socialization that gives women access to the social and cultural capital that ensures their success in the academy (Gopaul, 2011).

Living With Vulnerability and Establishing Trust

The value of vulnerability is highlighted as an essential element of supportive relationships for Black women in the academy. Transparency about challenges and difficult choices demystifies unchartered academic waters and creates necessary courageous spaces for (a) building trust, (b) the collaborative processing of problems, and (c) risk-taking and strategizing to develop solutions and innovative approaches. "We were both willing to take some risks. . . . We trusted each other and understood that our needs were essentially the same and if we supported each other we could make it through the process" (Fries-Britt & Turner Kelly, 2005, p. 231). Encouraging honest discussion about what one knows and what one has yet to learn fosters an environment free of pretense and the pressure to perform. This has been shown to empower Black women to resist and persevere in work environments that are unwelcoming, hostile, and largely unsupportive. The vulnerability that welcomes the admission of ignorance without judgment and encourages external processing contributes to mutual professional development among Black women. Identifying one's limitations and/or areas of weakness also illuminates opportunities for growth (Fries-Britt & Turner Kelly, 2005).

Maintaining Motivation and Momentum

Consistent with existing research on mentoring, and specifically mentoring relationships among women of color, Fries-Britt and Turner Kelly (2005) attributed their capacity to remain motivated and persist through the challenges of the academy to a strong work ethic and access to supportive networks both within and beyond academe. "Some of the mechanisms we have used to survive are through webs of personal and professional connection" (Fries-Britt & Turner Kelly, 2005, p. 236). Baker Sweitzer (2009) and Baker and Pifer (2011) found that students with broader networks of supportive relationships gain access to additional psychosocial and emotional support in the form of more opportunities to develop technical skills, affirmation, and increased understanding of subject matter in their respective fields of study. Similarly, Griffin et al. (2018) found in their study of underrepresented STEM doctoral students that students develop and depend heavily upon diverse developmental networks that include peers, faculty, administrators, and so on. The bonds created and sustained through these connections and communities are the mechanisms that Black women in the academy establish to both resist and survive racism, sexism, and other forms of oppression inherent to the academy, broader educational contexts, and society at large (Fries-Britt & Turner Kelly, 2005). These supportive relationships and networks also serve as incubators and think tanks created by and for Black women that ensure that their unique needs, experiences, success stories, and strategies are prioritized, valued, accurately chronicled, and shared among other Black women and marginalized populations (Fries-Britt & Turner Kelly, 2005).

"That's Fine, I'll Do It": Digital and Podcast Platforms by and for Black Women

The following sections describe five digital communities created to support and cultivate community among Black women students, faculty, and professionals at various stages of their academic and professional careers. These profiles detail a glimpse of the labor expended by Black women, many of whom are doctoral students and recent graduates, continuing the retention legacies of their foremothers.

Did You #CiteASista Today? Citation Praxis in Academe and Beyond

The CiteASista project advances a lineage of Black women building community and supporting one another. The founders describe the communal ethos with which Black women approach support and success as a form of community cultural wealth (Yosso, 2005) that exists within direct opposition to notions of rugged individualism and American exceptionalism permeating contemporary U.S. culture (Williams & Collier, 2016). As explicated by the cofounders, the CiteASista movement works to "provide encouragement for Black women to not only name the ways we actively resist against the silencing of our bodies and voices, but to also show that we can and do, after naming these experiences" (Williams & Collier, 2016, para 2). As such, CiteASista's online platforms are designed to prioritize, feature, and center the unique contributions, perspectives, and voices of Black women in the United States and abroad.

#CiteASista and CiteASista.com originated as an online forum and monthly Twitter chat(s). Founders Brittany Williams and Joan Collier established this digital platform to acknowledge, uplift, and appreciate the contributions of Black women. What began as a Twitter discussion to highlight how Black women's labor and ideas have been co-opted, misused, unpaid, and even outright stolen has morphed into an online platform sustained entirely through merchandise sales, donations, and cofounder contributions. Since the community's inception in 2016, CiteASista has well over 7,000 followers across online platforms, has inspired similarly named hashtags, and has ultimately functioned as a space to center citational practices as well as Black women's experiences broadly.

Together We Can Get PHinisheD: #SisterPhD

SisterPhD is a digital community for Black Women in higher education and is a model for communal support and retention. As explicated on SisterPhd.com, "The SisterPhD model is designed to facilitate friendships and sisterhood through talking out research, connecting about life experiences, allowing room to vent, and problematize opportunities for growth of self and the group" (McCloud et al., 2015, para. 2). The SisterPhD platform was conceived in the summer of 2015 by five Black women doctoral students from different programs across the country. Laila McCloud, who brainstormed the idea, connected with founding members DaVida Anderson, Shetina Jones, Mika Karikari, and Brittany Williams. This digital space was developed with the intention to "preempt the challenges of doctoral study by banding together" and has currently supported each member through coursework, comprehensive exams, ongoing dissertation projects, and a host of nonacademic life moments (McCloud et al., 2015, para. 3).

The SisterPhD.com website serves as an information hub for Black women doctoral students and recent graduates. Community members can apply to share their stories and advice in blog post form to enlighten and empower their peers. Prior blog posts cover a wide range of topics, including reflections on navigating the 1st year of doctoral training, imposter syndrome, managing distraction, balancing graduate study and parenting, and so on. The website's complementary social media presence, including both a Twitter handle and the hashtag #SisterPhd, is designed to recognize, celebrate, and encourage Black women's doctoral completion in higher education and student affairs. Since 2015, SisterPhD.com and #SisterPhD have grown into a community of close to 4,000 Black women followers and subscribers. The model has been recreated by master's-level students and non-Black women of color alike hoping to coalesce around successful graduate school study and completion.

Thoughtful, Impactful, and Affirming Conversations: Schoolin Life Podcast

Schoolin Life Pod, a weekly podcast hosted by two Black woman PhDs, was created to build community among women who are passionate about (a) personal and professional development, (b) telling their own stories, and (c) educating themselves and others. *Schoolin Life* provides women who may have limited access to affirming and empowering conversations among girlfriends the opportunity to listen in on and benefit from conversations between the show's hosts, Ashley and Marcy. The hosts use their doctoral training in higher education administration and clinical psychology, respectively, to discuss a wide variety of topics. Episodes explore dating/relationships, sexual health, religion/spirituality, professional networking, fashion/style, and other subjects important to Black women.

Schoolin Life Pod has evolved into a lifestyle brand engaging Black women listeners in live events, a bimonthly blog website, and merchandising. Moreover, the podcast averages over 2,000 listeners per month and has attracted over 20,000 listeners since the first episode. Listenership statistics reveal that the *Schoolin Life Podcast* audience mostly comprises Black women graduate students and young professionals aged 25–44. These women study and work in a wide range of fields and professions. The podcast affords listeners both on- and offline engagement and, to date, *Schoolin Life* has engaged over 300 women through live podcast recordings, a listener dinner party, brand collaborations with major retailers, and meetups facilitated in partnership with other digital communities that serve Black women in academe.

Adulting, for Real: Gettin' Grown Podcast

The *Gettin' Grown* podcast is by and for Black women navigating the realities of "adulting." Each week, hosts Jade and Keia, two Black women, share information, insight, and discussion to support one another in figuring out how to define and realize purpose, self-care, and success in their personal and professional lives. *Gettin' Grown* centers and celebrates the beauty, brilliance, and accomplishments of Black girls and women. Segments are designed to facilitate authentic and transparent conversations about the road to purpose with deference to not only the milestones and achievements but also the speed bumps, detours, and roadblocks. *Gettin' Grown*'s hosts and listeners engage and coalesce via comments, emails, and tweets sharing stories, advice, and insight to one another. *Gettin' Grown* averages approximately 270,000 listeners monthly and has engaged 11.3 million since their launch in March of 2017.

#TeamTypingFast: Community, Accountability, and Support

#TeamTypingFast (#TTF) is the brainchild of Tykeia Robinson, scholar-practitioner and cohost known as "Keia" on the *Gettin' Grown* podcast. As a doctoral student Tykeia used the hashtag #TeamTypingFast to chronicle her dissertation development and completion on social media. Other grad students, academics, writers, and professionals across the country started using the hashtag to document their progress on various projects. Thus, a community of practice was born. TTF empowers members to establish collaborative groups that meet (digitally and in person) to support one another through the various phases of academic programs, professional projects, and entrepreneurial endeavors (Robinson, 2018). The digital platform provides an infrastructure for building and sustaining communities of practice among women of color that ensures both our individual greatness as well as our collective success (Robinson, 2018). TTF members are able to connect with other like-minded hard workers, steadily pursuing purpose with passion at special events. These events are designed to be fun, *fly*, enlightening, and invigorating spaces for rich discussion about maintaining identity, navigating challenges, surviving and thriving at school and work, realizing and cultivating purpose, and more. TTF creates digital and in-person courageous spaces that afford Black and Brown women the information, resources, and community needed to get to work and meet their goals (Robinson, 2018).

Discussion

This discussion illuminates manifestations of the key qualities of supportive relationships as outlined by Fries-Britt and Turner Kelly (2005). These communities facilitate support and connection by and for Black women; establish trust, shared understanding, and make room for brave spaces; and help to motivate and build momentum for one another to not only persist but also to thrive. Though Black women are the target audience for these online and digital platforms, they are not race exclusive. In fact, the residual benefits of increased retention of Black graduate women and Black women serving in the academy translates to better prepared educators on the K–12 level, increased opportunities to shift campus policy and praxis associated with admissions and student support, as well as opportunities to begin and further national conversations on the experiences of Black girls. Much of the educational advocacy associated with Black identity focuses on the experiences of Black boys and men (Jacobs, 2017), including the work done by non-Black people. This makes it that much more important for Black women's success as Black women sit at the forefront of advocacy for Black girls.

Though none of these communities alone exemplify all the qualities identified by Fries-Britt and Turner Kelly (2005), each emphasizes and prioritizes one or more key qualities. Moreover, given the potential and actualized crossovers between these communities (see #HeySisMeetUp), it is possible that many Black women participating in these communities are more wholly fulfilled. Accordingly, the following sections reveal how the online communities presented here contribute to and facilitate supporting mentoring spaces, friendships, and relationships in ways that are not presented in the conceptual model given changes in digital and social technology. The section concludes by acknowledging the significance of these digital spaces and how they contribute to the retention, support, and success of Black women in educational spaces.

Connecting as Black Women

Fries-Britt and Turner Kelly (2005) lacked Black women support models and connected to collaboratively explore, process, and navigate how to be both Black and woman in academia. Their connection was not solely based on the shared academic and professional spaces they occupied nor on their academic and professional identities. Rather the development and sustainability of their connection were attributed to an intention to know each other first as women and then as Black women academics. Like Fries-Britt and Turner Kelly (2005), all of the Black women who have developed these communities and counterspaces have done so to fill a void within academe. Each of the digital communities profiled in this chapter offers holistic approaches to content and programming that emphasize connections among Black women. Moreover, these communities embrace and acknowledge the varied dimensional lives and positionalities that Black women have and hold in addition to their positionality within and adjacent to the academy. The women facilitating these communities are helping to bridge connections not only as professionals but as women who are also friends, spouses, mothers, daughters, colleagues, and so on.

The SisterPhd and CiteASista digital communities wholly recognize the multiple hats Black women wear and facilitate programming and discussion on a range of issues related to the safety, success, health, and wellness of Black women. On their respective websites, the posts and columns cover topics including, but not limited to, motherhood and parenting, music/pop culture/media, productivity and energy management, style and fashion, professional development, health care, religion and spirituality, and much more. Similarly, *Gettin' Grown Podcast* and *Schoolin Life Pod* content features a wide range of discussions and encourages listeners to prioritize their individual growth and self-care in every area of their lives, beginning with their academic and professional careers and expounding from there. In keeping with their communal ethos and commitment to Black women broadly, the websites for these digital communities offer online resource pages featuring links to external content and support spaces that prioritize the perspectives, unique needs, and lived experiences of Black women students and academics.

When these digital counterspaces offer opportunities to discuss pressing issues facing Black women, they also reveal evidence of the power in Black women's relationship and community building. Because online communities often serve as discursive spaces where participants tell their stories and process their experiences in an open forum, these communities offer opportunities to engage openly and in private by beginning the dialogue. Women grapple with their identities and the ways those identities intersect, converge, and influence how they navigate the personal professional spaces that they occupy and exist within. They examine historical practices, illuminate injustices, share their frustrations, and present and critique new ideas, strategies, and approaches. A blog published on CiteASista.com, for example, uses controversy surrounding tennis superstar Serena Williams's demand for an apology after a U.S. Open official falsely accused and penalized her for cheating during her match with Naomi Osaka. The piece unpacks the gross mischaracterizations of Black women in workspaces and the implications of existing harmful and misleading tropes about Black women on the professional development and advancement of Black women students, academics, and professionals. The author uses Williams's response to the official's ruling, and the media storm that followed, as a lens for unpacking the common and shared experiences of Black women as Black women, not as Black women academics, Black women professionals, Black women athletes, or any other role, because the common identity here is Black womanhood. Cokley (2018b) uses the blog as a digital forum, where she and other participants can acknowledge and explore the frustrations that often accompany the silence that we are expected to maintain while being misunderstood and treated unfairly and unjustly. The costs and risks of self-advocacy are also examined and presented with prompts for sharing strategies for coping with and combating the prevalence of these toxic professional environments via blog comments and tweets. This post, like the platforms themselves, offers a space to connect with Black women because it normalizes the frustration associated with the overpolicing of Black women's bodies, actions, and lived experiences.

Living With Vulnerability and Establishing Trust

Fries-Britt and Turner Kelly (2005) stressed the significance and necessity of vulnerability in facilitating and sustaining supportive relationships for Black women navigating academic spaces and environments. Cultivating a culture of transparency where women feel safe to share challenges, limitations, and areas of weakness in academic and professional development facilitates a sense of safety and trust that empowers all women to abandon the pretense and performance that can be so prevalent in academe, and learn from and with one another. This trust and vulnerability can be found throughout and across the online communities profiled in this chapter.

The #CiteASista Twitter hashtag often serves as a forum for sharing frustrations, grievances, complaints, and so on, and all the lessons learned through the difficult experience that women face in and beyond the academy. Women share mistakes made and lessons learned in ways that prompt the community for further discussion and future research and/or programming for women to process their experiences collaboratively. For example, an assistant professor who often engages both the #SisterPhD and #CiteASista Twitter communities published a series of tweets, or a thread, on her experience revising and resubmitting a manuscript that had been rejected. "Sometimes, what you initially thought was good, you realize falls short when looking with fresh eyes. So, embrace rejection. Sometimes it can lead to . . . not just getting work done but doing your best work" (FeleciaElana, 2018). This exemplifies the vulnerability encouraged by Fries-Britt and Turner Kelly and demonstrates how transparency about a failure breeds the opportunity for growth and skill development. Similarly, women utilize Twitter hashtags promoted through online communities to discuss and process the challenges in working with mentors and supervisors. For example, one woman postdoc of color shared the following tweets: "Today, I was reminded not all 'mentors' are in your corner . . . there is a perceived competition . . . senior scholars of color who would rather block your progress (and projects) than ensure access to the tools you need to grow" (OccScienceBae, 2018a, 2018b). Other members of the CiteASista community and other hashtags mentioned and responded to this woman's tweet citing similar experiences and agreeing with her sentiment. This prompted an opportunity for reimagining strategies for response and continuing success as it is often difficult for us as Black women to hold one another accountable when unstable power dynamics render us vulnerable to further reaction and/or retribution.

Maintaining Motivation and Momentum

Access to supportive networks of Black women both within and beyond academic spaces are identified by Fries-Britt and Turner Kelly (2005) as affirming sources of resistance and survival. These relationships, networks, and communities serve as lifelines to Black women navigating the dark, unpredictable, and often dangerous waters of undergraduate and graduate training, of life as a faculty member, administrator, scholar practitioner, and so on. They empower Black women to not only persist through their training and professional careers but to thrive personally and professionally and facilitate the success of others. Digital communities like those profiled provide infrastructure for building and sustaining these meaningful connections among Black women.

A review of the @CiteaSista, @SisterPhD, and #TeamTypingFast hashtags and handles on Twitter and Instagram reveal that engagement among Black women on these online communities exists in several different ways. Women use digital (counter)spaces to connect with other communities for the purposes of mentoring, finding friendship, support, and establishing accountability systems. Participants announce their accomplishments and recognize the accomplishments of their peers and colleagues for completing projects and meeting milestones across their academic/professional trajectories. Persons are affirmed and encouraged for publishing research, completing qualifying/comprehensive exams, defending dissertations/dissertation proposals, presenting research at national/regional conferences, faculty talks, job announcements, and so on. Women also promote themselves and their work posting flyers that announce when they and/or their scholarship will be featured on television/radio, and at conferences and events. Inspirational videos and stories of success and persistence are also shared, often with empowering quotes from notable Black women scholars such as bell hooks, Brittany Cooper, Venus Evans-Winters, and Lori D. Patton. The achievements of Black women and women of color colleagues are often featured, celebrating major milestones and the various ways that Black women scholars are breaking down barriers in unprecedented ways, leading institutions/organizations, excelling in research/scholarly practice, and so on (see Tmcf_hbcu, 2018).

Black academic women who experience feelings of physical and social isolation on campus use the space to find and connect with other Black women students/scholars who may be local or in close proximity to them (see ReadBlackademia, 2018). Similarly, women share "#protips" and "#gradschooltips," common characterizations for advice or instruction on how to optimize the advancement of their doctoral training, research, or professional development. For example, professors and advanced graduate students share professional etiquette tips such as advice for efficient communication via email (Tomiferg, 2018). These tips also emphasize the importance of physical care and illuminate common areas of struggle and difficulty in processes of research design, writing, and publishing (BrilliantBlkGrl, 2018a). Women offer encouragement, validation, strategies, and supports to colleagues and counterparts, often posting and sharing resources and encouraging dialogue around the unspoken and unwritten rules of the game. As cited in previous research, Black women and other marginalized populations are often precluded from relationships, environments, and/or socialization experiences where trade secrets and success strategies are typically shared (Gopaul, 2011). #SisterPhd, SisterPhD.com, and other digital platforms are filling that gap, serving as the discursive spaces where Black women can widely and accessibly discuss valuable information including articles detailing everything from choosing a graduate program through dissertation completion and the job search.

All of the digital spaces and online communities profiled in this chapter host in-person meetups and programming. CiteASista has hosted a meet and greet at the annual conference for American College Personnel International in 2017 following a presentation on a "Framework for Reimagining Digital Conversations." TeamTypingFast, CiteASista, SisterPhD, and *Schoolin Life Pod* joined forces to host an informal meetup at the 2018 conference of the Association for the Study of Higher Education (ASHE). The space was designed to build collegiality and community for Black women in higher education, and approximately 60 Black women doctoral students, faculty, and administrators participated. Similarly, *Gettin' Grown Podcast* has partnered with professional organizations like ASHE for the expressed purpose of promoting content and conversation about the experiences, needs, and support of Black women students and professionals. Lori D. Patton was featured as a special guest on *Gettin' Grown* in April of 2018. She shared her story as scholar and the ways that her Black woman identity shapes her research, her professional practice, and her leadership as the first Black woman president of ASHE (for 46,600 listeners). *Gettin' Grown* partnered with ASHE again in November 2018 to present a special episode featuring participants of the ASHE Town Hall Meeting on perspectives, needs, experiences, and educational attainment of incarcerated and formerly incarcerated Black women and Black girls. Each of these episodes reached more than 40,000 listener/downloads, respectively. Moreover, the content has catalyzed insightful discussion among listeners, both in the episode comments and via online discussion as observed on Twitter using the handles and hashtag @GettinGrownPod, #WokeAcademy, and #TeamTypingFast. Many were appreciative of the relatability of the content and conversation presented on each episode and how seeing themselves and their experiences was both affirming and empowering.

Implications, Limitations, Summary of Key Points, and Conclusion

The positive contributions of digital counterspaces by and for Black women cannot be overstated. For the Black women who stand as the *only* or among the *few* representations of Black women in their roles, these communities can and have proven to decrease their feelings of isolation. Moreover, online platforms also serve to demystify the hidden curriculum associated with graduate degree persistence and attainment as well as the success and productivity of Black women faculty, scholars-practitioners, administrators, and so on, thereby addressing existing disparities and issues of underrepresentation across the higher education landscape. Campus leaders may wish to operationalize the strategies presented in this chapter to promote the success and retention of Black women in academe. Leadership may even go a step further by consulting and enlisting the expertise of Black women scholars who are already integrated into their campus cultures, many of whom may be engaged in this service.

Implications

There are several implications for policy and practice as it relates to ensuring a more stable future for Black women in academe. First, given how many Black women, including those identified here and those elsewhere, are already doing the work of retention, institutions could benefit from learning and replicating these strategies across their own campus. This is not to suggest copying Black women's work that is being done and renaming it—a practice that has been done repeatedly within and outside of academe. Instead, consulting with Black women through paid opportunities, sponsorships, and sustained funding for program implementations could be mutually beneficial for Black women currently serving in these capacities for free when they should be paid and for helping institutions to improve their overall retention. For institutional researchers, collaboration with Black women students, faculty, and staff who have a better pulse on campus climate for Black women may prove of greater use than funding exploratory studies. Moreover, campus leaders may consider financially and socially supporting research projects and retention initiatives already underway to best support Black women.

Limitations

Though the communities identified here offer meaningful forms of support for Black women in and outside of the academy, they are not without limitations. An obvious pitfall of these digital and online communities is that of continuous access. Not all Black women hoping to join the academy may have stable internet and technological devices that allow them to engage. As the gender and racial wage gaps continue to rise in the United States this may prove to become a widening problem for many Black women hoping to learn and engage with the academy more. For those who have some access, cost effectiveness of internet and data plans as well as institutional support to engage in these initiatives might prove difficult for maintaining involvement. Beyond this, technology has and continues to advance rapidly. Another limitation could be the role of these communities shifting from forms of support to excuses for lack of self- and individual care. Though these communities are powerful, we would caution readers from solely engaging these spaces and failing to pursue individual counseling, therapy, and other forms of personalized care and wellness that may improve their success in the academy. Digital and online sisterhood are *a* form of care, support, and growth, inducing kinship—they should not be *the only* form for any one individual.

Summary of Key Points

- Black women create digital (counter)communities in response to cultural practices, systems, and institutional structures that have failed to prioritize, protect, and promote the unique needs, lived experiences, and contributions of Black women.

- The five digital spaces and online communities profiled in this chapter exemplify the key qualities of supportive relationships between Black women as outlined by Fries-Britt and Turner Kelly (2005) by (a) creating infrastructure for identifying, establishing, and cultivating meaningful and holistic connections by and for Black women; (b) serving as courageous brave spaces that encourage vulnerability, transparency, and trust; and (c) promoting and encouraging the motivation of self and others and the sustainability of professional productivity and success.
- Digital platforms can address existing barriers of proximity for Black women graduate students experiencing isolation despite the underrepresentation of Black women leaders in the academy.
- Online platforms also serve to demystify the hidden curriculum associated with graduate degree persistence and attainment, thereby addressing existing disparities and issues of underrepresentation across the higher education landscape.

Conclusion

When speaking about her experience as one of two Black girls in the gifted and talented program in her middle school, Brittany Cooper (2018) recalled her friend Holly. "We took to each other quickly because Black girls find each other as a means to survive" (p. 117). Similarly, in her best-selling memoir *Becoming*, First Lady Michelle Obama (2018) stressed the importance and impact of her relationships with Black girlfriends and Black women professional role models during her undergraduate years at Princeton University.

> It takes energy to be the only Black person in a lecture hall. . . . It requires . . . an extra level of confidence, to speak in those settings and own your presence in the room. Which is why when my friends and I found one another at dinner each night, it was with some degree of relief. (p. 75)

Isolation, whether physical, social, or professional, is a common experience for Black girls and academic women. Black women have always and continue to do the work of supporting and retaining one another within academe. For the communities discussed in this chapter, much of this work is done online; however, there are often complementary in-person events and joint ventures to help minimize the feelings of isolation Black women may negotiate on campus. Given the hostile climates Black women face in the academy, it is important for institutions to recognize the value of these online and digital counterspaces by not only acknowledging their existence but also financially and socially supporting these endeavors. For those of us with a vested interest in ensuring our campus leadership and faculty accurately reflect the student body, the efforts of the digital communities and online platforms presented here offer road maps for helping Black women to matriculate, thrive, and then graduate with advanced degrees to join the academy. Acknowledging Black women's labor in contributing to a more diverse academy has never been more critical.

Discussion Questions

1. Beyond the examples presented, what other ways might the internet and social media be used to build supportive relationships and communities among Black women across education?
2. What types of internet and technology access issues might we eradicate to ensure more women can engage with existing digital platforms and online communities?
3. How might we build stronger relationships between online communities of Black women in academe with Black women and Black girls in P–12 and undergraduate education?

Further Reading

Collier, J. N. (2017). *Using sista circle methodology to examine sense of belonging of Black women in doctoral programs at a historically White institution* [Unpublished doctoral dissertation]. University of Georgia.

Croom, N. N., Beatty, C. C., Acker, L. D., & Butler, M. (2017). Exploring under-graduate Black womyn's motivations for engaging in "Sister Circle" organizations. *NASPA Journal About Women in Higher Education, 10*(2), 216–228. https://doi .org/10.1080/19407882.2017.1328694

Morris, M. (2016). *Pushout: The criminalization of Black girls in schools.* The New Press.

References

Baker, V., & Pifer, M. J. (2011). The role of relationships in transition from doctoral student to independent scholar. *Studies in Continuing Education, 33*(1), 5–17. https://doi.org/10.1080/0158037X.2010.515569

Baker Sweitzer, V. (2009). Towards a theory of doctoral student professional identity development: A developmental networks approach. *Journal of Higher Education, 80*(1), 1–33. https://doi.org/10.1080/00221546.2009.11772128

Blackademia [@ReadBlackademia]. (2018, December 5). *Hey, fam! Anyone out there a grad student or prof at Rutgers? We're looking to help someone build community* [Tweet]. Twitter. https://twitter.com/ReadBlackademia/status/1070433345044144134

Cokley, R. [@BrilliantBlkGrl]. (2018a, December 4). *Random #gradschool tip: Figure out who in your cohort works at a similar speed as you* [Tweet]. Twitter. https://twitter.com/BrilliantBlkGrl/status/1070049936224542723

Cokley, R. (2018b). *Serena is all of us, #BlackWomenAtWork edition.* https://citeasista.com/2018/09/10/serena-is-all-of-us-blackwomenatwork-edition/

Cooper, B. (2018). *Eloquent rage: A Black feminist discovers her superpower.* St. Martin's Press.

Croom, N., & Patton Davis, L. D. (2011). The miner's canary: A critical race perspective on the representation of Black women full professors. *Negro Educational Review, 62&63*(1–4), 13–39.

FeleciaElana [@FeleciaElana]. (2018). *Sometimes, what you initially thought was good, you realize falls short when looking with fresh eyes. So, embrace rejection. Sometimes...* [Tweet]. Twitter. https://twitter.com/FeleciaElana/status/1068990729089949697

Ferguson, T. [@tomiferg]. (2018, December 7). *Professional etiquette tip of the day: Sarcasm should not be used over email, no matter how comfort you feel with an individual. #professionalism"* [Tweet]. Twitter. https://twitter.com/tomiferg/status/1071117474811133952

Fries-Britt, S., & Turner Kelly, B. (2005). Retaining each other: Narratives of two African American women in the academy. *The Urban Review, 37*(3), 221–242. http://doi.org/10.1007/s11256-005-0006-2

Gopaul, B. (2011). Distinction in doctoral education: Using Bourdieu's tools to assess the socialization of doctoral students. *Equity and Excellence in Education, 44*(1), 10–21. https://doi.org/10.1080/10665684.2011.539468

Griffin, K., Baker, V., O'Meara, K., Nyunt, G., Robinson, T., & Staples, C. (2018). Supporting scientists from underrepresented minority backgrounds: Mapping developmental networks. *Studies in Graduate Education, 9*(1), 19–37. https://doi.org/10.1108/SGPE-D-17-00032

Henderson, T. L., Hunter, A. G., & Hildreth, G. J. (2010). Outsiders within the academy: Strategies for resistance and mentoring African American women. *Michigan Family Review, 14*(1), 28–41. http://dx.doi.org/10.3998/mfr.4919087.0014.105

Henry, W. J. (2010). African American women in student affairs: Best practices for winning the game. *Advancing Women in Leadership, 30*, 1–19. https://doi.org/10.18738/awl.v30i0.306

Jacobs, C. E. (2017). Remember, black girls aren't doing "just fine": Supporting black girls in the classroom. In E. Moore Jr., M. Penick-Parks, & A. Michael (Eds.), *A guide for white women teaching black boys* (pp. 377–385). Corwin.

Johnson, K. [@OccScienceBae]. (2018a, December 7). *Today I was reminded not all "mentors" are in your corner. #PostdocLife #CiteASista @CiteASista #BlackWomenPhDs @BlackWomenPhDs . . .* [Tweet]. Twitter. https://twitter.com/OccScienceBae/status/1071075968142508032

Johnson, K. [@OccScienceBae]. (2018b, December 7). *I will not share details, but there is a need to discuss the perceived competition projected onto female post-docs of color by....* [Tweet]. Twitter. https://twitter.com/OccScienceBae/status/1071075970147381250

McCloud, L., Karikari, S., Williams, B., Anderson, D., & Jones, S. (2015). *Sister-PhD*. https://www.sisterphd.com/about-us/

McCloud, L., Williams, B., Karikari, S., Anderson, D., Jones, S. (n.d.). *The making of #SisterPhD*. [Unpublished manuscript.] Grand Valley State University.

Morris, M. (2016). *Pushout: The criminalization of Black girls in schools.* The New Press.

National Center for Education Statistics. (2012). *Integrated Postsecondary Education Data System, Table 314.40: Employees in degree-granting postsecondary institutions by race/ethnicity, sex, employment status, control and level of institution, and primary occupation: Fall 2011.* http://nces.ed.gov/programs/digest/d13/tables/dt13_314.40.asp.

Obama, M. (2018). *Becoming.* Crown.

Patitu, C. L., & Hinton, K. G. (2003). The experiences of African American women faculty and administrators in higher education: Has anything changed? *New Directions for Student Services, 104,* 79–93. https://doi.org/10.1002/ss.109

Patton, L. D. (2009). My sister's keeper: A qualitative examination of mentoring experiences among African American women in graduate and professional schools. *The Journal of Higher Education, 80*(5), 510–537. https://doi.org/10.1080/00221546.2009.11779030

Patton, L. D., & Croom, N. N. (Eds.). (2017). *Critical perspectives on Black woman and college success.* Routledge.

Patton, L. D., & Harper, S. (2003). Mentoring relationships among African American women in graduate and professional schools. *New Directions for Student Services, 104,* 67–78. https://doi.org/10.1002/ss.108

Robinson, T. (2018). *#TeamTypingFast.* https://teamtypingfast.com

Thurgood Marshall Scholarship Fund [@Tmcf_hbcu]. (2018, December 7). *Congratulations to Dr. Wilma Mishoe who will be installed as the 11th—and first female—president of @DelStateUniv! #HBCU* [Tweet]. Twitter. https://twitter.com/tmcf_hbcu/status/1071172213661945856

Williams, B., & Collier, J. (2016). *#CiteaSista.* https://citeasista.com/about/

Yosso, T. J. (2005). Whose culture has capital? A critical race theory discussion of community cultural wealth. *Race Ethnicity and Education, 8*(1), 69–91. https://doi.org/10.1080/1361332052000341006

17

MY SISTER'S KEEPER

Intergenerational Love and Commitment Between Black Women and Girls

Toby S. Jenkins and Vivian Anderson

Somewhere I read that liberty is words spoken
It's the strong voice that America allows to be heard
(that's only if your speaking kind words)
But my words are the truth, the conscious of America
You see I had words back when the dictionary was a foreign language
I had speeches when the alphabet was a dream denied
I spoke the truth even when my English was supposedly broken and my life
was threatened by the truth spoken
I was Nat Turner and that Lady Sojourner
I spoke of liberty—
My mere existence is liberation—
You are the one stuck in a dream
Wake up America

Magicians and Fairytales: A Theoretical View of Education and Community

In the *Wizard of Oz*, the story goes that Dorothy and her friends travel down an enchanting yellow road in search of their dreams. Each of them has a different goal. Oz is the magic place that will give each of them what they need. And so, they walk this path laid before them. They encounter all kinds of obstacles and scary experiences. But they ease on down the road. And when they get to Oz they find that it's not what they thought. Dorothy and her crew find that they really didn't need the magic of Oz to become whole, full people. Glinda the Good Witch tells Dorothy that she has always had the power, she just had to learn it for herself (Baum, 2000). Dorothy had the ability to fulfill her dreams from the start. A magical wizard didn't give her the tools of resilience and perseverance—it was Auntie Em and Uncle Henry—old folk who loved her with everything they had on a small, modest farm in Kansas.

Often targeted, punished, and pushed out of schools, Black girls' experiences within the field of education are no different. Fully capable, talented, resilient, and culturally equipped, young girls find themselves searching for magical teachers and educational wizards only to find themselves on a long, frightening, and disappointing journey to a pot of gold that does not exist— at least not for them to claim. In this chapter, we explore the complicated relationship between Black communities and education marked by the opposing feelings of both hope and disappointment. Black girls must often find alternative learning spaces that understand and appreciate who they are. These critical spaces filled with committed and loving family members, elders, neighbors, and community-based educators form an important intergenerational village that builds the capacity of Black girls to not only thrive but to also see and value their own magic.

Our examination of the experiences, beliefs, and needs of Black girls is informed by critical feminist theory, critical race theory, and intersectionality. Critical feminist theory encourages the examination of power and oppression, requires the construction of collaborative and co-operative relationships, and ultimately seeks to create a product that is transformative (Creswell, 1998; Gordon, 1993; Mohanty, 2003; Reinharz, 1992). In her critical work, Patricia Hill-Collins (1986) suggested that wrestling with the ways in which nontraditional knowledge has been used to educate, create self-awareness, raise self-efficacy, and steward social change among communities of color offers important insight into the complex relationship between culture and education in America. Critical race theory and the theory of intersectionality are also salient to this chapter due to their focus on the authentic voice and experiences of traditionally marginalized communities (Barnes, 1990; Crenshaw, 1991; Ladson-Billings, 1998; Ladson-Billings & Tate, 1995).

Both intersectionality and critical race theory acknowledge that traditionally marginalized community members might speak from a very unique life position that is critically important to hear. In essence, the critique that these communities bring to an experience is valuable. Intersectionality takes this a step further and acknowledges that these critical differences are often impacted by the intersecting identities of race, gender, and class. Black girls and women are uniquely experiencing life in America. Being a Black girl is one thing. But being a Black girl living in poverty creates a particular identity. Being a Black girl constantly terrorized by verbal or psychological assault is yet another. Being a Black girl attending schools and living in neighborhoods where her culture is marginalized and she is minoritized offers another lens. However, many Black girls are blessed with rich, loving families, neighborhoods and school environments that strengthen their sense of self-efficacy and belonging. In this chapter, we honor our families and neighbors who love and guide Black girls. To acknowledge the merit of community and culturally based education spaces is to challenge what education should look like, where it should reside, whose knowledge is real, and who is taken seriously as intellectual contributors to society.

American Dreams

The relationship between African Americans and "education" has always been complicated. Though there has been a very long history of educational exclusion and inequity, African Americans historically still viewed the opportunity to be educated as an important life goal (Jenkins, 2006). After emancipation, African Americans in the South entered schools as pupils from ages 6 to 60 (Fairclough, 2001). Many would argue that the first forms of activism toward equity were seen on hot summer nights in the South when enslaved Africans learned to read by candlelight. America has an almost 400-year history of higher education, yet for 200 of those years Blacks of any age were excluded from even being taught to read. Yet this never deterred the African American desire to be educated. Though African Americans have had to navigate their way through an oppressive history in America, progressive Black community members have always found ways to resist educational exclusion. Education was viewed as the means for upward mobility and it was a community-driven and culturally connected endeavor (Jenkins, 2006).

The African American community continued to fight for quality education during the civil rights movement, breaking down desegregation barriers. Today, many educational researchers and practitioners continue to champion the cause for quality and meaningful education (Adams, 1993; Bray, 2003; Landsman et al., 2015; Paul, 2003). What fuels the energy to fight for education (to receive it or to reform it) is a foundational belief in the value of education. There has been a historical sense of optimism and hope surrounding what it means for traditionally excluded communities of people to be educated and how an education will impact their life (Anderson, 1988;

Hine & Thompson, 1999; Williams, 2007). But after decades of strained relationships with the education system, why should Black youth still believe in the possibility that formal educational institutions will impact their lives in a positive way?

Reimagining Oz: When Dorothy Has an Afro

In the 2012 report *Race, Gender and the School to Prison Pipeline: Expanding Our Discussion to Include Black Girls*, Monique Morris argued that the traditional framework of the "school to prison pipeline" has largely focused on the experiences and conditions affecting Black males. Adopting a one-dimensional gender lens to study and address important work on inequality, exclusion, and the pushing out of students away from schools and into systems of criminal justice limits our full understanding of this phenomenon. Morris (2016) argued that, from a sociocultural perspective, Black women and men experience exclusion in education both together and differently. It is important to acknowledge that the work documenting, critiquing, and challenging exclusionary practices in education toward Black males has been extremely important and must continue. Similarly, a rich body of research is needed to focus on Black girls and the ways that their experiences within education systems often culturally isolate them, racially target them, push them out of school and into the criminal justice system, and more broadly destroy their sense of hope and belief in education.

In her classic text *Learning From the Outsider Within: The Sociological Significance of Black Feminist Thought*, Patricia Hill-Collins (1986) remembered the long history that Black women and girls have had being an "outsider within." Collins asserted that Black women and girls have gained a unique knowledge and expertise about the racially White and economically affluent populations who most often wield social control in the United States. From histories as "present but quiet" housekeepers and nannies, which brought them in close proximity to White families, to contemporary academic settings where Black women and girls are marginalized by the expectation for them to be "present but quiet" learners and colleagues, Black women and girls have a much more nuanced understanding of the White educational environment than White educators might have of the Black cultural and community experience. In this regard, Black girls enter educational spaces with a valuable expertise not only about their culture, society, and community, but also about the traditions, shortcomings, strengths, and weaknesses of schools and the educators within them. In the following we share our very personal insights and experiences with this issue. We are not only educators and community leaders who are dedicated to Black girls, we are educators who have been Black girls. And we also bring this experience and understanding into our work. It frames our commitment and it directs our steps.

Mama Love

Almost 20 years ago, bell hooks declared that, essentially, it's all about love (hooks, 1999). Our efforts to research and understand society and people; our efforts to create social change; our determination to transform schools, communities, governments, and societies are all rooted in love. Love is a basic requirement of change (hooks, 2001; Noddings, 2003; Tillich, 1960). This is the case in any realm of life. New parents radically change their lifestyle, schedule, temperament, and even their daily thoughts out of love. Your Google searches change once you become a parent. Newly married couples adjust, bend, and give out of love. Love demands that they be more and give more in order to make the relationship better. Love is at the root of all incredible change. And so, love really needs to be at the center of our examination of community needs. What role does love play in the field of education? What importance does love have in the effort to provide a better educational experience for Black girls? How do we teach Black girls? How do we communicate with them? How do we evaluate them? What type of skill, training, and praxis does it take for an educator to truly impact their lives? We argue that the most important skill is love.

More specifically, we need more mama love in education. To be clear, we don't need teachers assuming the role of mother. We don't need more cultures of paternalistic authority. Mama love is not literal; it is philosophical. It is a way of seeing and treating students. A mama's love is unconditional. A mama's love is genuine. A mama's love is fearless. A mama's love is visionary—it not only sees your magic, but also expects you to live up to your highest potential. A mama's love teaches you how to survive. A mama's love isn't perfect, but it always works. We need the ethic of mama love in educational practice. And we also need to love our mamas. In this regard, we are talking about acknowledging, valuing, and including all of the family and community members who dare to teach and mentor children (neighbors, aunties, grandmas, and activists who just care). We need to value and sit with our students' families and external support systems. I learned my greatest skills from my mamma. My mother is a Black woman who never went to college, who stayed at home with me for 5 years and then worked in factories, as a maid, and as a teacher's assistant. Hard and low-paid work. But I always saw her as beautiful, intelligent, and skilled.

Understanding the sheer brilliance that has allowed families to sustain through decades of poverty helps you to understand the resilience, creativity, and critical capacity that Black girls bring to the classroom. I brought an important consciousness and social awareness to the classroom as a daughter of farmers, janitors, maids, and factory workers. And although I was raised by very present, hard-working parents who came from a generation that definitely valued education, I can still push myself to try to understand those parents who fall short. Even when families fail and fall hard, they still generally manage to get their children to school. It is important to understand and ground what seems to be contempt for families who are careless and difficult. It's not easy dealing with some parents. But perhaps some parents don't have a critical capacity to make sound decisions because school failed them too—because society pressed them so far to the margins and segregated them in ghettos that limited their worldview.

As I came to work closely with Vivian Anderson, the coauthor of this chapter, what struck me about the power of her work was her incredible patience with parents. She often holds their hands and guides them through what is also a new experience for them (participating with an organization that cares, learning to be a supportive parent, and understanding the value of extra learning and leadership experiences). Many of them had none of these experiences when they were students. Vivian Anderson's story is a powerful testimony of intelligent, intentional, love-based work. Her organization is framed in both a research-based and street-level understanding of what Black girls need. But not only that, it is a testimony to the power that is present when Black women gather—when the act of teaching has no direction across generations.

Parents are both teachers and learners. Elders sit with the whole family—youth and their incredibly young parents. The community guides the community. The programs sponsored by Every Black Girl, Inc., are the physical embodiment of what mama love looks like in quality educational settings. In the next section, "The View From the Field," Vivian Anderson tells her story as a response to my critical question, "What do you see as the prevailing social issues and institutions that must be addressed in order to create loving growth environments for Black girls?"

The View From the Field

On October 26, 2015, a video went viral of a Black female student being assaulted by a White male resource officer in Columbia, South Carolina. The response to the video nationwide was split in empathy for the girl, but still the persistent initial question was "What did she do?" I was living in Brooklyn, New York, working with an organization focused on ensuring gender equality for girls of color, when the video was broadcast on the national news. We had been studying the root of school pushout and its impact on girls. This video was not only related to the work I had been doing with the girls in New York City, but it also actually became the visual representation for what many scholars such as Monique Morris had written about in her book *Pushout* (2016).

I would eventually travel to South Carolina to see how I could support the girls, their families, and any organization or groups protesting against the violent assault on this girl and the unjust arrest of the two girls involved (the one assaulted and another Black female classmate who stood in her defense). What I found when I arrived is what I started calling the "Pandora's Box of violence" against Black girls. Inspired by classic Greek mythology, the idea of Pandora's Box is a metaphor to refer to any source of great and unexpected trouble. Ultimately, the story is about a jar or container being given that when opened and accessed actually unleashes evil. Once it is opened, it can't be closed and trouble keeps pouring out (Hesiod, 2009). Has this not been the experience of African Americans with education—curiosity and desire to experience it followed by harassment, hate, denial, contempt, and pushout once they have tried to enter.

The contents of this Pandora's Box in South Carolina would include multilayered and systematic issues that have been oppressing and making Black girls invisible to society. The reason for the assault? The young lady allegedly did not give up her cellphone. She was sitting at her desk refusing to get up. She was not being violent in any way; she was being "noncompliant." She simply questioned what she did wrong to warrant being kicked out of class. That was her first offense, denying the request of authority, speaking up for herself. Her classmate, who after the resource officer began to pull the girl out of her seat, screamed out, "Why are you doing this to her?!" would also be arrested for the same issue of questioning authority and speaking up. I spoke to so many adults and young people after the incident, and the majority responded with statements like "She should have just followed orders," "She must have done something terrible," "She was a foster child so she must have been a bad kid." She . . . she . . . she. There was never a conversation about the officer's history of violence against students of color or why would a man be so violent against a young girl. But the girl was immediately assumed to be at fault because, as the old saying goes, "Children are to do what they are told."

Her first crime was being a minor questioning an adult. Her second layer of offense was being in Black skin challenging a person in White skin (Epstein et al., 2017; Rockett, 2019). Many want to say the incident was not racially motivated, but the officer's history would show it was. On top of the complications of race, this situation was also mired in sexist gender-based issues—she was a girl questioning a man. I would hear people say things like "Black girls are always talking back, being sassy and disrespectful." The ways that very particular stereotypes have been created for young people who are both girls and Black underline why it seems okay for them to be treated with contempt in schools.

All of this swirled in my head and drove me to act. I relocated my life to South Carolina to start working to create a world where Black girls thrive. After arriving in South Carolina, I would learn that the law under which the girls were arrested now numerically accounts for a significant amount of arrests in the state—it is in third place when it comes to the largest number of arrests for youth in South Carolina. Sifting through these cases and records affirmed that Black girls, as it had been studied, are penalized 10 times more than their White female counterparts (Crenshaw, 2015). Another issue that I would find is that South Carolina ranked in the top three for domestic violence incidences and deaths in the country (NCADV, 2015). This is a state which still has a law in place that says a man can beat his wife on the courthouse steps on Sunday, but prohibits the selling of alcohol and the operation of dance clubs on Sunday (Eubanks, 2017). These oppressive cultural norms play a role in why many folks would assume the girls were wrong and the officer was right without question.

These are all symptoms of a larger problem. The root is the systematic oppression that has existed since Black lives came to the shores of the United States. Black lives have never had value to our country unless they could be capitalized off of (Boston, n.d.). And some would argue that even when Black lives were directly tied to White wealth, there was still no hesitation to beat, dismember, or kill (Robinson, 2001). In looking at how Black women and girls were treated during the time of slavery, enslaved pregnant women (often carrying the master's child) were still required to be beaten as punishment. Flog holes were belly pits dug in the ground to ensure a pregnant woman could lay face down and be whipped without hurting the baby (Sadlier, 2012). And later, even movements for civil rights, voting rights, education equality, and women's rights often placed Black girls at the bottom of the totem pole on all these issues. The lack of concern for our well-being now that we are supposedly free is still present.

Education

The "Disturbing Schools Law" under which the girls in South Carolina were arrested was created in the early 1900s to protect White female students at all-girls schools against possible intruders coming in to harm them (Bowers, 2016). In his 2016 article in the *Charleston Post and Courier*, Paul Bowers offered the following explanation:

> In its earliest form, passed in 1919, the law prohibited "Disturbing Schools Attended by Girls or Women." At any school or college attended by women or girls, the law stated, it was illegal to interfere with students or teachers, to loiter, to "act in an obnoxious manner thereon," or to enter the premises without the permission of the school principal or president. Violators faced a penalty of up to a $100 fine or 30 days in jail. The law remained unchanged for decades. "Now in our more contemporary age, these same laws are used to essentially arrest kids—disproportionately black kids—for acting up in school," Elliott said [Jay Elliott, Columbia attorney and former police officer]. The most significant change to the disturbing schools law came in 1968, when the Legislature expanded the law to cover all schools for boys or girls. A 1972 act increased the penalty to $1,000 or 90 days, and a 2010 amendment specified that juvenile cases would be handled in Family Court. It remains unclear when police began applying the law to students, but by 1994 the state had endorsed its use as such. That year, a Jasper County School District official wrote to then-Attorney General Travis Medlock asking whether police could arrest students if they fought on campus, refused to leave campus when asked by a principal, or used profane language toward police or a principal. Medlock wrote back that all three offenses could be considered disturbing school. The widespread application of the disturbing schools law to South Carolina students in the 1990s came about as schools began bringing in school resource officers to patrol the halls, guard against terrorist threats and—increasingly—intervene in student behavior issues. (para. 4–6)

This follows a persistent historic trend in the United States where laws are used as tools to legally oppress and target certain communities. Although social trends make it unjust to racially target communities (discrimination is no longer socially accepted publicly), racist acts are wholeheartedly accepted and go unquestioned when disguised as laws.

When I started my organization EveryBlackGirl, Inc. (EBG), there was still the notion from others that there was only a certain type of Black girl who had the right to thrive. This is linked to the same underlying notion of which women deserved rights. The women's suffrage movement was a White woman's fight that did not stand for Black women, much less Black girls. Bold Black women suffragists like Sojourner Truth spoke directly to the issue of Black women not being valued and appreciated as women in her speech "Ain't I a Woman" during the women's rights convention in Akron, Ohio, in 1851. Other prominent activists like Anna Julia Cooper and Ida B. Wells continued the work of speaking out against the exclusion of Black women's issues in the cause for women's rights (Sadlier, 2012). Though this work of advocating for Black women's rights has been happening since the mid-1800s, we still find today that as Sojourner Truth stated, any Black woman or girl that does not fit the mold of what is acceptable in America does not get the constitutional right of liberty and freedom. Black girls in schools who wear head wraps, braids, distinctive clothes, or are self-expressive or ask questions are seen as unacceptable and at the rawest form as untamable. And this is because they are not seen as human, so they can be treated in any manner deemed acceptable by the other/society/world. The truth is that Black girls have no right to freedom, joy, or life outside of what they produce for others. They are not human, they are magical . . . which has made people feel like they can do or say anything to them, and they will be okay. The ability for Black women to simply sustain and survive has also been misinterpreted as a social strength only needed by the oppressed. The humanity of their lives and the fragility of their spirit is erased because they are not seen as people, but as objects. Objects can sustain wear and tear, but we don't intentionally do this to "real" people. And so, when Black girls start speaking against being treated as less than human, they are deemed out of control, wild, rebellious, and untamable. Words often used to describe how we interact with animals.

One of my students with whom I work shared that a White female teacher told her and her classmates that they should be lucky that she cares because everyone knows it is hard to educate Black children—especially Black girls. When girls are assaulted and harassed in schools and request support, they are often asked, "What did you do?" Or told that "boys are boys," so they must be mindful of their behavior so that they don't provoke the boys. They are punished for what others do to them. They are blamed and at fault at all turns.

EBG's vision is to create a world where Every Black Girl thrives. What that looks like is working with everyone in the life of a Black girl. Tangibly, we have started working with educators, policymakers, and community members in addressing how their unconscious biases and own internalized oppressions prevent Black girls from thriving. This is not from a place of blame or fault, but rather, awareness, so we can redirect and correct how adults and elders impact the lives of Black girls. It is our belief that no educator comes into teaching to harm a child. Holding this as our truth, we are able to work with educators from a place of what racial and gender equality beliefs they have been taught, or internalized oppressions they possess, that they continue to pass on to Black girls unconsciously.

An example of this work is our Legends Training that we provide for adults. We have graduated approximately 10 educators, community members, and parents since our start in 2017. The training pushes individuals to examine where they want to go in their personal lives and uncovers what have been their barriers to achieving it. Although many might expect our adult training to focus on parenting or supporting children in schools, we have found that we are working with a community where everyone needs educational love and redress. A parent, neighbor, or teacher can better help a young person to strive, dream, and achieve if they experience this magic for themselves. Intergenerational and multidirectional education is critical.

Home

On July 28, 2016, 14-year-old Bresha Meadows walked into the bedroom of her parents and shot and killed her alleged abusive stepfather with a gun that he had allegedly pulled on her and her family many times (Bromwich, 2017). A few months earlier, Bresha had run away from home, telling her family, teachers, school counselors, and social workers she was afraid for her life because her stepfather had been beating her mother and threatening to kill her, her mother, and her siblings. After the shooting, her mother commented that Bresha accomplished what she (the mother) did not have the courage to do. Bresha heard her mother's cry and acted. But unfortunately, Bresha's pleas went unheard.

As an organization, we took a closer look at this incident and started seeing patterns. Niya Kenny (the other student arrested during the Spring Valley High School incident) was arrested for doing all she could after her Black female classmate's pleas went unheard. Marissa Alexander, a Black woman in Florida who fired a warning shot at her abusive husband who was threatening to come into her home and harm her, was eventually arrested and jailed instead of the husband (Marissa Alexander Justice Project, n.d.). These are incidents where Black women or girls have reached out for support to people who are supposed to protect them and their pleas were answered with silence. When they decided to take the lead in protecting themselves, they were penalized.

EBG created the EBG Sanctuary to provide girls who are being harmed temporary shelter until we can find long-term solutions. Bresha's story could have been different had her calls for help been addressed. Bresha testified that she shot her stepfather because she felt that was the only way to stay alive (Bromwich, 2017). She felt that she had no other options because of the lack of support that had been given to her when she previously sought help. At EBG, we want Black girls to know they do matter. We want them to know that their pleas will be heard and addressed. To do so, we create and provide spaces where girls can speak their trauma and find solutions. The

EBG Sanctuary has been a place for girls to come, to just be, to heal, and start to thrive.

Institutions

In January of 2016, 16-year-old Gynnya McMillen was found dead in her cell after being arrested for arguing with her mother (Preston, 2017). Gynnya's mother called the police to assist her in handling her upset daughter, and the response from authorities was to arrest the teen. After being arrested and taken to a juvenile detention center, Gynnya would be physically handled by guards leaving her choking, gasping for air, and seizing as a guard watched, then walked away. Gynnya's story would resemble that of Sandra Bland—a Black woman arrested by police for a traffic violation and taken into police custody, where she would eventually die (Nathan, 2016). Gynnya's story was so appalling because she was a child.

The question looms, what if Gynnya was not looked at as a troubled Black girl, which is how many of the police reports revealed she was described? What if she were simply seen as a child with troubles? What if the police had brought someone who could deescalate the situation rather than arrest the child? These are the type of questions that EBG asks and seeks to answer. Our work now involves working with families and agencies as a referral for parents before calling in the police. We are committed to supporting families in deescalating and resolving first from a community base of love before involving the police. Currently we are working with school districts and shelters to be an alternative to incarceration for young people, specifically Black girls in South Carolina.

Community

In the early part of 2017, the nation would learn about hundreds of Black girls who went missing in the Washington DC and Maryland areas. It would be uncovered that many of the girls had gone missing for quite some time, but there was a lack of support from local authorities. In response, families and communities began to reach out to the media to bring awareness to this issue and seek support in bringing these girls home (Jarrett et al., 2017). Social media would be the tool used to spread this information. When community members addressed local officials at a town hall regarding the lack of response, officials suggested that somehow the girls were missing due to something they did (running away or dressing a certain way, such as wearing weaves and red lipstick). The overall feel was that it isn't important—these girls of color from the city were not important enough to take this as a crisis.

Research shows that runaways are most often not just rebellious youth. They are either running away from something or running to something. What if we actually looked at the child and not the behavior? As an organization, the women and men involved with EBG understand that there are major factors that go into a child going missing. In these cases, we want to know what we can do as an organization to have youth feel safe enough not to run, or to have abductors feel scared enough to know they would not do well in taking our children.

But beyond girls going missing on our streets, there is also the realization that Black girls often go missing in plain sight. They are often overlooked in classrooms, homes, and communities because they are Black girls. The missing girls in DC are a physical manifestation of a larger issue of how we make Black girls invisible. And so, our work is also about pulling together elders, community members, concerned neighbors, parents, dedicated educators, and Black girls themselves in an effort to fully see the experience of Black girls. We provide Black girls spaces where they are the rightful center of attention—the center of help, the center of education, the center of our love.

EBG was birthed out of a response to attacks on Black girls. We built ourselves from within, starting with community. We have created a space where the community became responsible for itself and others in the community. This concept of community accountability and responsibility is not a new one. We have historical context from which to learn. "It takes a village" is not just a quote we throw around, but a belief system that we live. We clearly understand that we must not put parameters on who can be a part of the village, who can help, and who can be a mentor. To do that is to engage in the same social pressures to conform that we fight against. Some of our adult educators and elders aren't perfect—but they are present. They care. Their experiences are important, and their wisdom is rich. They matter. If we all live by the principle that everyone matters and contributes to this world, then we might be able to make a real inroads toward change.

We have created a network for Black girls that goes beyond policing, or institutional interference. We focus on the needs of the girls guided by the voices of the girls. Then we engage with and invite adult community members in to address the needs. Our work seeks to dismantle the historical narrative of Black lives not mattering. We start within our communities to heal the pain, to address the psychological trauma that causes us to accept pain, and to confront the larger social systems and policies that cause us pain. We work and love girls—not certain types of girls, not girls who live in particular zip codes, not girls who quietly conform—but Every Black Girl. Because each of us deserves to be loved.

Vision Versus View: Imagining New Realities for Black Girls

As a result of conversation with community activists and scholar-activists like the authors who contributed to this volume, it is clear that transformation needs to occur within major social institutions across the globe. Anderson pointed to racist and gender discriminatory policies within the criminal justice system and educational institutions that cause Black girls to be targeted, harassed, and pushed out. She brings up violence against girls in their schools, homes, and communities and the lack of support and assistance given to them by the social institutions created to protect and advocate for all children. And she highlights the problematic view of Black girls: When the larger society does see them, it's typically as criminal and problematic; however, when they need help, assistance, and love, society overlooks them and is blind to their needs.

Being a Black girl in America is not easy. It never has been. The current view of how the world treats, understands, and cares for Black girls is disappointing and sad. A few years ago, as I was preparing a class lecture on racial stereotypes, I needed a few images to use in my presentation. I Googled "Angry Black woman." Michelle Obama's picture showed up numerous times. This was shocking. A highly educated lawyer and first lady of the United States was the number one hit for "angry Black woman." The negative stereotyping of Black women is powerful and pervasive. If this is how our first lady was interpreted, imagine what contempt must be awaiting an impoverished Black girl. Media propaganda has us viewing Black girls as disrespectful, loud, ignorant, and promiscuous ghetto babies.

It also views Black mothers and grandmothers as unimportant, comical buffoons. Movie after movie in our popular culture paints the African American grandmother, the "Big Mama" figure, as comical, buffoonish, and masculine. The way that girls and women who don't fit the social mold are represented is disgusting. I read a deeper meaning. I see it signifying that to be a big, Black woman is to be not seen as a woman at all—a man can play you in a movie. I'm offended by the way that the film industry has made a joke of the very real racial experience that would cause an older Black grandmother to carry a gun in her purse. One of my many grandmothers, Grandma Golston, ALWAYS had a gun in her purse—at Thanksgiving dinner, Christmas dinner, while walking down the street. The reasons why a Black woman in the South would learn to carry a gun to protect herself and her children both outside and inside of the home are not funny. We're talking about the realities of racial violence—a history of Black women being raped, beaten, and murdered at will. We're talking domestic violence and alcoholism—the many negative consequences that put Black lives at risk. It's not okay to present this cultural reality without context—to make a joke of the women who first died before women like Grandma Golston were taught to pack their purse.

These bold Black women taught us how to survive life in America—rural wisdom and street smarts. What we have learned from these histories of struggle are essentially politics of survival. A *politic* is a set of strategies that a group of people uses to advance themselves. Government officials have co-opted the word *politic* and made us automatically align it with public office. But all people—families and communities—establish politics of survival, success, and resistance. And so, ultimately, we need educators who understand and appreciate brilliance that is born of struggle.

We need a liberatory education of resistance. We need education that confronts political, social, and popular ideologies of hate. *Negro education, affirmative action, multicultural education, diversity,* and *social justice education* are all terms that trace this history of fighting for increased educational inclusion and service. But even behind the scenes of this good fight, we have seen the ways that specifically addressing issues of race can get lost in the use of broad terms like *multiculturalism, diversity,* or *social justice.* All are important issues, but they should not cause us to skirt the fact that we still have a race problem in the United States that must be addressed. This is why the unfiltered voices and experiences of older Black women are so powerful. They aren't constrained by theoretical ideas. Instead they are free to be honest and real. They whisper, speak firmly, or shout when necessary. We still need the dedication to radical (different, strong, bold) activism that we saw in the days when the fight against racism and sexism was priority number one. We need educators in all realms (in homes, in communities, in schools) to take bold visionary action toward change. Undoubtedly, we need folks that are critical of the current view of Black girls—critical of both how society views girls and also critical of the limited and oppressive landscape and worldview available to Black girls who are living in poverty in rural and urban communities. But we need more than criticism—we need action. A vision is meaningless without the action it takes to achieve it.

Recipes of Resistance

Although there is a significant amount of change that needs to occur in our educational system, we still don't need a magical wizard. Terms like these make everyday people feel powerless because they aren't magicians. So maybe instead of searching for the wizard, we need to search for a really good cook. That's a more approachable metaphor. Whereas becoming a world-class chef might require culinary training, being a legendary cook in our home communities is a feat achieved by many of our modest, humble grandmothers. We aren't talking Bobby Flay dominating the Food Network. We are talking about the type of creativity and talent that made Ms. Hattie Suber's fried chicken famous in my hometown of South Carolina. Loving and feeding the local community that you serve. Being a great cook takes time, consciousness, memory, awareness, and dedication. Social justice work requires much of this same diligence. Undoubtedly as educational leaders we must author a recipe of resistance. To take dry ingredients and give them life, give them taste, give them a new sense of purpose is an amazing thing. This is how we must educate our girls. And we must also address cultural illiteracy and ignorance in our society. We can stir the pot of pop culture and shake loose its hold on our children's psyche by teaching them critical media literacy directly focused on contesting issues of race, gender, and class. We can cook up a new image of what it means to be a Black woman and teach it to all of our children.

Ultimately, what revolutionary Black teachers in colored schools, visionary teachers in underresourced urban schools, dedicated teachers in impoverished rural communities, resistant teachers working to help Black girls in predominantly White schools, and brilliant community educators like Vivian are doing literally saves lives. This resistance takes the form of doing the important work of raising and educating whole, sane, positive souls who can contribute to the world. In this type of resistance, we teach Black girls to express themselves when society has told them to tone down their personality. We teach them to speak when society has told them to be quiet. We teach them to stand like Shirley Chisolm, to sit like Rosa Parks, or to take a knee like Representative Sheila Jackson Lee when it is necessary. We teach them to love. We teach them to laugh. We teach them it's also okay to cry. We teach them to resist.

Discussion Questions

1. This chapter begins by discussing cultural assets. What are the cultural assets that Black girls bring to education, and what aspects of your work can you transform to better include and tap into these cultural assets?
2. The chapter lists several social areas that are essentially failing Black girls; which of these examples were most salient to you and why?
3. The idea of being seen is another theme of this chapter. What can educational institutions do to impact the negative ways that Black girls are often seen in society and school? On the other end of the spectrum, what can educational institutions do to ensure that Black girls in need of help are seen and not ignored?

Resource

Blackpast.org. *Frederick Douglass, If there is no Struggle, there is No Progress.* http://www.blackpast.org/1857-frederick-douglass-if-there-no-struggle-there-no-progress#sthash.EXNXPCrp.dpuf

Further Reading

Baum, L. F. (2000). *The wonderful wizard of Oz* (100th anniversary ed.). George M. Hill.

Jenkins, T. S. (2013). *My culture, my color, my self: Heritage, resilience, and community in the lives of young adults.* Temple University Press.

Paris, D. (2012). Culturally sustaining pedagogy: A needed change in stance, terminology, and practice. *Educational Researcher, 2012*(41), 93.

Troutman, S., Jenkins, T., & Glover, C. (2018). *The invisible backpack: Narratives of family, cultural gifts and community assets on the academic journey.* Lexington Books/Rowman & Littlefield.

Yosso, T. (2005). Whose culture has capital? A critical race theory discussion of community cultural wealth. *Race Ethnicity and Education, 8*(1), 69–91.

References

Adams, D. (1993). Defining educational quality. *Educational Planning, 9*(3), 3–18. https://eric.ed.gov/?id=EJ487855

Anderson, J. (1988). The education of Blacks in the South, 1860–1935. University of North Carolina Press. https://uncpress.org/book/9780807842218/the-education-of-blacks-in-the-south-1860-1935/

Barnes, R. D. (1990). Race consciousness: The thematic content of racial distinctiveness in critical race scholarship. *Harvard Law Review, 103*(8), 1864–1871.

Baum, L. F. (2000). *The wonderful wizard of Oz* (100th anniversary ed.). George M. Hill.

Boston, N. (n.d.). *The slave experience: Living conditions.* Thirteen Media. https://www.thirteen.org/wnet/slavery/experience/living/history.html

Bowers, P. (2016, August 5). Law was written to protect girls' schools, not to arrest. *Post and Courier.* https://www.postandcourier.com/archives/law-was-written-to-protect-girls-schools-not-to-arrest/article_e2742436-32b9-5c06-8f32-c453d-3d6d0d4.html

Bray, M. (2003). Community initiatives in education: Goals, dimensions and linkages with governments. *Compare: A Journal of Comparative and International Education, 33*(1), 31–45. https://www.tandfonline.com/doi/abs/10.1080/03057920302598

Bromwich, J. (2017, May 23). Bresha Meadows, Ohio teenager who fatally shot her father, accepts plea deal. *New York Times.* https://www.nytimes.com/2017/05/23/us/bresha-meadows-father-killing.html

Crenshaw, K. (1991). Mapping the margins: Intersectionality, identity politics, and violence against women of color. *Stanford Law Review, 43*(6), 1241. https://www.jstor.org/stable/1229039

Crenshaw, K. (2015). *Black girls matter: Pushed out, over policed and under protected* [Report]. African American Policy Forum. www.aapf.orgrr

Creswell, J. (1998). *Qualitative inquiry and research design: Choosing among five traditions.* SAGE.

Epstein, R., Blake, J., & Gonzalez, T. (2017). *Girlhood interrupted: The erasure of black girls' childhood.* Georgetown Law Center on Poverty and Inequality. https://www.law.georgetown.edu/poverty-inequality-center/wp-content/uploads/sites/14/2017/08/girlhood-interrupted.pdf

Eubanks, C. (2017, February 14). *11 outdated and unusual southern laws.* https://www.thisismysouth.com/11-unusual-outdated-southern-laws/

Fairclough, A. (2001). *Teaching equality: Black schools in the age of Jim Crow.* University of Georgia Press.

Gordon, D. (1993). Worlds of consequence: Feminist ethnography as social action. *Critique of Anthropology, 13*(4), 429–443. https://doi.org/10.1177/0308275X9301300408

Hesiod. (2009). *Theogony and works and days* (Oxford World's Classics, reissue ed.). Oxford University Press.

Hill-Collins, P. (1986). Learning from the outsider within: The sociological significance of Black feminist thought. *Social Problems, 33*(6), S14–S32. https://doi.org/10.2307/800672

Hine, D., & Thompson, K. (1999). *A shining thread of hope.* Broadway Books.

hooks, b. (1999). *All about love.* William Morrow.

hooks, b. (2001). *Salvation: Black people and love.* Harper Perennial.

Jarrett, L., Reyes, S., & Shortell, D. (2017, March 26). Missing Black girls in DC spark outrage, prompt calls for federal help. *CNN News.* https://www.cnn.com/2017/03/24/us/missing-black-girls-washington-dc/index.html

Jenkins, T. (2006). Mr. Nigger: The challenges of educating African American males in American society. *Journal of Black Studies, 37*(1), 127–155. https://doi.org/10.1177/0021934704273931

Ladson-Billings, G. (1998). Just what is critical race theory and what is it doing in a nice field like education? *Qualitative Studies in Education, 11*(1), 7–24. https://doi.org/10.1080/095183998236863

Ladson-Billings, G., & Tate, W. (1995). Toward a critical race theory of education. *Teachers College Record, 97*(1), 48–68. https://eric.ed.gov/?id=EJ519126

Landsman, J., Salcedo, R., & Gorski, P. (Eds.). (2015). *Voices for equity and social justice: A literary education anthology.* Rowman & Littlefield.

Marissa Alexander Justice Project. (n.d.). *About Marissa.* https://marissaalexander.org/about/

Mohanty, C. T. (2003). *Feminism without borders: Decolonizing theory, practicing solidarity.* Duke University Press.

Morris, M. (2012, October). *Race, gender and the school to prison pipeline: Expanding our discussion to include Black girls.* Schott Foundation for Public Education. http://schottfoundation.org/resources/race-gender-and-school-prison-pipeline-expanding-our-discussion-include-black-girls

Morris, M. (2016). *Pushout: The criminalization of Black girls in school.* The New Press.

Nathan, D. (2016, April 21). What happened to Sandra Bland? *The Nation.* https://www.thenation.com/article/what-happened-to-sandra-bland/

National Coalition Against Domestic Violence. (2015). *Domestic violence national statistics.* www.ncadv.org www.speakcdn.com/assets/2497/south_carolina.pdf

Noddings, N. (2003). *Caring: A feminine approach to ethics and moral education* (2nd ed.). University of California Press.

Paul, D. (2003). *Talkin' back: Raising and educating resilient Black girls.* Praeger.

Preston, C. (2017, January 4). The story of the 16-year-old who died in custody after being arrested for arguing with her mother. *Jezebel.* https://jezebel.com/the-story-of-the-16-year-old-who-died-in-custody-after-1790335530

Reinharz, S. (1992). *Feminist methods in social research.* Oxford University Press.

Robinson, R. (2001). *The debt: What America owes to Blacks.* Plume.

Rockett, D. (2019, May 24). "They are totally overlooked": Young Black girls viewed as less innocent, study finds. To that, I cry foul. *Chicago Tribune.* https://www.chicagotribune.com/lifestyles/ct-life-black-girls-childhood-tt-20190523-story.html

Sadlier, R. (2012). *Harriet Tubman: Freedom seeker, freedom leader.* Dundurn Press.

Tillich, P. (1960). *Love, power, and justice: Ontological analyses and ethical applications.* Galaxy Books.

Williams, H. (2007). *Self-taught: African American education in slavery and freedom.* University of North Carolina Press.

Vivian Anderson is a healer-activist dedicated to building a world where all Black girls thrive. Anderson's work is rooted in youth, teen, family, and community health and well-being, as well as racial and social justice. In 2015, Anderson was inspired by two young Black girls, introduced to the world when a school resource officer brutally assaulted one, and arrested her and the other girl, who stood up for her classmate when nobody else did. Thus EveryBlackGirl, Inc was born, a 501c3 focused on creating the radical and systemic change that is needed to have a world worthy of the genius and heart of Every Black Girl.

Mildred Boveda, EdD, is an associate professor of special education at the Pennsylvania State University. In her scholarship, she uses the terms intersectional competence and intersectional consciousness to describe teachers' understanding of diversity and how students, families, and colleagues have multiple sociocultural markers that intersect in nuanced and unique ways. Drawing from Black feminist theory and collaborative teacher education research, she interrogates how differences are framed across education communities to influence education policy and practice.

Ruth Nicole Brown, PhD, founded and continues to co-organize Saving Our Lives Hear Our Truths (SOLHOT), an intentional social practice of celebrating Black girlhood with Black girls and those who love them. Brown is the author of *Hear Our Truths: The Creative Potential of Black Girlhood* (University of Illinois Press, 2013) and *Black Girlhood Celebration: Toward a Hip Hop Feminist Pedagogy* (Peter Lang, 2009), numerous journal articles, and anthologies. Brown is the inaugural chairperson of African American and African Studies at Michigan State University.

Janice A. Byrd, PhD, is an assistant professor of counselor education at the Pennsylvania State University. She earned her doctorate in counselor education and supervision from the University of Iowa. Her previous experience includes work as a school counselor, career counselor, and with counseling, teaching, and mentoring youth. Byrd's scholarship seeks to situate the lived experiences of Black students within the broader ecological context to systematically examine how their personal, social, academic, and career success is interrupted and/or enhanced by school, family, community, and policies throughout all stages of the educational pipeline (i.e., K–12, postsecondary, and graduate studies).

Mercedes Adell Cannon, PhD, is an associate director in a university disability office—an adjunct faculty in their school of education Indiana University–Purdue University Indianapolis with a deep interest in understanding oppression at the intersection of Black women's race, gender, and dis/ability. Inspired by her experiences with an invisible dis/ability label, she privileges Black women's pushback against systemic systems of oppression. Cannon uses a concept called "Subverted Truths" to describe how students with disabilities need to *reinterpret* socially constructed identities and *replace* them through transformative radical self-love. She is a recipient of the 2019 AERA Disability Studies in Education Special Interest Group Outstanding Dissertation Award.

Keeley Copridge, PhD, is a senior research associate with the United Negro College Fund Frederick D. Patterson Research Institute. She attained her Doctorate in Higher Education at Indiana University Bloomington. Her research interests include college access, college preparation, and enrollment of underrepresented populations, specifically Black women. She is well-versed in diversity, first-generation and low-income students, admissions, and residence life.

Erin Corbett, EdD, has spent over 2 decades in education access in a number of roles. With experience in independent school admission, enrichment programs, higher education policy, postsecondary financial aid, and criminal justice reform, her commitment to expanding postsecondary opportunities for all populations has served as the foundation of her professional endeavors. Currently, Corbett runs her community-based, educational nonprofit organization, Second Chance Educational Alliance, providing justice-impacted students a pathway to a bachelor's degree in business administration, in partnership with Southern New Hampshire University.

Lori D. Patton, PhD, is department chair of Educational Studies and professor of higher education and student affairs in the College of Education and Human Ecology at The Ohio State University. Patton Davis is known for scholarship on critical race theory, diversity initiatives on college campuses, Black women and girls in educational and social contexts, and college student development. She coedited *Critical Perspectives on Black Women and College Success* (Routledge, 2016) and is the author of numerous peer-reviewed journal articles, book chapters, and other academic publications. She has received national awards for her scholarship including being ranked among the top 200 educators in the United States. She is a frequently sought expert on education topics.

Cynthia B. Dillard, PhD (Nana Mansa II of Mpeasem, Ghana, West Africa), is the Mary Frances Early Professor of Teacher Education in the Department of Educational Theory and Practice at the University of Georgia. Her research interests include critical teacher education, spirituality in education, and African/African American feminist studies. Beyond numerous published articles and book chapters, two of her books have been selected as Critics' Choice Book Award winners by the American Educational Studies Association. Dillard also serves as executive director and president of GIVE.BUILD.SHARE, a nonprofit organization that supports educational opportunities for children and families by building schools in Ghana.

Venus E. Evans-Winters, PhD, is senior researcher at the African American Policy Forum. Her interests are educational policy analysis, Black girls' and women's psychosocial and education development, and critical race methodologies. She is the author of *Black Feminism in Qualitative Inquiry: A Mosaic for Writing Our Daughter's Body* (Routledge, 2019) and *Teaching Black Girls: Resilience in Urban Schools* (Peter Lang, 2011). She is coeditor of the books *Black Feminism in Education: Black Women Speak Up, Back, & Out* (Peter Lang, 2015) and *Celebrating Twenty Years of Black Girlhood: The Lauryn Hill Reader* (Peter Lang, 2018). Evans-Winters is also a clinical psychotherapist in private practice and founder of Planet Venus Institute.

Aria S. Halliday, PhD, is an assistant professor of gender and women's studies and African American and Africana studies at the University of Kentucky. Her research examines contemporary representations and cultural productions of Black women and girls in the United States and Caribbean. Her research is featured in *Cultural Studies, Departures in Critical Qualitative Research, Girlhood Studies, Palimpsest,* and *SOULS.* She is the editor of *The Black Girlhood Studies Collection* (Women's Press, 2019) and author of the forthcoming book, *Buy Black: How Black Women Transformed US Pop Culture* (University of Illinois Press, 2022).

Ayana T. Hardaway, PhD, is the Visiting Scholar for the Samuel DeWitt Proctor Institute for Leadership, Equity, and Justice in the Rutgers Graduate

School of Education and the Rutgers Center for Minority Serving Institutions. As a scholar-practitioner, her research explores Black girls and women in P–20 educational contexts, campus diversity initiatives and policies, and critical qualitative methods. She earned her PhD in education from Temple University and she's also a proud mother of two Black girls. Hardaway is a previous AERA Asa G. Hilliard III and Barbara A. Sizemore Research Fellow, and her most recent work was highlighted in *Urban Education Policy Annuals, Diverse Issues in Higher Education*, and the *HBCU Times*.

Dorothy E. Hines, PhD, holds a joint appointment as an assistant professor in the Department of African and African American Studies and in the School of Education at the University of Kansas. Hines works in collaboration with Black girls to amplify their voices at the intersection of race, gender, and policy. She is an award-winning author, mother of a Black girl, and a former high school history teacher from North Carolina. Hines previously served as a teaching fellow with the Harvard Graduate School of Education.

Charlotte E. Jacobs, PhD, is an adjunct assistant professor at the University of Pennsylvania Graduate School of Education. Her research interests focus on issues of identity development, race, and gender in education concerning adolescent girls of color, teacher education and diversity, and youth participatory action research (YPAR), which led her to recently cofound the EnGenderED Research Collaborative. Currently, Jacobs is the director of the Independent School Teaching Residency program at Penn GSE. Additionally, blending her work with independent schools and YPAR, Charlotte is the former research director of the School Participatory Action Research Collaborative at the Center for the Study of Boys' and Girls' Lives (SPARC-CSBGL).

Toby S. Jenkins, PhD, is interim associate dean of diversity, equity, and inclusion in the graduate school and an associate professor in educational leadership & policy studies at the University of South Carolina. Her work focuses on the use of culture as a politic of social survival, a tool of social change, and a creatively meaningful space of knowledge production. She is also interested in the examination of education as both a space of oppression and liberation. She has authored five books focused on culture, diversity, and inclusion in education.

Nicole Joseph, PhD, is an associate professor with tenure of mathematics and science education in the Department of Teaching and Learning at Vanderbilt University. She is also the Director of the Joseph Mathematics Education

Research Lab (JMEL), which trains and mentors undergraduate and graduate students in Black Feminist and Intersectionality orientations producing theoretical and methodological practices that challenge hegemonic notions of objectivity to emphasize humanizing, empowering, and transformative research. Joseph's research explores two lines of inquiry: (a) Black women and girls, their identity development, and their experiences in mathematics; and (b) gendered antiblackness, whiteness, White supremacy, and how these systems of oppression shape Black girls's and women's underrepresentation and retention in mathematics across the pipeline. Her research has been published in top-tiered journals such as *Educational Researcher, Review of Educational Research, Teachers College Record, Harvard Education Review*, and the *Journal of Negro Education*.

Monique Lane, PhD, is a proud mama, award-winning classroom teacher, and an associate professor of educational leadership at Saint Mary's College of California. Lane earned a doctorate in urban schooling from UCLA and served as a postdoctoral researcher at Columbia University's Teachers College. Her research advances Black feminist pedagogy and Black women's educational parenting strategies as disruptors to school-based stressors that threaten Black girl learners' opportunities to thrive. Her book, *Engendering #BlackGirlJoy: How to Cultivate Empowered Identities and Educational Persistence in Struggling Schools* (Peter Lang, 2021), explores how practitioners can harness youth oppositional knowledge as a bridge to self-discovery and academic empowerment.

Jamila L. Lee-Johnson, PhD, is the Diversity, Equity, and Inclusion Specialist for the University of Wisconsin system. A proud graduate of Clark Atlanta University, Michigan State, and the University of Wisconsin-Madison, Lee-Johnson is a critical Black woman scholar who studies the academic and social experiences of Black women in higher education. She is a strong advocate for helping Black girls and women pursue higher education and avid supporter of historically Black colleges and universities (HBCUs).

Gholnecsar E. Muhammad, PhD, is an associate professor of literacy, language, and culture at University of Illinois at Chicago. She studies Black historical excellence within educational communities with goals of reframing curriculum and instruction today. Muhammad's scholarship has appeared in leading educational journals and books. She has also received numerous national awards and is the author of the best-selling book, *Cultivating Genius: An Equity Model for Culturally and Historically Responsive Literacy* (Scholastic, 2020).

Nadrea R. Njoku, PhD, is a senior research associate for the Frederick D. Patterson Research Institute of the United Negro College Fund. There her research includes student success strategies and career pathways at histori- cally Black colleges and universities, with a focus on the influence of cam- pus environments. Her work outside of UNCF includes a multidisciplinary exploration of the footprint Black women have made on college campuses. She positions this work in a critical race and feminist framework that is devoted to disrupting issues of race and gender within the postsecondary education context. She's a proud graduate of Xavier University of Louisiana and Indiana University.

Christa J. Porter, PhD, is an assistant professor of higher education admin- istration at Kent State University. She critically examines policies and prac- tices that influence the development and trajectory of Black women in higher education, college student development, and research and praxis in higher education and student affairs. She was recognized by the American College Personnel Association as an Emerging Scholar in 2017. Porter's work has appeared in various refereed education journals and academic books; she coedited the book *Case Studies for Student Development Theory: Advancing Social Justice and Inclusion in Higher Education* (2020, Routledge).

Tykeia Robinson, PhD, is the associate director of research and policy in the Office of Undergraduate STEM Education at the Association of American Colleges and Universities. Her passion in higher education research is in illuminating processes of organizational learning and change and translat- ing research into tools for capacity building. Her current work focuses on empowering institutions to understand and interrogate barriers to inclusion and craft customized strategies that meet organizational needs with excellence and equity. Robinson also founded #TeamTypingFast (TTF), a community of practice that prioritizes the wellness and productivity of Black women academics, corporate professionals, and entrepreneurs.

Sacha Sharp, PhD, is an assistant professor of medicine in the Department of Medicine at Indiana University School of Medicine and an adjunct assistant professor in the program of Africana Studies at IUPUI. As a medical educa- tion specialist, she serves medical students, residents, and fellows through educational success initiatives. Sharp earned her PhD at IU Bloomington with a higher education focus in the Department of Education, Leadership, and Policy Studies. Her dissertation is titled *A Dramaturgical Analysis of Black Women Graduate Students' Use of Social Media as a Space for Reclamation, Resistance, and Healing.* Relatedly, Sharp's research interests include social media use, retention, and success initiatives for underrepresented populations, specifically Black women.

Tiffany L. Steele, PhD, is an assistant professor of education at Oakland University. Her research interest centers the lived experiences of Black girls and women in education, including students, faculty, and staff. Steele's dissertation research, entitled *Disciplinary Disruption: Exploring the Connection Between High School Sanctioning and Black Collegiate Women's Experiences,* examines how Black women's experiences with disciplinary action influence their collegiate realities. As her research expands, Steele plans to specifically explore the psychosocial development of Black collegiate women, their collegiate experiences, and intentional methodological alignment in the study of Black women and their life journeys through education.

LaWanda W.M. Ward, JD, PhD, is an assistant professor of higher education at The Pennsylvania State University. She was a student affairs educator for almost 20 years in residence life and career services prior to joining the professoriate. Ward's commitment to social justice, racially gendered equity, and inclusion in higher education is influenced by her family of educators. Her mother, a first-grade teacher for almost 30 years, marched during the civil rights movement. Ward's research agenda includes critically analyzing how legal interpretation of issues in higher education impacts Black women as collegians, professors, administrators, and staff.

Brittany Williams, PhD, is a national award-winning writer and speaker. She currently serves as an assistant professor of higher education at St. Cloud State University in Minnesota. Her research explores issues of career development, social class, and health disparities in and relating to college environments. Black women and girls serve as her primary point for scholarly inquiry. She is a cofounder of #CiteASista and one of five founding members of SisterPhD, two digital countercommunities for Black women within and beyond academe. Williams was a 2020–2021 American Association for University Women American Fellow.

Maisha T. Winn is the Chancellor's Leadership Professor and the cofounder and faculty director of the Transformative Justice in Education (TJE) Center in the School of Education at the University of California, Davis. Professor Winn's books include *Writing in Rhythm: Spoken Word Poetry in Urban Schools; Black Literate Lives: Historical and Contemporary Perspectives* (Teachers College Press, 2007); *Girl Time: Literacy, Justice, and the School-To-Prison Pipeline* (Teachers College Press, 2011); *Justice on Both Sides:*

Transforming Education Through Restorative Justice (Harvard Education Press, 2018). Winn is coeditor (with Django Paris) of *Humanizing Research: Decolonizing Qualitative Research* (Sage, 2015). Her new coedited book (with Lawrence T. Winn), *Restorative Justice in Education: Transforming Teaching and Learning Through the Disciplines* (Harvard Education Press), was published in the spring of 2021.

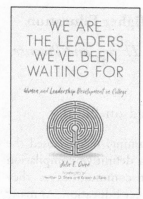

We Are the Leaders We've Been Waiting For

Women and Leadership Development in College

Julie E. Owen

Foreword by Heather D. Shea and Kristen A. Renn

"Julie Owen's book *We Are the Leaders We've Been Waiting For* is masterful. Far more than a book about women's leadership. Owen weaves a complex yet accessible narrative that is rooted in feminist and intersectional theory and exposes so much more than just barriers to women's leadership, but also a range of areas of gender inequality from the pay gap to sexual violence. In each chapter, Owen features the narrative of one of her students or colleagues, a strategy that makes accessing complex ideas feel like a conversation the reader is having with a trusted friend. The active learning exercises make this book a must-have not only for courses on feminist leadership, but also an ideal tool for anyone exploring their own leadership. I finished the book more confident that I can be and maybe am a leader I've always waited for!"—***Angela Hattery***, *Professor and Director, Women and Gender Studies, George Mason University*

"*We Are the Leaders We've Been Waiting For* is a compelling and necessary contribution to the scholarship on leadership and gender. Julie Owen integrates foundational and contemporary concepts and frameworks with powerful narrative in thoughtful and critical ways to advance our understanding of women's leadership. The book will undoubtedly transform students, educators, and our world. I can confidently say this is the book I've been waiting for."—***Paige Haber-Curran***, *Associate Professor, Texas State University*

Culture Centers in Higher Education

Perspectives on Identity, Theory, and Practice

Edited by Lori Patton

Foreword by Gloria Ladson-Billings

"Lori Patton's book is stunning! It has closed the decades-long absence of a definitive compilation to inform culture center communities as they function in American Higher Education. As many colleges and universities struggle with issues of recruitment and retention of underrepresented students, this work provides a splendid blueprint for the development of culture centers for years to come."—*Willena Kimpson Price, Director African American Cultural Center, University of Connecticut, Storrs*

"*Culture Centers in Higher Education* documents in one volume how ethnic and cultural centers have served as places and spaces where those who have been underrepresented in higher education have survived and flourished at predominantly white institutions. Throughout it documents how these centers honor and validate cultural and ethnic backgrounds, and inspire academic excellence and achievement among students without their having to lose cultural identity or values. The writers also speak to the future of cultural centers as places where multicultural centers will also have a place in order to ensure true pluralism on our campuses. As our nation becomes increasingly diverse, these centers serve as models of social justice and thus this book is a must-read for all who want to ensure that their institution provides environments that exude academic success and achieve graduation for all students with their soul and identity whole."—*Mildred García, President, California State University, Dominguez Hills*

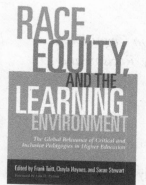

Race, Equity, and the Learning Environment

The Global Relevance of Critical and Inclusive Pedagogies in Higher Education

Edited by Frank Tuitt, Chayla Haynes, and Saran Stewart

Foreword by Lori D. Patton

"*Race, Equity, and the Learning Environment* could not be more timely and relevant for those who work in higher education. This work is a direct confrontation of race and racism and offers excellent examples from practice and research for how to center these important topics in the classroom. Readers are pushed to think in transformative ways about how to teach race and racism as well as confront their own power and privilege through critical self-examination. The urgency in this work to disrupt racist practices is needed and faculty at every stage in their career would benefit tremendously from the strategies discussed in the book."
—*Sharon Fries-Britt*, *Professor of Higher Education, University of Maryland*

From the Foreword:
"This volume bridges the gap from thought to action, providing the necessary context for educators around the world to either embrace or recommit to centering race in postsecondary classrooms and engaging in necessary conversations to ensure that students do not leave our institutions the way they came. I applaud the editors of this book as they dare to move beyond the conversation to engage in teaching and learning that reflects how progressive racial understandings promote equity in higher education."
—*Lori Patton Davis*, *Associate Professor, Higher Education and Student Affairs, IUPUI*

Bandwidth Recovery

Helping Students Reclaim Cognitive Resources Lost to Poverty, Racism, and Social Marginalization

Cia Verschelden

Foreword by Lynn Pasquerella

"Verschelden convincingly makes the case that many lower income and minority students struggle in college not because of lower ability or poor preparation, but because they deal with life situations that deplete cognitive resources that are needed for learning. Offering us a distinctly different lens through which to view these students, she describes concrete strategies we can implement to replenish their cognitive resources so that they don't just survive, but thrive in the college environment with recovered 'bandwidth.'"—**Saundra McGuire**, *(Ret.) Assistant Vice Chancellor and Professor of Chemistry; Director Emerita, Center for Academic Success, Louisiana State University; Author of* Teach Students How to Learn

"*Bandwidth Recovery* provides a roadmap for reversing the current trend, whereby only one in two high school students from low-income families enrolls in college in the first place, and the completion rate for those at the lowest socioeconomic rungs continues to lag far behind their wealthier peers. By drawing attention to the persistent economic and cultural barriers that continue to thwart the equity imperative upon which the American Dream is built, Verschelden brings us closer to being able to fulfill the true promise of American higher education—that of educating for democracy."—**Lynn Pasquerella**, *President of the Association of American Colleges & Universities*

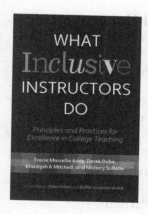

What Inclusive Instructors Do

Principles and Practices for Excellence in College Teaching

Tracie Marcella Addy, Derek Dube, Khadijah A. Mitchell, and Mallory SoRelle

Foreword by Peter Felten and Buffie Longmire Avital

"The authors have created an essential resource for college instructors by bridging the gap between theory and practice. Their practical, adaptable guidance is informed by a national faculty survey and integrated with evidence from the educational literature. The book addresses why inclusive teaching matters and goes beyond classroom practices to consider inclusive institutional culture. Instructors and administrators at all types of institutions will benefit from this timely approach to a critical topic."—*Jennifer Frederick, Executive Director of the Poorvu Center for Teaching and Learning, Yale University*

"This book is a timely and extraordinarily comprehensive resource for supporting instructors who wish to engage with inclusive teaching. Every facet of what makes teaching inclusive is unpacked and brought to life with quotes and examples from real instructors across different disciplines and institutional contexts, and the reflection questions embedded within each section create a natural way for instructors to engage more deeply with the text and think about applications in their own teaching. No stone is left unturned in connecting the practices shared and the research on why and how those practices support inclusion, making this a most valuable resource for instructors at any stage in their teaching careers."—*Catherine Ross, Executive Director, Center for Teaching and Learning, Columbia University*

Square Pegs & Round Holes

Alternative Approaches to Diverse College Student Development Theory

Edited by Fred A. Bonner II, Rosa M. Banda, Stella L. Smith, and aretha f. marbley

Foreword by Jamie Washington

Afterword by Amelia Parnell

"Previous examinations of student development theory have prompted scholars, researchers, policymakers, and practitioners to better understand the myriad ways in which students learn and engage. This book expands on those prior examples and creates new areas for discussion and inquiry. For example, as America continues to grapple with the many racial injustices and inequities that permeate the fabric of nearly every industry, this is the perfect time for a volume that uses critical race theory as a central frame. The selected topics stress the importance of not forcing conversations about students' development into previous models but instead reframing the dialogues in new and more appropriate ways. *Square Pegs & Round Holes* definitely fills a void in literature by providing an abundance of approaches that help practitioners better understand the nuances of students' progress. The effect should be a cadre of professionals who can make more precise adjustments to policies and procedures and thus positively impact student outcomes.

In this time of continued uncertainty regarding how the field of higher education will transform to address new demands and unanticipated challenges, professionals need an evergreen resource that focuses on students' development. This book's arrival could not be timelier, as the pressure on both campuses and students to succeed is arguably higher than ever. The approaches included in this volume certainly answer the call for new models and, in some ways, provide a glimpse of the kind of interactions that are possible when students are consistently placed at the center of campus strategies. This book contains a remarkable blend of historical contexts, current paradigms, and future aspirations and offers a means for connecting student populations that have traditionally received less attention in published scholarly works.

Advancing Black Male Student Success From Preschool Through Ph.D.

Edited by Shaun R. Harper and J. Luke Wood

"Harper and Wood have provided a timely and definitive text that offers rich conceptual, empirical, and practical analysis on Black males and education. This book explains the challenges Black boys and men encounter in pursuit of education, and offers meaningful ways to disrupt these troubling trends. It is mandatory reading for scholars, practitioners, and policymakers."
—*Tyrone C. Howard*, *Professor and Director, UCLA Black Male Institute*

"This book provides practical approaches for educators, parents, policymakers, and others who are committed to improving Black male student achievement. Instead of simply documenting challenges boys of color face, authors focus on proven structures, programs, and initiatives we can build upon. This is required reading for anyone committed to bringing out the genius in our youth."—*Jonathan Foy*, *Principal, The Eagle Academy for Young Men Bronx, New York Campus*

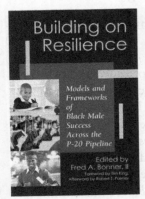